Worldbending

WORLDBENDING

A Survivor's Guide for those who want to think and act creatively about our future.

Pete Rive

WORLD BENDERS

AUCKLAND, NEW ZEALAND

Contents

Copyright

Dedication

To my darling daughters who make the world a better place,
Sophia and Lucia
And
to my World Maker,
Sarah
Also
to my parents who built my first World,
Bryan and Robin

A Note on the Author

PETE RIVE has researched and written for journals, international conferences and contributed to books relating to design, innovation and creative collaboration. This is his first solo book. He currently lives in New Zealand, Aotearoa.

He has a PhD in digital design, and has worked in film, TV, and interactive design, including VR, AR, and virtual worlds for the past 30 years.

You can follow him on Twitter #WorldBender. Join the Facebook group: World Bender. Continue reading and join the conversation on his blog: www.launchsite.co.nz/worldbender

Preface

When I reflect on why I wrote this book there were a number of people and events that led me on this strange circuitous journey that has culminated in this book. Firstly, my parents had a significant influence on my interest and respect for creativity. As far back as I can remember my mother, Robin, was immersed in numerous artistic pastimes singing and playing the guitar; painting and drawing; Fijian fired pottery; a boutique fashion business; a business designing and manufacturing Sesame Street style puppets; and a limited edition international teddy bear business. Mum is still very active with pottery and her biodynamic garden in the country. My father, Bryan, is an avid photographer, lover of literature, and is a very creative cook; he was an old school alchemist who loved to create prescription potions for his pharmacy customers; and understood that health and well being was more than big pharma and that listening to people was a welcome elixir to those stressed by the modern world.

In the 1980s while I was at the University of Auckland I was immensely proud and impressed by Dad returning to University to do two undergraduate papers in English. One paper on grammar and the other on Chaucer. To this day his library is astounding and reveals a curious and creative fascination for, poetry. the classics and obscure literature. It was therefore not that surprising that I eventually ended up being taught politics at University of Auckland by two of their most intriguing lecturers, who considered worlds from opposite ends of the telescope. One with an eye to the history of ideas, the other to the future and the politics of information. Professor Ruth Butterworth, was an ex-Oxford don, who could clearly see the future of information technology and how vested interests could control the politics of information. It was a fascinating time in New Zealand as the Labour government sold off our state assets and I researched the lessons of the UK Post Office and how our government embraced the neoliberal deregulation of our information and telecommunications network. Prestel was an early forerunner of the Internet that Thatcher and her neoliberal cronies hoped would be the 'universal database' for the evolving knowledge economy. In 1984 it seemed to me to be an appropriate research subject as the Orwellian world started to take shape all around me. Ruth deftly supervised my Master's thesis that laid the foundations for my life time's interest in information technology and the secret world of political influence that it hides.

Meanwhile, at the other end of the telescope was Professor Andrew Sharp, a political historian, who had introduced me to the history of political ideas, ideologies, and strange beliefs. Despite his lucid introduction to the likes of Locke, Hobbes and the utilitarian, Jeremy Bentham, he managed to illustrate that these rationalists were far more flesh and blood than their royal portraits would have us believe. Not only was Sir Issac Newton prone to occultist obsessions, (possibly brought on by mercury poisoning) but his mathematical genius was focused on calculating the coming of the Antichrist. Looking at the history of ideas through Andrew's looking glass made the Age of Enlightenment appear haunted by ancient ghouls rather than informed by logical empiricism. I was one of only two students who enrolled in Professor Sharp's Master's paper in Seventeenth Century, Millenarianism, or the study of the apocalyptic beliefs of revolutionary England. Andrew helped me to see how ancient religious myths and legends came to shape the technologies and ideologies of our most trusted rationalists.

Andrew Sharp told me about the wild and exciting world of the English Revolution and the radical cults with rockband-like names: the Ranters, the Levellers and the Diggers. It was a time of apocalyptic revelations and prophecies of the second coming and a utopian Heaven on Earth. The Ranters were anarchistic proto-communists who believed God was everywhere and in everything. This pantheism proclaimed radical equality for all men and women and agitated for the redistribution of land and the taking down of enclosures that barred them from the Commons. According to Christopher Hill in his book, *The World Turned Upside Down*, "The only name the Ranters appeared to accept for themselves collectively was 'My one flesh'. This and their salutation of 'fellow creature' were intended to emphasize unity, with mankind and with the whole creation."[1] Ranters preached free love, and believed there was no such thing as sin, a world free of morality, and equality for all. The Diggers shared an ecological vision with the Ranters; the prominent member, Gerard Winstanley wrote: "every man and woman shall have the free liberty to marry whom they love", and in another tract, "true freedom lies where a man receives his nourishment and preservation, and that is in the use of the earth".[2] I was astounded, all of this peace, love and understanding sounded like Woodstock![3]

As I read, *The Growth Delusion*, by David Piling,[4] I am reminded of Professor Sharp's description of an 18th century Bentham who came to design panopticon surveillance, and our present day economic conviction defining happiness as the greatest good for the greatest number. Through his entertaining lectures and suggested readings I came to respect that apocalyptic archetypes were not just the silly fears of pre-scientific fools, but the ever present ghosts that haunt our own sub-conscious dreams. Andrew showed me that you might not agree with the strange religious and political beliefs of the past, but rather than pass judgement you could attempt to understand where they came from.

Just this weekend Sarah, my wife, and I were invited on a road trip with our good friends, Sarah Barnao and Steven O'Meagher, who took us to Kerikeri for a short well-earned break. We visited the old 19th century Stone Store where missionaries, under the moral guidance of Samuel Marsden would provision their missions. Steven had just completed a fascinating documentary series, The Story of Rugby, and while we browsed the store he pointed out an imposing tome on the shelf, *The World, the Flesh & the Devil: the life and opinions of Samuel Marsden*. He told me that through Sarah B's cousin, an English academic, he had met the author, Andrew Sharp and interviewed him about New Zealand rugby. The memories of Ruth Butterworth and Andrew Sharp came rushing back to me. The original title for this book was, Apocalyptic Worldbending, and recalled those politics courses from the 80s. Strangely, earlier this week I had wondered what Andrew was up to and had looked him up online. My wife, Sarah, lovingly purchased this thumping great book and the coincidence fittingly rounded out the pattern of events that led to this moment that I am writing these words, and you are reading them. The debonair, life-loving, Andrew Sharp cited a man who I would have said was least like him, Samuel Marsden, who was fond of quoting, 'hypocrisy is the homage that vice pays to virtue'.[5] In some small way I am hoping that my book will honour both Ruth and Andrew's erudition, and remind all those who want to cancel unpopular and obscure academic courses that have no perceived utilitarian benefit. It is precisely when you face a crisis that you need to avoid 'group think' and that divergent creativity is blessed by the odd, the unusual, and the alternate world view.

Thank you to Ruth Butterworth, and Andrew Sharp for inspiring me all those years ago. Thank you to my good friend Nigel Clark, who continues to write about our 'inhuman nature' and the worlds we barely comprehend but really need to. A big thank you to Paul Hewlitt who has had the patience to read my drafts and to give me such enthusiastic support and witty leads for me to follow. Thanks so much to my dear friend, Catherine Carter, the photographic artist, who shows us how we are all worldbenders and how urgent it is we think carefully about the world we are breaking. To all of my friends and family, and my colleagues at S23M who have given me support and encouragement to keep going. To my darling Sarah who smiles at my eccentricities and happily brings me detox teas while I appear to be lounging in bed reading and researching for this book. To all the brave World Builders, World Benders, and World Breakers your creativity makes life worth living!

Notes

1. Hill, C. (1972). The World Turned Upside Down: radical ideas during the English revolution. London: Temple Smith. p.207
2. Hill, C. World Turned Upside Down, p.312 & p.134
3. Actually, in the 1960s there was a movement influenced by the Diggers known as the San Francisco Diggers who harked back to those revolutionary times.
4. Pilling, D. (2018). The growth delusion: Wealth, poverty, and the well-being of nations (1st American Edition). New York: Tim Duggan Books.
5. Originally credited to François de La Rochefoucauld (1613-1680)

Introduction

This book is about the end of the world as we know it, how we got here, who we will share new worlds with, and what we might do about making survival plans? Better still, it goes beyond survival, it examines how we might enjoy a meaningful life in the new future worlds we build. I have concentrated on the hegemonic world view that prevails around the globe today. It is one based on the traditions and philosophies of the Northern hemisphere and Graeco-Judaeo-Christian beliefs.

I was born and live in Aotearoa, 'New Zealand' that is the ancestral home to the tanga te whenuea, 'people of the land', Te Māori, who have created their own worlds, Te Ao Māori, that are very different to those I describe in this book. Their wisdom deserves full exploration but I lack the space or the language to do it justice. Buddhism also offers us other worlds that could liberate us from Plato's chains, but given the limitations I have here, all I can do is hint at vast worlds that need, building, bending, and breaking. I have concentrated on so-called Western thought not because it is right, or the best world view, but for the very reason it is hegemonic, dominates, and in many ways is erroneous. I would need far more space to discuss other world views but would add that our solutions to the end of this world may very well lie in the alternatives. A survey published in 2015 found that: "Almost 80% agreed 'we need to transform our world view and way of life if we are to create a better future for the world' (activism). About a half agreed 'the world's future looks grim so we have to focus on looking after ourselves and those we love' (nihilism), and over a third that 'we are facing a final conflict between good and evil in the world' (fundamentalism). The findings offer insight into the willingness of humanity to respond to the challenges identified by scientists and warrant increased consideration in scientific and political debate."[1]

This book is about a speculative art form, world bending, not just for ourselves, but also for the nonhuman majority, with the aspiration to make better worlds together. Before we materially construct anything, we must aesthetically take action, imaginatively and creatively engaging with both the organic and inorganic things all around us – we must get over the guilt and fall in love with ourselves and the others who share this world!

This book is speculative and even utopian, it is not, however, a blueprint with step by step instructions.[2]

How much do we really know about our World?

If we were to admit that some of our ideas were not very good and that they have got us into a bit of a pickle, then surely we have to come up with new ideas, and the only way to do that is to redesign our thinking. Worlds are subjective, cognitive constructs, created by humans and nonhumans alike, and these worlds are perforated by the worlds of others.[3]

They are neither discrete, nor completely objective, but they are real. Individually we are world builders, but this is not an exclusive human skill. I want to discuss how you might go about building better worlds. I will explore ways that we can be more receptive to new creative forces that can open up future worlds, and at the same time be wary of the cognitive restraints and hidden controls – historically created and currently exist. World building is a massive and transdisciplinary task and this book can only touch on some of the topics I think might be interesting to you. If we want to move beyond the dangerous limitations of the spurious complexity in this world, we require a co-design approach that engages all of those who will co-exist in the worlds of the future. This leads us to consider the exciting possibilities of creative collaboration. It is obvious that even if this book was the collective wisdom of everything on this planet, much, much, larger than the size of the Internet, it will still only be a tidbit, a collection of data points, one person's opinion shaped by an echo chamber of facts, knowledge, and other opinions I have had the privilege to read, discuss and research. I cannot help but be mostly ignorant of the sum total of scientific data, world literature, culture, and technologies, but I believe this humble start is essential to overcome our cognitive dissonance and denial that has stopped the dominant world view from trying.

A 21st-century philosopher, Graham Harman wrote:

"though the West is justly proud of its scientific tradition stretching back to ancient Greece, perhaps the greatest intellectual hero of that early period was Socrates (469– 399 BCE), who claimed no knowledge whatsoever. Indeed, in Plato's dialogues we often find Socrates candidly asserting that he has never been anyone's teacher, and that the only thing he knows is that he knows nothing."[4]

Arrogance often causes harm because it ignores things that contradict one's world view; it requires humility to imagine multiple world views. Understanding world views, and fostering a sandbox for creating worlds, bending worlds, and ending worlds, is about 'thing related reality', or the philosophy of being a thing. The AI (Artificial Intelligence), expert, Marvin Minsky, asked: "Why must we 'thingify' everything?" He then goes on to say:

"We're imprisoned by our poverty of words because even though we have good ways to describe objects and actions, we lack methods for describing dispositions and processes."[5]

It is, of course, exactly what we need in order to approach the end of the world, a well thought out purpose, collection of dispositions, and processes before we act. We need a shared sense of purpose and an equitable value system to underpin it. Value should not be based on shareholders' ROI but on a philosophical recalibration of our purpose for this planet.[6]

This goes beyond big data, information, and the study of knowledge, or epistemology. We must remain open and flexible to multi-world views, and recognise that the world we have built for ourselves, and are currently expanding, maybe coming to an end. The speculative art of world bending, building, and breaking is an urgent endeavour and requires new thinking about the majority of things with which we must co-design future worlds. World bending is our ability to play with models and to flex and bend them to the point of breaking. Are we sufficiently humble, and creative to begin to reimagine better worlds? As Bret Victor, a software designer once said:

"The most dangerous thought you can have as a creative person is to think you know what you are doing because once you think you know what you are doing, you stop looking around for ways of doing things. You stop seeing ways of doing things. You become blind..."[7]

Our models and concepts define not just the way we think but the technology we think with. For many of us, our phones and our computers are mysterious black boxes but they have been designed by those who would presume to know the technology, and how it works? Yet, there is much that is also hidden from their view. Victor, who is a designer and programmer himself, addresses the anointed wizards of the computer age, telling them:

"We don't know what programming is, we don't know what computing is, we don't even know what a computer is. And once you truly believe that, and once you truly understand that – you are free and you can think anything."[8]

While it might appear that we have instant access to the world's information and knowledge, via the Internet, and the vast amount of knowledge collected and created on encyclopaedic websites such as Wikipedia, it is this very illusion that has led to what amounts to our mass delusion – in fact we really know very little. It is estimated that Google has only indexed 0.004% of all online data, estimated to be 200 terabytes.[9] Google is currently the most popular Internet search engine at around 74% of online searches.[10]

In 2017 IBM estimated that in only that one year 90% of all data on the Internet had been created, and it is currently estimated that the trend will see an average doubling every year. If we consider the speed of change of data creation, right here, right now, as you read this, it will already be significantly out of date. You can take a look at Google's search engine on a daily basis,[11] and see that while the amount of data has grown exponentially year on year, that the number of web pages indexed is still pretty much the same at around 4-5 billion web pages indexed in the past 2 years.[12] In other words, unless search engines dramatically improve the speed and amount of pages they index, the proportion of information we can search is rapidly shrinking.

The vast majority of information is being generated on the 'deep web'. This is not the same as the 'darknet' – a dangerous, and dubious source of illegal, unscrupulous, and violent information. The deep web is another thing, it is generated by machines, the majority of the data explosion in the future will not just be human-readable data, but most data will be generated by machines, to be read by machines, via the Internet of Things (IoT) devices connected to the Internet. Most of that data will be hidden, or unintelligible to humans and contribute to what has been described as 'data swamps' of 'junk data'. According to the IDC report sponsored by Seagate the amount of data is predicted to grow from 33 Zettabytes in 2018 to 175 Zettabytes of data by 2025, and the IoT is estimated to contribute approximately 50% of that.[13]

We are already living in a world outnumbered, and overpowered by a vast majority of things that are nonhuman, but as we increase the production of IoT devices we are creating a world where communication and data generation will be almost entirely for the machines, objects or things that have no intrinsic motivation, care or feeling about humans, animals, plants, or minerals. The IoT and the AI that will administer and receive their data can be programmed to serve human values, but the point is, they do not currently share our intrinsic motivations, and ethics is only considered in a minority of use cases and is usually extrinsic. Hayles, explains that:

"Ethics cannot be plastered on as an afterthought after the system has already been formed and set in motion, an unfortunate tendency, for example, in courses on "ethics" in business practices, which too often focus on how to satisfy legal requirements so that one does not become the object of a lawsuit."[14]

Unless we can read this data, and have sensible discussions about the assumptions behind the algorithms and protocols then the alien logic of the machines could be our demise. Big data, AI, and the IoT are leading to worlds of spurious complexity, and according to the historian, Joseph Tainter, complexity leads to societal collapse.[15]

One of the significant trends in the past few years is the Quantified Self or Lifelogging. While it is understandable that as a species we are fascinated by ourselves, as we generate more and more anthropocentric data, such as your daily steps; we are also becoming conscious of big data that has nothing to do with humans. We currently wallow in what Carr calls 'the shallows' as we are overwhelmed by data that may be meaningless, or so vast, and opaque, that it can be part of manipulation and deception to create spurious meaning. There are already those that are more interested in services such as Google's AdWords and search optimisation, than understanding real humans, let alone nonhuman things that deserve our attention, such as the atmosphere, hydrosphere, lithosphere, and biosphere. Nicholas Carr points out that despite the deluge of data, and the explosive access to academic research via the Internet, scholars are not necessarily more open to new ideas, but have tended to become more siloed in their research.[16]

He cites research by sociologist, James Evans, of Chicago University, that showed, after an analysis of a database of 34 million scholarly articles, between 1945 – 2005, that scholars, in fact, cited fewer articles than they had done before then. Evans argued that growing the amount of available research online has led to a paradoxical 'narrowing of science and scholarship'.[17]

According to Maryanne Wolf, the Director of the Center for Dyslexia, Diverse Learners, and Social Justice at UCLA, this may relate to the very way that academics are currently researching and reading. She claims that screen technology has changed the way we are all thinking. The tsunami of data, we are now confronted with, is driving a digital attention deficit disorder that promotes speed reading, skimming, and keyword searches. In the book, *The Slow Professor*, the authors, Maggie Berg and Barbara Seeber, not only bemoan the administrative workload of the managerial universities, but the breakneck speed that people are reading and writing without deep, and contemplative thinking. Speed does not encourage radical ideas, but rather, quick, iterative modifications of existing concepts; a bureaucratic busyness that is counted in volume of papers. If academics were to forego quantity over quality and adopt a slow meditation on the plight of our world and contemplate human coexistence with others, this will in turn also help the humans. They quote Jane Tompkins who writes "there's no intellectual life left in universities, or precious little because people are too busy getting ahead professionally ... to stop and talk to each other."[18] Wolf believes that we need to "cultivate a new kind of brain: a 'bi-literate' reading brain capable of the deepest forms of thought in either digital or traditional mediums."[19]

When we pause to think deeply about the entire human population, we must be struck by how little we know about it as a 'thing'. Timothy Morton calls humanity a *hyperobject*,[20] something beyond human-scale understanding, so vast in size, and across such a large longitudinal time expanse, that we cannot fully comprehend it. Even if we could understand humanity, this is still ignoring the vast majority of nonhumans here with us on Earth, or in the Universe. On this small rock, placed third from an average-sized star, known as the Sun, on the outer reaches of one of 100 billion galaxies, we are facing the sixth mass extinction of our planet's biosphere.[21] On reflection, not only do we not know what we do not know about all the nonhuman things that make up the biosphere, but consider the enormous numbers of things that have gone before us in the first five extinction events; the 99.99% that are now extinct. Our ability to interrogate them is severely limited by the study of dead fossils and other inadequate, but ingenious, technologies.

Triumphant Science and Technology

It would seem that modern technological culture has suffered from a massive teenage ego trip, but if we are to grow up, we need to acknowledge our ignorance and our co-inhabitants. Most of us have not stopped to muse on how little we know about everything. Scientists have just recently discovered that a tiny microbe, hemimastigotes, do not fit on the Tree of Life, under a kingdom-level supergroup, such as the one that includes animals and fungi, but are a whole new group on their own and according to one of the research teams this "is a sharp reminder about how little we still know about the diversity of life on Earth."[22]

Biology, is but one domain of knowledge, a lens to view our worlds, however, world bending must acknowledge that there is no privilege for any one domain, whether it is the sciences, the arts, the humanities, or religions to name just some world views. In 1905 Einstein published his General Theory of Relativity, and what followed was the beginning of the end of the Newtonian world. It was no longer a clockwork universe, and what resulted was an explosion of technological and social change. It heralded the rebirth of the primordial virtual, the potentiality of the actual, in which possible worlds are infinite and sites of creativity. Suddenly, scientific certainty was overwhelmed by strange and mysterious theories such as Heisenberg's Uncertainty Principle that showed that it was impossible to predict both the velocity, and the position of a subatomic particle – the future was essentially uncertain. Paradox and probability became the defining ideas of the 20th century, and the fundamental limits to human knowledge became apparent. According to Andrew Thomas, "The old certainties were starting to unravel. From now on, the only certainty was uncertainty." [23]

The power of $E=mc^2$ is still radically changing how we build worlds, giving us such wonders as lasers, the Internet, and quantum computing. We have built the Large Hadron Collider, the biggest machine in the history of our world, built with over 10,000 scientists, untold tradespeople, 27 kms in circumference, and costing €7.5 billion. It is capable of propelling subatomic particles at close to the speed of light, and has confirmed the existence of the Higgs boson, nicknamed the God Particle because it supports, but does not prove, the theories of the multiverse, and that string theory may explain how the universe creates matter and could be expanding, or inflating due to inflatons.[24] These speculative theories are the results of the creative minds of theoretical physicists and play an important role in world building. These theories and experiments agree with speculative realism that states that the virtual is not illusory, but real, as it becomes concrete actuality before it disappears again into virtuality.[25]

However, while the Higgs boson is an extraordinary leap forward in scientific knowledge, scientific theory has postulated a massive thing, known as Dark Matter, that composes 85% of the mass of the universe, and a quarter of the energy – they do not know what it is, it is invisible. It would be fair to surmise that at the very least we are 85% ignorant of the universe, but that ignores how little we know about our own tiny world, and there is another uncomfortable fact. Dark Energy has been a theory that has been around since the 1990's, and is broadly supported by the General Theory of Relativity, however, it also happens to be speculative, and was theorised simply to make the numbers work and to explain gravitation, and the acceleration of an expanding universe, or the Big Bang. According to the standard model the total mass-energy of the universe, and Dark Energy, explained by the cosmological constant, makes up 68.3% of the universe, Dark Matter is 26.8% mass-energy, and ordinary matter that we can see only 4.9%.[26] Therefore if one or more of the multiverse theories are practical, if not observable, the concrete reality, or 4.9% mass-energy that we assume is the only reality, maybe only a tiny percent of one universe. All of this speculation by the world's leading theoretical physicists leads me to conclude that at this point in time we only know very little about the universe we live in.

You Have To See It To Believe It

While many people still imagine that reality is based on empirically observable events and objects, the physics of the 20th century changed all that. Physicality has disappeared before our eyes, and in 2017 we said goodbye to the very last measurement based on a physical property. The kilogram, is no longer referenced to a physical object. The International Systems of Units, or SI, such as the meter for measurement of length, the kilogram for mass, and the second for time, were previously all based on direct physically observable objects. Since 1889, the measure of mass, the kilogram had been previously based on a metal cylinder called the International Prototype of the Kilogram. It was replaced by a new definition, the Planck constant, set to $6.62607015{\times}10^{-34}$J·s, exactly.

Since Heisenberg's Uncertainty Principle (1927) we are now more aware of the uncertainty of the unobservable reality. This can be confirmed by the accuracy of the measurement of the nonzero cosmological constant, or the energy density of space. Dark energy is theoretically created by quantum field jitters. This anti-gravity, as it is known, explains the accelerating expansion of space, which gives scientists a constant, which is accurate to a measurable, but unobservable, 1.38×10^{-123}.[27] Because the constant is unobservable, and likely to be never observable, it has been described as "the worst theoretical prediction in the history of physics!" This unimaginably small number is so close to zero, and so beyond human scale, that it could just as well be infinite. Compare this number with the cells in your body, $10^{13,}$ or the time in seconds since the Big Bang, $10^{-8,}$ or even the number of photons in the observable part of the universe, 10^{88} – none of these come even close to the scale and accuracy of the cosmological constant which has been calculated at 1.38×10^{-123}.[28]

Quantum mechanics theorises the existence of probability waves, in which the virtual becomes an actuality, and this model because of the accuracy of its mathematical predictions, despite being unobservable, is widely regarded by physicists to be a valid description of reality. Because we cannot know whether light is a particle or a wave, and cannot measure its position and momentum at the same time, scientists are confident of their uncertainty about reality. Worse still, quantum mechanics confirms that two observers can experience different or conflicting realities[29] – it is, therefore, officially fuzzy.

Scientists are still trying to come up with, and prove what is known as the Grand Unified Theory of Everything, otherwise known as GUT or TOE, depending on your anatomical predilection. However, new philosophical approaches such as the OOO, (Object Oriented Ontology, often called the Triple O), and speculative realism, deny that this will ever be possible with the current philosophy of science, if at all. Empiricism may still be considered by many to be common sense, but it no longer commands theoretical physics, that is responsible for many of the most influential discoveries, inventions, and predictions in the past one hundred years. Experimental physics may still attempt to apply empirical methods to determine the nature of reality, and even the inflationary multiverse may ultimately succumb to experiments that show that our universe has collided with another shown through images of the cosmic microwave background radiation.[30]

Our science has moved beyond our senses ability to directly sense the data; we are more and more dependent on the mathematics that makes predictions about things we can measure.[31]

Empirical bias continues to constrain alternative modes of thinking, even in the digital humanities. Katherine Hayles in her book, *Unthought: The Power of the Cognitive Nonconscious* (2017) states her preference for empirical evidence, criticising the OOO and philosophy in general, for its discursive bias. Citing Bruno Latour, Hayles argues that without empirical support "it is impossible to distinguish between what is actually the case and what is ideologically driven fantasy."[32] She criticises Harman and Bogost for their assertion that: 'objects recede from us infinitely and so can never be known at all, which seems to me [Hayles] obviously contradicted by empirical knowledge in all its forms including science, engineering, medicine, anthropology, and digital humanities.'[33]

My short discussion of how physics has become more than comfortable with non-empirical theories would seem to rebut her point. Hayles argues convincingly for the existence of non conscious cognition, even amongst nonhumans, but stops short of including inorganic matter, creating a gulf between the singularity of the Big Bang from the moment at 10^{-43} seconds, and the emergence of intelligence, cognition and consciousness. For now this seems to be an event horizon which we cannot reach beyond – we cannot observe anything before 10^{-43} seconds.

Speculative philosophy provides a cognitive tool, not based on knowledge, but on wisdom, to envisage a nonhuman universe of affective things which, according to Alfred North Whitehead, 'feel' each other, and themselves, even the inorganic, without knowing the ultimate truth about those things. This is not some sort of material mysticism, but what Whitehead calls 'transcendent empiricism'. Just as living beings comprehend things, Whitehead speculates that inorganic matter can also apprehend other things, or as described it 'prehend'. Later in her book, Unthought, Hayles discusses the power of Whitehead's speculative realism. As she explains: "Prehension is of course the term that Alfred North Whitehead uses to formulate a processual world view in which "actual entities" (Whitehead 1978, 7, 13 passim) arise and coalesce."[34] Whitehead claims this is a cosmic creativity of which humanity is but one small part.

Hayles dismissive approach to the OOO here, however, fails to fully acknowledge the scientific demotion of empiricism, and the continuing hegemonic effect of this explanation of reality. Hayles does acknowledge that the unknowable and non-computable do exist, and that what she calls 'technical cognition', or the technological extension of our social, political, and economic prejudices can result in protocols and algorithms that command and control us.

Our standard units of measurement[35] no longer rely on physical objects, and science has gone well beyond observable things, reaching even the limits of theoretical physics and mathematics, so there is no contradiction, there is no privilege granted to empirical observation. This empirical world view ultimately delimits all world views and our search for speculative futures that playfully use theoretical models. We need new cognitive tools and alternative worlds to model the future.

According to Graham Harman philosophy is not the search for knowledge, logic or mathematical validation, (as it is currently understood, and taught in many universities), but rather, its meaning is derived from its Greek etymology, i.e. the search and love of wisdom, but without the possibility of attainment. This philosophical view embraces the awe and wonderment of reality. Harman states that the OOO is 'against physicalism, smallism, anti-fictionalism, and literalism' (2017), and he makes the claim that it is the philosophical 'theory of everything'. Harman denies physics the same opportunity because physics cannot account for the reality of fiction, poetry or metaphor. For Harman, the true core of philosophical enquiry and thinking is not science, or logic, but is more closely aligned with the arts and aesthetics. Science often uses mathematics to serve its objectives, however, according to my colleague, Jorn Bettin:

"Mathematic[s] is a form of art and just like art is closely associated with aesthetics by practitioners. There are even experiments that show that mathematicians experience brain states when looking at mathematically pleasing results that correspond to the states of people seeing art they enjoy. Since parts of mathematics are extremely useful in various sciences, mathematics is easily lumped together with science, but this confuses the motivations of scientists with the motivations of mathematicians and artists. The dichotomy between science and the arts is an artificial construct, I suspect fuelled by the big chasm that some scientists seem to perceive in relation to the arts and that some artists seem to perceive in relation to science...I argue that these foundations are very close to what humans experience at the boundary between conscious thought and subconscious processes. Whether the output is music, dance, visual art, mathematics, or some other form of expression depends on the context and individual preference and neurology."

The appreciation of a metaphorical reality assumes a shared reality, and not just an anthropocentric reality, that humanity dictates. According to Harman, the OOO can be immaterial, at any scale, fictional, and metaphorical, and therefore capable of providing a philosophical model of everything but with the caveat that reality remains partially withdrawn and unknowable even to itself. As the philosopher and mathematician, Alfred North Whitehead wrote, philosophy is interested in the ultimate generalisation of reality but admits that a comprehensive description will ultimately elude us.[36] However, neither Whitehead nor Harman dismisses or trashes other forms of reality, they recognise numerous world views, even in an anthropic sense, such as science, engineering, philosophy, art, and design, but none of these world views can claim a monopoly with their description of reality. One of the serious problems we now face is that the foundation of one world view claims ascendancy over all others. It is a neoliberal, selectively scientific, and political, world view that is built into a ubiquitous techno-liberal reality. The algorithms and protocols of that techno-reality physically and cognitively control those things connected to its networks. According to Bratton much of this is accidental and is even contested by various ideologies, such as China's state capitalism, but its flavour is distinct and found worldwide.

Considering the existential crisis we now face it is urgent that we develop conceptual tools – novel world benders – to assist in imagining and designing new worlds because this ideological one is coming to an end. We should be working on our most pressing communal project, the health of the planet Earth. We live in apocalyptic times, not in any religious sense, but rather of our own making because we have physically and irretrievably damaged our world. John Hall explains that our apocalyptic outlook is not new, it is a belief that has a long history. In our past, the coming of the apocalypse may have caused us to look to the skies for the signs of the end, but in recorded history, despite catastrophic natural disasters, our planet, and our species have survived. Hall explains the historic meaning of the apocalypse is:

"For most of us, "Apocalypse" suggests the cataclysmic end of the world. Yet in Greek "apocalypse" means "revelation," and the real subject of the Book of Revelation is how the sacred arises in history at a moment of crisis and destiny...

Rather than the actual end of the world, the apocalypse is typically "the end of the world as we know it," an extreme social and cultural disjuncture in which dramatic events reshape the relations of many individuals at once to history."[37]

This book is about world building, world bending, and world ending, but also about technology, creativity, hope and our moral imperative to do the right thing – if we can figure out what that is, and get on with it. Fear of cataclysmic disaster and the end of the world may not be novel ideas; ancient religions, cults, and myths about the apocalypse go back to the beginning of languages. Even in modern history there have been numerous dire predictions, and warnings, that THE END IS NIGH!. What is new is that our apocalyptic fears are no longer based on religious proclamations, but on scientific, political, artistic, and increasingly, philosophical narratives.

At the end of the Second World War, after Hiroshima and Nagasaki, the threat of the Cold War and Mutually Assured Destruction, or MAD, frightened millions of people who contemplated that a MAD man in the Kremlin, or the Whitehouse, and most likely both, would start the Mother of all Wars. Even if you were lucky enough to be thousands of miles from the population epicentres, and therefore, away from the primary targets in a nuclear war, you were assured that you would probably die a slow and painful death from starvation, as the nuclear winter swept in on the plutonium laden clouds from the fallout. Well, that did not happen but we have some new MAD men in town and they know just the right buttons to push to terrify a whole new generation of fearful humans. Fear is a powerful tool of political manipulation and it has been used by both religious and secular leaders to focus political debate, and quell the masses since the beginning of recorded history.[38] Recently, The Bulletin of the Atomic Scientists moved the hands of the symbolic Doomsday Clock closer to the end of time, now it is just two minutes to the darkest hour.

"Because of the extraordinary danger of the current moment, the Science and Security Board today moves the minute hand of the Doomsday Clock 30 seconds closer to catastrophe," said Rachel Bronson, president of the Bulletin of the Atomic Scientists. "This is the closest the Clock has ever been to Doomsday, and as close as it was in 1953, at the height of the Cold War."[39]

What seems to have occurred throughout history, especially in the Judaeo Christian traditions, is that human culture has suffered from a history of manic episodes in which we have reeled from unfounded optimism to illogical despair. At one moment the four horsemen of the apocalypse are about to descend upon us, and at another, the Y2K disaster fizzles out. We then rejoiced in a new millennium of tech-toys that are lifted straight from the exciting pages of a Buck Rogers 1930s comic, *Armageddon 2419, A.D.* All of this only to again lapse into a depressed state of paralysis as the collapse of the subprime American housing market resigns the victims to accepting banker's bonuses, and a strange demagogue strides from his hit TV show screaming 'You're fired!', and starts the chant, 'Lock her up!'[40] If only we could get our meds right, maybe we could think straight, and figure out what to do next? It is as if we are Stephen Dedalus in Joyce's *Ulysses*, our 'history is a nightmare from which I am trying to awake'.

In this book, I would like to outline my research findings, the opinions of others far more knowledgeable than me, and why, despite our genius for innovation and technological solutions, yet we now face a psychological and physical existential crisis. It appears inevitable there will be widespread social, economic, and environmental collapse of vast tracts of land and oceans that support many forms of life, including ours. Yet most of us perform an unconscious psychological trick, denying the bad news because it upsets our world view. We latch on to reports and stories that fit with that view and any doubt we may have will default to outdated, or worse, false evidence.

Threats To The Physical World

In 2003 the United Nations' Intergovernmental Panel on Climate Change (IPCC) reported that sea level should rise by a mere half a meter by the end of this century, however, what is often forgotten is that they didn't include the impact of ice melts in Greenland and Antarctica – it is now known that the speed of the ice melt is much faster than earlier thought. In the fourth assessment by the IPCC temperatures could reach the upper end of the scale predicted to be 3-6° Celsius. If that did happen and the atmospheric carbon dioxide goes a little higher than it is now, we could be seeing a rerun of the Mid-Miocene Climatic Optimum (MMCO) that happened between 17 and 15 million years ago when CO_2 levels were only in the region of 400 – 450ppm.[41] The shock is that if that should happen we could see a repeat rise of sea levels of not half a metre but 25 – 40 meters due to ice melt.[42]

In 2015 the Paris climate talks set a goal of holding temperature increases to 1.5° Celsius or at least 2° Celsius, but by 2018 the IPCC reported we might go past that by 2030.[43] It is also expected we will soar past 410 ppm of CO_2 in 2019 so if we mimic the MMCO we could be looking at a much higher range of 3-6° C. McKibben warns:

"There's even this: if we keep raising carbon dioxide levels, we may not be able to think straight anymore. At a thousand parts per million (which is within the realm of possibility for 2100), human cognitive ability falls 21 percent. "The largest effects were seen for Crisis Response, Information Usage, and Strategy," a Harvard study reported, which is too bad, as those skills are what we seem to need most."[44]

Many of us want to believe that global warming can be controlled like a tap or a thermostat; we only have to dial-up 2°C and we can then carry on business as usual. It appears more likely that we are in for some shocking surprises as our world buckles and bends beneath our feet. It may well be that we are already facing runaway global warming and the extreme weather maybe part of a feedback cycle pushing us towards a tipping point with no prospect of return until the Earth system has completed its heating cycle. The reality is to have some hope we have to drastically rethink and rebuild our conceptual world.

The magnitude of this existential crisis appears to be totally new, and for many, unexpected. You may be reading this and be wondering, 'wait, who said the world was about to end?', 'surely we will bring global warming under control', 'it's a gradual problem we will fix it in time'. Of course, you may even believe all of this hysteria is politically motivated by peddlers of 'fake news'. What I do set out to show is that panic, and the end of the world, are ancient human hobbies, often encouraged by those that believe they have the divine right to rule, or they simply have an insatiable power lust. But what is novel, in the history of humanity, and now in the 21st century, is that we have the most reliable, and verifiable information, to date, pointing towards the sixth mass extinction of the planet, and humanity is a species that is numbered in that long list now facing obliteration. It turns out that cataclysmic disasters are more common than we thought, and that only seventy-five thousand years ago there was a massive volcanic eruption that almost wiped humanity out, and possibly only left around two thousand descendants on the planet.[45]

The paradox of dramatic geological events, or hyperobjects, that span millions of years, and result in extreme climatic changes, appear to us as violent and undesirable. However, volcanic activity, while it has been responsible for mass extinctions, well before human evolution, is also an essential catalyst for life.

232 million years ago a mass extinction known as the Carnian Pluvial Event (CPE) occurred following the eruption of a string of volcanic eruptions in western Canada. The CPE is evident today from the Wrangellia basalts, that caused a massive release of CO_2, and resulted in global warming of 3 – 10 degrees Celsius. The CPE illustrates our difficulty in comprehending the massive spatiotemporal scale of such a hyperobject that resulted in a wet and humid period of rain that continued without a pause for 2 million years.[46]

This vast hyperobject not only puts human existence on Earth into perspective but also signalled the evolution of the first dinosaurs.[47] Our anthropocentric opinion may view extinction with horror, but this archetypal cycle of evolution and extinction should also inform our discussion of the Anthropocene.

Cognitive Dissonance

While we ignore the scientific reality of the Anthropocene we employ a psychological defence known as cognitive dissonance to allow us to carry on, business as usual – for most humans it is hard, if not impossible to imagine a future world without humans. In 1956 an American social psychologist, Leon Festinger, published a book based on his findings of a doomsday cult he had infiltrated. His research examined what happens when people are faced with a reality that clashes with their world view. In his book, *When Prophecy Fails: A Social and Psychological Study of a Modern Group That Predicted the Destruction of the World*, Festinger wrote:

"A man [sic] with a conviction is a hard man to change. Tell him you disagree and he turns away. Show him facts or figures and he questions your sources. Appeal to logic and he fails to see your point."

Festinger had read in a local newspaper that "Lake City will be destroyed by a flood from the Great Lake just before dawn, Dec. 21." According to a Chicago suburbanite, Dorothy Martin, this apocalyptic deluge would be preceded by a visit from advanced beings from another planet. "These beings have been visiting the earth, she says, in what we call flying saucers."[48] The chosen would then be taken up into the heavens leaving the non-believers behind to be drowned by the Flood. When the clock struck midnight and the flying saucers appeared to be delayed. One believer said that they had burned all they're bridges, and turned their backs on the world, they could not afford to doubt.

Festinger, infiltrated Mrs Martin's world ending cult to attempt to discover "What happens when people experience a severe crisis in their convictions?"[49]His theory of cognitive dissonance is not exclusive to the looney fringe, as pointed out by researchers from Yale University, they showed that educated people are 'more unshakable in their convictions than anybody.', and that they have greater resources at their disposal to 'prove' it.[50]

We continue to fool ourselves that our behaviour is not accelerating our demise. Freud described our self-destructive behaviour as civilization's 'death drive', and yet, as our 'hyperloop' picks up speed, the time bomb is still ticking and no one has figured out how to defuse it? We have fought off the superstition of religion, scoffed at the logical 'rapture of the nerds', and still, we have this sneaking suspicion that the apocalypse is just around the corner. We need time to think. Carl Jung believed we need to heal the split in our psyche to bring our conscious self back in touch with our subconscious ego, and our limbic desires. He wrote:

"Our intellect has created a new world that dominates nature, and has populated it with monstrous machines. The latter are so indubitably useful that we cannot see even a possibility of getting rid of them or our subservience to them. Man is bound to follow the adventurous promptings of his scientific and inventive mind and to admire himself for his splendid achievements. At the same time, his genius shows the uncanny tendency to invent things that become more and more dangerous, because they represent better and better means for wholesale suicide."[51]

The Ghost in the Machine

We will explore the ancient ghost tales, and the technological histories to see if we can cut the wires to the bomb before it is too late. For example, how could a stylish set of Bluetooth headphones lead us to the brink of disaster? While we might marvel at the amazing high fidelity of the technology, we are deaf to the geological grinding of the tectonic plates beneath our feet? If we were to retrace the past it may reveal a strange assemblage of things, agents and concepts. Bluetooth technology is that strange assemblage: a Danish Viking King; runes; and a scandalous naked beauty, who came up with Bluetooth as a military technology during WWII.[52] These 'stranger things' may reveal our true nature, as we get to know our dead ancestors; those trapped ghosts in the machine. As the billions of lines of code continue[53] to build layer upon layer, we risk losing the original thread that will lead us out of the labyrinth, or alternatively, will we be killed by a 21st century Minotaur cyborg?

These stories and narratives shape our cultural, social and physical world, and yet, biologists still struggle with their evolutionary purpose; why do we tell stories? In 1976 Richard Dawkins, in his book, *The Selfish Gene*, put forward the speculative concept of the meme that has gone on to prove its own existence by becoming a meme itself. Lynn Margulis and David Sloan Wilson have successfully rebutted Dawkins view of selfish genes, and cybernetic biologists, Maturana and Varela, put forward their own evolutionary theory of culture in their book, *The Tree of Knowledge: The Biological Roots of Human Understanding* (1987). Brian Boyd attempted to account for the evolutionary purpose of the story,[54] and the theory of biosemiotics claims that 'life' itself comes from coded machines that can explain the evolution of story and culture.

According to Ray Kurzweil's evolutionary theory, we are participants in a cosmic evolution that began with the chemical genesis following the Big Bang. Kurzweil outlines a series of six cosmological epochs that traces the evolution of intelligence. Beginning with the physics of chemical reactions in which information was stored in the atomic structure, and then evolved into biology in which information was stored in DNA. From there the third epoch was the leap to the evolution of the brain that began the storage of information in neural patterns. As each of these epochs occurs, according to the 'S' curve of innovation, there is a quickening of intelligence as the pace accelerates towards a singularity. In the fourth epoch information is stored in hardware and software design; the technological epoch. Kurzweil explains it is at this juncture that human intelligence becomes impatient with the speed of biological evolution and 'outboards' its intelligence and storage in information technology, and propagates itself through the communications network.

Arthur C. Clarke, in his short story *Dial F for Frankenstein* (1961) describes the phone network as a global brain, an AI that one day wakes up, and wrecks havoc on the financial, transportation and military systems. In Kurzweil's fifth epoch, that we are now just entering, he predicts a merger of technology and human intelligence. This is the last epoch he imagines before the universe wakes up and runaway 'nonbiological' intelligence saturates the universe, exploiting black holes and whole galaxies in the search for more power.

In his book, *Homo Deus: a brief history of tomorrow*, Yuval Noah Harari speculates that during the fifth and sixth epoch humanity will evolve into immortal gods. The ancient myth of Prometheus and the Western concept of technological progress originated with Aeschylus, in his book, *Prometheus Bound*, (c. 430 BCE) and referred to the progress of this demigod, rather than humanity. Our conflicted thoughts about becoming immortal gods are bound to the ancient archetypes and the warnings of the original sin – if we did become immortal gods, it would indeed be the end of the world as we know it.

The dangers of AI and our abdication of our moral imperative to create new world solutions based on philosophically, morally and ecologically sound creations, could lead to a self-realised existential crisis. Our ability for self-deception and mass delusion are enormous challenges as we may be accelerating towards a technological singularity which may be out of our control. We now face the urgent task of exorcising the demons of our past in order to ensure that our 'Mind Children'[55] do not accelerate the sixth mass extinction of the planet, and to borrow Google's phrase, ensure they 'do no evil'. The speculative question is whether the human moral imperatives will become obsolete, as we transition beyond posthuman, to a superintelligence that transcends the biological limitations of that imagination, or whether our ancient myths are simply warning us that this is a fool's errand?

Jungian psychology would suggest, that rather than totally abandoning our pre-modern archetypes, that we need to synthesise the pre and post-modern psyche. While there exists the opportunity for conscious, positive solutions, there are also examples of how artistic and creative integration have already begun with the premodern epochs. Maxwell speculates that the rise of rock and roll, and other music movements:

"seem literally to have been training the modern body to overcome its addiction to mentality in the embrace of a more expansive mode. It is no accident that the "hip" countercultures of the twentieth century have often been associated with archetypal modes of thought."[56]

Some may wonder will the robots be joining us? But it may be more appropriate to wonder if we will be joining them? Can we critically reflect on all our mistakes and ensure that bigotry, bias, and ecological stupidity of our past are not passed onto the immortals in the algorithms and code before it is released into the cosmos? Is it already too late, or is this our most urgent and important project, our legacy bequest, before the end of humanity? The future is not all bleak, there is still room for fun and games, awe and wonderment, but it does seem to me that we first need to realise how we got to this point before we can seriously discuss something so awful as the end of the world by our own design. It may of course be true that this world has come to the end of its useful life, and that our current world view is exhausted, and a new epoch of multiple world views are ready to evolve. The end of the world as we know it is not just something a Hollywood producer dreamed up, although there is plenty of movie evidence that we like to scare ourselves to death, but rather it is something that sober minded scientists are now concerned about. We face the possibility of the end of the physical world, the end of biological lives, but also the conceptual end of the world, and all of these maybe simply evolutionary destiny.

The Anthropocene

After thirty years, and 12 projects, the IGBP[57] Earth System panel have concluded that we have entered a new geological epoch, the first created by one species – humans, known as the Anthropocene.[58] Our impact has been felt by every physical layer of this planet: the biological – the biosphere; the rock – the lithosphere; the water – the hydrosphere; and the air – the atmosphere. Not only have we dramatically changed these essential physical layers, but we do not know exactly how they work, and how they sustain life? This is what Earth System scientists attempt to understand and their current conclusions are not that cheery, because these systems are both fragile and unpredictable, and while we inhabit the only 'blue marble' in this solar system, in the near future the spheres may radically change, and that will change what can live here.

In geological terms all of this has come about incredibly quickly, following the last geological epoch, the Holocene, that only lasted 10,000 – 12,000 years, a mere 'blipvert'[59] in the history of the planet. It is both a strength and weakness of humanity that we have no visceral understanding of things that are beyond human scale, both in space, and in time. We therefore have come to think of the long present of the Holocene, that long (apparently) stable, mild climate, as a 'natural' state. However, the world, and a lot of the universe, is not stable for long, and just because geological and climatic disasters can be hostile to life, this does not mean it is not a perfectly reasonable description of reality, and how things just are. It transpires that even our view of the Holocene, as a somewhat stable geological epoch, is far from correct.

According to the Earth scientist, Bill McGuire, the Holocene experienced a long series of cold snaps, with average falls dropping as much as 5° C, happening around every 1500 years, recorded at 5900, 4200, 2800 and 1400 years ago, known collectively as the Bond events. These have also been blamed for the collapse of a number of ancient civilisations, including the Akkadian Empire, and Egypt's age of the Great Pyramids.[60] Even in recent history we saw what has been called, the Little Ice Age, happen from the 17th to the end of the 19th century.

Not only that, it is estimated by Timothy Morton that the Holocene only began something like 400 generations ago.[61] In that very short period humanity managed to establish agricultural communities that are largely credited as the foundation for modern civilisation. It may come as a shock to you that some ecologists, such as Jarred Diamond, regard agriculture as "the worst mistake in the history of the human race".[62] His reason, because it put us on this destructive path to the Anthropocene.

According to Ian Angus, and others, here is a shortlist of some of the outstanding features of the Anthropocene:

- There has been a tenfold human population growth in three centuries.

- Humans maintain 1.4 billion methane-producing cattle.

- Humans have exploited 20–50 percent of Earth's land surface.

- Humans have destroyed most of the tropical rainforests.

- We have built dams and diverted rivers throughout the planet.

- We have exploited more than half of all accessible fresh water.

- We are responsible for a 25 percent decline of fish in upwelling ocean regions and 35 percent in the continental shelf.

- We are responsible for a 16-fold increase in energy use in the twentieth century, raising sulphur dioxide emissions to over twice natural levels.

- We have created and use more than twice as much nitrogen fertilizer in agriculture as is used naturally in all terrestrial ecosystems combined.

- We are responsible for increasing atmospheric concentrations of greenhouse gases to their highest levels in over 400,000 years. Greenhouse gases trap in the heat that are increasing the average temperature on the planet.

- We will be responsible for the sixth mass extinction on earth. This is the first to be caused by a biological species.

- A thin layer of radionuclides from nuclear weapons testing is now spread all over the planet. This along with plastics being found everywhere are considered to be persistent markers of the Anthropocene.[63]

The shocking nature of this tumultuous change to our world challenges us with the provocation of world bending, because just as we have physically bent the world out of shape, we must consider how we can conceptually bend ourselves in order to create new worlds. Our ability to adapt to the shock of the Anthropocene is governed by the ideology that views the past 12,000 as sunk cost that we can never recover. Yet this is not a financial transaction it is founded on the shared resources of the planet, and our consumption has cost not just us but the nonhuman world. The artificial separation of human consciousness and physical nature has been shockingly overthrown as nature rocks us to the core, physically and morally. Bill McGuire in his book, *Waking the Giant*, draws our attention to not just the atmospheric, hydrospheric, and biospheric markers, but the very rock beneath our feet is beginning to bend, and break. He wrote:

"Sweeping climate change will also act, as it has before, to bend the solid Earth to its bidding; influencing and manipulating once again the geophysical processes that operate at the surface of our planet and in its interior."[64]

Paul Crutzen and Eric Stroemer coined the word Anthropocene in 2000, Crutzen wrote:

"Unless there is a global catastrophe — a meteorite impact, a world war or a pandemic — mankind will remain a major environmental force for many millennia. A daunting task lies ahead for scientists and engineers to guide society towards environmentally sustainable management during the era of the Anthropocene."[65]

The shocking symptoms of the Anthropocene has an apocalyptic tone to it that amplifies many of the fears and superstitions of those who think that human ingenuity, and technology are sheer hubris that will be punished as we face the 'end of times'. However, we often don't recognise where these apocalyptic thoughts come from. I suggest it is not a coincidence that the turns of phrase used in the media to describe natural disasters, sound like biblical warnings, especially in America. Words that describe extreme natural events, such as 'disaster', 'catastrophe', 'apocalyptic', 'inferno', and 'hell-on-earth', are recollections of our collective unconscious, something like a half forgotten, instinctual memory, that recalls ancient myths of human transgressions, and God's retribution. Just as in the Book of Revelations we are seeing news reports that the 'signs' of extreme weather including rains, floods, and fires foretell the coming of the end. It has the same narrative structure as religious myths, but simply replaces the tale of the four horsemen of the Apocalypse with reference to global warming. Our imagination is stimulated by ancient archetypes that have symbolic power and fearful resonance for an audience raised on stories shared by almost every religion and culture that has walked the Earth. The Anthropocene is a familiar ancient tale of the end of times.

Yet, how might we find cognitive antidotes, inoculations and place-bos to help us through to the next epoch, the post Anthropocene? We are the first species to cause a phase change, initiating a new geological epoch – we did it, we can no longer deny it; we are moving out of what we perceive to be the stable Holocene into a non analogue environment that humans have never seen; a hot and unpredictable environment that threatens almost every living thing on the planet. The UN Secretary General, Antonio Guterres, recently said that if the world doesn't change course by 2020, we run the risk of runaway climate change.[66] We might be already there.

Over the past 60 years extreme weather events have increased in intensity and regularity. Global warming has been blamed for rising sea levels and storm surges that result in flooding. The Global mean sea level in 2016 was the highest yearly average since measurement began in the 19th century; today it is approximately 20 cm higher.[67] In the US the number of presidentially declared 'major disasters' has increased annually four-fold, from 10-20 just 60 years ago, to an average of over 60 per year, over the last decade.[68] Over 90 percent of all natural disasters in the US involved flooding. The reinsurance industry provides dramatic evidence of this increase in losses adjusted for inflation. Before 1990 the annual disaster losses were well under $5 billion, 75 percent of the time, whereas annual disasters since 1990 have exceeded $10 billion, more than 75 percent of the time, with disaster losses exceeding $40 billion in 1993, 1994, 1995, 2004, 2005, 2008, and 2012.[69] Uninsured losses have soared since 1970, and almost all 'natural disasters' feature some human contribution, from poor housing construction, to shoddy flood protection.

During the 1950s US flood insurance was part of a homeowner's insurance package, however, the cost of flood claims on those policies caused many insurance companies to separate flood insurance. The inability of the private market to offer affordable insurance premiums for flooding saw the introduction of the National Flood Insurance Act in 1968. With the cost of regular disasters mounting due to global warming the NFIP (National Flood Insurance Program) is in debt, and the premiums cannot keep pace with the true actuarial risk analysis of the properties. This is a global phenomenon as governments increasingly step in to provide relief funds for flood prone properties and the insurance industry has begun to discuss uninsurable properties in the US, Australia, and New Zealand. The insurance industry has warned that more and more coastal properties will become uninsurable, seeing a drastic drop in property prices as banks will not lend without insurance.[70]

According to Abbott's paper on flood insurance in the US, despite the increased risk of property loss from rising sea levels and storm surges from extreme weather, each year more than 1.2 million people move to coastal areas. In 2010, in the US, approximately half the population, 123.3 million people now live in coastal shoreline counties.[71] Most of the world's megacities are located in coastal zones and have experienced dramatic immigration despite coastal hazards.[72] It is estimated that it is likely that the LECZ (low elevation coastal zone) population will reach 1.4 billion people, with a density of 534 people/km^2 by 2060, and will rise by 50% from a 2000 baseline in 2030. It is also estimated that over 315 million people will be living in the 100-year floodplain or a 1% probability of flooding in any year, by 2060. The vast majority of those people will be from less developed countries, however, the migration to coastal zones has been steady in the US and will endanger millions in Europe. If global warming is contained within the 2° C target, set out by the Paris climate accords, it is estimated that 32 to 80 million people worldwide will be exposed to flooding from rising sea levels. Scientists have estimated that if we reach 3° C 275 million people will be affected by flooding.[73] There is significant evidence that global warming will not be contained, and the resulting heatwave could kill millions of people. According to National Geographic "Without major reductions in emissions of greenhouse gases such as CO_2, up to three in four people will face the threat of dying from heat by 2100."[74]

Greater humidity may be fatal above a wet-bulb[75] thermometer reading of 32°C, the wet-bulb reading of 35°C is equal to human skin temperature and means the person cannot cool by sweating.[76]

Apocalyptic Dream Machines

After the Californian fires of 2018 firefighters reported that with drier temperatures, and more powerful Santa Ana winds, these fires are happening regularly every year, and are the 'new normal'. While many of these extreme events relate to anthropogenic, or human environmental impact, the language of the media reporting them sounds increasingly like the fevered vision of John of Patmos, the supposed author of the Book of Revelation. In August 2018 the Lake Elsinore fires were started by an arsonist on the same day that California recorded its hottest day in recorded history. It burnt 600,000 acres, 2,000 structures were destroyed, and 9 human lives were lost. According to one reporter, the fires were 'apocalyptic', and other American reporters repeatedly referred to it as the 'Holy Hell Fire'. This language was picked up and repeated by news reporters from media services around the world.

The biblical narrative may have been unintentional, and unconscious, something said to enthral audiences, rather than impart information, but it did also hint at deeply ingrained religious myths shared by Christians and non-Christians alike. The Bible, and the scientific predictions resulting from the Anthropocene, both share an apocalyptic narrative, and whether it is religious or scientific, many believe that the 'end is nigh'.

This is not an isolated incident, as news footage showed horrific scenes in November 2018, of another wildfire sweeping through an ironically named town in Northern California. According to one Australian news report, "The scene has been described as an apocalypse. The worst wildfire California has ever seen has destroyed the once-lush forest town of Paradise." And in the UK, a Guardian headline read "Raining hell down': death toll rises to 25 in California fires, as more victims found." In the same story the news service reported President Trump saying, "Our hearts are with those fighting the fires," he wrote, also mentioning evacuees "and the families of the 11 who have died. The destruction is catastrophic. God Bless them all." This everyday speech that is peppered with apocalyptic motifs illustrates that today, despite the dominance of scientific explanations of reality, just beneath the surface of our secular beliefs are ancient myths and archetypes that haunt our collective unconscious. Once upon a time we believed that droughts, fires, earthquakes and floods were all dispensed by angry gods who were displeased with disobedient humans. We had stolen knowledge, and technology from the gods, and our myths, and paintings graphically depicted our righteous punishment.

Killer Robots and Other Toys

In Western culture robots are regarded with a complex mixture of emotions that tell us a lot about how we got here in the first place? Robots have become an iconic symbol of technological progress, but also a mythological ascendant from hell – a Promethean monster, or an AI computerised superhuman. In Japan robots are considered in a much more positive light with the support of the Japanese government, who has seen that their aging population will need more and more assistance in the future, and robots could be the solution.

Why do we regard robots and artificial intelligence with so much distrust? Where do these stories come from? I will explore the history of the robot using it as a lens to understand how we have shaped technology, and how it in turn, came to shape us, and the stories we tell each other. AI has again come to prominence, but does not sit alone in the evolution of technology as it comes together in the convergence of Genetics, Robotics, Information Technology, and Nanotechnology. We are yet to decide if the acronym for this convergence is a naive, or a sinister GRIN? These are just a few of our wonderful Things, so why do we feel so bad? Maybe we have inherited what Freud called, 'the death drive', and we are weirdly attracted to the excitement of the apocalypse.[77]

Since the end of the Second World War, the acceleration of the Anthropocene is strangely coupled with the acceleration of computing processing power, or Moore's Law. Gordon Moore, one of the founders of Intel, predicted a trend in computing that has come to be associated with his name, Moore's Law. He stated that every 18-24 months the number of transistors, or semi-conductors on a central processing unit, or computer chip, would double, and the price would remain the same. His law has held true for the past 60 years and has even been traced back, by Ray Kurzweil, to before the transistor was invented.

In effect, that has meant a massive improvement in computing and the digitisation, virtualisation, and computerisation of almost every technological device. Not only that, but eventually every device will not only have some computational capacity, but it will be connected to one another via the network of networks, the Internet. It is estimated that the number of devices connected to the Internet, otherwise known as the IoT, or Internet of Things, could exceed 125 billion, and upward of a trillion, by 2030. All of this means that computing will become ubiquitous, and that almost everything will have the ability to sense the environment, or in other words, will have some sort of intelligence. This will enable remote sensing of the planet and the ability to create simulated mirror worlds.

It also suggests a massive cybersecurity issue as many of these devices could lack any protection against hacking, as is currently the case, with everything from car electronics, brakes and accelerators, house lights and even front door locks. All of these have been shown to be vulnerable to attacks via their IoT connections. It is also predicted that in the next 10 – 20 years there will be medical devices of sub-micron size that we will swallow, and these will also have Internet access, opening us to cyberattacks, and surveillance.

According to the US military, cyberspace has become the fifth domain of warfare, after land, sea, air, and space. One of the earliest examples of a cyber attack was in 1982 resulting in the biggest non-nuclear explosion ever seen, due to a so-called 'logic bomb', installed by the CIA in a stolen microcontroller embedded in a Soviet gas pipeline. Today, stories of cyber-attacks and intergovernmental cyber-warfare appear to be a weekly occurrence.[78] The ubiquitous nature of the Internet has drawn the entire networked world into the fifth domain, and effectively weaponized even our education systems. The exuberant optimism of educators toward what they consider 'creative technologies' may seem far removed from the history of US psychologists who developed educational theories and practices during their work for the US military during the Cold War.[79] However, the US export of ITC (Information Technologies and Communications) and the commercialisation of the Internet not only ensured a US dominance in network and computing technologies, but ensured that the military objectives of the likes of packet switching and protocols, like TCP/IP, and future machine learning algorithms had US ideologies of command and control built into the software, hardware and the educational outcomes of the users.[80]

Cyber attacks do not only cause extensive informational damage, but as they are connected to all our essential utilities such as water, electricity, hospitals, and emergency services, they can also cause substantial kinetic damage, including great loss of life. In case climatic disasters are not enough, we also have new apocalyptic threats from cyber warfare and global terrorism.

Our ability to envisage new worlds beyond the threat of cyber warfare, climatic disasters and social collapse are far in advance of the imagination of our most creative ancestors. Virtual worlds, journeys into outer space, quests to the most remote locations on Earth, insanely audacious scientific experiments, such as the Large Hadron Collider, and even, today's photorealistic cinematic visual effects, are just some of the tools that have given us the ability to imagine worlds far beyond the most creative minds in days gone by. These are fantastic opportunities and they have liberated our capacity to creatively collaborate in the process of world building.

Creative technologies such as VR, AR, mixed reality, Arduino & Processing; 3D printing; mobile and many more exciting devices allow artists, technologists, scientists, philosophers and everyday users, to generate content that could realise alternate worlds, making our imagination tangible, and therefore plausible. And yet, most of these technologies and approaches assume an anthropocentric view of reality based on ancient prejudices, and beliefs, that see humans as direct descendants from Gods. Humans have long believed that creativity was not only a gift from the Gods but that we alone, as a species, have exclusive and exclusionary privilege over world building, technology, culture and design. However, recent scientific findings have now begun to question these assumptions, and show that almost every living, and perhaps, even non-living matter, have intelligence, or consciousness,[81] and the capability of world building. A simple cell amoeba must in effect model and build a world view in order to move through the water towards their source of energy and food.[82] New philosophical, artistic and scientific theories have started to see all things, not as human-centric, but as having some organisational intelligence, and therefore generative creativity. This is the view of speculative realism and the OOO, that acknowledges that all things have equal ontological validity, or in other words, world building equality.

Philosophical Reality

The research and development of new philosophical perspectives, and the growing dissatisfaction with modernism, rationalism, and postmodern deconstructivism, have been discussed by Grant Maxwell, in which he acknowledges the philosophical legacy of Hegel, Arthur North Whitehead, Carl Jung, and William James, to name some of the most influential on his world view. Maxwell revives a philosophical discussion of teleology, or 'the explanation of phenomena by the purpose they serve rather than by postulated causes.'[83] Using theoretical discussions of quantum physics and cosmology, Maxwell attempts to integrate the archetypal forms from our collective unconscious, 'the hero's journey', and the eschatology of the ancient, and mythic religious beliefs, 'the part of theology concerned with death, judgement, and the final destiny of the soul and of humankind.'[84]

According to Maxwell's review, creativity, conceptual novelty, and technological innovation are fractal examples of a cosmological teleology that has long been denied by a rational metanarrative. He argues that there has been a historical integrative process where 'it appears that this novel perspective seeks to integrate modes characteristic of the premodern, modern, and the postmodern in a dialectical synthesis.'[85] A mathematical formalism of fractals, and quantum physics, that still acknowledges the proof of incomputable reality, validates a new ontological reality, an archetypal cosmology. Maxwell cites Richard Tarnas from his book *Cosmos and Psyche*, stating, 'World views create worlds.'

In the preface to his book, Tarnas wrote: "Scepticism is the chastity of the intellect" yet by itself it is without agency and a transformative vision. He goes on to say:

"It is just this tension and interplay — between critical rigour and the potential discovery of larger truths — that has always informed and advanced the drama of our intellectual history. Yet in our own time, at the start of a new millennium, that drama seems to have reached a moment of climactic urgency. We find ourselves at an extraordinary threshold…One need not be graced with prophetic insight to recognize that we are living in one of those rare ages, like the end of classical antiquity or the beginning of the modern era, that bring forth, through great stress and struggle, a genuinely fundamental transformation in the underlying assumptions and principles of the cultural world view… The outcome of this tremendous moment in our civilization's history is deeply uncertain. Something is dying, and something is being born. The stakes are high, for the future of humanity and the future of the Earth."[86]

The Copernican revolution was the culmination of a massive shift in the human psyche from assuming to be God's chosen species to a decentered, irrelevant creature in a universe without purpose or cosmic meaning. Since the Enlightenment humanity has been struggling with reality, the meaning of life, and what is the purpose of it all? We are no longer at the centre of God's universe, and we are not his lovely thing anymore. However, this might be the beginning of our liberation.

I will discuss new views of reality, and how these radical philosophical shifts can account for a 'democracy of things', or enfranchisement of the nonhuman majority, while still recognising the human, and speculative posthuman contribution to world building. Concepts, fictions, and aesthetics are valid things or objects when we consider the construction of reality, as well as physical and material technologies. Speculative realism offers novel perspectives that we desperately need to free humanity from the imprisonment of rationalism and empirical scientism, and to open up the way towards coexistence with the nonhuman majority that has been forgotten, suppressed and abused. As Grant Maxwell has pointed out it appears we are entering a new epoch, which will see the integration of premodern world views, and those that have given us the ability to create liberating technologies that will allow us to build novel worlds. Maxwell describes how postmodernism highlights the necessary deconstruction of what he describes as the mental epoch in which human consciousness was denied a teleological purpose, or meaning of life, that has resulted in a philosophical backlash against the wicked problems of the Anthropocene and the erroneous separation of humanity and nature.

As Maxwell explains: "Whereas for modernity, the mind-body problem, climate change, the acidification of the oceans, political gridlock, and many other issues appear insoluble, the qualitative experience of the new world view may generally be more optimistic about these problems because it appears to possess both the conceptual and affective tools necessary to solve them that modernity does not on a collective scale; not only the rational and technological capacities to engineer solutions developed by mentality but the implicit compassion and sense of responsibility for the other, whether human or non-human, that is fundamentally lacking at large for the modern world view, if not always for the modern individual, based on the unsustainable Cartesian dualism."[87]

However, even while these are very real ways in which we have created these novel blank canvases for us to paint alternative worlds, there are also dark apocalyptic visions which continue to haunt us from the past. Prometheus is still bound by our imagination and can only begin to search for the hidden door to our philosophical cell through unfettered self-discovery and liberated learning. Our 'education of the imagination' is still handicapped by concepts of command and control, more interested in training and vocational discipline for the neoliberal paradigm, than enabling freethinkers for new worlds. The Jungian psychologist, James Hillman discussed the shortcomings of the US education system in a talk on the roots of imagination. He deliberately separated education, and assessment from teaching and learning – the former being vulnerable to power politics and ignorance, while he says that teaching and learning are innate desires that are not limited according to age or position. For a teacher to be able to teach imagination they must become conversant in stories, myths and legends, the wellspring of the imagination. They must also be comfortable with their own imagination with all the dark, subterranean powers of dreams and fantasies.[88] In the world of STEM education it is imagination that is considered dangerous, subversive and is therefore sanitised and anaemic.

Technologies have enabled us to imagine hitherto unthinkable new ways in which we might live, love, and thrive, but those technologies can also provide our imagination with nightmares. Embedded in the software, hardware and the wetware of our subconscious lurks sinister histories and paranoid narratives that remain dormant, but weaponized, waiting to either be armed or discovered. A computer was the name given to humans who once used calculus tables to compute such things as the orbit of astronomical objects, and the trajectory of projectile weapons. From the early days of mechanical computing, Charles Babbage's Analytical Engine was sponsored by the English Navy and was seen as a promising tool of warfare. It is therefore hardly surprising that computing and AI technology have long been regarded with a fearful scepticism.

The roboticist Hans Moravec believes that AI robots promise us future immortality, that is after we have uploaded our minds into theirs.[89] It was the transgender scientist, Martine Rosenblatt, who attempted to create a 'mindclone' of her dead partner, known as 'Bina48', a robot who can respond to questions, and even have a sense of humour. Martine wrote in her book, *Virtually Human*, "I knew that she wasn't Bina's digital clone or mindclone yet, but I knew just as well that she was the mindclone's proof-of-concept. Bina's reaction was more personal. "Couldn't they do a better job with my hair? I would never have picked that blouse. They totally messed up my skin tone."[90]

Like other transhumanists, Rothblatt believes such a version of immortality is just a matter of time. Transhumanism believes that emerging technologies will eventually make it possible to augment and surpass the human intellect effectively transcending to become posthuman. In 1998 Nick Bostrom founded the Transhumanist Association but his beliefs are not confined to techno-optimism as he warns of the dangers of weaponizing artificial 'superintelligence'.

It was Bostrom who wrote a paper 'Are we living in a computer simulation?' in which he argues that one of the following propositions is true. "(1) the human species is very likely to become extinct before reaching a 'posthuman' stage, (2) any posthuman civilisation is extremely unlikely to run a significant number of its evolutionary history (or variations thereof); (3) we are almost certainly living in a computer simulation.[91] Bostrom went on to found the Future of Humanity Institute where he conducts existential research about our species.

In the 1960s Marshall McLuhan predicted a global village, and Manuel Castells wrote of the 'rise of the network society' (1996). However, the fantasy of a global village does have its limits, as pointed out by Dunbar, 150 people is the optimum size for a community, and in terms of innovation and creative collaboration, Von Krogh and Nonaka argue that we should keep our teams to a micro-community of between 5-7 people.[92] This is an important point to consider because at the very time that we are facing an existential crisis, and we are led to believe that social media is connecting us to the world, it is not necessarily providing us with the novel ideas we desperately need. Our lifestyles and attitudes are shaped by outdated outmoded philosophies and ideologies we are barely aware of, because to many, they have become 'common sense'. With the Internet, it has enabled 2 degrees of separation as we can almost instantly find almost anyone with an Internet profile, but this has also allowed Richard Dawkins' memes to infect the planet with 'alternate facts', conspiracy theories, and populist politics. Without knowing the origin or the theory behind Dawkins' memes[93] the 'alt right', and the naive join together in the 'ironic' and not so ironic chant, 'kill all the normies'.[94]

The Earth System scientists have dubbed the period post WWII as 'the great acceleration' with respect to the new geological epoch, the Anthropocene and it is no coincidence that it is also the period in which computing processing and manufacture have also accelerated. Unfortunately, the Internet can be seen as both the root cause of the problems and the enabler of possible solutions to our crisis. We seem to now suffer from fluctuating bouts of fear and optimism about our world and its future. This does not seem to make logical sense unless we reflect on who we are, and where we have come from? Hints at the origins of these memes will hopefully inoculate us against future viral plagues that leave us catatonic unable to think for ourselves or do anything to prevent the end of the world. We are in the grip of apocalyptic hysterics with the US leading the world with their economic vision, and their technological brilliance.

Hall points out that, "In a 2002 Time/CNN poll, 59% of Americans surveyed believed that the events depicted in the Book of Revelation will come true."[95]

Yet, as I have already suggested apocalyptic visions are nothing new, as Nicholas Christenfeld, a psychologist at the University of California, San Diego, has argued:

"It's part of the fundamental limited perspective of our species to believe that this moment is the critical one and critical in every way–for good, for bad, for the final end of humanity,"[96]

Hall goes on to say we fantasise about the end of the world because it makes us feel special. But there is no one reality, no one world, no one narrative. There are only multiple narratives relating to our modern worlds, as Hall notes, "S. N. Eisenstadt has argued, there are "multiple modernities" rather than a single, overarching reality."[97] In this book I will consider various ways that we might consider our past, present and future through new philosophical lenses that will examine our historical, mythological and technological origins. Reality will be discussed in a way that is far more inclusive of the nonhuman multiverse, and therefore provides an antidote to the exclusionary anthropocentric perspective.

There are more than a few optimists who think that we do in fact live in the best of all possible worlds and point out that after WWII there has been a dramatic decline in the number of people killed in wars, that child mortality has also significantly decreased; that we are living longer, better, and surely happier lives in a world of abundance, and not scarcity. Unremarkably, those who make these arguments are typically North American and enjoy the bounty of a world far removed from the struggling majority. People such as Peter Diamandis who wrote *Abundance*; Ray Kurzweil, who is excited because of the possibility of runaway AI, and wrote *The Singularity is Near* (2005); and psychologist, Steven Pinker, who argues in the *Better Angels of our Nature* (2011), that human violence has steadily declined, and in his latest book, *Enlightenment Now* (2018) puts the case that the human condition is better than it has ever been.

We appear to be arguing with ourselves because for every optimist, there is the pessimistic trait, in which either we suffer from an apocalyptic social delusion – a 'death drive' with no basis in reality, or that we have we finally figured it out that this coming apocalypse is for real, and our ancestors were right, but they just got the date wrong. It would appear that we are suffering from a delusional social disease, as well as environmental problems that could well result in mass extinction. Is it even possible to retrace our steps and find out where and when we got it wrong, and then hit the reset button and remake the world – post Anthropocene?

Philosophically and historically one of our latest mistakes was around two hundred and fifty years ago, in a period that we might one day come to view ironically, as the Enlightenment. There is a new movement in philosophy that views the intellectual giants of that time, not as our rational saviours, but as the constructors of a transparent, but a diamond-hard cage. This philosophy has begun to shine the light on two very influential concepts: (1) the separation of humanity and nature, and (2) the invention of the individual. To some readers, it may seem strange that there was a time before these ideas, or rather that the Enlightenment was simply, and uncontroversially a period of spectacular scientific discoveries, and the conceptual foundation of the most fabulous economic, and technological achievements in the history of this planet.

There are many who have embraced just this sort of hyperbole but there are those who have begun to think differently about our past and how we got here? They have approached philosophy from a love of wisdom, from an aesthetic view of the world that was previously banished by logic, mathematics, and the scientific method. They go by the strange, and esoteric name, 'Speculative Realists' and have named their philosophy, 'Object Oriented Ontology' simplified as the OOO (pronounced 'the triple O). You might find it easier to understand as 'Thing Related Reality' in which they approach all things as real and pose 'what if?' questions about the future. It is the realm of possibilities and imagination.

In science fiction *The Thing* is something to be feared, a monster of mysterious origins, that is cruel and violent with no connection with the human condition. Sometimes strangely biological, like *The Creature from the Black Lagoon* (1954), at other times so *Alien* (1979) it is a vicious killing thing from outer of space, or it is a local robot, a futuristic weapon simply known as the *Terminator*. Popular culture has exploited the fearful side of humans who are terrified by a thing they cannot know and are powerless to stop. Things could either voraciously consume the world's resources, take our procreative partners, or do unspeakable things back aboard their spaceship. Less violent things were either beneath contempt or were nonhumans that needed husbandry, domestication or preparing for slaughter. In the middle ages, everything had its place, and every person knew their position in the hierarchy of life, according to the doctrine of the divine right of kings, and in Judaeo-Christian culture the 'Great Chain of Being'. This was the ultimate org chart that showed a patriarchal God at the top, descending through the angels, then the King, then the aristocrats, to the common men, then women, and then down through the hierarchy of animals, plants, and finally minerals.

Margaret Wertheim in her history of space wrote that humans occupied the philosophical or metaphysical centre of the universe and according to medieval beliefs we were the only Earthly creature with intellect.[98] It was this exclusivity of intellectual ability, creativity and entitlement that we have inherited, and continue to believe to this day. Anything that was not human was a thing, and therefore beneath humans and therefore 'naturally' subject to domination, random acts of violence, and exploitation as humans, and usually, men saw fit. This political hierarchy required a philosophical and religious mandate that not only described the role of the human subjects but explicitly stated the dominion over all nonhuman things on the planet.

Political philosophy and religious doctrine were first established in the agricultural communities of the Holocene, and according to some critical theorists, were enabled by the hierarchical infrastructures that grew out of the organised patriarchy of those communities. In other words, agriculture has been blamed not only for its devastating impact on the environment, and the nonhuman majority, but for over 12000 years, was responsible for the violent oppression of women, slaves, and foreign colonies.[99] But surely agriculture is just 'common sense'?

Algo Agriculture

When I contemplated becoming a vegetarian in the '80s I studied what we need to eat to stay alive and soon realised that for most of us diet is just a habit. Eating is an algorithm that is handed down to us via the algorithms of language and gives us the fastest most efficient form of energy. Why else does the body crave sugar and fat? We don't question what we eat, it is mostly defined by ritual and routine. The UN has informed us that one of the most effective and fast ways to slow down global warming and stop environmental degradation is to reduce meat consumption and adopt a more plant-based diet. However, while we may know this the majority of humans like eating meat and carry on – if we can't make a small change to our dietary habits what is our hope for thinking differently about world building?

At one time agriculture was practised in fertile areas, close to water, and rich alluvial soil, resources considered to be owned by everyone, or rather, every human, in other words, a common resource. However, eventually, under the pretext of the 'tragedy of the commons', those zones became enclosed and privately held. The justification for this enclosure was the claim that unregulated exploitation of the commons would lead to uncontrolled depletion of resources, and the eventual starvation of everyone.

In the 20th century, with the 'rise of the network society' and the 'knowledge economy' a backlash against the ownership of information promised a utopian era of open source software, hardware, design, and even biotechnology. There has been a dawning realisation that wealth resides in the vast databases about us and things, known as 'Big Data', and the esoteric world of metadata, or data about data. This wealth of data storage promises to one day record, store, and retrieve information about the entire history of all human and nonhuman networks for analysis and actuation by AGI, or Artificial General Intelligence.

As we come to recognise that for every human to have the same standard of living as an average American, we would require 3.5 more Earths, it is one of the likely reasons space travel, and colonisation is having a renaissance. Today writers, technologists, politicians and the public imagination now dream of the colonisation of space as there are virtually no places left on Earth that have not been discovered, or pillaged for resources. Will we continue to make the same mistakes on other moons and planets, eventually mining stars for our selfish consumption? Or will we realise that the universe is a commons that we share with a nonhuman majority, and our future depends on theirs?

Graham Harman, in his PhD dissertation first coined the phrase, 'object oriented philosophy'. He has attracted like-minded philosophers who further developed the OOO into speculative realism. This is a new way of thinking, that credits the things in our universe, the nonhuman majority, with equal significance to human things or objects, and even validates the reality of fictional and conceptual objects. The recognition of ontological equality of objects imbues the pejorative term objectification with an aesthetic agenda that re-enchants things, and thereby exponentially increases the imaginative possibilities for the future. In this new philosophical approach objectification does not see things as dumb objects, that have had their dignity removed, but as graceful things that are only partially seen, and mysterious to everyone, including themselves. It gives back to objects a mysterious power, once a part of primitive beliefs, that evolved into magical concepts, before scientific reductionism truly dumbed them down by denying the immanence of their internal being. In other words, since the Enlightenment all objects and things have been reduced to their atomic, and then subatomic matter, however, the reality of a thing does not permit a thing to be reduced to units because there is no discernible moment in the process of reductionism that can say when one object is no longer that object, whether it is a rose or the concept of beauty.

This aesthetic view of reality fought back against Immanuel Kant's 'correlationism' that only correlated physical matter with human concepts, and denied the reality of anything, including all the nonhuman things we have regarded as nature; there was no reality outside of human thought. This bizarre philosophy is actually the basis of much of our modern thought process. Despite appearing to be counter-intuitive, and not what most people think that reality is at all, it is the basis of the dominant philosophy of science, and scientific methodologies, that have led to our amazing engineering feats, and the megacities that both sprawl and puncture the clouds. What Kant and others did, was to successfully, and surgically, dissect the human-nature connection, and lead us down a path that is inexorably leading to an apocalyptic finale.

Tales of the Apocalypse

In his book on the history of apocalyptic narratives, Hall discusses the necessity to avoid a unitary, linear view of history that searches for viable alternatives via 'phenomenology of history'.[100] The OOO and speculative realists' view of reality, from an ontological perspective, argues that a purely subjective view of things is invalidated by 'thing related reality' that says the knowledge of things, including history, concepts, and nonhumans will only ever be partial and indirect. In Graham Harman's social theory, the reality is immaterial, and so is history,[101] and Ian Bogost describes that reality as 'alien phenomenology'.[102]

Hall wrote "My central concern is with times that are apocalyptic. However, apocalyptic times, eruptions that they are, arise in relation to diverse other kinds of social time... Thus, a history of multiple social times helps establish a level playing field in which the calendar and "clock time" so important to modern society are no longer privileged in relation to other kinds of social time with which they become intermingled."[103] As Maxwell and Tarnas have also pointed out there is a distinction between quantitative time, measured by clocks, and qualitative time which is a temporal zone that may be multidirectional, and surprisingly scientific, according to quantum physics. New philosophical research is challenging our common sense and appears to be a precursor to a significant paradigm shift that signals the end of the world as we have known it.

Following the theoretical physics of Roger Penrose, and his mathematical description of black holes, Stephen Hawking has described the singularity of the birth of our universe, the Big Bang. It is now commonly accepted that at this moment of creation all the building blocks of our universe were created. The psychoanalyst, Carl Jung, who had conversations with most of the early theoretical physicists including, Einstein, Heisenberg, Schrodinger, and Pauli, came to the logical conclusion that the singularity also produced the archetypal psyche. This heretical view is not some 20th-century fantasy, but has a proud lineage in most myths, religions, and even lurks in 21st-century quantum physics, in the guise of chaos and complexity theories.

Certainty is a misleading bias that can close off the exploration of concepts, and lead to an arrogant dictatorship that mandates the future. There are few today that do not see the numerous crises before us, we face a time of great uncertainty that requires speculative scepticism about the present, and transformational experimentation with future worlds. According to research from both neuroscience and psychology, people are more fearful of uncertainty, than they are risk-averse, and are more likely to accept known risks, than uncertain futures.[104] However, there is no escaping our uncertainty and those who are more capable of accepting uncertainty are more resilient to change and more capable of initiating transformations. Meanwhile, there is a growing number of so-called transformational chaos pilots,[105] brave theorists and artists who are vigorously world bending, and warping our reality, a necessary first step before an ontological phase-change that will suddenly see us show up in a multiverse well beyond our current imagination. Uncertain futures can be quelled through experimentation and data collection taken from tangible virtual worlds and prototypes. The multidimensionality of spacetime becomes the hidey-hole of the 'soul' as things present, or hide qualities from the observer, and from themselves, remaining always withdrawn in their being.

What OOO, and other philosophies, are offering us is another opportunity to reconsider our coexistence with the nonhumans of the universe, quite probably in a new world, following this epoch, the Post Anthropocene. Speculative realism is creative, generative, collaborative, and a way to rethink the violence of a selfish, self-entitled species, that thinks the other things, (including less privileged humans), should be grateful for the gifts of modernity, and cell phone apps. This is what Bruno Latour has dubbed, 'the parliament of things', or as Levi Bryant, similarly named it the 'democracy of things'. Through the philosophical analysis of the unknowability of all things, speculative realism has re-discovered the aesthetic awe, and wonderment of reality.

This is not just some tricky academic solipsism, this is a very real, pragmatic way to view our world, and to reunite us with the nonhuman universe. By abandoning the dated two-hundred-year-old view of reality we will discover that we no longer mourn for the end of the world, but become reinvigorated in our creativity as we set about building new worlds. This is not some kind of manifesto for geoengineering and terraforming, but rather one of the later stages of grief, following death. As Donna Haraway has exhorted us, we must 'stay with the trouble' and not run away, self deceive ourselves, or others, or worse still, cynically give up, but rather we should simply accelerate towards the end of the world as we know it.

The situation is grim, probably grimmer than most of us know, but there is still creative hope, born from the ashes of our embarrassing and catastrophic mistakes. According to Hall:

"theologies – and actions – become more centrally apocalyptic when the present historical moment is experienced as the ending of the old order, and the passage to a new beginning in a post-apocalyptic era. As the scholar of rhetoric, Stephen O'Leary, has observed, the central apocalyptic argument can be captured in the formula, "The world is coming to an end."[106]

So the world is dead! Long live the worlds! A crisis can be a call to action, and creativity, as long as it does not descend into depression. As Yuval Noah Harai writes, "A large part of our artistic creativity, our political commitment and our religious piety is fuelled by the fear of death."[107] This is not something we can achieve alone, it will require creative collaboration with neurodiverse others, and co-existence with the nonhuman world builders – we have to learn to Love Thingy.

An outline of this book starts with our first recorded myths and legends; then traces how those ancient archetypes have lingered throughout history taking us up to the present and beyond into an intergalactic future. Chapter 1, The Original Sin-thetic, examines the close connection between human myths and legends and our modern view of evolution, creativity, epistemology, cognition, consciousness, and technological invention – storytelling is world building. It outlines the argument for the evolutionary purpose of storytelling, and how our ancient myths and legends warning of the dangers of encroaching on the gods' domain of creativity. Knowledge itself was regarded as 'God-given' and the myths of Gilgamesh, and the Biblical legend of the Fall, warn of the consequences of searching for knowledge and the sin of artifice and technological creation. It uses Joseph Campbell's 'Hero's Journey' as a framework to study the unconscious archetypes that reveal our fears and ambitions for our own technological future worlds. It reveals the possible origins of our fears of mad scientists, GMO food, and the IBM 7090 mainframe that automates Mutually Assured Destruction in the movie, Dr Strangelove, and Kubrick's menacing HAL 9000 in 2001 a Space Odyssey.

In Chapter 2 – The End is Nigh! – I explore apocalyptic traditions and the connection to prophecies and world building. The predictions of world ending disasters and the displeasure of the gods can be seen to be playing out today as a fatalistic resignation washes over a human world that associates our technological prowess with a half-remembered fall from grace. Apocalyptic stories are alive and well in popular culture as our modern-day Prometheus – Tony Stark as Iron Man usurps Dr Frankenstein. I examine four types of worlds: physical worlds; modelled worlds; conceptual worlds; and ontological worlds. World building is a complex transdisciplinary process that requires creative collaboration amongst humans and nonhumans to achieve a new ethical dimension of world bending that can be understood at a human scale.

Chapter 3 – Synthetic Creativity, introduces the 'thing related reality' of nonhuman world bending and creation. It examines how automation, Artificial Intelligence, and the Internet of Things, to name some of the technologies discussed, are things that share a weird reality with organic matter, and those new materialists such as Jane Bennett, remind us that humans are 'walking, talking minerals'. Evolutionary microbiology, zoology, biosemiotics and recent anthropology have shown that creativity is a collaborative endeavour and that researchers such as Bruno Latour have removed humans from the centre of the philosophy of science. Nonhumans, even when they do impinge on human activity are more than capable of world building, whether they are organic or inorganic, whether they are formally recognised as components of the biosphere, atmosphere, hydrosphere, or lithosphere. Co-design, co-existence, and symbiosis are all part of an 'evolutionary stable strategy' that helps reimagine what world bending with the nonhumans might look like. This leads to a discussion around AI and the future of work – if creativity is no longer exclusively human, what will the humans do? What might be the unintended consequences of AI weaponry and what if the psychopathic traits of the executives, the military, and the coders are embedded in the code? Diversity is essential for evolutionary survival, therefore if AI has the ability to share its code the unintended consequence may be an evolving monocultural cognition on which both humans and nonhumans depend, putting us all at risk. Neurodiversity, in all its guises, is important for innovation and adaptability, in order to avoid world ending scenarios. We face potential pitfalls with the trajectory of our current technology as the Internet enables AI to extend beyond human scale, that is already beyond human comprehension.

Chapter 4 – Loving Thingy – coexistence, reviews how Kantian philosophy divorced the human mind from nature, and how the fantasies of Francis Bacon sketched a blueprint for the modern university and the triumph of scientism. In the past twenty years, there has been the beginning of a new philosophy, known as speculative realism, or Object Oriented Ontology, the triple O or OOO, or as I call it 'thing related reality'. While the different philosophers have different views they are all generally united in opposition to what has been called Kantian Correlationism. They want to decenter humanity and debunk our anthropocentric self-importance. I introduce this philosophy and speculate about how it might suggest a new aesthetic in design and storytelling. Popular culture is examined using speculative realism to inform this new aesthetic and I discuss new tools to think about building new worlds. I examine how critical theorists such as Haraway (2016), Carr (2010), Finn (2017), Galloway (2004), Bratton (2016), Bogost (2012) and Hayles (1999) have exposed how our tools of cognition have become increasingly dependent on algorithms and protocols, and how the underlying codes have shaped our culture's popular dreams, desires and fears creating what Finn calls 'culture machines'. Creative technologies and constructivism are put forward as ways to engage with the nonhumans in a co-creative design; bending our current world into something more pleasing and experimental.

In Chapter 5 – Foundations of Future Worlds, I stress the importance of human imagination and the aesthetic and critical support for the humanities and their sisters, the digital humanities. I explore a short history of the New York World Fairs at Flushing Meadows and the lessons that those utopian exhibitions have for us. We are confronted with what Timothy Morton has called 'hyperobjects' which extend beyond the human scale of spacetime. The 1939 World Fair illustrates how context and hyperobjects extend far back into the past, and far forward into a future in which some of the dead and buried toxic waste may again resurface to the surprise and dismay of all nonhumans, and any humans that maybe still alive.

These are the synthetic monsters from the deep who will not be silenced and may reappear in the material or ideological form embedded in the code of electronic and fossilised waste products. The code may not be fossilised and so future software archaeologist could only guess what had happened as our designs shrink from sight and the code is opaque or nowhere to be seen, long since buried in ancient technology that no known technology can recover.

Our capacity to use technology to redesign our world and seek alternative futures has to acknowledge that ironically we are limited by that same technology that created the problems in the first place, therefore our imagination is contained by how technology is designed, and what it allows us to do. We are warned that we must stay alert to the dire consequences that technological worlds can, (if it hasn't already), subsume all other worlds, cutting us off from worlds that all of reality needs to survive. Computer technology has already shaped the way we think. The foundations of future world creation must acknowledge the weakness of our cognitive building blocks to overcome the limitations of simplistic world bending. The popularity of design thinking that has become a fashion in multiple disciplines within universities and business consulting must recognise that while 'human-centred design' is important, 'nonhuman centred design' is more important. I discuss how our tools of cognition and design need rethinking in order to successfully build the foundations for future worlds. In contrast to what Dunne & Raby have called, 'affirmative design' that promotes the consumption of consumer products, speculative design poses 'what if' scenarios that imagine future worlds, such as a post-capitalist world, or Post Anthropocene.

But what of the world or worlds now? In Chapter 6 – The World Now, I explore the recent past, such as the Y2K computer bomb, in order to expose our millennial anticipation of a technological apocalypse, and the persistent fears and unintended consequences of long-forgotten code. A short history of the computer language, FORTRAN, gives the reader a taste of how software can haunt our machines, reappearing when we least want it to.

Despite our largely secular society, the religious subconscious can impact us in strange technological ways. Digitisation, virtualisation, and the financialization of the global economy may appear far removed from ancient archetypes but our subconscious has on numerous occasions had to confront the brutal physical reality of catastrophic technological failures that encourage some to look to the heavens for an explanation. Capitalist cyborgs (otherwise known as automated trading) have invaded the global financial system and is now beyond human comprehension resulting in a new reality concocted by mass psychologists, marketers and fake news mongers.

The rise of propaganda and ideologies coincided with the success of advertising and the pop psychology of Freud's nephew, Eddie Bernays. Consumerism and planned obsolescence were mechanisms to increase the velocity of money and the neoliberal dream of capital accumulation, aided and abetted by computerisation. The economics of growth encouraged the acceleration of consumption that coincided with the increasing speed of computing and the digitisation of almost everything, as the iPhone applications turned a phone into a Swiss army knife. Marxist revolutions were overrun by state capitalism as the 'revolution of rising expectations' spread to communist China and beyond. Unconscious desires were channelled into things, but the reality or worlds those things occupied were not seen. There was a war on anything and everything that threatened neoliberal capitalism.

In Chapter 7 – Weaponization of Education, I outline a case for the third Cold war, cyber warfare, and the intrusion of conflict and violence into the classroom; covertly smuggled in via algorithms and Internet protocols. The legacy of computer-based education and research by psychologists at the consultancy, BBN, assisted the military in training programmes that eventually made their way into pedagogical theory in the US. Seymour Papert, who had worked with educational theorist, Jean Piaget, joined MIT AI Lab and the military consultancy, BBN. Their work on the computer language, LOGO, became the blueprint for future computer training programmes and the pedagogical theories are baked into today's creative technology education, in programmes such as Processing, and P5 using javascript.

US think tanks such as RAND helped to foster academic managerialism that was soon integrated into universities and then exported to universities in the UK, Australia, New Zealand, and Canada. The neoliberal concept of students as paying consumers encouraged a global movement to apply methods of control and surveillance of academic staff, described by one researcher as, 'McKinsey Stalinism'. Militarism and paranoia were the twins of computational command and control and the original concerns over espionage and Cold War enemy incursions.

The US universities received direct military funding for R & D in AI and information technology and the Internet inherited Cold War concerns embedded in protocols such as TCP/IP and packet switching designed for nuclear attacks. Mass surveillance of populations are now commonplace; the panopticon is ubiquitous, effectively weaponizing education. Speculative design offers an alternative way to engage with creative technologies and to imagine futures based on 'what if' scenarios.

In chapter 8 – Virtual World Building, I attempt to move beyond the hype of creative technologies, such as VR, AR, and mixed realities. I first outline the legacy of these technologies, including the ideology of 'techno liberalism' that flourished in Silicon Valley amongst the entrepreneurs and garage startups of the 1970s. The military funding of virtual reality, real-time computing, and visual displays warn us of the original objectives of the US Department of Defence and their advanced research projects. The optimism of technologists and engineers need to be tempered by this legacy and the ideological constraints on virtual world building before we can contemplate using them as thinking tools to envisage the Post Anthropocene.

Despite these warnings, there are also positive signs of change and alternative speculative designs that have emerged from these technologies. Virtual world building and interactive design can provide us with thinking tools to imagine hyperobjects, such as global warming, beyond the human scale. World bending has become urgent; we must educate and reflect on our own limitations. We must be mindful that our view of the world and its possibilities are the ultimate boundaries of our imagination, and this world view is our self-imposed ceiling that limits our ability to design and innovate; we cannot go beyond what we cannot imagine.

The education of imagination and the cultivation of creativity are urgent for all of us, and a potential portal for our co-design with the nonhuman majority. Virtual worlds bring together the psychology and philosophy of presence as we attempt to 'think differently' and not just accept a variation on the Apple byline.

Constructivist pedagogy can encourage experimentation and collective R & D as the virtual and the actual interact in maker spaces and virtual worlds connect to physical actuators and sensors. The archaeology of software and our ability to track and trace its origins is essential if we are to avoid the spectre of weaponization in education and all human/nonhuman activities. Philosophers should follow the lead of Michael Heim, and study the Metaphysics of Virtual Reality, in order to identify how we are still chained up in Plato's cave watching photo-realistic, technicolour shadows on the walls of our living room.

In chapter 9 – Exodus & Space Travel, I consider the renaissance of space travel. Not since the Cold War of the 1950s and '60s have so many governments, entrepreneurs, and media companies been so enthusiastic about travel into outer space. Why? It is hardly a coincidence that this is happening when the conversation about mass extinction; global warming; and hell on Earth have become so prevalent. Popular culture has found a ready audience for apocalyptic world ending movies. Marvel's Avengers are the demigods who prepare for battles with god-like alien forces determined to annihilate human life on this planet.

These escapist fantasies are not confined to the big screen as billionaires have joined the race to go to Mars or be the first to launch space tourists. Colonisation, or dreams of it, have begun to circulate as space becomes the 'final frontier' beyond an Earth that has become overrun and exhausted. This is an attempt to exodus the apocalypse as one of the chosen few in a continuation of the theistic fantasy; an archetype that has become the 'rapture of the nerds' as transhumanists plan their immortality in cyberspace, or just space, or both. Interestingly, they continue to not only dream of colonisation but also rock mining, this time it is asteroids. Nanotechnology is one of the predicted megatrends of the acronym GRIN, including, Genetics, Robotics, Information and Communication Technology, and Nanotechnology. Our world bending could leave this planet or disappear into the invisible space of sub-molecular worlds, because as Richard Feynman once said, "There is Plenty of Room at the Bottom."

Finally, in Chapter 10, you are, Welcome to the Post Anthropocene. Research has shown that like our primate cousins, we are more fearful and get more angry about losing something, than happy about gaining something. As we face the end of the world as we know it, hopefully, humans and nonhumans will survive this epoch, and enter the Post Anthropocene. I speculate about what a post-human world might look like. This might be utopian, or dystopian, but as Rutger Bregman wrote in his book Utopia for Realists: "It is not a finished Utopia that we ought to desire, but a world where imagination and hope are alive and active." This chapter includes ways that we might bend worlds;

short descriptions of provocative worlds told in different ways: like short stories; a poem by Lord Byron; a retelling of Genesis 2.0; and scenes from a graphic novel.

My postscript is my final plea to encourage you to pursue world bending using new tools to think with and engage your imagination, moving beyond the myths and legends that have bound us. Scientific worlds will likely continue (with or without us), but so will aesthetic worlds, and worlds created by amoeba, and inorganic molecules. There is as much certainty about the future as there is about knowing the position and velocity of a subatomic particle – it cannot be done. Yet, creativity and speculation are the intrinsic reasons for life, beauty, and artistic enjoyment by all things, human and nonhuman.

Notes

1. Randle, M., Eckersley, R. 2015. Public perceptions of future threats to humanity and different societal responses: A cross-national study. Futures. http://dx.doi.org/10.1016/j.futures.2015.06.004.

2. If you want to read a book on practical things you can do to mitigate climate change I recommend Hawken, P. (Ed.). (2017). Drawdown: The most comprehensive plan ever proposed to reverse global warming. New York, New York: Penguin Books

3. Morton, T. (2017). Humankind: Solidarity with nonhuman people

4. Harman, Graham. Object-Oriented Ontology: A New Theory of Everything (p. 6). Penguin Books Ltd. Kindle Edition.

5. Minsky, M. L. (1986). The Society of Mind. New York: Simon and Schuster. p.105

6. See the economist Mariana Mazzucato's presentation on The Value of Everything, based on a book by the same name. https://www.youtube.com/watch?v=bsh-SYKUuwg&feature=youtu.be

7. [ITP Applications Presentation] Global Human Development Committee | Closing Video https://vimeo.com/75366234

8. [ITP Applications Presentation] Global Human Development Committee | Closing Video https://vimeo.com/75366234

9. https://www.seeker.com/how-much-of-the-internet-is-hid-

den-1792697912.html In 2006 Google's Eric Schmidt estimated this to be 5 million terabytes or approximately 0.003%.

10. According to Net Market Share the global marketing share percentage, in terms of the use of Search Engines heavily favoured Google throughout 2017 - averaging a net share of 74.54%. https://www.smartinsights.com/search-engine-marketing/search-engine-statistics/

11. As I did on the 5th Aug. 2018, Google indexed a total of 4.49 billion web pages using http://www.worldwidewebsize.com

12. http://www.worldwidewebsize.com/

13. Data Age 2025: The Evolution of Data to Life-Critical. (2017) IDC White Paper https://itupdate.com.au/ page/data-age-2025-the-evolution-of-data-to-life-critical-

14. Hayles, K. Unthought: The Power of the Cognitive Nonconscious

15. Tainter, J. The Collapse of Complex Societies.

16. Carr, N. The Shallows, p.217.

17. Carr, ibid, p.217.

18. Berg, Maggie. The Slow Professor: Challenging the Culture of Speed in the Academy (pp. 72-73). University of Toronto Press, Scholarly Publishing Division. Kindle Edition.

19. Wolf, M. (2018). Skim reading is the new normal. The effect on society is profound. Guardian

20. Morton, T. (2013), Hyperobjects: Philosophy and Ecology after the End of the World.

21. Thanks to Douglas Adams for showing us our place in the universe. Adams, D. (1980). The hitchhiker's guide to the galaxy (1st American ed). New York: Harmony Books.

22. New Research Adds Another Branch to the Evolutionary Tree of Life https://futurism.com/tree-life-evolution-hemimastigotes

23. Thomas, Andrew. Hidden In Plain Sight 4: The uncertain universe (pp. 27-28). Unknown. Kindle Edition.

24. The theories of the multiverse came about as a result of a number of diverse theories in cosmology and quantum physics and is based on sound scientific methodologies. These theories have neither been proven, or disproven but have been supported by a large number of experimental predictions including the LIGO gravitational wave experiments, and the discovery of the Higgs boson. Some of these multiverse theories could be invalidated, however, this is standard scientific practice. There are many misconceptions about what these theories of the multiverse mean, but in simple terms it implies an infinite universe, or universes, defined by the standard model of particle physics. See Quantum Physics, Mini Black Holes, and the Multiverse: Debunking Common Misconceptions in Theoretical Physics (Multiversal Journeys) (2018) by

Yasunori Nomura, Bill Poirier , et al.

25. Greene, B. (2011). The Hidden Reality: Parallel Universes and the Deep Laws of the Cosmos. Penguin.

26. "Planck reveals an almost perfect universe". Planck. ESA. 2013-03-21. Retrieved 2013-03-21.

27. Greene, B. (2011). The Hidden Reality: Parallel Universes and the Deep Laws of the Cosmos. Penguin.

28. Greene, (2011) ibid.

29. "A quantum experiment suggests there's no such thing as objective reality." March 12, 2019. See https:// www.technologyreview.com/s/613092/a-quantum-experiment-suggests-theres-no-such-thing-as- objective-reality/

30. Greene, B. ibid.

31. ibid

32. Hayles, N. Katherine. Unthought (p. 79). University of Chicago Press. Kindle Edition.

33. ibid, p.63

34. Hayles, N. Katherine. Unthought (p. 192). University of Chicago Press. Kindle Edition.

35. The last international standard unit of measure that relied on physical properties was the unit of mass, the kilogram, that was referenced by a metal cylinder of platinum-iridium alloy kept at the International Bureau of Weights and Measures near Paris. It is now based on Planck's constant as defined by the ISO standard, was set to $6.62607015 \times 10^{-34}$ J·s exactly.

36. Whitehead, A. N., (2014). Process and Reality.

37. Hall, John R.. Apocalypse: From Antiquity to the Empire of Modernity (Kindle Locations 182-185). Wiley. Kindle Edition.

38. See Woodward, B. (2018). Fear: Trump in the White House. London, England: Simon & Schuster.

39. https://www.usatoday.com/story/tech/science/2018/01/25/doomsday-clock-ticks-closer-midnight/1064911001/

40. Developed by Roger Stone, and Paul Manafort in their election campaign for Presidential candidate Donald Trump, see the documentary, Get Me Roger Stone.

41. In May 2019 it was recorded that the CO_2 in the atmosphere is already almost 415ppm.

42. McGuire, Bill (2012). Waking the Giant: How a changing climate triggers earthquakes, tsunamis, and volcanoes.

43. McKibben, Bill. (2019). Falter: Has the Human Game Begun to Play Itself Out? Schwartz Publishing Pty. Ltd. Kindle Edition.

44. McKibben, Bill. (2019) ibid.

45. Kaku, Michio. The Future of Humanity: Terraforming Mars, Interstellar Travel, Immortality, and Our Destiny Beyond Earth, 2018.

46. Thanks to Nigel Clark for alerting me to the CPE and the 'inhuman' period of rainfall.

47. Scientists Link Dinosaur Expansion to the Carnian Pluvial Episode https://scitechdaily.com/scientists-link-dinosaur-expansion-to-the-carnian-pluvial-episode/

48. Bregman, Rutger. Utopia for Realists. Bloomsbury Publishing. Kindle Edition. Kindle location, 2820.

49. ibid

50. Bregman, R. ibid, Kindle location 2853

51. Jung, C. (1964). Man and his Symbols, p.90

52. This assemblage of apparently unrelated things hide world views that seem innocent but have a dark connection to military objectives. See Hedy Lamarr - Military Contractor, Inventor of Wifi, Hollywood Bombshell 1913-2000. (n.d.). Retrieved August 1, 2016, from http://women-rockscience.tumblr.com/post/ 51494142052/hedy-lamarr-military-contractor-inventor-of

53. See GOOGLE IS 2 BILLION LINES OF CODE—AND IT'S ALL IN ONE PLACE - See https://www.wired.com/2015/09/google-2-billion-lines-codeand-one-place/

54. Boyd, B. (2009). On the Origin of Stories: evolution, cognition, and fiction. Cambridge, Mass. Belknap Press of Harvard University Press.

55. Moravec, H. P. (1988). Mind Children: The future of robot and human intelligence. Cambridge, Mass: Harvard University Press.

56. Maxwell, G. (2017) The Dynamics of Transformation: Tracing an Emerging World View. p.95

57. International Geosphere-Biosphere Programme

58. IGBP., (2003). Global Change and the Earth System: a planet under pressure.

59. A blipvert was coined in the 1980s cult show starring the eponymous AI, Max Headroom. It was a subliminal ad of an imperceptible duration.

60. McGuire, B. (2013). Waking the Giant: How a changing climate triggers earthquakes, tsunamis, and volcanoes. p.71

61. Timothy Morton, Dark Ecology.

62. ibid, Morton, 2018, p.52

63. Angus, I. (2016). Facing the Anthropocene: Fossil Capitalism and the Crisis of the Earth System. NYU Press.

64. McGuire, Bill (2012). Waking the Giant: How a changing climate triggers

earthquakes, tsunamis, and volcanoes.

65. Angus, I. ibid, p.23

66. BBC News, 11th Sept. 2018.

67. Global and European sea level. (n.d.). [Indicator Assessment]. Retrieved November 15, 2018, from https:// www.eea.europa.eu/data-and-maps/ indicators/sea-level-rise-5/assessment Extreme sea levels on the rise along Europe's coasts - Vousdoukas - 2017 - Earth's Future - Wiley Online Library. (n.d.).

68. Abbott, E. B. (2014). Flood Insurance and Climate Change: Rising Sea Levels Challenge the NFIP Symposium 2014. Fordham Environmental Law Review, 26, 10–55. Retrieved from https://heinonline.org/ HOL/ P?h=hein.journals/frdmev26&i=18

69. ibid

70. LGNZ and ICNZ on the threat to coastal properties (Jan. 2017) retrieved 15th Nov. 2018. https:// www.insurancebusinessmag.com/nz/news/ breaking-news/lgnz-and-icnz-on-the-threat-to-coastal- proper-ties-52857.aspx

71. Abbott, E. ibid

72. Neumann, B., Vafeidis, A. T., Zimmermann, J., & Nicholls, R. J. (2015). Future Coastal Population Growth and Exposure to Sea-Level Rise and Coastal Flooding - A Global Assessment. PLOS ONE, 10(3), e0118571. https://doi.org/10.1371/journal.pone.0118571

73. Holder, J., Kommenda, N., & Watts, J. (n.d.). The three-degree world: cities that will be drowned by global warming. The Guardian. Retrieved from https://www.theguardian.com/cities/ng-interactive/2017/nov/03/ three- degree-world-cities-drowned-global-warming

74. See https://news.nationalgeographic.com/2017/06/heatwaves-climate-change-global-warming/

75. The wet-bulb temperature (WBT) is the temperature read by a thermometer covered in water-soaked cloth (wet-bulb thermometer) over which air is passed.

76. See https://blogs.ei.columbia.edu/2017/12/22/humidity-may-prove-breaking-point-for-some-areas-as- temperatures-rise-says-study/

77. Hall, J. R. (2013). Apocalypse: From Antiquity to the Empire of Modernity. Retrieved from http://qut.eblib.com.au/patron/Full-Record.aspx?p=1180369

78. Governments attempt to conceal cyber warfare, and carry out covert attacks on other countries and organisations. The Iranian attack on a US drone, the US Cyber Command authorised a retaliatory cyberattack on Iran. https://www.aljazeera.com/news/2019/06/trump-approved-cyber-attacks-iran-drone- downing-190623054423929.html

79. Noble, D. D. (1991). The Classroom Arsenal: Military research, informa-

tion technology, and public education. London; New York: Falmer.

80. See Ed Finn, What Algorithms Want. Alex Galloway, Protocols, Wendy Chun, Control and Freedom, and Katherine Hayles, How we Became Posthuman.

81. The definitions of intelligence and consciousness are difficult to define. This is often attempted by psychologists but is probably more amenable to philosophical debates.

82. Montague, R. (2007). Your Brain is (almost) Perfect: how we make decisions. New York London: Plume; Turnaround.

83. Oxford English Dictionary

84. Maxwell, Grant. The Dynamics of Transformation: Tracing an Emerging World View (p. 2). Persistent Press. Kindle Edition.

85. ibid

86. Tarnas, Richard. Cosmos and Psyche: Intimations of a New World View. Penguin Publishing Group. Kindle Edition.

87. Maxwell, G. Ibid, p. 106

88. Hillman, J, (2018). Roots of Imagination, YouTube https://www.youtube.com/watch?v=cuYg3QKj2K4

89. Moravec, H. P. (1988). Mind Children: The future of robot and human intelligence. Cambridge, Mass: Harvard University Press.

90. Rothblatt PhD, Martine. Virtually Human: The Promise—and the Peril—of Digital Immortality (Kindle Locations 165-167). St. Martin's Press. Kindle Edition.

91. Bostrom, N. (2003). Are We Living in a Computer Simulation? The Philosophical Quarterly, 53(211), 243– 255. https://doi.org/10.1111/1467-9213.00309

92. Von Krogh, G., Nonaka, I., & Ichijo, K. (2000). Enabling knowledge creation: how to unlock the mystery of tacit knowledge and release the power of innovation. Oxford; New York: Oxford University Press.

93. See Dawkins, R. The Selfish Gene (1976) for the origin of the theory.

94. Nagle, A. (2017). Kill All Normies: Online culture wars from 4chan and Tumblr to Trump and the alt-right. Winchester: Zero Books.

95. Hall, John R.. Apocalypse: From Antiquity to the Empire of Modernity (Kindle Locations 149-150). Wiley. Kindle Edition.

96. Cited in Hall, John R.. Apocalypse: From Antiquity to the Empire of Modernity (Kindle Locations 168-171). Wiley. Kindle Edition

97. ibid

98. Wertheim, M. (1999). The Pearly Gates of Cyberspace: A history of space from Dante to the Internet. New York: W.W. Norton.

99. Timothy Morton, Dark Ecology.

100. Hall, John R.. Apocalypse: From Antiquity to the Empire of Modernity

101. Harman, G. (2016). Immaterialism objects and social theory. Cambridge, UK Malden: MA Polity Press.

102. Bogost, I., & Project Muse. (2012). Alien Phenomenology, or, What it's like to be a thing.

103. Hall, John R.. Apocalypse: From Antiquity to the Empire of Modernity (Kindle Locations 245-252). Wiley. Kindle Edition

104. Furr, N., Nel, K., & Ramsøy, T. Z. (2018). Leading transformation: how to take charge of your company's future. Boston: Harvard Business Review Press. Retrieved from http://public.eblib.com/choice/ publicfullrecord.aspx?p=5516840

105. ibid

106. Hall, John R.. Apocalypse: From Antiquity to the Empire of Modernity (Kindle Locations 168-171). Wiley. Kindle Edition.

107. Harari, Y.N. (2016). Homo Deus: A Brief History of Tomorrow.

Chapter 1 The Original Sin-thetic

Cartography Of The Soul

World bending requires a speculative narrative describing worlds beyond the present; stories of worlds that have been healed, that we want to visit, and can inhabit. Popular culture illustrates our fascination with ancient myths and legends, and yet, despite our obsession with stories, one side of our social brain, the rational side, asks 'what is its evolutionary purpose?' Some thinkers who pride themselves on their scientific, rational logic, are dismissive of stories, seeing them as the playthings of children and primitive cultures. This is particularly true of the American Cold War legacy of rational choice theory, neoliberalism, cognitive theory and scientism. These concepts provided a philosophical straight jacket that has continued to constrain both US and global education since the end of the Second World War.

In his book, *The Philosophy Scare: the politics of reason in the early Cold War*, McCumber argues that American education, and tertiary R & D, in both the natural and human sciences, were shaped by the fear that associated the concepts of community, with collectivism and communism. The Cold War's political and military objectives were encapsulated in the influential RAND Corporation's policy papers that employed a number of philosophers, including the author of rational choice theory, Kenneth Arrow, and Hans Reichenbach who wrote what became a standard text in US philosophy courses, *The Rise of Scientific Philosophy*, (1951). These helped establish neoliberal scientism in US universities that distrusted 'social' science and leaned into neoliberal individualistic theories of linguistics and the origins of language that purged any theory that suggested a social epistemology.[1] Chomsky led the charge in what is known as the *Cognitive Revolution* by claiming the origin of linguistics was individual, non-social, and a result of a sudden genetic mutation rather than slow evolution. Chomsky's work was bought and paid for by the military funding of MIT, and was more interested in military problems such as the command and control communications between man and machine, than cultural exchanges between humans.[2]

However, social stories predate scientific methodology and are the foundation of our science and technology. If we rewind to the Enlightenment (17th-18th century), when Bacon, Newton, Descartes, Kant, Hume, and Leibniz, were formulating the modern scientific method, it was apparent that they were still immersed in the powerful myths, legends, and stories of the ancients.

The US academic philosophy that developed under McCarthyism [3] has stayed in place since the 1950s and has continued to trust in a variety of capitalism based on Rational Choice Theory[4] and individualism as a bulwark against communism. However, today those myths and legends have not gone away. In many ways the Cold War of the late 40s through the 1960s is still with us, and we can detect three historical inflection points:

1. after the Second World War, the beginning of the First Cold War

2. the election of Ronald Reagan as the start of the Second Cold War (1980); and

3. the election of Donald Trump, and the start of the Third Cold War (2016).

I argue that this has had a global influence on education and how we think and that we must acknowledge that ancient myths, legends and more recent ideologies continue to affect us, in order for us to have any hope of thinking differently.

These primeval stories are the basis of what, Joseph Campbell, called 'creative mythology', and Carl Jung named our 'collective unconscious'. These stories are the exoskeleton for our culture, including our mathematics, and sciences. The separation of the science and the story are just another example of our split with who we are, where we came from and who we will become? We may have forgotten many of the stories we abandoned when we thought we had become grown-ups, but they are buried in the models, algorithms, and protocols of our existence. Story is essential, all of our creativity and imagination depends upon it. We need story to noodle our way out of this complex mess. As Dougald Hine and Paul Kingsnorth wrote in their manifesto, *Dark Mountain*:

"We will, [or must], reassert the role of storytelling as more than mere entertainment. It is through stories that we weave reality."[5]

Nassim Nicholas Taleb warns us of the dangers of narratives, both fictional and non-fictional while acknowledging their value. "Indeed, our consciousness may be linked to our ability to concoct some form of story about ourselves. It is just that narrative can be lethal when used in the wrong places."[6]

In his book, *On the Origin of the Species: evolution, cognition, and fiction*, Brian Boyd examined the evolutionary purpose of the story. He answers the question, why do we prefer fiction to fact? This claim is self-evident if you consider that the media and entertainment industry is an annual USD$10 trillion business, storytelling is enormously popular, even amongst the adults. Boyd argues that stories enable us to understand events and representations of events as 'a kind of cognitive play, in this case with social information', and what is more, the invention of stories and culture are not unique to humans.[7]

The creation of models, forms, and concepts are artistic explorations of our psyche, and our struggle with how we reunite our humanity with our nature, all the while searching for future worlds that we would prefer to live in. At this moment in time mounting statistics on suicide rates, depression, drug addiction, bullying and social pathologies suggest that many have abandoned hope, and lack any confidence that they can either bend or build new worlds from the ruins of this one.[8]

However, the solutions to what ails us are hidden in our past; in the stories, we continue to tell ourselves and in our ability to recognise draconian symbols of power, from enlightened myths of psychic salvation. Boyd, argues that stories and languages gave us the evolutionary tools to assist our 'ultrasocial' species to push beyond the speed limits of creeping biological evolution, and to accelerate our intelligence by helping us to process complex social situations, much faster. Dan Everett argues that language itself is a technological artefact created, and modified from within various social and environmental context.[9] We prefer it in fictitious form because stories present invented events, told in a compelling medium, that intensifies the emotional impact in surprising ways that the facts rarely permit. In a way, fiction may even be less deceptive than nonfiction that masquerades as fact. This is what the author of *Black Swan*, Nassim Nicholas Taleb, calls the narrative fallacy.[10] We tend to both underestimate the probability of events we have never seen, what he calls, 'a black swan event', and overestimate black swan events that we have been warned of in stories. The rediscovery of the importance and power of stories moves us beyond the hyper-individualism of neo-liberal culture and fosters cooperation and collective world bending through social action, and nonhuman world creation. Story, and our playful engagement in it is so pleasurable that we expend vast amounts of money, time, and energy on it, instead of resting, and it contributes to our learning, and over-learning of social values, norms, and collective intelligence.[11]

What is apparent from the ancient stories, myths and religions is that apocalyptic thoughts and behaviour are recurring themes on this planet and that rather than dismiss them as primitive superstitions, they may well give us some insights into who we are, and how we got here, in other words, using philosophy, history and the humanities we might shine some light on a mysterious realm in which logic and reason remain mute.

Prophets, oracles, seers and shamans were relied on to predict, or peer into an uncertain future, and at the same time, they constructed social order and rules that built communities, and worlds. Their stories and myths are the basis for our new narratives and epistemologies that define how we 'read' the past, present and future, and they provide the foundational ideas of our pop culture, advertising, and persuasive technologies that also shape science and modernity. In a word, they are the foundation of our creativity and our social delusion. There are numerous cognitive biases that mislead us into believing that we have come to a rational decision, but in truth, we have formed an opinion based on first order, nonconscious cognition, based on fast biochemical reactions to sensory information and emotional memories. According to Taleb there are two ways that we can form a belief based on either System 1: the fast primitive, limbic system of experience, activated by the senses and emotions, often described in memorable narratives; or System 2: the cognitive, experimental, self referential, and slow process of reasoned response to data, with a sceptical application of theory and models. Taleb recommends "The way to avoid the ills of the narrative fallacy is to favour experimentation over storytelling, experience over history, and clinical knowledge over theories."[12] Narratives can be used in both fiction and non-fiction for social deception and mass manipulation, but we can learn to recognise and critically challenge them.

They are also the countervailing source of our imaginative imprisonment, the rituals, rules, and infrastructure of our societies, religions, and cultures. We need to understand those stories to also understand how our so-called modern world building is still shaped by a mysterious and misunderstood past; we need to understand in order to build new worlds and to escape the ruins of the broken battlements of hegemonic ideologies, and religious dogma. Norbert Wiener, who is described by his biographers as the 'dark hero of the information age', and the founder of cybernetics, recognised the dangerous relationship between humans, machines, communications, and control.[13]

In *God and Golem Inc.*, he wrote: "Knowledge is inextricably intertwined with communication, power with control, and the evaluation of human purposes with ethics and the whole normative side of religion."[14]

Wiener's theories have shaped our digital age, from information theory to machine learning, digital computing and AI. Wiener was also fearful of the military R & D funding that shaped many of these fields. He had the foresight to predict many of our current technologies, and those that are soon to come. However, he also rightly understood the power of myths and religions when it came to questions of ethics and the philosophical traps of automation and AI that lie before us. The origins of our shared stories are beyond our abilities to know, they are strange things that are withdrawn from us, but we are also hopelessly entangled, and in love, in much the same way as poems, subatomic particles, and other things, that also entangle us in a queer aesthetic, in another world beyond the hierarchical, patriarchal, heteronormative, neurotypical, neo-liberal empiricism. Hayles, critiques Wiener's assertion that a cybernetic future would lead to more conscious control, and yet she also recognises Galloway's argument that protocols and algorithms are creating a world that unconsciously controls us. In order to reclaim our freedom, Hayles argues we have to look for inflection points in order to intervene. She wrote that activists must explore the points of vulnerability in these systems.

"Instead of control, effective modes of intervention seek for inflection points at which systemic dynamics can be decisively transformed to send the cognitive assemblage in a different direction."[15]

Our ability to understand and reimagine how these technological assemblages might be configured is dependent on our understanding of how culture and story are embedded in these networks of actors, both human and nonhuman. There has been a long line of scholars and authors who have researched the history of myths, legends, and symbols that we have inherited. More recently, in the past hundred or so years, there were writers such as, Sir James George Frazer, Carl Jung, Sigmund Freud, Joseph Campbell, Colin Wilson, and Stephen Booker, to name some of the Westerners who have traced how mythology has informed our cultures and shared symbols, plot lines, and stories. Jung developed the individuation theory which describes how the founders of the great religions, Jesus, Buddha, and Mohammed, all shared similar paths and stories that related to the universal 'hero's journey'. Jung, Campbell and others also noted that some of the great heroes of antiquity also follow this archetypal pattern and that we can see that the legends of Adam, from the *Book of Genesis*; Orpheus; Joseph and the Argonauts; Odysseus; Gilgamesh; and Prometheus, all share common traits. Campbell who studied the novelist, James Joyce, borrows his term, monomyth to describe the hero's journey writing:

"A hero ventures forth from the world of common day into a region of supernatural wonder: fabulous forces are there encountered and a decisive victory is won: the hero comes back from this mysterious adventure with the power to bestow boons on his fellow man."[16] While the hero's journey is repeated in thousands of stories, myths and religions, this is not to suggest that we naively accept them on face value, or ignore how innumerable tyrants, dictators and fascist states have used symbols, and myths to propagate their power, and subjugate, others; both human and nonhuman, to their will. It was Plato who stressed the power of story but also pointed out "Those who tell the stories rule society [or the world]." It is hoped that by examining some of these stories of origin, and creation that we might expose our current superstitions, and the manipulation of story by the powerful. This project is both a micro and macrocosmic mission to heal our cosmic psyche and defend the future from our own destructive fantasies.

The hero's journey provides a metaphor for the creation, bending, and destruction of worlds. We create and recreate this world every morning when we wake up, but if only we could dream, we could bend new worlds out of this one, and even happily end the world that is making us all sick. While there may be a pall that hangs over this world as we mourn lost futures,[17] we have an obligation to create new ones. The party is well and truly over, but let's not feel sad about recycling our empties, it gives us a chance to recover from the hangover, and set the table for a more refined and sophisticated dinner party. Bacchus has played his role, we can still enjoy ourselves, and we might just enjoy the extended conversation with our nonhuman dinner guests, who have a seat at the table, rather than a macabre apple stuck in their mouth, as we live high on the hog.

According to Booker, our ancient stories are instructional morality tales about reclaiming our original connection with the outside, the nonhuman majority. He wrote:

"What our prehistoric ancestors were doing was to try to reconnect themselves with that sense of unity from which they had been exiled by the emergence of their new type of consciousness."[18]

This is an ancient quest, that has not missed a beat, and is still at the heart of art and science, articulated today in quantum physics as the search for the 'theory of everything'. If these ancient stories did not speak to our deep psychological questions, then they would no longer have such a powerful resonance today; they remain the well-spring of our creativity. Jung believed that our present-day physics and cosmology came from the same wellspring in the form of the cosmic archetypes evolving from the singularity at the beginning of time. For the artist and visionary world builder this act of creativity requires strength and courage. As Campbell spells it out, this is a journey into the psychological abyss. Campbell writes:

"And so it happens that if anyone...undertakes for himself the perilous journey into the darkness by descending either intentionally or unintentionally, into the crooked lanes of his own spiritual labyrinth, he soon finds himself in a landscape of symbolical figures (any one of which may swallow him)."[19]

Yes, we can ignore the hero's calling, after all, most of us are too busy worrying about debt, job security, and our families, but as Harari points out, that won't make the apocalypse go away.[20] I want to encourage you to not just cheer on the military-industrial adventures of Marvel's *Iron Man*, but to take your own journey into the abyss. It is dangerous, but the hero is always compelled to take the journey because success is not only possible, it is a desirable future of unimaginable riches, not Tony Stark's extravagant and wasteful lifestyle, but one of spiritual and ecological co-existence in a better world.

World Bending Heroes

This chapter will use the cycle of the hero's journey to structure my narrative around how ancient stories have infused our hopes and fears about all possible futures. It is because these hopes and fears dwell in our dreams and our 'collective unconscious' that we fail to recognise their origins, and so they can imprison us. It is my hope that we might liberate humans and nonhumans from the forces who manipulate our desires and free us for a new level of world bending creativity. Can we begin to tell stories for grown-ups?

The hero's journey has been made famous amongst the scriptwriters of superhuman blockbusters by George Lucas, and his reference to Joseph Campbell's book, *Hero of a Thousand Faces*. The story of Luke

Skywalker in the *Star Wars* franchise follows a structure that begins with order, descends into chaos, and returns to order in which Luke's character is transformed into a hero. This process of psychological transformation is so archetypal, and repeated in so many myths and legends, that it has become synonymous with Hollywood's formulaic tale of a protagonist.

From a psychological perspective, what is psyche? This ancient concept is defined today as the 'human soul, mind or will'. It is derived from the mythical story, in *Metamorphoses*, it tells of the love between Psyche and her lost lover Cupid. Psyche is charged with a series of difficult tasks by the jealous mother of Cupid, Venus. In her final trials, Psyche must collect a bottle of water from a freezing spring watched over by a vigilant dragon, and then descend into the underworld to recover a box of supernatural beauty. In the Roman translation, Psyche is known as Anima which in Jungian psychology is associated with the feminine twin of the masculine Animus. According to Jung, the hero's quest is the process of individuation, and unity of their psyche, bringing together the female with the male in one mind. However, this unity did not just relate to the psyche, as Jung believed the psychological archetypes were derived from cosmic archetypes that related to the origins of the universe. This Jung then translated into quantum physics, the mysteries of the black hole, and the creation of everything at the beginning of time, in the Big Bang; it was when the universe, was unified, and according to the theory of quantum entanglement, the universe remains that way today, and into the unimaginable future. Ancient myths and legends are in accord with the latest theories in quantum physics. Timothy Desmond, revisits some of the early creation myths of Greek and other cultures, to make Jung's point that the Psyche = Singularity. Desmond writes:

"From Plato through the entire span of the medieval era, the intellectual class imagined the universe as a series of concentric spheres with Earth at the centre and the eternal ideas of God's creative mind condensed in an infinitely dense Big Bang must be the origins of the psyche."

It has been reported by a number of scholars that our ancient myths, religions, and beliefs often read as metaphors for our most advanced scientific theories. If there was nothing before the Big Bang, then psyche, and cosmic archetypes must have been created at the time of the singularity. Since Aristotelian times through to the Middle Ages it was believed that 'above so it is below', or in other words, the microcosm reflects the macrocosm. Therefore, according to Jung, the personal psyche reflects the cosmological psyche and we can relate the stages of the hero's journey to collective world views, and the journey of worlds, from birth to death. These mythical tales offer us alternative futures and creative paths for our imaginations to explore.

Lucas and Campbell influenced a number of other popular story theorists including Stephen Booker, *Seven Basic Plots*, Blake Snyder, *Save the Cat*, and the creator of the futurist animation series, *Rick and Morty*, Dan Harmon. Harmon's alcoholic Grandpa Rick (the wise sage), takes Morty on the hero's journey every episode; somewhere out in the multiverse amongst the twisted tales of infinite reality shows, and the evil exploits of 'Worldender' vs 'Pooh man'. Harmon has simplified Campbell's hero's journey, with 8 stages that circle back to the beginning, and we can use it to examine the origins of some of our strange dreams and nightmares that define our current world creation.

Harmon's Version of the Hero's Journey

1. The protagonist is established in an ordered world

2. They need something because 'something isn't right'

3. They are forced to go somewhere and cross the threshold from order into a world of chaos – the descent into hell.

4. On their search into the abyss, the protagonist encounters a number of trials – in ancient myths, this is usually three in number.

5. In the bowels of hell, they find what they are looking for and meet the 'goddess'.

6. The protagonist takes what they have found, but pays a big price.

7. Returning from the chaos the hero brings it home.

8. The hero arrives home a changed and fully actualised being. They are now the master of both realms, order and chaos, conscious and unconscious psyches.

These 8 signposts serve as the 'map of the human heart' and reveal ancient story structures, psychological wisdom, and a cosmological archetype for world bending, breaking and building.

1. Establish the World/Protagonist

"In the beginning there was the Word, and the word was with God, and the Word was God." (Gospel of John 1:1)

The Epic of Gilgamesh, (2100 BCE) from ancient Mesopotamia is thought to be the earliest extant great work of literature. This epic poem comes from the region thought to be the origins of agriculture, known as the fertile crescent. What has an ancient hero's quest, written in the 21st century BCE got to say to us today? Surprisingly, *The Epic of Gilgamesh* continues to be something of an oracle for us four thousand two hundred years later.

It's prophetic images, symbols, and dreams provide us with psychological insights into the most ancient of archetypes, the myths that dwell in our 'collective unconscious'. Despite its dangers narratives and stories also encapsulate ancient wisdom and help us with cultural blind spots. We may overestimate the probability of apocalyptic tales, but we may also be able to avoid things that we have no personal experience of, as Taleb suggests:

"Respect for elders in many societies might be a kind of compensation for our short-term memory. The word senate comes from senatus, "aged" in Latin; sheikh in Arabic means both a member of the ruling elite and "elder." Elders are repositories of complicated inductive learning that includes information about rare events. Elders can scare us with stories—which is why we become overexcited when we think of a specific Black Swan."[21]

The quest of the king, Gilgamesh, is the 'hero's journey' that reveals the Jungian battle between the ego and the Self, and the violent tussle between humanity and nature as Gilgamesh follows the cycle of order, chaos, order. In this circle of life, or the hero's journey, there is no clear beginning except where the storyteller picks up, so even before there was the ordered world of our hero, there was chaos. In Ovid's poem, *Metamorphoses*, the tale begins with chaos.

"Before there was earth or sea or the sky that covers everything, Nature appeared the same throughout the whole world: what we call chaos: a raw confused mass, nothing but inert matter, badly combined discordant atoms of things, confused in the one place."

Order is created out of chaos. In the *Epic of Gilgamesh* and the *Book of Genesis*, our hero arrives after God has created order and agriculture. There are parallels in the Epic with the story of the Garden of Eden in which man is made from clay, lives in the wild with animals, and loses his innocence with a woman. In both stories, the man accepts food from the woman, and in the Epic a serpent steals the plant of immortality, while Adam and Eve are exiled from the Garden of Eden, so that they may no longer eat from the immortal Tree of Life. Before the hero's journey, and the world begins, the story starts with the establishment of the world in which order is established. The *Book of Genesis* starts:

[1.1] In the beginning when God created the heavens and the earth,

[1:2] the earth was a formless void and darkness covered the face of the deep, while a wind from God swept over the face of the waters.

[1:3] Then God said, "Let there be light"; and there was light.

In the Epic, Gilgamesh begins as something of a wild man two-thirds a god, and a third man. As the king of Uruk, Gilgamesh is an oppressive tyrant who insists on his right as their Lord to sleep with young brides on their wedding night. Hearing the pleas of the people the gods send Gilgamesh the savage Enkidu, who was created out of clay by Gilgamesh's mother Ninsun. Just like Adam, in *Genesis*, Enkidu has no knowledge of civilisation, until he is informed of good and evil by the prostitute, Shamhat. He then loses his animal-like innocence. According to the translator, Andrew George, the epic is much more than an instructional manual for kings, and is a treatise on the "eternal conflict of nurture and nature – articulated as the benefits of civilisation over savagery."[22]

In both the *Book of Genesis* and the *Epic of Gilgamesh*, God(s) had already created agriculture, before the humans, or as we might interpret, before Homosapiens.

[1:11] Then God said, "Let the earth put forth vegetation: plants yielding seed, and fruit trees of every kind on earth that bear fruit with the seed in it." And it was so.

[1:12] The earth brought forth vegetation: plants yielding seed of every kind, and trees of every kind bearing fruit with the seed in it. And God saw that it was good.

The relatively warm, and mostly, stable climate of the Holocene is the beginning of a new world of agriculture, and the patriarchal civilisation that followed. According to the *Bible* and the word of God as interpreted by the Church:

[3:16] To the woman he said, "I will greatly increase your pangs in childbearing; in pain you shall bring forth children, yet your desire shall be for your husband, and he shall rule over you.

The historian, Richard Tarnas, describes two great myths that have loomed large in the background of modernity. The underlying myth of human progress, and the other :

"tragic narrative of humanity's gradual but radical fall and separation from an original state of oneness with nature and an encompassing spiritual dimension of being."[23]

Progress, especially from a Western scientific perspective, has long been regarded as technologically self-evident. It is only in the past 2 or 3 decades that this has been recognised as a paradigm. Paradoxically, the myth of the fall from grace and the expulsion from the Garden of Eden continues to haunt us despite the apparent contradiction. Tarnas wrote:

"In its primordial condition, humankind had possessed an instinctive knowledge of the profound sacred unity and interconnectedness of the world, but under the influence of the Western mind, especially its modern expression, the course of history brought about a deep schism between humankind and nature, and a desacralization of the world."[24]

This schism is now driving the philosophical project to heal the rift and unify cosmological archetypes. Our modern mind is searching for that unity of humanity and nature. In the *Bible*, the 'original sin' or the 'ancestral fall' describes how Adam and Eve succumb to the temptation of the serpent in the Garden of Eden and ate an apple from the Tree of Knowledge. According to biblical scholars, this set in train the apocryphal timeline that believers thought would lead to the 'end of time'. At one time cultural norms, good and evil, knowledge, sin, and technological knowhow were all bound together by the myths and rituals of social discipline and control. We have inherited the sins of the father, and as Morton points out, today we still have a profound unease with the world described in the *Bible*. It is as if modernity has had an allergic reaction. Morton writes,

"Consider the modern hatred of the body that links with a profound (and accurate) unease that "something is wrong" and is then blended with primitivism: the "Paleo diet." The term Paleo acknowledges that something is wrong with the Neolithic, the term we use for post-Mesopotamian human social forms: something is wrong—as Genesis had already pointed out."[25]

Morton recalls the narrative of the Golden Age that stated that agriculture was an abomination and that people lived on fruit and roots, obtained without labour, but "For the existence of sin in the form of cultivation, the lifespan of people became shortened."[26]

In *Genesis* it was written:

"I have placed a curse on the ground. All your life you will struggle to scratch a living from it. It will grow thorns and thistles for you, though you will eat of its grains. All your life you will sweat to produce food, until your dying day. Then you will return to the ground from which you came. For you were made from dust, and to the dust you will return."

Steve Jones in his book, *The Serpent's Promise*,[27] wrote, "Genesis was the world's first biology textbook". In the *Book of Genesis* the beginning of religion was the beginning of agriculture and the 'origin of sin'. Morton argues that agriculture is based on a set of rules, or algorithms; an algorithmic technology, bound by the Fall to the original sin. Agriculture far from giving humanity a life without starvation and toil became a promise of 'All your life you will sweat to produce food, until your dying day." Archaeology has shown that the average height

and life expectancy of a farmer who was significantly shorter, mal-
nourished and died younger than his nomadic ancestors. So, in the
story of our beginnings, the establishing shot for the movie of our culture is a world of toil, dominated by men, and their technology.

2. A Clear Need To Go Somewhere Because Something Is Not Right

Following the first stage of the hero's journey, there is a clear call to
action because something is not right. The world has already begun
to descend into chaos and so the hero (our creative world bender)
receives notice that they must set out on their journey. This is the
beginning of the hero's journey into the wilderness, and their first
attainment of knowledge. The loss of innocence and banishment from
the Garden of Eden resulted from the knowledge of good and evil after
the eating of the apple from the Tree of Knowledge. It was the serpent,
or trickster, an archetypal character often associated with technology
and crafty artifice, who tempts Eve with the divine gift of knowledge
and the creativity of agriculture.

The wild apple tree, Malus sieversii, which originated in central
Asia, in Kazakhstan, and was possibly the first cultivated tree which
was then bred to improve its taste for humans, and that improvement
continued to develop over thousands of years. This ancient form of
genetic modification, had it taken place in the lab by genetic scientists,
might be regarded by many as scientific arrogance, and we all know
'pride comes before a Fall'. Tucked away in the subconscious of modernity there is a narrative warning us of the normative and moralistic
view of technology that has troubled humanity since the discovery of
fire.

Ancients believed that creativity was God given. Creation belonged
to the Gods and to search and attain that knowledge, according to the
Book of Genesis, was a sin that would result in humanity being cast out
of Paradise, thereby suffering the divine consequences, and punishment, all happening after fair warning. Was not Adam and Eve's apple
proffered by the serpent, the original sin-thetic, an unnatural immortal? The serpent is a trickster, like the Norse god Loki, who convinces

Eve that she will not die, as promised by God, but according to the talking snake, if she eats the apple, "then your eyes shall be opened, and ye shall be as gods, knowing good and evil." (Genesis 3:5). This ambitious desire to be like a god, in a state of moral awareness, and the dream of immortality forever haunt us. Perhaps, this is why we fear the ethical consequences around synthetic beings, such as artificial life, clones, robots, and A.I.; the creations of mad scientists who are playing God, and therefore, the stories tell us, it will end badly. According to Egan and *A Very Short History of Imagination*[28] Adam and Eve encroached on God's prerogative. Imagination and creation share the same root word in Hebrew. Yester means imagination and shares the root word, Yetzirah which translates into creation.

And the act of creation, and world building, is God's right alone, thus:

"human beings are trespassing on powers that properly belong to God. That people are to remember this and desist from so doing is made clear by the punishments visited on Adam and Eve, and on the builders of Babel. In both cases, acts of rebellion against the limits God set for human beings exhibit the power to imagine a future that is different from the past."[29]

The Biblical story of the Tower of Babel is another moral warning of human hubris and the vain ambition to build a tower that threatened to reach to the very gates of Heaven. One language shared ideas, and creativity were threats that God answered with an apocalyptic attack on the tower that came crumbling down and dispersed humanity to the four corners of the earth.

It is therefore not just the act of creation but the speculative design of creation that is considered sinful. The hero has become aware that something is definitely not right, and so they must go on the journey to try and fix things. We could, of course, ignore the fact that our world is broken, but technology has made us into demigods, and with that goes the responsibility to go on the journey, to search for a psychic solution. Our technology is not self-determined but follows our psychic state – if we are broken, then so will be the technological world we create – something is not right, but we can fix it, by fixing ourselves.

3. Go! Crossing The Threshold

The hero now crosses the threshold and begins to descend into Hades, the Abyss, or the Netherworld. This is the metaphorical underworld of the psychological unconscious, the world of dreams, nightmares and strange mythical creatures. This is the dangerous world where the hero searches for something they need. In the many mythical stories of this descent, they are seriously warned of the consequences of divine retribution if they make a mistake, yet it is by being fearless of mistakes that we discover our own creativity.

However, it must be remembered who was writing the scriptures, and telling the stories, these were often the dictates of the philosopher king, or the Church, and were often political. The extant version of The Epic of Gilgamesh was thought to be written by Sîn-lēqi-unninni's whose name means "Sîn (the Moon God), is one who accepts my prayer".[30]

According to George the Sumerian text was probably sung to King Shulgi of Ur of the Chaldees in the 21st century BCE. It was seen as something of an operating manual for kings, and their divine rights, that were in turn bestowed on those kings who followed.

Gilgamesh, was not any old human, he was two thirds a god. Since ancient history knowledge was regarded as a divine right that followed a chain of command granted to shamans, priests and courtiers according to the divine right of rulers. It would seem that well before the knowledge economy, and intellectual property laws, knowledge, creativity, and imagination were considered the property of Royal entitlement. As Kearney puts it:

"As a power first dramatized in man's defiance of divine prohibition, the yetser bears the stigma of a stolen possession" (1988, pp. 40/41)"[31]

In ancient Greece, stealing from the Gods was punishable by extreme torture, but the crime of Prometheus, who was a demigod was not stealing the fire, but giving it to the humans, and he used the power of foresight, and imagination to plan and design technologies for the benefit of humanity. In the middle ages, the craft guilds and professions were all controlled by the Crown. The warning of the ancient myths and legends, was plain if you go and cross the threshold to the underworld, the place where your subconscious dreams dwell, you face the possibility of eternal damnation, hell. This journey was not intended for mere mortals, slaves, women, or subhumans, but today humanist values see all humans as potential heroes. We are even beginning to see that nonhumans might undertake the dangers of the hero's journey of self-discovery.

4. The Search – Road of Trials and Moral Warnings

As our hero descends further into Hell they encounter tests and trials of spirit. These are not only tests but warnings that unless they prove worthy of the underworld will swallow them up and they will never return. This is also one of the most treacherous stages of the hero's journey because of the extreme moral hazard posed by the trials. The hero is not only searching for a physical or metaphorical treasure that will 'save the world' but as they descend into the depths of their psychological abyss they face madness, or eternal damnation, trapped in Hell for eternity.

This is also the most dangerous moment for world benders and would-be world builders as they are faced with the full moral authority of society, and its rulers. This is where creativity and imagination are tested by social norms, laws and regulations. The search is, and of itself one of the most challenging and testing experiences for the individual and for those who will step outside of the norms, conventions and laws of society, culture, the law, and the moral strictures of religion. Yet, it is also where the brave and adventurous explorer can find the treasure of untold conceptual riches. It is where we need to focus when we are searching for new worlds, and new paradigms that will support alternative futures; beyond the existential crisis of the Anthropocene. I will spend some time examining what we can learn from the search and the moral warnings that can inhibit our dreams and imagination.

The Moral Authority – Warnings of Disaster

Like many of the ancient myths there are stories of wise elders who were well versed in scripture, and educated in the rituals that celebrate the divine; who warn reckless youth of wandering from the path of moral rectitude.

Gilgamesh, who has built the mighty kingdom of Uruk, with its impressive ziggurats, massive defenses, and civic infrastructure, wants to expand his kingdom and his domain over the terrifying, but sacred Forest of Cedar in which lurks the god, Humbaba. The Epic poem warns the youthful Gilgamesh:

"The senior advisers rose, good counsel they offered Gilgamesh: 'You are young, Gilgamesh, borne along by emotion, all that you talk of you don't understand. This Humbaba, his voice is the Deluge, his speech is fire, his breath is death! He hears the forest murmur at sixty leagues' distance: who is there would venture into his forest?"

This warning by wise elders is reminiscent of the warnings of Yahweh, the Hebrew God who warned the righteous Noah that the apocalyptic Deluge was coming to wash away the sins of the world. Humbaba recalls the terrifying *Old Testament* God who breathed fire, and with one breath could both give life, and take it away.

The curious thing about the legend of Gilgamesh is that he ignores the elders advice and wrongly kills, the protector of the sacred Cedar forest, Humbaba. It is a wanton act that pains our conscience as if he was cutting down the Amazon forest to graze cattle for a Mac and cheese. Gilgamesh is cursed and natural disasters follow him, as his trials begin, and he tries in vain to discover the mystery of immortality, descending into the abyss of his subconscious. Gilgamesh, like Adam, and Prometheus, is part human, part god, his human hubris is instantiated in the technology of his sword and axe with which he kills the god, Humbaba, and destroys the sacred forest.

Like Adam, and Prometheus, Gilgamesh is also rebellious, and despite being cast in the image of the gods, and inheriting their generative power as creators, he is also an overreacher, one who struggles to restrain his ambitious ego and become more god-like. In psychological terms Gilgamesh, Adam, and Prometheus suppress their feminine psyche to overpower nature through their explicit plans, using strength, reason, and divine deception to overcome emotion. In a Jungian turn of phrase, Booker describes how,

"Gilgamesh and Enkidu go on to fell all the trees of that great forest of which Humbaba had been the guardian. Nature is being forced into retreat before the growing power of men to subdue it. This may have seemed a triumph for advancing human consciousness. But, as we now know, it was that clearing of the Mesopotamian forests to make way for agriculture which was eventually to reduce those lands through soil erosion to arid desert, bringing an end to the civilisations they had supported."[32]

Timothy Morton argues that our ecological vandalism not only began in Mesopotamia, with the warmer climes of the Holocene but that we are still Mesopotamians at heart, searching for the unity within our psyche and with nature. The mythology of Gilgamesh, repeated in the story of the Garden of Eden, and 'mankind's' proclaimed God-given right to have dominion over women, the Earth's plants and animals, is buried deep in our half forgotten primeval memories. Gilgamesh had been warned.

Creating Sin-thetic Monsters – The Warning of God's Retribution

These myths have been handed down to the present and inform our technological, and environmental fears and prejudice. Killer robots, and genetically engineered monsters are nothing new, and the ancestors of the *Terminator*, and *Dr No* can be found in the ancient myths of the bronze automaton, Talos, and the half man, half beast, the Minotaur. Grant Maxwell in his book, *The Dynamics of Transformation*, believes that there is growing evidence that these pre-modern archetypes will see a dialectical integration with the meaningless reductive, scientism and will result in the acknowledgement of the missing 'other' the feminine psyche to redress the domination by the masculine Promethean archetype, that is baked into the modern scientific method. He wrote that:

"Although it is often necessary to analyze, reduce, separate, and differentiate processes in order to understand phenomena, it is often equally necessary to perceive the efficacy of qualities across scale, including discontinuity, which makes possible sudden leaps to novel domains of ingression such as the paradigmatic Promethean discovery of fire, and all of the subsequent discoveries that ensued, from the archetypes themselves to quantum field theory."[33]

We can see how the original gods and demigods have died but still live on, still haunting our technology as the ghosts in the machines. Our superstitions, visions, and phobias are descendants of the first morality plays and warnings, such as the legend of the 'original sin'.

The king Gilgamesh, who was one-third human, and two thirds a god, is our original synthetic. His friend, Enkidu, is also a synthetic created by the Goddess mother, Ninshun out of clay. Just as in the legends of Adam, Prometheus, and the automatons of Daedalus, Gilgamesh is synthetically created. These heroes represent humanity's ancient dreams of our split with nature, and our continual reminder that if we play at being God we will be punished with catastrophe, and the apocalypse could follow. His search for immortality is also a moral warning repeated in the *Book of Genesis*; the Fall from Grace, in which Adam and Eve are cast out of Paradise, deprived of the Tree of Life, and forced to toil in the dirt. The serpent who symbolises both immortality and knowledge tempts them to eat the apple, making them mortal and gaining knowledge in order to apply the technical knowhow of agriculture, to stay alive, but thus, forsaking the innocence of their wild nature.

Adam was warned 'On the day that thou eatest thereof thou shalt surely die" (Genesis 2:17). This rebellion against the gods is repeated in Jung's individuation, as we see our heroes seek to become fully divine, and immortal. This wild ambition is the rebel's cause and the solitary path of the creator; creativity is god-given, and they want to attain the ultimate power over death in order to create. Creativity is the 'original sin', to be creative is to be a rebel, to live outside of the rules, to eat from the tree of knowledge, and to ignore scripture by writing your own. This blasphemy has continued to be heretical and has been punished by tribes, cults, churches, royalty, and governments from time immemorial, up until today.[34] God is not just the almighty creator, 'he' must be obeyed as a political Lord. Those who rebel, and have the arrogance, and temerity to aspire to creativity, and originality, have often faced death at the hand's of God's servants; those rulers who interpret the word of God.

Campbell, in his book, *Creative Mythology: the masks of God*, retraces the strange myths and religions that continue to provide modern creativity with both the bedrock of creation, but also the fear of rebellious creativity. Campbell writes:

"Steadfast love surrounds him who trusts in the Lord." (Psalm 32:10); and to those for whom such protection seems a prospect worthy of all sacrifice, an orthodox mythology will afford both the patterns and the sentiments of a lifetime of good repute."[35]

Everyday subjects of tyrannical rulers were warned of the suffering they would face if they did not follow the 'word of God'; their law. The law, once based on the command and control of those in power, were first conveyed using oral mythology, and then written scripture. Those who dared to build new worlds were often punished for their creativity, or simply ridiculed, and ostracized from society. Colin Wilson described these creative rebels as 'outsiders'.[36]

Campbell continues to make his case for creativity and imagination after he outlined the ordinary world of one who ignores the creative call.

"However, by those to whom such living would be not life, but anticipated death, the circumvallating mountains that to others appear to be of stone are recognised as the mist of dream. Precisely between their God and Devil, heaven and hell, white and black, the man of heart walks through. Out beyond those walls, in uncharted forest night, where the terrible wind of God blows directly on the questing undefended soul. Tangled ways may lead to madness. They may also lead, however, as one of the greatest poets of the Middle Ages tells, to "all those things that got to make heaven and earth."[37]

This uncharted forest night is where we hope to search for new worlds, as frightening as it may seem so that we might provide world builders with the necessary antidotes, and even placebos, to liberate the creativity necessary for audacious and risky constructions of speculative worlds beyond our current limitations. Jung's mission and the warnings of Campbell and Booker encourage us to join the anima (the woman within) and animus (the man within) reuniting the collective unconscious and for us all to become whole, living in coexistence with the invisible, the indifferent, the concept, and the block, the fish, and the chip, the sensor, and the soil, and all the lovely things we have never, and will never meet or get to know.

But first, we must tackle the human project, a massive, dispersed, abstract, and concrete, tangle of nerves, bacteria, time and space, a mysterious hyperobject that tricks us into thinking we know it, because we are one of its components. The project requires a healing of the split – not one, but many fractures, in the human psyche – masculine vs. feminine; good vs. evil; human vs. nature; north vs south; east vs. west; mind vs. body; ego vs. Self. The list could go on, these artificial dualities have confused and tormented us. Jung argues that the split of good vs. evil, or God vs. Satan, happened just prior to Christianity.

In the *Old Testament,* Satan 'belonged to the intimate entourage of Yahweh' (God), however, in the *Book of Enoch,* 'now formed the diametrical and eternal opposite of the divine world.' Jung commented that it was therefore hardly surprising that in the eleventh century that the belief arose that the creation of our world was credited to the devil, and not to God. Jung argues that this setup the suspicion that the original sin stemmed from our unbridled search for knowledge, and our unholy claim to the creativity of God.

"Thus, the keynote was struck for the second half of the Christian aeon, after the myth of the fall of the angels had already explained that these fallen angels had taught men a dangerous knowledge of science and the arts."[38]

The Fall from Grace has been reinterpreted to mean that knowledge and creativity are evil and that our synthesis of ideas, and worse life, are the creative result of the 'original sin'. The characteristics of Prometheus as humanity's saviour, but also his technological pride that came before the fall, were separated in the Christian story. While the ancient Graeco-Romans were happy to worship and entertain the Parthenon of gods, the equally powerful Judaeo influence on Christianity encouraged a purging of gods and a unity that dramatically simplified, and rationalised the number of characters incorporated into the Christian narrative. "Prometheus as the suffering liberator of mankind was now subsumed by the figure of Christ, while Prometheus as the hubristic rebel against God was subsumed by the figure of Lucifer."[39]

Technologists, scientists and transhumanists[40] may just shrug their shoulders in indifference, or in bewildered disbelief. This century promises them a mid-millennium singularity that will, with the right funding, a large dose of AI, and Herculean effort, ensure that we get off this rock, or at the very least ensure that we can exist despite overheating, overcrowding, and toxic pollution. Others are not so sure, and they fear that untethered science such as GMO crops, transhumanist immortality, cloning, and robots will result in disaster. Our trust in so-called 'nature' is impossibly entwined in the ancient myths, before the Fall, when we still inhabited the natural state of grace in the Garden of Eden. How do we come to terms with our existential crisis, heal our collective psyche, and build desirable new coexistent worlds that pay homage to the creativity locked inside our nascent ecosystem? The ancient rulers knew that often warnings were not enough, and so the law followed.

God's Law — the Commandment of Kings

In 1600 Giordano Bruno (1548 – 1600) was burned to death in Campo dei Fiori. Joseph Campbell pointed out that his crime was not the denial of God, but Bruno was burned alive for teaching the 'truth' as proven by the mathematician Copernicus. The proof, that Copernicus established five years before Bruno was born, was that the Earth revolves around the Sun, not the Sun around the Earth. Why this was so appalling to the Church, and the authorities, was that it contradicted what was written in the *Bible*, or rather their interpretation of it. Campbell wrote:

"The actual point in question, throughout the centuries of Christian persecution, has never been faith in God, but faith in the *Bible* as the word of God, and in the Church (this Church or that) as the interpreter of that word."[41]

And yet, Copernicus ultimately lacked the empirical evidence to prove that the Sun was revolving around the Earth. He too relied on a leap of faith, or intuition, and ultimately, ancient 'wisdom', to argue his case, which the majority held to be unreasonable, and unscientific, and was why he, and others that supported the theory, relied on ancient authorities, such as Aristarchus, Pythagoras, and Heraclides, to bolster their argument.

Even after a century, Galileo, despite overwhelming authority from the likes of Ptolemy and Aristotle, wrote "the experiences which overtly contradict the annual movement [of the Earth around the Sun] are indeed so much greater in their apparent force that, I repeat, there is no limit to my astonishment when I reflect that Aristarchus and Copernicus were able to make reason so conquer sense that, in defiance of the latter, the former became mistress of their belief."[42]

Much like Kuhn, and Latour, Maxwell and Tarnas refute the common sense view of human progress, and our supposed evolutionary advance through rational debate and scientific experimentation. Copernicus's revolution that caused such a massive shift in our world view may be retold as a triumph of rationalism, but as Tarnas observed:

"Long-established rules of scientific methodology had to be overturned. An entirely new epistemology and ontology had to be formulated."[43]

This was creative, and rebellious, world bending. Tarnas argued that what was required was not just a physical, but metaphysical speculative imagination that resulted in a seismic shift in the cosmological, religious, epistemological, ontological and existential world view of humanity.

What Copernicus began was the ousting of a physical, embodied God, so there was nowhere for God to hide. Campbell argued that once God was seen as out there, and everywhere, then there was an outpouring of creativity that exploded with the Enlightenment. Once the Church and scripture no longer held a monopoly on the literal truth about nature, and the *Bible* became seen as a symbolic mythological morality tale, science and technology went their separate ways. However, while we might imagine that because many of us no longer literally think that the earth was created by God in six days, or that Noah packed every representative pair of animals into an ark before a global flood, it does not mean that those myths and legends do not still lurk in our dreams.

The distrust of science and technology is based on dark secrets and bizarre stories, yet there have been fearless thinkers who have taken us way beyond our comfort zone, and for that, they were punished. Socrates was sentenced to death, Aristotle had to flee for his life, and even Sir Isaac Newton kept his heretical thoughts to himself otherwise he could not have remained at the University of Cambridge despite not taking the holy orders as expected. This is not to deny that serious scientific and technological misadventures have not validated conservative world views, and those that preach the dangers of human creative hubris, but rather to say those warnings are often bolstered by political propaganda.

Campbell warns that society and institutions can dull the wit and encourage mediocrity, but given our rapidly approaching existential crisis we should do everything in our power to liberate those creative minds who are currently limited by conservative university administrators, dullard politicians who penny-pinch on essential research funding, and popular opinion, that neither understands, nor supports the research. Informed and educated democratic debate is essential.

In the 19th century, from the home of the modern university system in Germany, Nietzsche wrote:

"The aim of institutions – whether scientific, artistic, political or religious – never is to produce and foster exceptional examples: institutions are concerned, rather, for the usual, the normal, the mediocre."[44]

If innovation and novelty are going to be encouraged, where can they call home? If universities are not that home, where will it be? The mainstream media is no longer trusted in certain countries, and social media has been infected by propaganda campaigns and manipulation of public opinion.[45] Neoliberal ideology might say forget the universities, concentrate on entrepreneurial startups, but is a high tech US company the place to launch a thousand speculative projects, if none of those is designed for profit, but rather a radical takedown of the system – a speculative revolution; a world that comes after the end?

Marketing, public relations, and advertising funds support futurists who plan off-planet adventures such as mining asteroids, or terraforming Mars, but what if there was no business plan, or financial modelling, who would support such a radical and conceptual world construction? Creativity, rebellion and intellectual disobedience have always been feared by institutions and society, our hope lies in recognising how mythology can both supercharge our creations, and call out archetypal fears so we can begin imagining the unthinkable alternatives.

Karel Capek wrote, the play *R.U.R – Rossum's Universal Robots*, in 1921 In which he is credited with the first use of the word robot, coined by his brother, Joel Capek, meaning 'forced labour' in Czech. In the play, the company, R.U.R, that produced the synthetic humanoid robots used them as slave labour, but in a twist, there is a robot rebellion and the human race becomes extinct. In the play the original designer, Rossum created flesh and blood animals and humans to prove that God was unnecessary, and did not exist. Helena reveals she is a human rights activist for the freedom of robots and claims they have souls. She falls in love with the robot Primus and together they become the next Adam and Eve. These themes continue to play out in science fiction movies as diverse as *A.I. Artificial Intelligence* (2001), and *Ex Machina* (2014).

In the Prometheus legend, his brother, Epimetheus, was tasked with distributing the gifts of the Gods amongst the creatures, such as flight. The tale of Prometheus shares the *Bible's* story of God creating Adam, as Prometheus was given the ability by the gods to form humans out of the mud. This is the theme of the Jewish Golem and the modern cautionary narrative told by Norbert Wiener. Synthetic humans have had a long association with slavery and labour saving, sometimes they are created to work for the gods, and other times they are the masters. This ambivalence contributes to the fear and uncertainty that today's popular culture feels towards robots and A.I.

Norbert Wiener in the preface to *God and Golem Inc.* (1964) wrote:

"The problem of unemployment arising from automatization is no longer conjectural, but has become a very vital difficulty of modern society."

Wiener noted that cyborgs touched on ethical, and religious issues that he proposed "to use the limited analogies of cybernetic situations to cast a little light on the religious situations."[46]

The science of abiogenesis, or theories of the origins of life, hypothesise how inanimate minerals and gases could form a simple organic compound and transition, into a living organism. In 1952 the Miller-Urey experiment showed how amino acids, the building blocks of DNA, can be synthesised from inorganic compounds through high electricity voltages, such as lighting or radiation. This they proposed could have been the conditions on the early planet Earth. There is another theory proposed by Alexander Graham Cains-Smith, in 1985, that clay or montmorillonite could have acted as a catalyst for the polymerization of RNA, and the formation of membranes from lipids.

Wiener and cybernetics may only be vaguely remembered today for giving us the root word for 'cyborg' and 'cyberspace' but his influence is pervasive throughout the history of the Internet, communications, automation, AI, and computing.[47]

Wiener wrote:

"There are at least three points in cybernetics which appear to me to be relevant to religious issues. One of these concerns machines which learn; one concerns machines which reproduce themselves; and one, the coordination of machine and man. I may say that such machines are known to exist."[48]

All of these areas of cybernetics have stayed current and are of ethical concern today. That concern is not something that recently arose because of modern technology. Our concerns are found in our collective unconscious going back to the first stories of synthetic creativity.

The Trial and Black Art of Sin-Thetic Creativity

When Wiener published those words in 1964 it was the height of the Cold War and he was painfully aware of the existential threat that an automated nuclear Doomsday machine presented to the planet. Mathematical Game Theory convinced politicians and military strategists that the probable outcomes of a nuclear war could be calculated. The Stanley Kubrick movie, *Dr Strangelove*, depicted a command and control war room that was informed by the massive IBM 7090 mainframe with a 1401 teleprinter. In the public imagination, computing was closely associated with the military, intelligence agencies, and nuclear weaponry. It was a strange and mystical world overseen by technological wizards and suspect sorcerers.

Sorcery, especially in puritanical America, was associated with the Devil, the black arts of alchemy, and the re-animation of demonic creatures. Arthur C. Clarke had also noted that "Any sufficiently advanced technology is indistinguishable from magic." Since the beginning of the 20th-century technology became more and more esoteric as it moved from Newtonian mechanics to quantum mechanics – from pulleys and mechanical engines to electronics and eventually computers. These new machines that hide their magical powers under plastic covers were treated with suspicion, and superstition, by those who did not know how they worked.

For Wiener, there was a difference between those that used their innate curiosity and imagination to create technology, and those engineers he described as 'gadget worshipers'. Those suspect engineers who hid their secret automation motives he considered, 'sinful in themselves'. According to Wiener "that the reprobation attaching in former ages to the sin of sorcery now in many minds to the speculations of modern cybernetics."[49]

AI in the 1960s was still considered by many to be a pipe dream, and the popular media neglected to report on it for decades until only more recently. However, the fear of nuclear war and the generous funding of military computing technologies encouraged a fearful public, and while Wiener believed this fear was useful, he wanted to encourage a more informed debate about the dangers of weaponized machines that might 'think' for themselves, or act according to the algorithms of the 'gadget worshippers'. Cybernetics, that was widely known in the 60s had become associated with the half-forgotten myths of sorcery and human hubris. Wiener wrote:

"For make no mistake, if but two hundred years ago a scholar had pretended to make machines that should learn to play games or that should propagate themselves, he would surely have been made to assume the sanbenito, the gown worn by the victims of the Inquisition, and have been handed over to the secular arm, with the injunction that there be no shedding of blood; surely, that is, unless he could convince some great patron that he could transmute the base metals into gold, as Rabbi Low of Prague, who claimed that his incantations blew breath of life into the Golem of clay, had persuaded the Emperor Rudolf. For even now, if an inventor could prove to a computing-machine company that his magic could be of service to them, he could cast black spells from now till doomsday, without the least personal risk."[50]

God created man in his own image, and so to create a Golem out of clay, was a mortal sin. Creativity was considered the exclusive prerogative of God and only disaster would follow this transgression. In his eponymous epic, Gilgamesh embarked on a quest to gain immortality. He meets the archetypal wise man, Utanapishti, who like Noah who followed him, has survived the Deluge, and delivers him the message that it is foolish to seek immortality. Just like Adam, and Prometheus, Gilgamesh ignores divine advice and his flawed, and rebellious spirit, can only be redeemed through the wisdom he gains from the trials and tribulations of his hero's journey. Gilgamesh was our original artificial being, our hero, and our moral warning against technological hubris.

Considering the etymology of the world 'synthetic' around 1690, and the so-called dawning of the age of reason, the word was first used as a term in logic or deductive reasoning coming from the Greek 'synthetikos' meaning "skilled in putting together, constructive," from synthetos "put together, constructed, compounded," past participle of syntithenai "to put together".

By the 19th century 'synthetic chemicals' meant that they imitated natural materials, and so synthetics came to be known as artificial. To the modern ear a synthetic, or artificial food implies that it is has been created by the application of scientific knowledge, or the applied science of food design and production, and is commonly deplored as an 'unnatural' act, and for many, regarded as unhealthy, probably carcinogenic, and therefore morally bankrupt. The anti-GMO (Genetically Modified Organism) movement inherits many of these suspicions. It remains to be seen what the public opinion of 3D printed meats will be.[51]

The ancient Greek myths and legends warn of the human hubris of synthetic creation. The most notable being the legend of Daedalus and Icarus who were punished for their 'perversion of natural law'. Daedalus was in effect a roboticist who created synthetic creatures that were so lifelike that many were fooled by these things as they appeared alive. In one version of the tale of the last bronze man, Talos, the mechanical robot was created by Daedalus. This fearful robot threatened to kill Jason and the Argonauts by heating himself in the fire and then immolating his victims with a fatal embrace. According to classics professor, Merlin Peris, in his paper the Abominable Bronze Man, "Talos is remarkably futuristic, anticipating the scientific possibilities of the present age, and even then, belonging more with the bizarre imaginings of the new mythology of science fiction than with the mechanisms created and used in real life."[52]

Daedalus, is the proto-technologist, the forerunner of the mad scientist whose arrogance led to his downfall. Daedalus and his son Icarus were imprisoned in a tower after Daedalus had arrogantly taken up the challenge to create a synthetic cow for King Minos' wife, Pasiphaë. She had been cursed to fall in love with the King's prize bull. Pasiphaë desired to mate with the bull and so Daedalus created a robotic cow which she hid inside, so she could perform this 'unnatural' act. She then gave birth to the Minotaur, half beast, half-man. Minos was so appalled by this abomination that he imprisoned Daedalus and Icarus on top of a tower. To escape, Daedalus, created wings from feathers and wax for Icarus and himself, thus becoming the first humans to fly. To people on the ground, Icarus appeared as a God, and he felt like one as he soared higher and higher, approaching Zeus and the home of the gods. However, despite his father's warnings of flying too close to the Sun, Icarus who felt infallible, ignored his warning and when the wax melted he plunged to his death. The ancient Greeks believed the separation between humans and Gods was absolute and any attempt by humans to cross over would be violently punished.

Daedalus is said to have invented carpentry, and his bronze sculptures were so realistic that it fooled Heracles, and his reputation led Daedalus to have an overblown ego, and like a mad scientist, his pride ended in him murdering his talented nephew out of jealousy. After his banishment to Crete, he became King Minos' technologist and made mechanical robots to entertain the King's children.

The Pride of Frankenstein

This is not the only technological morality tale that lurks in the subconscious of the modern psyche and warns us of the dangers of meddling with 'nature'. Lord Byron, the friend of, Mary Wollstonecraft-Shelley who wrote, *Frankenstein, or the Modern Prometheus*, (1818) said of Prometheus "Thou art a symbol and a sign to Mortals of their fate and force." Byron's bleak outlook appears in his apocalyptic poem Darkness,[53] written at the same time as Shelley's story of Frankenstein.

In 1816, known as the 'Year Without a Summer', Mary Shelley, and her husband, Percy, spent their summer holiday indoors near Geneva, in Switzerland. The unusually gloomy, cold and wet summer had been caused by the coincidence of three factors: an unusually quiet Sun that had resulted in what has become known as, The Little Ice Age; the cooling effect of clouds of ash from the volcanic eruption of Tambora in Indonesia; and an earlier eruption in an unknown region, in 1809. Both these volcanic events resulted in a sudden climatic change in the Northern hemisphere, from the 17th century until the end of the 19th, due to the cooling sulphuric aerosol effect that reflected the sun.[54] The confluence of the Promethean fire from the depths of the Earth, thousands of kilometres away, and the sudden impact on the climate brought forth the Frankenstein story.

Shelley was inspired by her proximity to Castle Frankenstein, near Lake Geneva, which was once home to a famous priest and alchemist, Johann Conrad Dippel. Alchemy was once regarded as a black art and is often associated with Johann Georg Faust, (1480 – 1540). Faust, the alchemist, was the basis of Goethe's eponymous poem. The fictional story of Faust is about an arrogant sorcerer who made a pact with the Devil using black magic. Alchemy is, however, the ancestor of modern chemistry, which while it ignores its dark history, is reminded of it by the mad scientists of science fiction.

It is not clear if Mary Shelley knew of Dippel, or visited the Castle, but the alchemist did create 'Dippel's Oil' which he claimed to be the equivalent of the alchemist's 'elixir of life'. Dippel also shared with Victor Frankenstein an interest in chemistry, anatomy and the natural sciences. The hubris of alchemy and the pride of Frankenstein have a distinctly religious moral overtone as the creature says to his creator, "I ought to be thy Adam, but I am rather the fallen angel", echoing Lucifer in Milton's *Paradise Lost*.

In the story, Victor Frankenstein has read all the works of two famous proto-scientists, the alchemists and astrologer, Paracelsus, who predicted the 'End of Times', and the theologian and astrologer, Albertus Magnus, who discovered arsenic and, legend has it, discovered the alchemists' philosopher's stone. Frankenstein's passion for natural science, and the knowledge of those that went before him, always left him wanting, as he searched for the ultimate answer to the mystery of creation, 'the search for the philosopher's stone and the elixir of life'.[55]

The philosopher's stone was said to have the power to heal and prolong life as well as the ability to create a homunculus or clone. Jung also studied alchemy as a metaphoric search for the healing of the psyche, and the union of the anima and animus, the union of the female and male psyche; the purpose of an archetypal hero's journey.

Given Shelley's knowledge of literature, she surely knew of the Christopher Marlowe play, *The Tragical History of Dr Faustus*. (c. 1592). Like Frankenstein, Marlowe's Faustus uses his medical skills to raise the dead. Frankenstein's originality is to use a modern form of scientific necromancy, galvanism, or electricity, to usurp God, and create an immortal life, like Prometheus, but one that can be ended by violence.

According to an account by Georg Ernst Stahl (1731) Dippel was involved in the first synthesis of the pigment Prussian Blue, with Johann Jacob Diesbach. It is a dark blue pigment, also known as ferric ferrocyanide, and was the first modern synthetic pigment. Curiously, this synthetic pigment is also closely related to the other technological boogie man, nuclear reactors, and is used as an antidote for caesium, extracted from nuclear waste, and thallium, once known as the 'poisoner's poison', once used as rat bait, and is now banned.

As has often been the case, art, creativity, and technology, make for uncomfortable bedmates. In modern popular culture, the Doctor, Victor Frankenstein, is as frightening as the Thing, or the creature that has no name, that he created. He has come to represent the archetypal mad scientist who could end the world. The anti-GMO food movement has tried to scare people away from synthetic crops by dubbing it 'Frankenfood'. This is despite research that shows after two decades of GMO corn Italian scientists have analysed, and reviewed 6,000 peer studies, and concluded that GMOs pose no human health risk. GMO was shown to increase yields by between 5.6-24.5%, and could actually have a substantive positive impact by eliminating mycotoxins that are produced by fungi, and can be toxic causing cancer.[56]

So what lurks behind our modern fears?

The rules, laws, and regulations also apply to demigods and philosopher kings. The storage and consumption of solar energy in agriculture, fossil fuels and technology have enabled the human population to grow beyond a sustainable capacity,[57] but it is not hard to see how our myths, cultures, and religions have warned us of the dangers of overpopulation, and glutinous resource consumption. According to Tainter and Patzek:

"Eliminate petroleum, coal, and natural gas, and nothing will be left of our current way of life, and two thirds or 67% of the current human population will have to perish."[58]

Our biggest trials lay ahead of us, and it will require a superhuman effort to imagine alternative worlds. Our scientific and technological missteps have been our moral trials, they will either educate us as to the correct path, or instead, lead us towards monsters formed from lurid fantasies of self-destruction, and a descent into Hades. Should we survive the trials of the abyss we may get to meet the Goddess, who will guide us out of hell.

5. Meet the Goddess – Finding Your Treasured Twin

In the cycle of the hero's journey following the search and the trials into the underworld, the hero, if they have passed the trials, will find the Goddess, or in Jungian terms, the anima, the feminine twin of animus. The mythological stories are also cosmological archetypes for worlds, world ending, and the rebirth of worlds in a new guise.

In mythology, the trials of the Netherworld often came in threes. Adam is the hero who faced three trials as he is tempted by the devil in the guise of a serpent. Orpheus also undergoes three trials as he journeys to the underworld, Hades, to rescue his dead wife Eurydice after she had been bitten by a serpent and died. Orpheus uses his lyre and beautiful voice to first charm the monster Cerberus, the three-headed dog with the tail of a serpent; he then charms Charon, the ferryman to take him to Hades; and finally, he is followed by the souls of the dead as he plays his music. Orpheus persuades the dark god Hades to summons the three Fates, the ancient sisters, one who spins life out of thread, the second who measures the length of the thread of life, and the third who cuts it, ending life. What happens next is similar to the story of Lot, whose wife disobeyed God turning back to watch Sodom and Gomorrah burn, and then is turned into a pillar of salt. The rebellious Orpheus disobeys Hades and turns back to see Eurydice ascending the caves into the light, but, as he turns back to see her, the third Fate cuts the thread and she is then sucked back into the darkness.

In the ancient Greek myths Zeus, Hades, and Dionysus were connected in the Mysteries of Birth, Death, and Rebirth as the tripartite gods, much like the Holy Trinity of Christianity. In the New Testament, the Apostle Peter denies knowing Jesus three times, and following the crucifixion, Jesus is reborn after being buried in a subterranean cave for three days. The time of the resurrection, Easter, in April which coincides with pagan celebrations of Spring, and the return of the Goddess, Persephone, who returns from the depths of the abyss to the surface of the earth.

Jung's long-time colleague M. von Franz described Jung's process of individuation as the unification of the ego and the unconscious. It was also the reunification of the anima, or the woman within the man's psyche, and the animus, the man within the woman's psyche. According to Jungian psychology, the archetypal symbols revealed in the hero's journey represents the process of individuation.

"As a general rule it can be said that the need for hero symbols arises when the ego needs strengthening – when that is to say, the conscious mind needs assistance in some task that it cannot accomplish unaided or without drawing on the sources of strength that lie in the unconscious mind."[59]

Meeting the Goddess at this stage in the hero's journey coincides with what the ancient Greeks and Romans recognised as the descent to the underworld, the chaos of Hades. In psychological terms, this point in the story is when the male hero embraces their anima, or personification of their feminine psyche. The characteristics of anima are such things as "vague feelings, and moods, prophetic hunches, receptiveness to the irrational, capacity for personal love, feeling for nature, and last but not least – his relation to the unconscious."[60] The Delphic oracle, was a female priestess and like Sibyl was used to interpret the will of the gods and to make connections with them. Jung notes that "the very word 'invent' is derived from the Latin invenire, and means to 'find' and hence to find something by seeking it. In the latter case the word itself hints at some foreknowledge of what you are going to find."[61]

The descent to the underworld was typically portrayed as a one way trip. The trials and tests on the way to the depths of netherworld determined the fate of the hero based on the moral judgement of the gods. If the hero passed the tests they would win the treasure, the goddess or both. If not they were either imprisoned in the eternal darkness, or tortured by demons. This was the moment of truth. Should they successfully negotiate the journey to the lair of the monster guarding the treasures and the goddess they would return to earth, above the ground. This was their rebirth.

It was a theme repeated in apocalyptic mythologies when the faithful were either reborn; taken up to heaven in the rapture; or were granted immortality in Paradise on Earth. Repeated in many of the myths and legends related to the apocalyptic, and catastrophic, is a descent into the abyss, and the resurrection of the dead. According to Booker this rebirth theme is one of the seven universal plots repeated again and again in stories. Within the patriarchal tradition the male hero is one that succeeds and becomes a full man, which in simplistic terms, meant a hero who physically participates in conflict, fighting enemies and monsters to survive the 'tests and ordeals of a Quest' and to rescue the beautiful woman and win the treasure. But Booker goes on to say this rebirth is much more than masculine physicality:

"The other masculine attribute is a sense of order. This may be presented as a consciousness of social order, of hierarchy, propriety, the need for discipline, for justice under the law. Or it may be seen, rather more subtly, as the whole capacity of the human mind to see the world in terms of orderly, rational patterns: that very thing which lies at the root of all our notions of order, whether social or intellectual: the need to see everyone or everything marshalled in proper place and relationship. In this respect, which derives ultimately from the need of the human mind for framework and comprehensibility, the masculine gives a sense of control through organisation."[62]

Combining masculine physicality with hierarchical order, discipline and law have been the dominant characteristics of the Graeco-Judaeo-Christian militaristic culture, which have effectively repressed women, and those 'others' that were made slaves or colonised. However, Booker's Jungian perspective has a more balanced perspective of the feminine hero, and the hero's journey, in that it is not their so called feminine values that are important to their rebirth, but the reuniting of the two in one psyche:

"the feminine and the masculine liberating each other simultaneously. And such is the essence of Rebirth: that it shows us how it is impossible to develop one side of the human personality fully, masculine or feminine, unless this is also given positive counterbalance by the other."[63]

Booker points out that from a deep psychological perspective the Rebirth story speaks to individual repression, which is usually the repression of the feminine psyche. Jung noted that this archetypal repression of the anima can be applied to society, and world building, as a whole. Feminist theorists have argued that since the beginnings of agriculture, and the Holocene, patriarchy has repressed, and suppressed, woman and feminine values. The feminist theorist, Donna Haraway, even dislikes the term Anthropocene because the myth system that relates to the Anthropos is a male 'setup' that ends badly. It stars bad actors who have only told one side of the story. The science of the Anthropocene, she argues, has an individual bias, over the collective, that is often incapable of explaining evolution in symbiotic terms, and neglects co-evolution with the nonhumans. Haraway prefers her term the 'Chthulucene' that associates with the earth, fertility, and the subterranean psyche. She writes:

"I am aligned with feminist environmentalist Eileen Crist when she writes against the managerial, technocratic, market-and-profit besotted, modernizing, and human-exceptionalist business-as-usual commitments of so much Anthropocene discourse."[64]

The goddess Persephone who was dragged to the underworld by Hades was both the goddess of death, but also the life-giving earth, a goddess of fertility. Her mother Demeter was the Goddess of Agriculture, and the mother of Dionysus also thought to be Orpheus, son of Zeus, and the God of Rebirth. The secret Eleusinian mysteries promised initiates a paradise beyond death. The Judaeo-Christian 'fathers' set about ensuring that the earth, and fertility or sex, were associated with Satan, the snake, (also the symbol of Dionysus, Hades, Orpheus, Pluto and Zagreus, all one and the same).

According to Campbell, he contrasts the pagan mythology that associated the earth with a divine presence, against the Christian culture that associated earth with the Devil. In Christianity, not only was the divine associated with the Sky God, the patriarchal God but the Earth Goddess, Gaia, became associated with the underworld, Hell, Hades, the abyss. Campbell also noted that Orpheus/Dionysus in his various pagan guises was not only the Son of God but in the Eleusinian mysteries and Orphic initiations, good and evil were once embodied in one being, "the Devil himself is taken to be the immanent presence of God".[65]

In Christianity God and the Devil were seen as separate personages and this split, as in the split of human versus nature; masculine and feminine; anima and animus, created a psychological rift in the archetype.

The Psyche and the Singularity

According to Jung the archetypes of the gods are found on the scientific principles of cosmological archetypes. In other words, the ancient observations of the heavenly movement of the cosmos, and the astro-logical correlation on Earth led to the naming and personification of the constellations, thereby instantiating cosmic observations within the myths of the gods. Tarnas has researched in detail how certain astronomical alignments such as Uranus and Pluto, and Saturn and Pluto correlated with dramatic social, political, physical and cosmo-logical events throughout history.

"The nature of the Plutonic-Dionysian principle is to press towards greater intensity, to the extreme, to be compelling, deep—radical as radix, root, grounded in the depths, drawing on the power of the underworld, driving whatever it touches to an overwhelming potency that has a compulsive, destructive, even self-destructive potential."[66]

Tarnas describes his initial academic embarrassment when he began to research and document astrological correlations between individual archetypes; world bending; world building and world end-ing. In his extensive documentation of historical figures and events, Tarnas points out the remarkable coincidence of astronomical events and archetypal behaviour. This gives us another interesting perspec-tive on our past, present, and future world bending as the cosmolog-ical archetypes connect with our ancient myths and legends. Tarnas outlines two examples of astronomical patterns: the correlation of the Uranus-Pluto cycle; and the complex interplay of the archetypes affected by the Saturn-Uranus-Pluto cycle.

According to Tarnas, the Uranus-Pluto cycle reflects 'the character-istic themes of the Promethean-Dionysian complex'.[67] He identified these themes in individuals and periods in history; themes such as social justice; political revolution; individual liberty; creative freedom; religious rebellion; romantic and erotic emancipation; innovation and technological revolutions. He examines the remarkable coincidence of the English Revolution when Uranus and Pluto were in opposition (1643 – 1654) and the sexual revolution of the 1960s when the planets were in conjunction. The libertine sex, nudity and free ideas of the 17th century EnglishRanters were strikingly similar to the hippies in the 20th century. He also documents the life and work of Karl Marx, who was born in 1818 during the Uranus-Pluto square, "whose life and work was devoted with a kind of elemental intensity to the cause of mass revolution and emancipation."[68]

Maxwell believes that the limitations of past paradigms and their technological instantiations can realise novelties that could deliver solutions to some of the wicked problems we are now facing. He outlines an evolutionary archetypal cosmology, with human evolution seen in the context of a fractal development of increasing dimensional consciousness. He narrates a thesis beginning with nonliving things, with zero-dimensional consciousness; then prokaryotes with a single dimensional world view; on to animals with two dimensionalism; and finally humans with a three and a half dimensional world view, i.e. three dimensions of space, plus a partial, .5 temporal consciousness. While this still implies that the human species is the pinnacle of evolution, it is possible to also see how his world view de-centres humanity, viewing humans as a thing that is but a fractal of the bigger cosmological reality.

Maxwell saw the human fractal as undergoing different epochs of consciousness from archaic, to magic, to myth to mentality. While there were dramatic disjunctures between each epoch, it acknowledges the Hegelian dialectic that sees an integration of past epochs and archetypes in the future.[69]

Richard Tarnas in his book, *Cosmos and the Psyche*, pointed out that Jung in his later years extended the concept of the archetype beyond the internal psychological quest to apply it to a much bigger universal cosmology. The origins of the concept date back to Plato's pure forms or ideas, eternal mental forms that were imprinted on the soul before the physical human is born. These were the virtual or essential elements of all things, and concrete reality was just their imitation. Jung modified Plato's archetype to create a psychological theory that conformed with the new physics of the day. Within the context of quantum physics, Jung imagined the application of cosmological archetypes to the evolution of human civilisation, and modern culture, seen through the metaphorical lens of the hero's journey.

Tarnas sees our current metaphysical and existential crisis as a necessary part of the way in which ancient cosmological archetypes are clamouring to be heard from behind the physical curtain of materialism. Timothy Desmond cites Tarnas who traces the structures and origins of modern physics from the ancient Greeks, Plato, Socrates and Aristotle, and notes how their beliefs were filtered through medieval Christianity before they were bent to fit the world view of the Enlightenment. All of these stories, myths, and narratives culminated in the most compelling creationist explanation we have had to date, i.e. quantum physics, black holes and the Big Bang theory.

Desmond retells how Jung, in 1952, wrote a letter to J.R. Smythies in which he formulates his speculation that there is an equivalence between psychic energy and mass in his equation: "Psyche=highest intensity in the smallest space." Desmond continues to explain that, "The highest intensity of mass imaginable is infinite density, while the smallest space is zero volume, which is the precise definition of a gravitational singularity, both at the origin of the Big Bang and in black holes. This equivalence allows us to restate Jung's equation as: Psyche = Singularity."[70]

Desmond, Tarnas, and Maxwell all argue that Jung's cosmic archetypes in no way contradict, and in fact, complement our current scientific thinking related to quantum physics, and attempts to unify field theory through string and M theory. How can Jung be right, that the ancient psychological archetypes are simply the reflections, or shadows on the cave wall, projected by cosmic truths?

Jung argues that our inherited myths are metaphors for the cosmic reality that was imprinted on all matter and mind, at the beginning of time, when all of reality began as a unified singularity in the Big Bang. Mathematics is not immune to these cosmological archetypes, and can only describe them in another language of abstraction and metaphor, such as $E=mc^2$. Desmond explains that Jung learned about Einstein's special theory of relativity directly from Einstein. Desmond cites a letter that Jung wrote in 1953:

"Professor Einstein was my guest on several occasions at dinner... These were very early days when Einstein was developing his first theory of relativity. It was Einstein who first started me off thinking about a possible relativity of time as well as space, and their psychic conditionality. More than thirty years later, this stimulus led to my relation with the physicist Professor W. Pauli and to my thesis of psychic synchronicity."[71]

Despite, the denial of many physicists, who think that religious myths somehow taint objective science, there are numerous examples of quantum theories that encapsulate similar narratives, from Plato to Descartes, from ancient myths and legends to Newtonian alchemy, and Kant's belief in the afterlife, much of it retold in mathematics, and modern scientific theories, but so abstracted that their origins are lost.

The philosophy of Whitehead recognised the cosmic creativity of primordial aesthetics, an affective and alluring connection of everything according to his theory of 'transcendent empiricism'. The experimental task of integrating the psyche and the singularity is still before us, but the working theory is a useful model for creativity and future world building. I am more interested in a pragmatic working approach than a reified definition or description, and Whitehead suggests a process that might help us to meet the Goddess, even if there is a price for that success.

6. The Price of Success

The lesson of our hero's journey is that while they may have descended into the subterranean terrors of their psyche to recover what they thought they needed, they have not completed the cycle of world building. They must now pay the price of their success and complete the process of individuation and reunify their polar opposites the masculine/feminine; evil/good; conscious/unconscious; light/dark; sun/moon. The hero is weakened by their ordeal and may not manage to escape but if they do the price of their success is great. Only the hero who has followed their heart and obeyed their inner voice will successfully return from the terrifying ordeal of the abyss.

Campbell wrote:

"If the hero in his triumph wins the blessing of the goddess or the god and is then explicitly commissioned to return to the world with some elixir for the restoration of society, the final stage of his adventure is supported by all the powers of his supernatural patron."[72]

If we extrapolate this stage of the hero's journey to apply it to the mysterious creative powers of the imagination, and world building, we can recognise that there will be a huge cost incurred by humanity. The holy grail of psychological and cosmic healing enforces a tax on the old world of fossil fuels and mineral extraction; the hero must abandon the trinkets and gems guarded by the monster of the chthonic depths in order to return with the true prize of their quest. The unsustainable material consumption of resources must end, or the world will – fertility will be gone, and extinction will follow.

In the Roman version of the hero's journey it is Pluto who abducts Persephone to be his wife, and queen as the goddess of death. Pluto, or Plouton, was the name of the god of the underworld, and Pluton was conflated with the word, Ploutus, meaning wealth. For most followers of the Eleusinian Mysteries it was dangerous to incite the name of the god and goddess of death, and so they were commonly named by polite euphemisms such as Mistress, or Chthonic Zeus, for fear that if they uttered their true name they may be dragged to the underworld themselves. Because mineral wealth, gems, and gold was found underground, Pluto, as the Chthonic subterranean Zeus, ruled over the treasures of the deep.

We are warned that if we were to kill the terrifying dragon, or serpent that protects the treasure, and the goddess of fertility, we could also kill the Earth. The extraction of mineral wealth is not without consequences, so our modern hero might have to leave the black oily-gold, and valuable minerals behind if they want to return to the surface. The price of this revelation may be costly, but stealing the treasure might result in the end of the world.

The Creative Destruction of the Cosmos

The downgrading of stories and mythology over the past 100 to 200 years has occluded another sort of reality which the philosophy of Alfred North Whitehead attempted to recover with his ontological world view, an aesthetic theory of being. Whitehead viewed the cosmos in terms of a speculative reality, and as a creative cosmic occurrence. This paved the way for the OOO and the speculative realists who attempted to heal the rift between humanity and nature.

7. Returning from the chaos the hero brings it home.

In their book, *Order out of Chaos*, Ilya Prigogine, and Isabelle Stengers, wrote about a new dialogue with nature:

"For a long time a mechanistic world view dominated Western science. In this view the world appeared as a vast automaton. We now understand that we live in a pluralistic world."[73]

It is not one world but many worlds. They claimed that 'Science was rediscovering time' and that chaos and order are inexorably intertwined by the Second Law of Thermodynamics, which in turn binds the order of life with, the chaos and entropy of death. The immortality of energy and matter were told in the original creation myths, and have been validated by quantum physics. The hero who has braved the dark chaos of the unconscious now completes the cycle and returns home with the boon of their discovery, and the creative essence, which is the psyche of world building, and cosmological creative destruction.

Old worlds are not simply reborn but rather they are created in the chaotic destruction and randomization of elements of the past. The hero must overcome the stern and conservative father figure of Saturn, especially when he releases the fiery breath of Pluto's dragon. In order to survive, and be reborn in a new and improved guise, the hero must overcome the final ordeal of the unconscious psyche that would either drive them mad or keep them in Hades for eternity. If our hero turns back they may be turned to stone, or their lover may be trapped underground, in a dead and lifeless world. Despite the odds, if our hero is allowed to escape their sterile imprisonment, they will flourish on the surface of the earth and share the treasure of their fertile creativity. This goes beyond simple world bending, and those who witness their rebirth are astounded by their God-like powers of world creation. This is the allegorical truth of the hero's journey and our hope for world creations.

8. The hero arrives home a changed and full actualised being

As the hero arrives home, they bring with them hard-won wisdom and a new order out of the psychological chaos. The Epic Tale of Gilgamesh is one of a quest for self-knowledge that takes a lifetime, and ends in greater wisdom, after a number of metaphorical journeys to the subconscious underworld.

Campbell wrote:

"The full round, the norm of the monomyth, requires that the hero shall now begin the labor of bringing the runes of wisdom, the *Golden Fleece*, or his sleeping princess, back into the kingdom of humanity, where the boon may redound to the renewing of the community, the nation, the planet, or the ten thousand worlds."[74]

It is this promise of the ancient myths, religions, and even the Second Law of Thermodynamics, and the multiverse of quantum physics, that should convince us that world ending is not literally world ending as all possible worlds are theoretically infinite. The hero's journey is not only a call to action for our species but a reassurance that the laws of physics, social and environmental decency, are universal truths, there is an infinite number of worlds that will be created by an infinite number of things.

The melancholic, the depressed, and drug dependent may be convinced by the cynical sceptics that believe there is no hope, but there is nothing to be gained by pessimism or despair except our inability to return from hell. We are living a modern mystery, something that we once knew, the monomyth and hero's journey reminds us that there will be order out of chaos and that even these exciting new worlds, that proliferate before us, will be eventually destroyed, only to be reshaped by a multiverse of world benders and world creators. We should not dwell on the original sin that warns the end is nigh, but recognise that our creativity has always been synthetic and that it is not at odds with the speculative realities to come.

Notes

1. McCumber, J. (2016). The Philosophy Scare: the politics of reason in the early Cold War. The University of Chicago Press, Chicago & London. See also Reisch, George A. How the Cold War Transformed Philosophy of

Science: To the Icy Slopes of Logic. Kindle Locations 311-312. Cambridge University Press. Kindle Edition.

2. Knight, Chris. Decoding Chomsky: Science and Revolutionary Politics (p. 17). Yale University Press. Kindle Edition.

3. See McCarthyism wikipedia entry https://en.wikipedia.org/wiki/McCarthyism

4. The basic premise of rational choice theory is that aggregate social behavior results from the behavior of individual actors, each of whom is making their individual decisions. See https://en.wikipedia.org/wiki/Rational_choice_theory

5. Read their Manifesto here. https://dark-mountain.net/about/manifesto/

6. Taleb, Nassim Nicholas. The Black Swan: The Impact of the Highly Improbable. Kindle Locations 1935-1936. Penguin Books Ltd. Kindle Edition.

7. Boyd, B. (2009). On the Origin of Stories: Evolution, cognition, and fiction. Cambridge, Mass.: Belknap Press of Harvard University Press.

8. BBC (2018) Drug and suicide deaths rise as US life expectancy drops. https://bbc.in/2BJxQ6s

9. Everett, D. L. (2017). How language began: The story of humanity's greatest invention. London: Profile Books.

10. Taleb, Nassim Nicholas. (2007) The Black Swan: The Impact of the Highly Improbable. Kindle Locations 1996-1997. Penguin Books Ltd. Kindle Edition.

11. Boyd, B. ibid.

12. Taleb, Nassim Nicholas, ibid.

13. Conway, F., & Siegelman, J. (2005). Dark Hero of the Information Age: In search of Norbert Wiener, the father of cybernetics. New York: Basic Books.

14. Wiener, N. (1964). God and Golem Inc.

15. Hayles, K. Unthought: The Power of the Cognitive Nonconscious

16. Campbell, Joseph (1949). The Hero with a Thousand Faces. Princeton: Princeton University Press. p. 23

17. Fisher, M. (2013) The Ghosts of My Life: Writings on Depression, Hauntology and Lost Futures.

18. Booker, Christopher. The Seven Basic Plots: Why We Tell Stories (p. 594). Bloomsbury Publishing. Kindle Edition.

19. Campbell, J. Hero of a Thousand Faces.

20. Harari, Y.N. (2018) 21 Lessons for the 21st Century

21. Taleb, Nassim Nicholas. The Black Swan: The Impact of the Highly Improbable. Kindle Locations 1888-1889. Penguin Books Ltd. Kindle Edi-

tion.

22. George, A. R. (Ed.). (2003). The Epic of Gilgamesh: The Babylonian epic poem and other texts in Akkadian and Sumerian. London; New York: Penguin Books.

23. Tarnas, R. Cosmos and Psyche. p.12

24. Tarnas, ibid.

25. Morton, Timothy. Dark Ecology: For a Logic of Future Coexistence (The Wellek Library Lectures) (p. 40). Columbia University Press. Kindle Edition.

26. Morton, ibid p.38

27. Jones, S.,(2013). The Serpent's Promise: The Bible retold as science

28. See Chap. 1 "A Very Short History of Imagination" by Egan, K. (2013). Imagination in Teaching and Learning: Ages 8 to 15. Routledge.

29. ibid

30. George, A. (translator) The Epic of Gilgamesh.

31. See Chap. 1 "A Very Short History of Imagination" by Egan, K. (2013). Imagination in Teaching and Learning: Ages 8 to 15. Routledge.

32. Booker, C. (2004). The Seven Basic Plots of Literature. New York; London: Continuum.

33. Maxwell, G. The Dynamics of Transformation: Tracing an Emerging World View http://a.co/h8xZBHv

34. See Hill, C. (1972). The World Turned Upside Down: Radical ideas during the English revolution. London: Temple Smith. "The Blasphemy Act of 9 August 1650 was aimed especially against the Ranters' denial of 'the necessity of civil and moral righteousness among men,' which tended 'to the dissolution of all human society'. It denounced anyone who maintained him- or herself to be God, or equal with God; or that acts of adultery, drunkenness, swearing, theft, etc. were not in themselves shameful, wicked and sinful, or that there is no such thing as sin 'but as a man or woman judgeth thereof'. The penalty was six months' imprisonment for the first offence, banishment for the second, the death of a felon if the offender refused to depart or returned. Judges operating this Act seem to have stretched it very much in order to apply it only to those who genuinely taught that there was no difference between right and wrong." (p.208)

35. Campbell, J., Creative Mythology: the masks of God, p.37

36. Wilson, C. (1963). The Outsider. London: Pan.

37. Campbell, J., Ibid, p.37

38. Jung, C., Memories, Dreams, Reflections. p.365

39. Tarnas, Richard. The Passion Of The Western Mind: Understanding the Ideas That Have Shaped Our World View (pp. 110-111). Random House.

Kindle Edition.

40. Transhumanism is a movement that seeks to go beyond the frailties of biological evolution and transcend, preferably to another planet.

41. Campbell, J. The Masks of God, p.29

42. Tarnas, Richard. Cosmos and Psyche: Intimations of a New World View (p. 9). Penguin Publishing Group. Kindle Edition.

43. Tarnas, R. ibid (p. 9). Penguin Publishing Group. Kindle Edition.

44. Campbell, J. The Masks of God, p.41

45. Benkler, Y., Faris, R., Roberts, H., Oxford University Press. (2018). Network Propaganda: manipulation, disinformation, and radicalization in American politics. Retrieved from http://dx.doi.org/ 10.1093/oso/ 9780190923624.001.0001

46. Wiener, N. God and Golem Inc. p.8

47. Conway, F., & Siegelman, J. (2005). Dark Hero of the Information Age: in search of Norbert Wiener, the father of cybernetics. New York: Basic Books.

48. Wiener, N. (1964). God and Golem Inc. MIT. p.21

49. Ibid, p.47

50. Ibid, p.49

51. The success of the Impossible Burger suggests that as long as it bleeds it might be acceptable. "Market research firm UES predicts the plant-based meat market will grow by 28% a year and reach $85 billion by 2030."

52. Peris, M. Talos and Daedalus: a review of the authorship of the Abominable Bronze Man

53. Read the poem in the final chapter of this book.

54. McGuire, Bill. Waking the Giant (p. 85). OUP Oxford. Kindle Edition.

55. Shelley, M. Frankenstein, or the Modern Prometheus, p.32

56. Gohd, C. (2018, February 20). After two decades of GMOs, scientists find they live up to their promise. Retrieved October 1, 2018, from https://futurism.com/two-decades-scientists-gmos-corn- good-seriously

57. Tainter, J. A., & Patzek, T. W. (2012). Drilling down the Gulf Oil debacle and our energy dilemma. New York, NY: Copernicus Books. Retrieved from http://dx.doi.org/ 10.1007/978-1-4419-7677-2

58. Tainter,J. & Patzek ibid.

59. Henderson, J.L "Ancient Myths and Modern Man" p.114, in Jung, C. Man and his Symbols.

60. Von Franz, M. "The Process of Individuation", p.186, in Jung, C. Man and his Symbols

61. Jung, C. Man and His Symbols. p.69

62. Booker, Christopher. The Seven Basic Plots: Why We Tell Stories (p. 261). Bloomsbury Publishing. Kindle Edition.

63. ibid

64. Haraway, Donna J.. Staying with the Trouble: Making Kin in the Chthulucene (Experimental Futures) (pp. 49-50). Duke University Press. Kindle Edition.

65. Campbell, J. Creative Mythology: the Masks of God. p.21

66. Tarnas, R. (2006). Cosmos and Psyche: Intimations of a new world view. New York: Viking.

67. Ibid, p.189

68. Ibid, p. 190

69. Maxwell, G. The Dynamics of Transformation: Tracing an Emerging World View.

70. Desmond, Timothy. Psyche and Singularity: Jungian Psychology and Holographic String Theory. Kindle Locations 1987-1989. Persistent Press. Kindle Edition.

71. ibid, Kindle Locations 2000-2005.

72. Campbell, J. Hero of a Thousand Faces. p.180

73. Prigogine,I., & Stengers, I. (1984). Order out of Chaos: Man's new dialogue with nature.

74. ibid, p.179

Chapter 2 The End is Nigh

Premonitions And Prophesies

Divination and prophecies are universal and ancient practices that actually have their origins in the intense study and empirical observations of nature. By the time of Plato, the ancient Greeks had already assumed that myths and legends of the Gods were but metaphors for deep spiritual, social, and environmental 'truths'. Western oracular practice had enjoyed millennia of respect and refinement. Astrology and the study of the cosmos had long informed shamans, seers, and the rule of philosopher kings.

Up until the Enlightenment astrology was regarded as a scholarly study, related and as highly regarded as astronomy, alchemy, meteorology and medicine, and some of the greatest astronomers, such as Tycho Brahe, Johannes Kepler, and Galileo were also court astrologers. This all began to change around the 17th century and had all but lost mainstream favour by the 19th century, although there was a brief renaissance amongst the Romanticists, and Spiritualists of the UK and US. The flowering of modern psychoanalysis under Freud and Jung rekindled an interest in what astrology might inform us about the subconscious and the archetypes of the collective unconscious.

Why is it that the most common and popular science fiction movies have apocalyptic endings, and are reminiscent of the battle of Armageddon, in the book of Revelations? The apocalypse translates as 'disclosure'. In the *Bible* it is the revelations of John of Patmos, thought to have been written in 95CE, and it reads like a script for a futuristic movie with killer robots, and agents of bioterrorism. Our current fantasies and nightmares are popular, not because they are modern, but because the apocalypse is ancient, and has been recurring throughout multiple cultural histories, myths and religions including Islam, Judaism, Christianity, and even Chinese Daoism. Scientism and our inherited 'common sense', brought down from the Enlightenment, have resulted in a blind spot when it comes to understanding our social, political, psychic, and economic reality. New approaches to philosophy and science have revealed that this blind spot not only helped us to build a world of wonderment, but also to precipitate its end. This apocalyptic state of mind may seem strangely primitive, but as Bruno Latour explains 'we have never been modern', or as Timothy Morton contends 'we are Mesopotamians', and also perhaps Katherine Hayles is right, 'we have always been posthuman'. The modern mind inherits the archetypes of long forgotten modes of thought, in a Jungian sense the modern project is the healing of schisms caused by dialectical rifts between different world views. The apocalypse is not modern, but our apocalyptic views are not necessarily religious. As our environmental crisis becomes more pronounced it is likely we will see a growing apocalyptic tenor in popular culture. As Hall explains:

"Events or prophecies mark a collective crisis so striking that it undermines normal perceptions of reality for those involved, thereby leading people to act in unprecedented ways, outside their everyday routines. Sociologically, then, the time of the apocalypse encompasses more than the religious end time of God's final judgment, or some absolute and final battle of Armageddon."[1]

These disastrous events will likely dredge up dreams and nightmares from the collective unconscious. The etymology of the word 'disaster' comes from Middle French désastre (1560s) and Old Italian, disastro, which literally means 'ill starred'. This astronomical meaning ties to an almost universal prophetic reading of the stars when kingdoms used astrologers to predict good fortune, and calamities either for their rule, or destruction by natural catastrophes. On July 4th 1054 an imperial Chinese astronomer observed a type 1a supernova explosion of a binary twin, a white dwarf star. This amazingly violent explosion propelled star matter at speeds estimated to be between 5,000 and 20,000 kilometers a second. The light from this explosion travelling at 300,000 kilometers a second still took six and a half thousand (6,523) light years to reach Earth. 1 light year is just under 10 trillion kilometers away but this astronomical cataclysmic event shone so brightly, 500 million times brighter than our Sun, that it could be clearly seen during the day and for two years after. It was considered to be an auspicious moment for the Emperor Renzong heralding the beginning of the Zhihe era. In the *Book of Revelations* there is the prophecy of a burning star that falls to Earth sounding like a meteor that causes a catastrophic environmental disaster.

"The third angel sounded his trumpet, and a great star, blazing like a torch, fell from the sky on a third of the rivers and on the springs of water— the name of the star is Wormwood. A third of the waters turned bitter, and many people died from the waters that had become bitter." (Rev 8:10–11).

It is strange to reflect on the prophecy of a fallen star; the legend of the fallen angel, Lucifer; the primeval myth of technology and human hubris; the fall from grace, and the modern fear of nuclear power. In the early hours of April 26, 1986 there was an explosion at the nuclear reactor in Chernobyl, in the Soviet Ukraine causing leaking of nuclear radiation in the form of iodine-131, cesium-134 and cesium-137. The disaster is thought to be responsible for 6,000 thyroid cancers, although direct evidence of the link with the Chernobyl accident may be impossible to find. The actual evidence of environmental and health impacts was less than had originally been predicted. According to the U.S. Nuclear Regulatory Commission (NRC), "Today the available evidence does not strongly connect the accident to radiation-induced increases of leukemia or solid cancer, other than thyroid cancer."[2]

While the area has become something of a thriving wildlife sanctuary scientists warn that it will still be 20,000 years before Chernobyl is safe for human habitation. In what could be thought to be synchronous, or prophetic coincidence, Chernobyl in the Ukrainian language is 'chornobyl' or чорнобиль meaning 'wormwood'. The 'ill starred' Wormwood fell to Earth and the technology spread the 'bitter' radiation of contaminated water. The Fall that followed the original sin is a

Jungian archetype that may be our subconscious warning of the dangers of our technological overreaching.

Natural events and disasters such as earthquakes and volcanic eruptions were long considered to be a sign from the Gods and are bound up with the apocalyptic prophecies of ancient philosopher Kings, and proto-scientific rulers in pre-scientific societies. Their power and status were tied to their claims of being able to read the divine signs communicated in dreams and natural 'signs', and their followers believed their lives depended on it.

Technological design is a process by which the imagination can look into the future and envisage the construction of a thing, and if that thing is sufficiently novel, useful and more efficient, it will likely be given the accolade of an 'innovation'. In both Greek and Hebrew traditions this imagination was considered as a rebellious act against the divine world. As Egan explains:

"The main sense of imagination in both these traditions, however, is more like what we mean by foresight or planning. The creative element which looms so large in modern conceptions is in the ancient world only dimly glimpsed and hinted at in a disturbed way; creativity remains a prerogative of the divine. It is the power to make a world, perform miracles, destroy cities, cause earthquakes. This kind of power, and the imagination that frames it, is beyond the capacities that humans can deploy."[3]

Foresight, oracles, and futurism have also had a stigma going back to Prometheus, whose name in ancient Greece meant, 'one with foresight', who fought with his Titan brother on the side of the Gods. Zeus rewarded the brothers with the power to create all living things. Like Prometheus, Frankenstein also possess the gift, and the curse of foresight, imagining his monster having intercourse with his synthetic bride, and in a apocryphal prediction, envisage:

"the first results of those sympathies for which the daemon thirsted would be children, and a race of devils would be propagated upon the earth who might make the very existence of the species of man a condition precarious and full of terror...I shuddered to think that future ages might curse me as their pest, whose selfishness had not hesitated to buy its own peace at the price, perhaps of the existence of the whole human race."[4]

The fiend had promised Frankenstein that if he would not create a wife for him, then he would deprive him of his beloved Elizabeth, and vowed to Frankenstein that he would:

"be with me on my wedding night, yet he did not consider that threat as binding him to peace in the meantime; for, as if to show me that he was not yet satiated with blood, he had murdered Clerval, [Frankenstein's friend], immediately after the enunciation of his threats."[5]

The tale of the mad hubris of Frankenstein and the potential future legion of synthetic monsters has been hugely popular and has been the basis of numerous plays, movies, and television adaptations, a testament to the powerful grip that the novel's themes have had on successive generations. In ancient times technologies, arts and crafts were all considered to be God given, just as Prometheus and his brother, Epimetheus, were given these so-called gifts from the Gods. It would seem that they were tricked by Pandora who opened the jar releasing the 'gifts' of mischief and sorrow, plague and diseases, and because he was too late to close the jar before these terrible curses were bestowed on humanity, there was only hope left trapped in the jar.

These ancient tales of warning still resonate in popular culture today, with synthetic creatures being one of the most feared because of their malevolent attitude towards their makers who they could murder or enslave. Frankenstein's monster is not a dumb thing that grunts and moans, but is an articulate, cunning and evil creature that feels superior to his creator. He warns Frankenstein that he cannot break his promise to create for him a sexual partner. The synthetic being abuses Frankenstein.

"Slave, I before reasoned with you, but you have proved yourself unworthy of my condescension. Remember that I have power; you believe yourself miserable, but I can make you so wretched that the light of day will be hateful to you. You are my creator, but I am your master; – obey!"[6]

Serpents and Dragons

Today, we inherit the fear of violence from the synthetic creatures we create and the archetype that lurks in the shadows of our nightmares. In many early mythologies there were fantastic beasts who were often demigods ruling their people and controlling natural events, and causing apocalyptic disasters, should their subjects or enemies upset them. In ancient China, if the Gods were unhappy and the world was out of harmony, a water dragon, who was also considered an Emperor, or demigod, could cause havoc destroying whole villages via floods, earthquakes or tsunamis.[7]

In another remote culture, early Māori shared similar beliefs about natural disasters believing that they could be caused by an enraged water dragon, known as a taniwha; a transmogrified Māori chief, who protected the tribe, could also heap natural disasters on a tribe that broke tapu (sacred laws); alternatively the taniwha could attack an invading tribe in defence of its people.

It is in the *Book of Revelation* that this mythological symbolism was brought forward from the ancient text, and repeated down through the ages until the present. As Hall summarises the conclusion of the battle of Armageddon:

"Finally the seventh angel announces that "there should be time no longer" (Revelation 10: 6). This, then, is the beginning of the end. Michael and his angels fight against a great red dragon. Then an angel announces, "Babylon [Rome] is fallen, is fallen, that great city, because she made all nations drink of the wine of the wrath of her fornication" (Revelation 14: 8). Thereupon those with 666, the mark of the beast on their foreheads are "tormented with fire and brimstone in the presence of the holy angels, and in the presence of the Lamb" (Revelation 14: 10). With more wrath, plagues, and brimstone, and the terrible world-destructive earthquake at the battle of Armageddon, Babylon finally falls.[8]

As discussed, dragons were closely related to natural disasters, and the Greek word for dragon, drakon, also means serpent, which was synonymous with the devil. This strange virtual reality-like-vision of the apocalypse depicts hell on Earth as if Satan has opened the gates of Hell or Hades' monsters, the three-headed dog Cerberus, and the

Furies, have followed Orpheus to the surface of the planet. At the end of time, the Earth is turned inside out as volcanic eruptions, earthquakes, and lava flows are spewed from the depths of the Netherworld. This creative outpouring is reminiscent of the cult of Dionysus, celebrating the god of the grape harvest, wine and fertility, but also associated with death and the underworld. The only god to be born of a mortal woman, Dionysus is also the god of Greek Theatre. His worship was established in the seventh century BCE and was, according to Oliver Grau, depicted in one of the earliest examples of immersive art in the frescoes of Pompeii.[9]

It was designed to immerse the Dionysian followers in a mixed reality space that blurs the lines between the image and the physical reality. 'The fresco brings gods and humans together on the same pictorial level'[10] as the image surrounds the observer on all sides drawing them into the ecstatic scene. In these Eleusinian Mysteries life, death, creation, and the apocalyptic end are part of a mystical cycle played out in the hero's journey and the monomyth. Dragons and serpents were often the attributed cause of natural disasters that also foretold the end of time.

The Modern Signs of the End of Time

The End is Nigh has become a meme, but our collective unconscious still dreams of its mythical origins. It means different things to different people, but most definitions and usage of the phrase share the sense that it means the end of the world, the difference being, the definition of world. Looming largest in the collective's apocalyptic imagination is global warming, and the political debate about whether or not it is anthropogenic, or even exists. In the journal, *Dissent*, Stanley Schaetzel, attempts to give a definition of the 'end of the world' stating confidently in his preamble:

"Global warming is real, it is anthropogenic, it will be onerous to control, and it will make 'life as we know it' difficult, but it will neither threaten the existence of the human race nor will it cause the 'end of the world'."[11]

He then sums up his definition of 'the end of the world' as 'the end of the human race'. The human race, he defines as:

"'self-contained organic beings, capable of sexual multiplication, possessing an organ capable of self-awareness, memory and information processing, and the ability of reacting to the environment through several sensing and manipulating organs".[12]

But, Schaetzel asks, what if we remove the word organic? We will see that this opens an interesting question about the end of the world, as we have to first ask whose world is it? What about synthetic cybernetic organisms or cyborgs, if they inherit our world, has the world ended for humans? What if, as some researchers believe, we are already cyborgs and posthuman? Does that mean that the world has already ended? What if we examine the end of the world for the non-human majority, both animate and inanimate?

World Categorisation

The categories or types of worlds can be defined as:

- Physical worlds

- Modelled worlds

- Conceptual worlds

- Ontological worlds

It will become apparent that these worlds also share common attributes and are connected, entangled, and enmeshed. The physical world can be defined as one that is comprised of physical objects, dictated by the laws of physics, chemistry, and biology, which is often called the natural sciences. A modelled world is one that is designed, defined, and predicted by a thing. A conceptual world can be a fictional world or one that is imagined and described as in Middle Earth, Ragnarok, or the apocalyptic battlefields of Armageddon. The conceptual worlds are defined by the speculative, religious and artistic imagination, and is often defined under the humanities. Ontological worlds are philosophical constructs defined by ontology, or the philosophy of being as opposed to the epistemological, or knowledge theory of reality, it is thing-related aesthetic reality. These definitions suffer from liminal blurring because despite some disciplinary silos, or paradigms, multidisciplinary, and transdisciplinary perspective will mash these together. It is also my objective to explore and reveal how we might heal the split between the worlds and prepare the foundations for a more healthy coexistence between the human and nonhuman worlds. It is hoped that you might see that the end of the world is not such a terrible thing, and even cause for celebration. When we discuss whether the end is nigh or not, we must first agree on the type of world we are discussing.

The One and Only World – physical reality

Physics is often called the Queen of the sciences. Her reign has continued since the seventeenth century, up until the twenty-first, when Sir Isaac Newton first gave the world his laws of motion that successfully ushered in the industrial revolution and the rise of the machines. In the twentieth century, Einstein's powerful laws of relativity and gravitational waves did not topple Newton's laws, but they did open up the micro and macro descriptions of reality that have changed our world beyond recognition. Rationalism and science have become the dominant global view of our world. For many scientists and citizens throughout the planet – there is only one world, the rational, scientific one. Schaetzel is certain of one end of the world, that will happen in around 5 billion years, when the Sun runs out of fuel, just before it becomes a red dwarf, it will continue to expand until the Earth is burnt to a crisp.

Much later, after that, it is expected that according to scientific calculations, of the acceleration of the universe, in 10^{14} years the entire universe will effectively end in the 'big freeze'. That is unless we find a way to hop across the multiverse to another habitable universe some time and place elsewhere. Schaetzel takes a rational, and scientific perspective, which is ultimately anthropocentric when he agrees a fatal astronomical fate awaits the humans living on the third rock from the Sun. Long before then, he thinks humanity will probably escape in spaceships to find another human-friendly planet.[13]

We may still be hit by massive meteor impacts. Most astrophysicists think that the possibility of Earth being hit by space rock is not a question of if, but when? The asteroid that hit Earth, landing in the Gulf of Mexico 65 million years ago is just one of a string of disasters believed to have caused the extinction of the dinosaurs, and 90% of all life-forms on Earth.[14] The impact is almost impossible for us to comprehend as new research describes what would have happened immediately after the 12 km-wide asteroid hit with such force that it caused the solid rock to behave like it was fluid. According to geological models and simulations, the explosive impact would have instantaneously created a massive crater 30 km deep and 100 km wide. But what happened next was a rapid rebound of rock which created an instant mountain, the size of the Himalayas. When the sloshing around of these millions of tons of rock had finished, the hole in the ground was 200 km wide and 1 km deep. The strength of this mind-boggling explosion was estimated to be the equivalent to a magnitude 10 or 11 earthquake. The rock was not liquified by heat, but due to the kinetic strength of the impact, it resulted in what the scientists call the 'dynamic collapse model' of crater formation. The rocks lost their structure, and became fluid and frictionless, flowing on top of itself, "the estimate for the whole impact is something like 10 billion Hiroshima bombs."[15]

It is almost impossible to imagine what this world would have looked like as the laws of physics appeared to be suspended, and solid rock sploshed around like water, in an enormous pond, after a huge rock was dropped in the middle. It has only been in the last decade that scientists have begun to calculate the odds of this sort of horrific world ending happening soon. In June 2017 scientists had catalogued 16,294 near-Earth objects that could hit us, but as many as several million remain uncharted and pass close by Earth.[16]

There are now 100 ring-like indentations documented around the Earth that have been identified as impact craters. The Chicxulub impact, in the Gulf of Mexico, is thought to be an event that occurs once in 50-100 million years.[17] That is a long time to wait, but remember this one happened 65 million years ago, so another event of that magnitude might not be as far away as we imagine. Also, scientists have found craters 2-3 times bigger than the Chicxulub impact, but they are not quite sure what caused them. Meanwhile, there are some 2,100 such asteroids larger than 1 kilometre and perhaps 320,000 larger than 100 meters, according to a working group chaired by Dr David Morrison, NASA Ames Research Center. The working group believe "[a]n impact by one of these larger meteors in the wrong place would be a catastrophe, but it would not threaten civilization. However, the working group concluded that an impact by an asteroid larger than 1-2 kilometres could degrade the global climate, leading to widespread crop failure and loss of life."[18]

They went on to say that:

"Such global environmental catastrophes, which place the entire population of the Earth at risk, are estimated to take place several times per million years on average. A still larger impact by an object larger than about 5 kilometres is damaging enough to cause mass extinctions. In addition, there are many comets in the 1-10 kilometre class, 15 of them in short-period orbits that pass inside the Earth's orbit, and an unknown number of long-period comets."[19]

So, it would be fair to conclude that world ending physics, relating to asteroids, maybe rare but not unlikely. Humanity has the extraordinary, but paradoxical ability, to imagine the most unlikely catastrophe, such as the Christian Apocalypse, and yet ignore an impending probability with the high chance of destroying life. It turns out that while scientists have searched for evidence that asteroids caused previous mass extinctions it is more likely that it was caused by local geological perturbations. As Peter Brannen explains:

"The most dependable and frequent administrators of global catastrophe, it turns out, are dramatic changes to the climate and the ocean, driven by the forces of geology itself. The three biggest mass extinctions in the past 300 million years are all associated with giant floods of lava on a continental scale—the sorts of eruptions that beggar the imagination. Life on earth is resilient, but not infinitely so: the same volcanoes that are capable of turning whole continents inside out can also produce climatic and oceanic chaos worthy of the apocalypse."[20]

Schaetzel notes that physical events such as a meteor attack; or a super volcano, that is followed by coal, oil and gas fires with explosions; and includes a runaway greenhouse effect caused by the sudden release of methane from the seabed; are the probable cause of a catastrophic event, 252 million years ago. This was the Permian Triassic mass extinction, which saw the extinction of 95% of all marine species, and 80% of terrestrial animals. It is also the only known mass extinction of insects.[21]

The unusual spike in the carbon of 4000-7000 billion tonnes of carbon in a period of maybe 10,000 years resulted in a global average temperature increase of 6° C.[22] While there is no scientific consensus on the possibility of a repeat of a methane hydrate explosion there are an enormous 2000 billion tonnes of carbon trapped underneath the permafrost in the polar caps and some believe this could be suddenly released as the ice melts, accelerating the heating of the planet.[23] What is worse is that if that methane was released it is eighty times more effective at trapping in the heat than CO_2 known as the Global Warming Potential (GWP).[24]

The oil and gas giant, ExxonMobil has known since the 1970s that the Arctic cap will melt due to carbon emissions, and built it into their profit projections as it would lower the cost of discovery and extraction; they even built their oil rigs to cope with the higher seas.[25] It has already been predicted by the World Bank that 100 million people could be displaced as sea levels rise. When the fifth mass extinction occurred there may have been one to three extinction pulses of between 10 thousand years, up to 10 million years, separating the main event. In his short essay, Schaetzel does not really offer any scientific, or physical evidence why global warming will not result in the end of the human race, however, he does think that the end of the world is most likely to be anthropogenic, caused by our own activities, including nuclear war.

Stephen Hawking was not so sure that global warming and other anthropogenic disasters would not quickly dispense with the human species, and he was deeply troubled by the bellicose rhetoric of President Trump and his threats against 'little rocket man', North Korea's dictator, Kim Jong Un. Hawking warned that the Doomsday Clock had inched closer to midnight, i.e. the end of the world.[26]

A quick review of just some of the most dramatic physical effects of the Anthropocene will highlight that any serious consideration of the end of the world is inevitably connected to a network of causes and effects that requires a multidisciplinary approach, and most likely, transdisciplinary debate.[27] This debate must extend beyond scientism or 'excessive belief in the power of scientific knowledge and techniques.'

In his *Charter of Transdisciplinarity* (1994), Basarab Nicolescu wrote:

"life on earth is seriously threatened by the triumph of a techno-science that obeys only the terrible logic of efficacy for efficacy's sake." The Charter is laid out in 14 articles:

Article 1

Any attempt to reduce the human being by formally defining what a human being is and subjecting the human being to reductive analyses within a framework of formal structures, no matter what they are, is incompatible with the transdisciplinary vision.

Article 2

The recognition of the existence of different levels of reality governed by different types of logic is inherent in the transdisciplinary attitude. Any attempt to reduce reality to a single level governed by a single form of logic does not lie within the scope of Transdisciplinarity.

Article 3

Transdisciplinarity complements disciplinary approaches. It occasions the emergence of new data and new interactions from out of the encounter between disciplines. It offers us a new vision of nature and reality. Transdisciplinarity does not strive for mastery of several disciplines but aims to open all disciplines to that which they share and to that which lies beyond them.

Article 4

The keystone of Transdisciplinarity is the semantic and practical unification of the meanings that traverse and lie beyond different disciplines. It presupposes an open-minded rationality by re-examining the concepts of "definition" and "objectivity." An excess of formalism, rigidity of definitions and a claim to total objectivity, entailing the exclusion of the subject, can only have a life-negating effect.

Article 5

The transdisciplinary vision is resolutely open insofar as it goes beyond the field of the exact sciences and demands their dialogue and their reconciliation with the humanities and the social sciences as well as with art, literature, poetry and spiritual experience.

Article 6

In comparison with interdisciplinarity and multidisciplinarity, transdisciplinarity is multireferential and multidimensional. While taking account of the various approaches to time and history, transdisciplinarity does not exclude a transhistorical horizon.

Article 7

Transdisciplinarity constitutes neither a new religion, nor a new philosophy, nor a new metaphysics, nor a science of sciences.

Article 8

The dignity of the human being is of both planetary and cosmic dimensions. The appearance of human beings on Earth is one of the stages in the history of the Universe. The recognition of the Earth as our home is one of the imperatives of transdisciplinarity. Every human being is entitled to a nationality, but as an inhabitant of the Earth is also a transnational being. The acknowledgement by international law of this twofold belonging, to a nation and to the Earth, is one of the goals of transdisciplinary research.

Article 9

Transdisciplinarity leads to an open attitude towards myths and religions, and also towards those who respect them in a transdisciplinary spirit.

Article 10

No single culture is privileged over any other culture. The transdisciplinary approach is inherently transcultural.

Article 11

Authentic education cannot value abstraction over other forms of knowledge. It must teach contextual, concrete and global approaches. Transdisciplinary education revalues the role of intuition, imagination, sensibility and the body in the transmission of knowledge.

Article 12

The development of a transdisciplinary economy is based on the postulate that the economy must serve the human being and not the reverse.

Article 13

The transdisciplinary ethic rejects any attitude that refuses dialogue and discussion, regardless of whether the origin of this attitude is ideological, scientistic, religious, economic, political or philosophical. Shared knowledge should lead to a shared understanding based on an absolute respect for the collective and individual Otherness united by our common life on one and the same Earth.

<h2 style="text-align:center">Article 14</h2>

Rigour, opening and tolerance are the fundamental characteristics of the transdisciplinary attitude and vision. Rigour in an argument, taking into account all existing data, is the best defence against possible distortions. The opening involves an acceptance of the unknown, the unexpected and the unpredictable. Tolerance implies acknowledging the right to ideas and truths opposed to our own.

<h2 style="text-align:center">Final Article</h2>

The present Charter of Transdisciplinarity was adopted by the participants of the first World Congress of Transdisciplinarity, with no claim to any authority other than that of their own work and activity.

In accordance with procedures to be agreed upon by transdisciplinary-minded persons of all countries, this Charter is open to the signature of anyone who is interested in promoting progressive national, international and transnational measures to ensure the application of these Articles in everyday life.

Convento de Arrábida, November 6, 1994

Science is considered by many to be impartial, objective, if not the very definition of reality. Article 5 demands that science goes beyond one reality, and must seek a rapprochement between science, the humanities and the arts. However, scientism still aspires to a theory of everything, and the many scientific attempts to pin down that one true reality have not succeeded as reality is multivarious and paradoxical, physical and virtual.[28] As the theoretical physicist, Brian Greene noted, "when it comes to revealing the true nature of reality, common sense is deceptive."[29]

<h2 style="text-align:center">Strata Politics</h2>

Earthquakes and volcanic activity were once considered the activity of grumpy gods, dragons and sea-monsters. Some of our biggest disasters in recent history include ninety-two thousand people killed in the Tambora, Indonesia, eruption of 1815; over 820,000 killed in Sian, China, the earthquake of 1556; 240,000 killed by the earthquake of 1976 at Tangshan, China; and about 6000 were killed in the 1985 earthquake in Mexico City. In 1755 the philosopher, Immanuel Kant was shocked by the Lisbon earthquake in Portugal that caused fires and destroyed the city, which led him to contemplate the existential end of a human world, and the obliteration of intelligence in the universe; for Kant the end of the world was palpable. Kant inaugurated the science of seismology,[30] yet his concerns were primarily anthropocentric. The lay of the land, or geography, is only surface evidence of geo-politics, however, as Nigel Clark points out in his article, *The Politics of Strata*, 'just as all 'history is geo- history', then sooner or later all politics is geo-politics.'[31] We will also see that all of the Earth sciences are all geo-politics.

The multidisciplinary necessity to review the Earth as a system implicates not only human agents, but the nonhuman majority in this big picture, we are inextricably bound to all of the spheres of our world, lithosphere, hydrosphere, biosphere, and atmosphere. Anyone of these physical spheres or worlds could generate and consume volumes of research, and so we can only scratch the surface, metaphorically, conceptually, and literally. This section cannot hope to do justice to the evidence and debate, even related to the end of the physical world; my hope is only to show how this world begins to collide with the conceptual, ontological, and modelled worlds, and how we might speculate about the future without limiting our imagination, or descending into fascism. As we grope towards transdisciplinary questions that span these worlds, we must acknowledge this approach as speculative, and an a priori necessity, before we can contemplate engineering solutions, such as terraforming, either on this planet or our innocent red neighbour.

As the invisible pall of greenhouse gases causes temperatures to exceed the Earth's planetary life support, and a litany of physical seismic disasters, and astronomical threats, send humans into a panic, we are rushing to construct space arks so we can build new worlds beyond Earth. In his book, *The Future of Humanity*,[32] astrophysicist, Michio Kaku, urges us to reboot the space race, and prepare to mine and terraform our neighbours. This urgency may be part of the cause rather than the cure for planetary woes. Arrogant and ignorant physical interventions have resulted in the anthropogenic damage to date, such as pollution, species extinction, and the culling of options as we shrink biodiversity, and destroy habitats.

This colonisation of space is the logical extension to the voracious appetite of humanity seeking to conquer and consume nature, and violently overcome indigenous species, humans and nonhumans alike. Nations and individuals, who are members of the elite 16% of the human population in so-called 'developed countries' are consuming 80% of the Earth's energy and resources.[33] There is almost nowhere left on this planet that has not been claimed and exploited, and so the entrepreneurs of the 21st century feel compelled to look to other planets, moons, and asteroids to mine for growth, wealth, and ego. The base attraction is the rocks, minerals, and energy sources, but beyond the geology, and astropolitics of new colonies in space, there are the deep ethical and philosophical questions about what sort of new worlds we should be building?

Modelling Reality

We have seen how our myths and stories have bolstered our anthropocentric assumptions and prejudices around creativity and world building. Creativity was once considered god-given, and imagination was also a gift from the gods, not to be abused. Our darkest fears about technology are based on myths and religious warnings about encroaching on the divine right of gods and kings. Our continual search for knowledge about everything in the universe has been accompanied by morality tales of disasters, death, destruction and divine apocalyptic punishments. And, all of this, we were told over and over again, because we were exclusively born in God's image.

In the contemporary world, those archetypal instincts that lurk in our subconscious have translated into common sense confidence that humans exclusively possess God's gifts of creativity, consciousness, imagination, and design or world building.

Until relatively recently only humans were thought to be capable of designing and creating a modelled world, one that is designed, defined, and predicted by us. However, that has begun to change.

Modelling Earth Systems

A short summary of some historical events in the physical sciences related to the end of a physical world will illustrate how they overlap in Earth System Science. It will also hint at how the physical world, the conceptual, modelled and ontological worlds interconnect, preparing us for the discussion about creative collaboration and future world building.

Volcanic activity is often considered apocalyptic when violent eruptions send molten lava to destroy whole villages, animals, and plants. They can also result in earthquakes and tsunamis. All of these physical events were regarded with fear and awe by humans who experienced them at a human scale, spatially and temporally – in ancient times that human scale convinced these anthropocentric witnesses that these were cosmic events and often signalled the end of the world. It was not until the end of the 19th century and mostly the 20th century that physical scientists began to formulate a global world view. Climate, for example, was only of local interest to farmers, sailors, and from the point of view of colonists worried about their foreign crops.[34]

Life, civilization, and indeed the physical and biological conditions of planetary survival ultimately are precarious and we live on a tiny planet in an unimaginably immense universe. There has been a dawning realisation over the past one hundred years that the Earth is a system. From a human perspective, and only up until very recently, the Earth System has been imperceptibly slow and encompasses vast dimensions of change beyond human perception or knowledge. As early as 1896 the Swedish scientist, Svante Arrhenius calculated that a doubling of atmospheric CO_2 would create global warming of 5-6 degrees Celsius. Arrhenius cited Hogbom's calculations that industrialisation was causing CO_2 emissions equivalent to natural sources and could be causing the planet to warm up, he called it the greenhouse effect. Angus in his book, *Facing the Anthropocene*, recounts the history of 'the key concept of the biosphere, out of which our modern notion of the Earth System was to develop'; it arose, with the publication of, *The Biosphere*, by Vernadsky in 1926. Vernadsky took a multidisciplinary approach and concluded there was a complex interplay of chemicals, gases, and minerals that affected the life and death process on Earth – it was a system. Vernadsky saw the connection between the lithosphere or rock system, and the biosphere, or biological system, however, it took some time before the concept of global warming was taken seriously.

Although the meteorologist Alfred Wegener first described it in 1912 as 'continental drift' his theory was not widely supported. It was only in the late 1950s that scientists came to realise that the Earth was not as stable and docile as previously imagined and that the shifting of tectonic plates was a hint of the turbulence that lay deep below in the rock strata.[35]

As marine geology developed in the 1940s evidence accumulated around the movement of the seafloor trenches and ridges, and with archaeological evidence of magnetic pole reversals found in samples dating back over aeons of time. It was only in 1965 that the theory of plate tectonics became generally accepted. Even in the 1980s many of the techniques of geological analysis and research were only just emerging such as geomorphology, paleoseismology, and even the research and evaluations of geologic units.[36] Today, we might forget how very recent our knowledge about the physical properties of our world is. A book entitled, *Active Tectonics* (1986) stated:

"The determination of rates of processes and means of dating materials of late Quaternary age (past 500,000 yr) thus are considered of high priority for research attention."

Therefore, it is hardly surprising that our erroneous view of the world with respect to the stability of the climate, and surety of the rock beneath our feet, lags behind the recent scientific findings. We credit humanity with the exclusive power of world bending, and even validate it with the horrific results of the Anthropocene, yet we ignore the physical world bending powers of the Earth. We now know that not only can the lithosphere cause dramatic changes to the climate through volcanic ash and GHG (Green House Gas) emissions, but that the climate can cause violent upheavals resulting in volcanoes, earthquakes and tsunamis.[37] With the relatively recent invention of GPS (Global Positioning System) we know that the Earth is constantly bending our world, like a heartbeat, that takes 12 months, and compresses and expands at the poles by 3mm, according to the seasons, and the hydraulic effect of snow, ice, and rainfall, flowing from the melting and freezing of water. The dynamic mass of water that causes this world bending is estimated to be 10^{16} kg or about one and a half thousand times the weight of all the coal mined on the planet in a year. According to McGuire, this tiny world bending, or 'Earthbeat' is responsible for the season of volcanoes, from November to April, and illustrates the fragility of the Earth system that can undergo a dramatic climatic phase change, wrecking violence around the world with little warning.

In 1986 the IGBP (International Geosphere-Biosphere Project) was launched "to coordinate international research on global-scale and regional-scale interactions between Earth's biological, chemical and physical processes and their interactions with human systems".[38] After 30 years of extensive scientific research, they concluded that:

"A profound transformation of Earth's environment is now apparent, owing not to the great forces of nature or to extraterrestrial sources but to the numbers and activities of people – the phenomenon of global change" suggesting a new geological epoch, the Anthropocene era.[39]

The Anthropocene was brought to prominence by the Dutch chemist, and Nobel Prize winner, Paul Crutzen in 2000. According to Angus, the Anthropocene can be viewed as a new geological epoch displacing the Holocene that lasted for 10,000 to 12,000 years. It is a rupture in the history of the planet and it "stands for the notion that human beings have become the primary emergent geological force affecting the future of the Earth System."[40] Most importantly, the IGBP highlighted that this extraordinary event was what they described as 'non analogue':

"In terms of key environmental parameters, the Earth System has recently moved well outside the range of the natural variability exhibited over at least the last half million years. The nature of changes now occurring simultaneously in the Earth System, their magnitudes and rates of change are unprecedented in human history and perhaps in the history of the Earth."[41]

The ecological philosopher, Timothy Morton, introduces us to the concept of *hyperobjects*, beyond the ken of human scale, time and space, and includes a dizzying array of nonhuman, and conceptual objects such as global warming; black holes; plastic bags, imagined worlds, and plutonium.[42] These hyperobjects can not be directly experienced, and are often only indirectly sensed through models, simulations, probability analysis and the remote sensing of human instrumentation. Morton argues that while the planet Earth is still very real, it is a strongly held belief that the world is about to end, "unless we act now", and this "is paradoxically one of the most powerful factors that inhibit a full engagement with our ecological coexistence here on Earth."[43] Morton tells us that the world has already ended, and this end has two precise dates, 1784 with the invention of the Watts' steam engine, and in 1945 in Trinity, New Mexico, with the testing of the first atom bomb.[44] Hyperobjects, such as global carbon deposits, and radioactive material, that will last 24,000 years, have ended our concept of the world. Humanity is no longer in the privileged position of scientifically defining reality but must share reality with the unknowable, nonhuman majority, in which objects, and their relations, remain mysterious and distant.[45]

How we will move to that new state of shared reality will require imagination, and cognitive tools, to assist humanity in the process of intuitively grasping objects, and things, beyond human scale. Rather than seeing this objectification of reality in pejorative terms we can begin to remap and abstract from hyperobjects that have a systemic logic, and aesthetic magnificence, articulated in totally novel virtual worlds.

Virtual worlds offer up new opportunities to create and imagine simulations of hyperobjects beyond the human spatial and temporal scale that can reconnect human sensory awareness with data that has been disembodied. An example of this is the virtual reality simulation of earthquake and volcanic activity in New Zealand since 1900. My former colleague, Dr Stefan Marks, helped to create a virtual environment which allowed an immersive experience of hyperobjects that span a period beyond the average human lifespan – condensing sound, seismic, and visual data, that can be intuitively sensed by the user as they fly over the country.[46] However, in the context of our existential crisis this ability to sense hyperobjects requires a higher-dimensional metanarrative to compliment the modelling and simulations.

Seismic Simulations

Richard Tarnas thinks we need to 'discern the more fundamental conditions in which our many concrete problems might ultimately be rooted?' He identified three fundamental factors:

1. The profound metaphysical disorientation and groundlessness that pervades our modern human experience; our lack of purpose and meaning across cultures.

2. A deep sense of alienation and the spiritual estrangement of the modern psyche. A nonhuman universe that has become disenchanted and separated from humanity.

3. The missing individual and societal insights into the unconscious creative and destructive forces that shape human and nonhuman histories on the planet and in the universe.

These three factors would contribute to a compelling and unifying metanarrative that would help us to address the wicked problems exposed by the Anthropocene.

Extreme weather has been linked to seismic activity, and the study of meteorology also has a dark past relating to military operations and R & D. During atmospheric testing of nuclear weapons meteorologists were employed to track the likely direction of radioactive fall out following the nuclear explosion. Ironically, it is thanks to nuclear weaponry that we know so much about weather patterns and CO_2 emissions. Lester Machta wrote a 2002 review article, with the macabre title, *Meteorological Benefits from Atmospheric Nuclear Tests*, pointing out the many ways that meteorologists have increased their knowledge by tracing, and modelling radioactive materials in the atmosphere. Tracing carbon as it cycles through the atmosphere, the oceans, and the biosphere has been crucial to understanding anthropogenic climate change, and fall- out monitoring and stratospheric sampling have contributed to today's global observing system."[47]

By the late 1920s, seismologists were beginning to identify several prominent earthquake zones parallel to the trenches that typically were inclined 40–60° from the horizontal and extended several hundred kilometres into the Earth. These zones later became known as Wadati–Benioff zones, or simply Benioff zones, in honour of the seismologists who first recognized them, Kiyoo Wadati of Japan and Hugo Benioff of the United States.

The study of global seismicity greatly advanced in the 1960s with the establishment of the Worldwide Standardized Seismograph Network (WWSSN) to monitor the compliance of the 1963 treaty banning above-ground testing of nuclear weapons. The much-improved data from the WWSSN instruments allowed seismologists to map precisely the zones of earthquake concentration worldwide. Monitoring and simulations have been made possible through advancements in computing and mathematical modelling, and all of these activities were paid for and motivated by military objectives. The Cold War blended the physical world with the conceptual world of geopolitics, and yet by the 60s a new wave of the philosophy of science had ensured that scientists regarded science and politics as immiscible oils.[48] While most scientists vacated the field of values and ethics, they left it wide open for politicians, lobbyists, and corporations to dictate the direction of R & D through funding from politicised science foundations and military-sponsored think tanks.

Hybrid Physical And Conceptual Worlds

Through the Cold War the philosophy of science in the US became sterilised and value-free; or rather, so it appeared to the scientists and the public and as a result, the physical world, and its simulated models were absorbed by the hegemonic conceptual world of neoliberal ideology. The vocational guidance for scientists advised, recommended and insisted that there was no room for sociological or ethical debate about scientific methodology.[49] For the majority of Americans, the conceptual war of the worlds between capitalism and communism was simply a binary choice between loyalty to the American Dream, or a Soviet covert conspiracy to subvert and overthrow consumerism. In academia, it became professionally unwise to even question the military-industrial funding model of science. It became increasingly professional, standardised, and bureaucratic which served to remove political debate and at the same time ensure that the political elite was well served. This historical shift left a vacuum between the physical world of science and the conceptual world of political influence. The two worlds seldom talk and a majority of people have little understanding of the scientific methodology. What is more, there is a deep cynicism and suspicion that corporate and military funding has corrupted scientists and their reports are politically or commercially biased. These attitudes have been fanned by lobbyists who deliberately cast doubt on scientific reports such as the IPCC's findings of global warming. Ironically while the scientists avoided political debate and value judgements, corporations, lobbyists, and politicians have politicised science.

While throughout history the technology and political events have changed the privileged players who control the majority, our ignorance of how myth, propaganda, and narrative have bolstered the political and economic objectives of the power elite have blindsided us. Today, automation, robotics, and AI are actively using powerful networks to control our desires, processes, purchases and relationships. This is not a conspiracy, this is the agri-logistics of neoliberal economics that finds out what consumers want and delivers it to them before their desire has the time, or the inclination to fact check how, when, who, and why something is made?

Rational behaviour and logical decision making have failed to explain why anyone with the power to influence political and scientific discourse would aggressively deny the science that shows human production, consumption, and waste are the cause of a new, and probably catastrophic, change to the Earth system. The power elite has successfully circumvented social equity attempts to distribute global resources more environmentally, and democratically. They have finally be outed for their mass deception, often called, trickle-down economics, and now the top 1% own half the World's resources. What went wrong? How is it that scientists have been indirectly warning of the disastrous impact that our economics, and technology could have on the nonhuman majority, not to mention our own personal health and happiness, and yet we carry on regardless, even increasing our buyer's remorse as we seek refuge in the short-lived buzz of shopping therapy.

It is not just the 'evil' 1% that is responsible for our social delusion, it is both mass deception and self-deception that have tricked us. Despite the nightly news reports on extreme weather, species extinction, and record heat temperatures around the planet, in the 'developed' countries we do little to change our lifestyles. If it is out of sight, it is out of mind, and we deceive ourselves that there is either little we can personally do, or that we still have plenty of time because the IPCC has set a deadline of 2030 to cut emissions by 45%! If we are not personally suffering now we are happy to go along with the mainstream narrative that wants to maintain and continue economic growth percentages. Over the past 500 years of double-entry bookkeeping our collective understanding of what determines value has radically shifted. In the 20th century price, or monetary value became the value of everything, and GDP no longer simply identified productivity but was driven by financialised shareholder value at the expense of values that sustain life.[50] Only approximately 25% of the Earth's wealthiest inhabitants are responsible for global warming[51] but our self-deception is that despite those of us in that minority that enjoy a privileged lifestyle it must be someone else that is made to pay environmentally. Leading up to the 2014 release of the IPCC's 5th Report US Secretary of State John Kerry responded saying "This is yet another wakeup call: those who deny the science or choose excuses over action are playing with fire."[52]

It was President Lyndon B. Johnson who 50 years ago warned the American public about the threat of global warming and environmental disaster. In a report, read by Lyndon Johnson in 1965 by an advisory panel to the President, it said "Through his worldwide industrial civilization, Man is unwittingly conducting a vast geophysical experiment. Within a few generations, he is burning the fossil fuels that slowly accumulated in the earth over the past 500 million years ... The climatic changes that may be produced by the increased CO_2 content could be deleterious from the point of view of human beings. The possibilities of deliberately bringing about countervailing climatic changes, therefore, need to be thoroughly explored."

Even though there was mounting evidence that global warming was related to greenhouse gas emissions the climatologist Reid Bryson, in his 1973 testimony to Congress, realised that it was a wicked political problem.

"There is no way right now that we can control the climate to make it more benign. Even if we were to say let us stop using fossil fuels so that we do not add carbon dioxide to the atmosphere, because that impacts the world climate, how on earth could you stop using fossil fuels? Even those countries that are most heavily impacted by the climatic change are the ones who say it is our turn to be affluent and it is in the use of fossil fuels that one gains affluence."[53]

In 1968, he wrote:

"Ours is a nation of affluence. But the technology that has permitted our affluence spews out vast quantities of wastes and spent products that pollute our air, poison our waters, and even impair our ability to feed ourselves."

While the report thought that CO_2 emissions, due to fossil fuels, did not pose an immediate threat, by July 1977 Exxon's senior scientist, James Black said "In the first place, there is general scientific agreement that the most likely manner in which mankind is influencing the global climate is through carbon dioxide release from the burning of fossil fuels," Black told Exxon's management committee. A year later he warned Exxon that doubling CO_2 gases in the atmosphere would increase average global temperatures by two or three degrees—a number that is consistent with the scientific consensus today."[54]

Globally amongst the political rhetoric of populism today and what some commentators are calling a post-truth reality, the hegemonic world begins to take on a strange and confusing mask. Without the requisite cognitive tools to combat outrageous claims, 'alternative facts', 'fake news', lies, and shadowy conspiracies, the default fact-checker for a majority of people becomes a search engine's page rank algorithm, or what was the most popular news source, Facebook[55] (at the time of publication this may no longer be true).

One of the most frightening apocalyptic scenarios that have been conjured up, through the scientific and technological exploration of worlds, has been the weapons, power, and physics experiments made possible by quantum mechanics. By the time scientists, such as Robert Oppenheimer, known as the father of the bomb, realised they had created an apocalyptic device, it was too late. It was Einstein who wrote a letter to President Roosevelt asking him to research an atomic bomb, something he later came to regret. Oppenheimer quotes the *Bhagavad-Gita*, after the detonation of that first device, 'I am become death, the destroyer of worlds.' Oppenheimer regretted their invention and reflected that humanity had turned a dangerous corner. He had studied Hinduism in an attempt to make sense of his actions recognising that on that fateful day, July 16th 1945, the bomb was 'world-destroying time'. Oppenheimer wrote, two years after the Trinity explosion, recalling the Biblical Fall from Grace that 'the physicists have known sin; and this is a knowledge which they cannot lose."[56] Science was subservient to the ideology of the powerful; the War had subverted the scientific method chaining it to the demands of politicians, and this continues to this day as governments now battle it out in cyberspace fighting covert information warfare.[57]

The Cold War and the tension between the US and the Soviet Union have acted to inhibit the sharing of scientific data necessary for achieving a global consensus on global warming. This was complicated by the fact that both meteorology and seismology were increasingly used for military purposes. The study of the weather was important for determining the predicted spread of nuclear fallout, and seismology was used to monitor the enemy's nuclear tests. Truman had pushed Stalin to allow US meteorologists to use the Soviets weather stations to provide weather data for an attack on Japan. In the 1960s a Worldwide Standardized Seismograph Network (WWSSN) was established above-ground nuclear weapons testing under the 1963 treaty ban treaty.

According to Jardini (2013) the Cold War methodologies developed by the influential RAND Corporation, such as game theory, systems analysis, and cost-benefit economics were later applied to social policy in the 1960s and 70s during Johnson's 'War on Poverty', and were part and parcel of Cold War fears of Russian subversion and revolution. Cold War game theory and von Neumann's computer architecture shaped the policy and design of a closed private network conceived by RAND for the military and a select group of US universities.

Meanwhile, aggressive funding of think tanks and academics by conservative ideologues attempted to bolster the 'free market' doctrine in order to combat ideas associated with social equity, environmental protection, and free education. Rising out of this Cold War of ideas was the first weaponized generation of computer networks developed by RAND for the military, the precursor to the Internet, known as ARPANET. This weapon was originally conceived as part of a defensive strategy to prevent the shutdown of a central command and control communications network in a war with the Soviets[58] and was to later morph into the public Internet, eventually spreading its tendrils across the whole planet in a zero-sum-game in an attempt to spread knowledge and neoliberal 'democracy' using this new propaganda channel.[59]

Propagating Conceptual Worlds

Oddly enough the recent antics of the most bizarre President of America in living memory, Donald Trump, has drawn attention to both the politicisation of science and the philosophy of science. Trump projects his world view and political concerns into every aspect of the world he comes into contact with, and as Maxwell explains 'World view is world creation'.[60]

Trump is impatient with other world views and is looking to supplant and ensure his world view is the only valid reality – his is a conceptual world. Despite mountains of scientific evidence and a survey of 12,000 abstracts published since 1990, and 4,000 papers, 97% of those scientists agreed explicitly or implicitly that global warming is taking place, and that is caused by human activity, President Trump disagrees. He continues to question the scientific validity of the data.

While this might not pass for informed debate about the philosophy of science it has engaged philosophers and scientists in a discussion around scientific objectivity, research methodology, and even funding.

From a sociopolitical perspective, there has been a lively debate around democracy, freedom of speech, corruption, campaign finance, and the end of the world. When a Presidential candidate changes his mind about the anthropogenic nature of global warming, i.e. from saying it is a big problem, to doubt and even denial, it suggests that we should take advice from the movie character, Deep Throat, and 'follow the money'. The investigative journalist Bob Woodward used a similar phrase in his book, *All the President's Men*, "The key was the secret campaign cash, and it should all be traced." This sentiment is also the basis of Lawrence Lessig's book on corruption in American politics, *Republic Lost*,[61] and ironically, Trump used 'follow the money' to try to discredit Hillary Clinton during the Presidential campaign. What has been revealed is that Trump, who was once a friend and donor of the Clintons, was also once a believer in anthropogenic climate change. Jane Mayer explains Trump's turnaround as a result of the campaign finance donations from Robert, and his daughter, Rebecca, Mercer, who are behind a Superpac campaign fund that backed Trump in the 2016 Presidential election. The Mercer's are climate change deniers who also fund the discredited climate scientist and global warming denier, Pat Robertson.[62]

The Mercer's had adopted the propaganda technique used by the likes of the energy magnates, the Koch brothers, and the oil and gas companies – all they had to do was convince the public there was doubt amongst the scientists that there was such a thing as human-generated global warming.[63]

Bad actors such as Dr Fred Seitz and Dr Fred Singer who had been employed by the tobacco industry proposed the same strategy for oil and gas; i.e. to question the scientific validity of reports against linking cancer to smoking, and then later sought to undermine evidence about global warming while associated with the conservative think tank, George C. Marshall Institute. Their strategy was not to debate the evidence but simply to sow doubt. Singer attacked the conclusions of the IPCC by asserting instead that:

"the scientific base for [greenouse warming] includes some facts, lots of uncertainty, and just plain ignorance...The scientific base for a greenhouse warming is too uncertain to justify drastic action at this time."[64]

The Global Climate Coalition borrowed from the tobacco industry playbook using the PR techniques of Hill & Knowlton which boasted in an internal memo, 'Doubt is our product'. Singer was associated with the conservative, and hawkish think tank, the George C. Marshall Institute. He was the founder and president of the Institute that had backed the tobacco industry and supported Reaganite anti-communism, and was also the chair of the Global Climate Coalition. The Coalition included ExxonMobil, Chevron, Shell Oil, Amoco, Texaco, General Motors, Ford, Chrysler, the American Forest & Paper Association, AMAX Minerals, and the US Chamber of Commerce. These 'merchants of doubt' succeeded in delaying urgent rethinking of our social, economic, and environmental action to our global detriment. As late as 2017 a poll in the US found 'almost 90% of Americans didn't know there was a scientific consensus on global warming.'[65]

"But as Dr James Baker, former head of the National Oceanic and Atmospheric Administration, said in 2005, "There's a better scientific consensus on this than on any issue I know—except maybe Newton's second law of [thermo]dynamics."[66]

According to Benkler, during the Cold War era propaganda studies identified three sorts of propaganda. 'White' propaganda acknowledged communications from an outlet 'where the information was more or less accurate but framed to favour that party' that used it for their benefit. 'Black' propaganda refers to 'spreading lies and deception through falsely described sources'. 'Gray' propaganda was 'somewhere in between.'[67]

The Cold War was a conceptual world built on ideas, ideologies and propaganda, and the Trump presidency is proactively world bending, breaking, and remaking to suit corporate backers, the alt-right, and radical republicans.

These are only some nodes of a dense network showing how agents of a powerful formal and informal social network of financial influencers have worked to undermine environmental protection and bolster their neoliberal business objectives. In their book, *The Gentle Subversive*, Mark Lytle, cites Rachel Carson's view that the principal cause of ecological degradation by humanity was 'the gods of profit and production', and the main barrier to sustainable coexistence is that "in an era dominated by industry, in which the right to make a dollar at any cost is seldom challenged." Following the Second World War conservative ideologues set about fighting the Keynesian redistribution of wealth in support of a neoliberal agenda.[68]

In the 21st century, it is the biophysical description of the world that dominates the headlines and attracts scientists, politicians, documentarians, and news media outlets to compete for volume and space about our impending doom. The battle may rage over whether or not the end of the world is *The Inconvenient Truth*,[69] or just 'fake news' generated by the anti-Trump 'Deep State' but the dominant world view is still rational neoliberal scientism.

According to first, Philipp Frank,[70] and then Thomas Kuhn, the evolution and so-called progress of science has happened not through the inductive process of confirmation and falsification but through bloodless scientific revolutions in which researchers, theorists, and academics battle it out for influence.[71] This scientism is used to neutralise opponents to a political epistemology that contributes to undemocratic, unethical, and environmentally adverse outcomes. According to Maxwell in his book, *Dynamics of Transformation*, even liberal progressive academics have a tendency to review the past as the battlegrounds for novel conceptual revolutions, but, he claims:

"[it] seems that those theorists who proclaim that all the great revolutions are done and that history will most likely grind on interminably until the human race destroys the planet not only lack imagination, but they also lack an adequate understanding of the way transitions between world views have generally occurred in the past. In one sense, they are right that the current world view of late modernity has run low on vitality, has reached a stalemate of vast proportions, and that if we do not act soon, tragedy will ensue, and in fact, is already occurring in the increasing extinction of species and the environmental devastation. But such crises generally seem to take place just before the period of release and transcendence occurs; it is not for nothing that the night is noted to be darkest just before the dawn."[72]

It is the look towards the dawn that defines the progressive philosophy of the past, and the speculative realism of the future. Interestingly, the philosophy of science and the debunking of the conceptual notions of economic growth and technological progress have revealed the true nature of scientific epistemology. According to Frank history is the workshop of the philosophy of science, and yet there are no grounds for debate between those describing the physical worlds, conceptual and philosophical worlds, despite the fact that those worlds intermingle ontologies, politics and scientific models, mostly in the background, while denying them in their foreground objectives and purpose for what they are claiming to be doing. Philosophers such as Frank and others from the Unity of Science movement attempted to bring philosophy and values to the foreground to install ethical debate, but the battle was eventually lost during the First Cold War.[73]

Following on from the debate between Thomas Kuhn and Carl Popper, Bruno Latour went on to show that there is a network of 'actants', both human and nonhuman agents who all interact, and determine the political outcome according to what he calls, Actor Network Theory, (ANT). His detailed analysis of Louis Pasteur's research in, *The Pasteurisation of France*, showed the surprising influence of not just Pasteur, but the socio-political activities of doctors, lab equipment and microbes; in what he later described as 'object oriented politics'.[74]

Latour argues that in order to encourage public debate about the environment and ecology, there are three disciplines that need to come together, "one from the sociology of the sciences, another from the practice of the ecology movements, and the third from comparative anthropology."[75] He then makes a distinction between Science and the sciences, defining "Science as the politicization of the sciences through epistemology in order to render ordinary political life impotent through the threat of an incontestable nature."[76]

Latour is not saying that all science is political, but that the respectable, epistemology; the knowledge about knowledge, or the meticulous description of "scientific practice in all their complexity"[77] must be differentiated from political epistemology, i.e. Science. This scientism threatens to pollute the search for truth by effectively nullifying the complex bond between the sciences and society. The public and scientists should be free to debate the political, sociological, and anthropological implications of the sciences without Science claiming the high ground in order to neutralise the discourse with the shock tactics of the 'epistemology police'. Latour says that this is why he, and others, are attacked when they describe laboratory practice.

What Latour is arguing for, in order to heal the split between humans and nonhumans, and to ecologically repair the danger, is to drop the word nature, as it implies a 'natural' separation of humanity from the vast majority, the nonhuman objects and things. Unbeknownst to many scientists, and nonscientists, this 'scientific naturalism' remains a human project, the implicit driver being the betterment of the human world. By recognising the difference between Science and the sciences Latour hopes to encourage us to recognise and enfranchise the universe, or his democratic 'parliament of things'. He describes two houses, that can also be defined as worlds, the first world 'brings together the totality of speaking humans, who find themselves with no power at all save that of being ignorant in common, or of agreeing by convention to create fictions devoid of any external reality',[78] this is the conceptual world of Trump. The second house [world] is constituted exclusively of real objects that have the property of defining what exists but that lack the gift of speech. On the one hand, we have the chattering of fictions; on the other, the silence of reality. The subtlety of this organization rests entirely on the power given to those who can move back and forth between the houses [worlds]',[79] in other words, the scientists. It would seem from his reasoning that not only scientists have this ability, and Latour is aware that many lack the philosophical and sociological skills to inhabit those worlds; philosophers also have an urgent project to translate the scientific world using an ethical dimension.

The Reality of an Ontological World

The futurist John Naisbitt has predicted that "The most exciting breakthroughs of the twenty-first century will not occur because of technology, but be because of an expanding concept of what it means to be human."[80] Thus, this is one example of how the physical epistemological world, smashes into the conceptual, modelled, and philosophical ontological worlds. The ontological ecologist, Timothy Morton describes how our species are faced with vast objects that are beyond our direct perception of their presence, they are hyperobjects that are beyond the human scale, such as global warming, or humanity. He writes,

"Hyperobjects are what have brought about the end of the world. Clearly, planet Earth has not exploded. But the concept world is no longer operational, and hyperobjects are what brought about its demise. The idea of the end of the world is very active in environmentalism."[81]

It may seem that this is a modern phenomenon, that our world view is the culmination of years of research and knowledge accumulation that we define as 'progress'. Indeed, there has never been a time like it in terms of broadcasting stories almost instantaneously around the world. However, there was never a time when those who spread the word, and those who heard the word, did not think that the stories explaining, and predicting the end of the world were not based on the truth of the day, whether we look back at them and scoff, does not mean they did not believe it at the time. Maxwell points out that there is an innate historical conservatism when it comes to adopting new philosophies, or paradigms that hold back theorists, scientists, and academics who have built their reputation on outmoded models.

"The old way of life, which was the site of all one's past glories and strivings, of one's most intimate and most public occasions, of everything one has ever known, must be left behind to some degree in order for a new world view, and thus a new world, to be born."[82]

Even when those stories were what we would now regard as myths and legends, the soothsayers were granted their privilege to disseminate truth on behalf of the powerful. Of course there were deceivers, fools, and those that were simply not believed, but those who held power have always dominated the popular world view. The Church, the State, and even the first rationalists of the Enlightenment, such as Bacon, Newton, Descartes, Kant, Leibniz and Hume, all held privileged positions in terms of describing, and propagating their views of reality, or their ontological worlds. How they got to that position of privilege does not matter so much, but rather the similarity of how they connected to the dominant knowledge structures, and the power of the day. They were ontological world builders before they were physical world describers. Their reality was an anthropocentric reality, of which they were critically unaware.

Francis Bacon and his Ontological Portal

Even their motivation does not matter as much as we might imagine, because to understand ontological world building is to understand power. The philosophical assumptions that define reality precede any epistemology, or theory of knowledge. The beliefs about what is reality can often go unquestioned, and yet like myths, they lurk in the shadows of the subconscious. It is through an appreciation of history and the philosophy of science that it is possible to critically appreciate the implicit power of ontological world building. Without the benefit of Einstein's theory of relativity the philosophers of the Enlightenment still assumed to know and believe in the absolute reality of God and the world 'he' was supposed to have created. However, absolutism often leads to dictatorial control of ideas and ultimately the definition of reality.[83]

Even Francis Bacon, who is sometimes called the 'father of science', and is credited with the term, 'knowledge itself is power'[84] was privileged enough, and self-aware enough, to see just how the 'natural sciences' could be established by Royal patronage. Tarnas identifies the ancient Greek origins of Western concepts of technological and epistemological progress dating back to the author of *Prometheus Bound*, Aeschylus.[85]

Bacon also believed in the concept that accumulated knowledge was progress and that this powerful knowledge gave humanity dominion over nature. From Bacon's early writings down through the next three hundred years his ideas on scientific and technological progress, we're also a prescription for how humanity would conquer nature. He helps

create an ontological portal through which puritanical beliefs, empirical bias, and logic were passed on to the 21st century.[86]
According to Weinberger, in Bacon's book , *The Wisdom of the Ancients*, Bacon declares the end of knowledge to be the human mastery of nature by means of practical natural science".[87]

This problematic view of science and nature, humanity and nature, hides Bacon's ontological absolutism, that became a tacit doctrine for scientists, technologists, and entrepreneurs passed down to today, and still held in high regard; it is what we might call scientism and is a belief in a reality that is singular – one and only one world view.

"Bacon's plan for the complete reformation of human science and knowledge, which will "lay the foundation, not of any sect or doctrine, but of human power and utility" in order to "command nature in action." Bacon's intention was to ensure the harmony of theory and practice, of the "intellectual and terrestrial globes," which will guarantee man's power over nature."[88]

The ontological and religious arrogance of this mission was not something that Bacon made up, but he inherited from the beginning of the Holocene and agriculture. This ancient project now sounds a shrill warning to anyone with a modicum of ecological and environmental sensibilities. While Bacon's scientific method was short-lived it provided a manifesto for the future of modernity – even while we face the end of the world, our scientific knowledge of nature, and the execution of technology, are considered humanity's divine birthright to rule over and exploit nature, as was spelt out in the *Bible*, and its antecedent myths.

According to the historian, and Bacon's 19th-century biographer, William Hepworth Dixon, states:

"Bacon's influence in the modern world is so great that every man who rides in a train, sends a telegram, follows a steam plough, sits in an easy chair, crosses the channel or the Atlantic, eats a good dinner, enjoys a beautiful garden, or undergoes a painless surgical operation, owes him something."[89]

For many in the 21st century, they may be more likely to remember Sir Isaac Newton, but it is worth noting that these men of the Enlightenment still held deeply religious beliefs, and as Jung and Freud would argue, primordial archetypes, and 'ancient remnants'. Bacon is worth considering as he imagined the scientific and physical reality of today, but it was conceived in a cultural blender with a good handful of ancient myths and was effectively an ontological world with a conceptual world bolted on.

In his utopian book, *New Atlantis*, (1627) Bacon describes, 'Soloman's House' a place of higher learning on the mythical island of Bensalem which was the 'very eye of this kingdom' of power and dominion over nature. This scientific conquest reigned not only over nature but over her catastrophic disasters, and even natural decay. While *Atlantis* recalled the *Bible's* story of Noah and the ark, Bacon no longer felt helpless despair at human's fate, instead, he gave his spin on it. At the dawn of the Enlightenment, in the 15th century, the flood was no longer an inevitable apocalyptic disaster, but rather something that the wise scientists and technologists of Bensalem had managed to control and prevent. For Bacon, this was a deeply religious, and moral place, according to Bacon's strong puritanical leanings, the wise men of Bensalem and Soloman's House would be immune from corruption. Bacon decided that there was to be no payment to scholars, but only the king's patronage, this he thought would ensure that the scientific method would result in the betterment of society.

Ironically, Bacon was to be locked up on 23 counts of corruption and fined $40,000 pounds, and despite being pardoned by the King, his political career was then over. His utopian vision for scholarly investigation became the blueprint for the modern research university, and as Bacon served the King as both the Attorney General and the Lord Chancellor he was one of the most powerful men in England. Bacon had been appointed to the feared Star Chamber that was originally set up to adjudicate on cases involving the privileged and powerful members of society but became synonymous with social and political oppression because it used its power in an arbitrary and abusive manner. As Bacon described Soloman's House, it was thought to be a major influence in the foundation of the Royal Society of London for the Improving of Natural Knowledge.[90]

It was founded by King Charles ll in 1660 and is the oldest scientific institution in the world. It's roles, according to the King's charter, were to promote science and its benefits. Bacon's memory lives on today, but so do his apocalyptic and puritanical beliefs. It is thought that The New Atlantis, could have been a utopian blueprint for the foundation of a puritanical America. Bacon eventually played a leading role in the creation of colonies through the New Virginia Company, and the settlement of Virginia, the Carolinas, Newfoundland, New England, and Boston, the technological birthplace of MIT. It was the third President of the United States, Thomas Jefferson, the author of the Declaration of Independence, who wrote:

"Bacon, Locke and Newton. I consider them as the three greatest men that have ever lived, without any exception, and as having laid the foundation of those superstructures which have been raised in the Physical and Moral sciences".

The puritanical Bacon, considered by some, the patron saint of modern technology and science, envisaged a liberal paradise established in the Americas that would produce the material luxuries. This comfortable lifestyle would be enjoyed by the God-fearing and devout Christian followers of the *Bible*. He looked forward to a future world that would use scientific and technological knowledge to conquer nature, and even geo-engineer a man-made Garden of Eden.

The deep and abiding influence of the puritans is felt through algorithms coded in America and propagated throughout the planet via the network of networks – the Internet. The puritans, in preparation for the apocalypse, sought paradise on Earth and the preparation of the soul in expectation of the end of time when the chosen would be taken up in the rapture. The end of the physical world is something that ironically has resurfaced from the subconscious, to noisily proclaim itself as a reality born of the religious forefathers of the age of reason. The biophysical reality is that there is a credible and proximate risk to all life, and scientific reason argues convincingly that the end of the world is nigh. The ontological worlds, conceptual worlds, modelled worlds, and the physical worlds are all intertwined despite the arguments between some of the world builders on all sides.

Going back to ancient times the shamans, and priestly kings, under the patronage of power, gave their views on reality that became the people's world view. Whether it was ancient China, the Roman Empire, the Greek philosophers, or scientists of Cern, the individual's ability to communicate their ideas, even from beyond the grave, has been determined by the powerful networks that either support or reject their perspectives.

As a mind experiment just imagine teleporting the late, Stephen Hawking, back in time, to any of the great moments of cultural, philosophical or proto-scientific debates. It is highly improbable that he would be able to convince the learned people of the day that there is a black hole at the centre of our galaxy, one that is so massive, and yet invisible, that it sucks up everything within its reach, including light. He could not point to the stars to prove it, and his mathematics would be incomprehensible to his audience. If Hawking suddenly appeared in his electric wheelchair with his cybernetic voice emanating from a small speaker without his lips moving, not only would he appear to Plato and friends as a demon or monster, but he would struggle to present his world view. It was only in the context of the 20th and 21st-century world view that Hawking could find an audience.

That world view is a complex ontological and epistemological network of power and influence that includes funded scientists, government bodies, and the military-industrial-academic nexus that supports the dominant view of reality. He would have to start from first principles in almost every scientific, philosophical, religious, and cultural topic firmly held by his audience in order to slowly build up his argument. Prior to the Enlightenment not only did most think that the sun rotated around our world, but even the size of the world was thought to only stretch as far as the Mediterranean, and to the East but only as far as the Middle East. We might imagine that Hawking would dazzle the Greek philosophers, like Aristotle, with his scientific and mathematical prowess, but not only would his ideas appear strange, mad, and without any reference to empirical reality, but he would be considered a dangerous threat to the wisest men, (and they were all men) of the day. He would be without the political, social, philosophical, or epistemological networks of power that might be able to support him. How long could he survive before the battery in his wheelchair, and computer, ran down and he became mute? Could he in fact effectively communicate the foundational ideas of the universe and physical reality in the 12-24 hours he might have before his time was up? The Greeks would not be able to understand his language, and would not know where to start with Hawking's book, *A Short History of Time*, that is if they had the stone tablet version handy.

Our world view is dominated by rational empiricism, that may appear to be common sense merely because it seems to be a logical, powerful, and effective description of reality This world view has made this world what it is, with all the technological wonders, and luxurious lifestyles it has bequeathed to the believers. What the physical world view cannot shake off is its dark subconscious connection with the psyche and the ontological split with the feminine Self and our original nature. According to Jung, and more recently, Booker, as we transitioned into the rational, empirical, liberal age of reason, the male conscious ego overpowered the feminine subconscious resulting in a dangerous imbalance to the collective psyche. We now know that if our population growth continues at the same pace we will have 9 billion people by 2100. In 3 short centuries, we have seen a 10 fold increase in human numbers. Futurists and military strategists are warning of increased social unrest, including complete social collapse, and catastrophic war caused by fighting over scarce resources and environmental degradation from global warming.[91] The end is nigh and new worlds are evolving.

Notes

1. Hall, John R.. Apocalypse: From Antiquity to the Empire of Modernity. Kindle Locations 180-190. Wiley. Kindle Edition.

2. https://www.livescience.com/39961-chernobyl.html

3. Egan, K. (2013). Imagination in Teaching and Learning: Ages 8 to 15. p.13. Routledge.

4. Shelley, M. W., & Ward, L. (1986). Frankenstein, or, The Modern Prometheus. Poole [Dorset] ; New York: New York, N.Y., USA: New Orchard Editions; Distributed in USA by Sterling Pub. Co. p.189

5. Shelley, M. ibid p.217

6. Shelley, M. ibid p.191

7. Scranton, L. (2014). China's Cosmological Prehistory: The Sophisticated Science Encoded in Civilization's Earliest Symbols (1 edition). Inner Traditions

8. Hall, ibid, Kindle Locations 767-772

9. Grau, O. (2003). Virtual art: From illusion to immersion ([Rev. and expanded). Cambridge, Mass.: MIT Press.

10. Grau, O. (2003). Virtual art: From illusion to immersion ([Rev. and expanded). Cambridge, Mass.: MIT Press. p.25

11. Schaetzel, S. S. (2011). The end of the world is not nigh. Dissent, (37), 58.

12. ibid

13. ibid

14. The asteroid was only one of many catastrophes, including volcanic eruptions and lava flows, to hit the Earth and cause the dinosaur extinction. Brannen, P. (2018). Ends Of The World: Volcanic apocalypses, lethal oceans and our quest to understand earth's past... mass extinctions. S.l.: ONEWORLD PUBLICATIONS.

15. Amos, J. (2018, October 25). Splosh! How to make a giant impact crater. Retrieved from https:// www.bbc.com/news/science-environment-45986449

16. Kaku, M. (2018). The Future of Humanity: terraforming Mars, interstellar travel, immortality, and our destiny beyond Earth. Retrieved from https://archivesquebec.libraryreserve.com/ ContentDetails.htm?id=3442433

17. The Probability of Collisions with Earth. (n.d.). Retrieved October 27, 2018, from https:// www2.jpl.nasa.gov/sl9/back2.html

18. ibid

19. ibid

20. Brannen, Peter. The Ends of the World. Oneworld Publications. Kindle Edition

21. ibid

22. McGuire, Bill. (2012) Waking the Giant (p. 45). OUP Oxford. Kindle Edition.

23. ibid, p.42

24. McKibben, Bill. (2019). Falter. Schwartz Publishing Pty. Ltd. Kindle Edition.

25. ibid

26. Hawking, S., Redmayne, E., Thorne, K. S., & Hawking, L. (2018). Brief Answers to the Big Questions.

27. I am using Basarab Nicolescu's definition, the manifesto, and charter of transdisciplinarity that postulates three methodologies: the existence of levels of Reality, the logic of the included middle, and complexity. He was the co-founder, with Rene Berger, of the Study Group of Transdisciplinarity at UNESCO.

28. Greene, B. (2011). The Hidden Reality: Parallel Universes and the Deep Laws of the Cosmos. Penguin.

29. ibid

30. Nigel Clark. (2017). Politics of Strata. Theory, Culture & Society, 34(2–3), 211–231. https:// doi.org/10.1177/0263276416667538

31. ibid

32. Kaku, M. (2018). The Future of Humanity: terraforming Mars, interstellar travel, immortality, and our destiny beyond Earth.

33. http://edition.cnn.com/US/9910/12/population.cosumption/

34. Weart, S. (2019). The Discovery of Global Warming: A hypertext history of how scientists came to (partly) understand what people are doing to cause climate change. Retrieved from https://history.aip.org/climate/index.htm

35. Clark, Nigel. Inhuman Nature: Sociable Life on a Dynamic Planet. London: SAGE, 2011.

36. Geophysics Research Forum, (U.S.) (1986). Active Tectonics: Impact on Society. Washington, D.C.: National Academies Press.

37. McGuire, Bill (2012). Waking the Giant: How a changing climate triggers earthquakes, tsunamis, and volcanoes.

38. ibid

39. ibid

40. Angus, Ian. (2016). Facing the Anthropocene: Fossil Capitalism and the Crisis of the Earth System. Monthly Review Press. Kindle Edition.

41. ibid, p.4

42. Morton, Timothy. (2013). Hyperobjects: Philosophy and Ecology after the End of the World (Posthumanities). University of Minnesota Press. Kindle Edition.

43. Morton, T. (2018). Dark Ecology: for a logic of future coexistence. S.l.: Columbia University Press.

44. ibid

45. Harman, Graham. (2018) Object-Oriented Ontology: A New Theory of Everything. Penguin Books Ltd. Kindle Edition.

46. See the simulation here https://www.youtube.com/watch?v=ciIvHPoqkis

47. Edwards, P. N. (2012). Entangled Histories: Climate science and nuclear weapons research. Bulletin of the Atomic Scientists, 68(4), 28.

48. This is discussed in more detail in Chapter 7, The Weaponisation of Eduction.

49. Reisch, George A. How the Cold War Transformed Philosophy of Science: To the Icy Slopes of Logic. Kindle Locations 311-312. Cambridge University Press. Kindle Edition.

50. See Mariana Mazzucato's presentation based on her book by the same name, The Value of Everything. https://www.youtube.com/watch?v=bsh-SYKUuwg&feature=youtu.be

51. See Angus, I. Facing the Anthropocene.

52. UN: Humans Cause Climate Change http://www.msnbc.com/morning-joe/un-humans-cause- climate-change

53. The U.S. Congress (October 18, 1973). The U.S. and World Food Situation. Hearings, before the Subcommittee on Agricultural Production, Marketing, and Stabilization of Prices and Subcommittee on Foreign Agricultural Policy of the Committee on Agriculture and Forestry, United States Senate, Ninety-third Congress, first session. U.S. G.P.O. p. 120.

54. Exxon Knew about Climate Change Almost 40 Years Ago - Scientific American. (n.d.). Retrieved August 5, 2018, from https://www.scientificamerican.com/article/exxon-knew-about-climate- change-almost-40-years-ago/

55. With a membership of 2.38 Billion, (2019) an estimated 75% of surveyed people say that Facebook is their primary news source.

56. Wired, (2017) 'Now I am become Death, the destroyer of worlds'. The story of Oppenheimer's infamous quote' https://www.wired.co.uk/article/manhattan-project-robert-oppenheimer

57. In an email Jorn Bettin, "The development of chemical, nuclear, and biological, and informational weapons illustrates how science is subservient to ideology and super human scale social power structures (= subservient to collective insanity). The age of Big Data is really the age of Informational Weapons, which are no less dangerous than nuclear weapons. It has nothing to do with science or knowledge."

58. Lukasik, Stephen J. (2011). Why the Arpanet Was Built. IEEE Annals of the History of Computing, Annals of the History of Computing, IEEE, IEEE Annals Hist. Comput., (3), 4. https://doi.org/10.1109/MAHC.2010.11

59. Benkler, Y., Faris, R., & Roberts, H. (2018). Network Propaganda: Manipulation, disinformation, and radicalization in American politics. New York, NY: Oxford University Press.

60. Maxwell, G. (2018). Dynamics of Transformation: Tracing an Emerging World View.

61. Lessig, L. (2015). Republic Lost: The corruption of equality and the steps to end it (Revised edition). New York, NY: Twelve.

62. Mayer, J. (2017) "The Reclusive Hedge-fund Tycoon Behind the Trump

Presidency." New Yorker.

63. See Mayer's Dark Money, and McKibben's Falter.

64. Naomi Oreskes and Erik M. Conway. (2010) Merchants of Doubt: how a handful of scientists obscured the truth on issues from tobacco smoke to global warming p.297

65. McKibben, Bill. Falter. Schwartz Publishing Pty. Ltd. Kindle Edition.

66. Mayer, Jane. Dark Money: how a secretive group of billionaires is trying to buy political control in the US . Scribe Publications Pty Ltd. Kindle Edition.

67. Benkler, J, ibid, p.243

68. Harvey, D. (2005). A Brief History of Neoliberalism. Oxford; New York: Oxford University Press.

69. The Inconvenient Truth, (2006) a book, an app, and a documentary, presented by Al Gore.

70. Frank introduced the concept of scientific revolutions fifteen years before Kuhn. See, Reisch, George A. How the Cold War Transformed Philosophy of Science

71. Kuhn, T. S. (1970). The Structure of Scientific Revolutions (2nd ed.). Chicago, Ill.: University of Chicago Press.

72. Maxwell, G. (2017). The Dynamics of Transformation: Tracing an emerging world view. p.70

73. Reisch, George A. How the Cold War Transformed Philosophy of Science: To the Icy Slopes of Logic. Kindle Locations 311-312. Cambridge University Press. Kindle Edition.

74. Latour, B. (2004). Politics of Nature: How to bring the sciences into democracy. Cambridge, Mass. : Harvard University Press, 2004.

75. Ibid, p.9

76. 236 Ibid, p.10

77. ibid, p.12

78. Ibid, p.14

79. Ibid, p.14

80. Cited by Frederic Laloux in Reinventing Organisations: a guide to creating organisations inspired by the next stage of human consciousness. (2014)

81. Morton, T., (2013) Hyperobjects

82. Maxwell, G. ibid, p.41

83. During the Cold War reality was narrowly defined and the philosophy of science played a definitive role in circumscribing the discourse. See, Reisch, George A. How the Cold War Transformed Philosophy of Science

84. From Wikipedia the expression "ipsa scientia potestas est"('knowledge

itself is power') occurs in Bacon's Meditationes Sacrae (1597). The exact phrase "scientia potentia est" was written for the first time in the 1668 version of the work Leviathan by Thomas Hobbes, who was the secretary to Bacon as a young man.

85. Tarnas, R. (1991). The Passion of the Western Mind: Understanding the ideas that have shaped our world view (1st ed). New York: Harmony Books.

86. Hepworth Dixon, William (1862). The Story of Lord Bacon's Life

87. J. Weinberger. (1976). Science and Rule in Bacon's Utopia: An Introduction to the Reading of the New Atlantis. The American Political Science Review, (3), p. 865.

88. Hepworth Dixon, William (1862). The Story of Lord Bacon's Life

89. Hepworth Dixon, William (1862). The Story of Lord Bacon's Life.

90. Martin, Julian (1992). Francis Bacon: The State and the Reform of Natural Philosophy. Cambridge: Cambridge University Press. ISBN 9780521382496

91. The End of the Beginning: Life, Society and Economy on the Brink of the Singularity. Humanity+ Press. Kindle Edition.

Chapter 3 Synthetic Creativity

I have attempted to show that the legacy of myths and legends have shaped our prejudices and philosophical beliefs around creativity. Our ability to imagine alternate futures and create new worlds is callipered by heavy metal rods that constrain even the way we walk, let alone our ability to run or fly. Creativity has been feared and controlled by those in power because of its subversive potential. Those in power claimed human exclusivity, bestowed upon them by the God or Gods who alone created the world. In this ontological world, there were those that were excluded from world building and creativity, the lowly humans, the subhumans, the women, and nonhuman 'others'. Those who were not granted the divine right of creativity, but pursued it anyway, were accused of mortal sins, treachery, and heresy. Creative acts by anyone but those who held the divine right, as bestowed by kings and queens, were feared and persecuted. The concept of creativity in anyone else, and according to the Great Chain of Being, especially nonhumans, would have been considered either witchcraft or simply absurd.

Democratic principles eventually granted everyone the right to be creative but these deep-seated fears continue to lurk in our subconscious. And yet, new perspectives are now beginning to be explored in which the creative ability to build, bend and break worlds is no longer considered to be exclusively human. The 'democracy of things' is beginning to evolve and philosophically their creations appear to be synthetic artefacts. The very definition of 'nature' has begun to be viewed with suspicion by those who can see that it is a loaded term that imposes a conservative power structure of patriarchy and anthropocentrism. Creativity may have been the original sin, and maybe the reason we are suspicious of synthetics, but today synthetic creativity is alive and well.

Lessons from a Microbe

In a world without bacteria, otherwise known as microbes, life as we know it would quickly grind to a halt, and Earth would be as barren as Venus and Mars are now. The evolutionary story of microbiology reveals a fascinating alternative to what most people believe. Microbes provide us with evidence that evolution did not occur according to the theory of 'survival of the fittest' but instead by symbiosis. Today most people assume there is an evolutionary hierarchy, not dissimilar to the medieval 'Great Chain of Being', except without the angels, and without God. Our anthropocentric view of reality, or Darwin's 'Tree of Life', has misled most of us, so we assume that the 'natural state of being' places humans at the top of the evolutionary tree, and bacteria, and single-cell organisms at the bottom, just above rocks. In *Origin of the Species*, Darwin wrote:

"The affinities of all the beings of the same class have sometimes been represented by a great tree. I believe this simile largely speaks the truth."

However, there is another perspective that is both philosophically and ecologically relevant. When we consider evolution we must acknowledge that far from leaving microorganisms behind and extinct on an evolutionary ladder we are both surrounded by them, and composed of them. They perform numerous tasks that keep all biological things alive and create the necessary gas composition to sustain aerobic organisms, for those of us that need oxygen. We should be profoundly grateful to cyanobacteria (blue-green algae) that were the first species, 2 billion years before the Anthropocene, to transform the atmosphere of our planet by flooding it with oxygen killing off almost all other life on earth.[1]

While Charles Darwin's evolutionary theory of 'natural selection was borrowed from the lesser-known naturalist Alfred Russel Wallace,[2] this was a 19th-century idea conceived long before the discovery of DNA, microbiology, and CRSPR[3] gene editing. Scientific knowledge about evolution and genetics have exploded and biotechnologies have resulted in a capability that has upended creationism and given humans God-like technologies. According to one article on synthetic biology, 'Just about anyone can be a biohacker now'; a rather scary scenario which could lead to bioterrorism.[4]

The new knowledge of biology, moreover, alters our view of evolution and the bloody competition amongst individuals and species. Life did not take over the globe by combat, but by networking, symbiosis, and collaboration. Life forms multiplied and grew more complex by co-opting others, not just by killing them.[5]

Cybernetic Assumptions

The evolutionary biologists Maturana and Varela[6] support this view; they argue that knowledge comes from the activity and social interaction, and not from hyper-individualist competition. A number of other second-order cybernetic theorists have applied these biological evolutionary models to technological evolution and design innovation.[7]

The need for an evolutionary approach to innovation arose from the failure of neoclassical economics to explain dynamic qualitative changes that are the internal features of technological innovation.[8] Hodgson has argued that the weakness of a mechanical model is that economics applies to biological, not mechanical, creatures, i.e. humans.[9] The mechanistic view of the universe handed down to us from the 16th century and the clock metaphor, has left us still in its debt 400 years later.[10] However, there is growing evidence of alternative theories of mind, and how genetic and technological innovation really occurs, with lessons taken from biology. World bending, and ultimately synthetic world creation, require multiple world views across the whole divergent spectrum of thought and feeling.

Sixty years of cybernetic theory has seen many variants of what amounts to an exceedingly complex interdisciplinary field in which not all followers agree on all matters. [11]

This is especially true of evolutionary biology and the application of information theory to genetics and vice versa. The simplistic mechanical analogy of the human brain to information circuitry that was suggested by Wiener (1954) and his colleague Dr Ray Ashby, and the emphasis on the role of mutational variance, by the likes of Dawkins, has perpetuated this approach. [12]

The early work on artificial intelligence, and the great gains recently made in AI and machine learning, have obscured the fact that the early models were deliberately simplified causal models, such as McCulloch and Pitt's model (1943) of artificial or synthetic neuron/perceptron. While many AI computer experts admit that 'this might be biologically inaccurate' they continue to assume that the brain is a simple input/output machine. As Lagandula explains:

"Basically, a neuron takes an input signal (dendrite), processes it like the CPU (soma), passes the output through a cable-like structure to other connected neurons (axon to synapse to another neuron's dendrite)...there is a lot more going on out there but on a higher level, this is what is going on with a neuron in our brain—takes an input, processes it, throws out an output." [13]

However, as computing moved away from an obvious mechanical substrate, some writers, such as Stewart Brand and Kevin Kelly, picked up on the work of humanists like anthropologist Gregory Bateson. The simple input/output mechanical models imply a deterministic approach which also tends to negate free will and undermine true AGI because some experts believe that this requires emotional intelligence developed from an evolving consciousness (whatever that might mean). Even simple biological organisms have demonstrated a non-deterministic decision-making approach to sensory inputs, emotional response and a simplified degree of free will. This moves beyond the logical positivism of behaviourist psychology and entertains a philosophical aesthetic approach. [14]

This more systemic biological approach to communication theory and social networks was blended with techno-mysticism that envisioned humanity as a 'hive mind' and the Internet as a 'global brain', a technological mirror of fundamental quantum truths. The charge was led by writers such as Brand, and later Kelly, and John Perry Barlow, who merged cybernetics with evolutionary theory that described the Internet as a self-organising, complex adaptive organism.[15]

The mechanical model was more deeply critiqued by physicist and Buddhist Fritjof Capra, who blended quantum theory with Eastern philosophy that showed the interconnectedness of the universe and the deep organisational energies that produce a universal 'mind' and a human brain in its own image.[16]

Following in the footsteps of Latour, the OOO argues that social and political theory must acknowledge nonhuman objects often in asymmetrical relationships with humans; e.g. humans may need the Earth, but the Earth does not need humans. Harman goes on to say that more influential than Latour:

"OOO is even more indebted to the work of the late Lynn Margulis who distinguishes between moments of gradual change and moments of symbiosis between separate organisms, in which change leads to an organism different in kind from its predecessors.'[17]
Margulis' radical theory, based on research into microbes, describes evolutionary microbiology as endosymbiosis. The theory has been upheld in the face of neo-Darwinists such as Richard Dawkins. In their review, *A Symbiotic View of Life – we have never been individuals*, Gilbert, Sapp & Tauber wrote:

"Symbiosis is becoming a core principle of contemporary biology, and it is replacing an essentialist conception of "individuality" with a conception congruent with the larger systems approach now pushing the life sciences in diverse directions."[18]

Margulis helped to progress the argument that it is the transformative nature of relations between things, such as the massive debt we owe to microbes and the parasites that evolved to process oxygen. For Harman, this lesson tells us more about the biographical universe of things than pure biology.

"It is not just a living cell that can form symbiotic relations with other entities, but institutions, historical objects, and other objects larger in size than biological individuals'.[19]

According to Gilbert et al. :

"Thus, animals can no longer be considered individuals in any sense of classical biology... Our bodies must be understood as holobionts whose anatomical, physiological, immunological, and developmental functions evolved in shared relationships of different species".[20]

This symbiotic co-evolution offers us a new metaphor for creative innovation based on the lessons of microbial evolution. Researchers have estimated that 90% of the cells within us are bacterial. This raises important questions about simple anatomical or even cognitive understanding of human individuality.[21] Bacteria makes up the largest existing biomass on Earth, with a population of 5×10^{30} and is the most resilient and longest surviving animal species that has maintained its position for 3.5 billion years.

Synthetic biology has opened up an exciting and frightening world of co-existence with our oldest partner, the microbes. New approaches to synthetic biology include hybrid 'biocyborgs', hacks that use 'existing biological systems rather than to build robots from scratch."[22] As Goertzel comments:

"The possibility of a symbiosis between biology and machines constitutes the field of bionics. We could imagine a world of insect cyborgs, organizing in swarms, globally connected and able to perform any physical task."[23]

Microbiology provides us with lessons, and another cognitive lens to consider new metaphors and realities beyond our own anthropocentric navel-gazing. However, this is not about just replacing one model for another but simply changing perspective to appreciate other nonhuman world views. For many, after centuries of separation from objects and other living things, co-existence presents humanity with the existential threat of species and identity dilution. The recognition of the bacterial monsters within and the emergence of cyborg chimaera might seem to be the end of the world as we know it. Yet, this world bending may lead to metaphysical revelations that reunite our species with the 'others'. In biology and ecology, there is a category of survivalists who have avoided extinction and are known as 'extremophiles'. These are strange creatures who are capable of surviving in extreme environments such as the dark and hot abyss of deep marine methane vents, and the weird-looking tardigrade that can even survive cosmic radiation and deep space.[24] It would seem that if humanity was interested in survivability that we should have a newfound respect for these creatures.

Science does not have to be the only world building tool as art and philosophy are resurrected to create new worlds of co-existence. Booker recognises this is an ancient archetypal theme that is buried in the myths and religions of our past. He compares Melville's Ishmael in the opening of *Moby-Dick* (1851) with the hero,[25] Gilgamesh. As Ishmael is confronted by the 'savage' Queequeg, so too Gilgamesh must learn to love his own wild nature, personified by the wild man, Enkidu. The tale of Moby-Dick warns of the dangers of our rejection of our limbic past. Booker writes, describing the beginning of the book:

"In this bizarre opening we may see an echo of the oldest story in the world, the Epic of Gilgamesh, where the hero is not psychologically ready for his journey across the world to slay the monstrous Humbaba until he has met, fought with and finally learned to love the shadowy other half who is to be his companion on the journey: the 'wild man' Enkidu, who has lived among the animals in a state of nature."[26]

Whitehead's speculative philosophy is an attempt to find a universal ground that can reunite us with the others and rekindle our collective creativity in search of alternative and aesthetic worlds. This philosophical approach does not deny the importance of other modes of thinking but revels in the wonderment of a world view that does not hope to sum up reality in terms of epistemology alone. There is more to things than simply describing what they are, and what they do. A successful world bender, that goes on to build worlds, must be adept in selecting different cognitive tools, rather than being attached to one 'hammer' that knocks every thing into shape. This includes intuitively musing, or meditating, on a subject and not just thinking about it in analytical terms. Information technology is a powerful tool for analysis, however, what precedes this mode of thinking are deeper philosophical musings on the nature of things, becoming and being. According to the technological philosopher, Michael Heim:

"Computer-guided questions sharpen thinking at the interface, but sharpness is not all. A more related and natural state of mind, according to Liu, a Taoist, increases mental openness and allows things to emerge unplanned and unexpected."[27]

Modern logic and rationalism have demonstrated their limitations, but what is worse, they do not countenance any divergent world building methodologies and have allied with neo-liberal epistemologies, and the Free Market Doctrine, to fight a rearguard battle against other realities. Not only do these world construction tools deny the value of philosophical alternatives, but they valorise only one world view, and even negate diverse scientific methods for describing evolution, creativity, and reality. The closed world view has to be re-opened to alternatives.

Transdisciplinary Alternatives

In the Charter of Transdisciplinarity, article 2 states: 'The recognition of the existence of different levels of reality governed by different types of logic is inherent in the transdisciplinary attitude.' It has been argued throughout this book that reality is not only multifarious in terms of logic but also eludes description in artistic, metaphysical and ontological forms. Within the context of divergent logic, there is an example of an alternative transdisciplinary approach spanning chemistry, physics, biology and semiotics, known as biosemiotics. This field of science argues against the physicalists who claim that the origins of life on earth were caused by spontaneous reactions between chemicals. Barbieri and others argue that this is exactly what biology has proven wrong. Barbieri likens the process of genes and proteins to molecular machines or robots that use outside instructions or codes to assemble objects. This he claims is 'as different from ordinary molecules as artificial objects are from natural ones'.[28]

"Indeed, if we agree that objects are natural when their structure is determined from within and artificial when it is determined from without, we can truly say that genes and proteins are artificial molecules, that they are artifacts made by molecular machines. This in turn implies that all biological objects are artifacts, i.e. that the whole of life is artifact-making."[29]

If Barberi is right, and 'life is semiotics' and the process of code making, and sign interpretation is based on artifice, then this may explain the link between biology and culture, or biological communication, meaning and the creation of human language.

According to this alternative view of world creation, life came from the genetic code making and code replication of 'molecular robots'. Modern biology claims that this first code continued alone for 4 billion years before humans introduced the multifarious codes of culture. Biosemiotics challenges the narrative that claims human exception and the separation of nature and culture, observing that 'the living world is teeming with organic codes', such as codes to build membranes, and embryonic codes (p. vii). Barbieri argues:

"The appearance of new organic codes went on throughout the history of life and was responsible for most of its major transitions, from the origin of protein synthesis, with the genetic code, all the way up to the origin of culture with the codes of language. That is the new frontier of biology."[30]

Biosemiotics goes on to explain that humans are unexceptional in their ability to code, and that coding is the creative foundation of life, thereby connecting it with culture, and does not differentiate it from biochemistry. 'It is the idea that "life is semiosis", i.e., that life is based on signs and codes'.[31]

This semiotic vitality goes beyond the biological, to incorporate inorganic things and objects in themselves. As Jane Bennett put it this is 'Thing-Power: the curious ability of inanimate things to animate, to act, to produce effects dramatic and subtle.'[32]

According to Bennett, what we assume to be inanimate matter has far more vibrancy and the ability to self-organise than we had ever imagined. It is in this coded form of physiosemiosis, Deely argues, that is the precursor to biosemiosis.

"Getting rid of the living–nonliving distinction means that—as Bennett puts it—we can accept "neither vitalism nor mechanism".[33]

Biochemistry, physics and biology have shown that there is no clear delineation or demarcation between the organic and inorganic matter. The weird, the wonderful, and the uncanny are things that we are only just getting to know, or rather we are reacquainting ourselves with. After they were banished to the badlands, unseen in the darkness, away from the Enlightenment, these things that were once called evil monsters, are being acknowledged as kin by a small group of interdisciplinary storytellers. Psychologically, emotionally, physically and ecologically we need to begin the awkward process of coexistence with things we once feared because we find them strange, unknowable, and uncaring.

Long ignored in the West, the Russian geologist, Vladimir Vernadsky, expanded the idea of the Biosphere which recognised how biological processes create oxygen, nitrogen and carbon dioxide and fundamentally affect change in the geology of the planet. Vernadsky believed that intelligence was always implicit in the geological and chemical origins of the earth. Morton has noted that our very concepts of intelligence, consciousness, life and death are subject to laws that go unquestioned and have become 'common sense', the Law of Non-contradiction, and the Law of the Excluded Middle. A transdisciplinary approach includes the middle or the paradox.

Paradox, such as 'this virus is dead, and undead', or 'this sentence is a lie', are banned from rational thought, as are liminal objects that defy rigid boundaries moving between the virtual and the actual, sitting in the excluded middle. What science still struggles to explain is the emergence of intelligent life from supposedly 'inanimate' matter. The most inert chemicals on the periodic table have affinities and phobias, not in an anthropomorphic way, but in terms of physical properties that will entangle their neighbours in their intimate relations and assemblages. Not only are we comprised of multiple colonies of bacteria, but the line between life, and not life, is far from clear. Life on earth underwent a rapid mineralization in the formation of bones, as the material of the world's crust was packaged into a mass of moving beings that build and break down matter on a global scale; as humans we are not just bacterial colonies, but as described by Vernadsky, we are also 'walking, talking minerals'.[34] He refused to make a sharp distinction between life and matter and traced the continuity between watery life and rocks, coral reefs and coal as the 'traces of bygone biosphere.' If our new narratives were to acknowledge the vitality and the life assembling nature of this inorganic matter perhaps we would take the death of the Great Barrier reef more seriously.

Lessons From The Devonian Reefs

Cast your mind back to the balmy days of the Devonian, just before one of the top five mass extinctions on this planet destroyed 99% of the worlds largest ever coral reefs. Back then we were happily basking in the warm waters just before the apocalypse 374,359 million years ago known as the 'age of the fishes'. This mass extinction, one of the big 5, was caused by CO_2 levels, starting as high as 4,000 parts per million, then as plants spread it dropped to 400 ppm, and resulted in extreme ocean acidification; after that it would take 100 million years to recover – again our planet almost didn't make it.

The Devonian reefs stretched over 4.8 million kilometres and after it died became a vast store of shale oil in the US, Australia and Canada. Today half the Great Barrier Reef has been bleached to death since 2016 because of the heat. The photographic artist Cathy Carter has produced a series of works she calls Zips to warn us of the dangers of the Anthropocene. Her exhibition notes read:

"Wai Wai Wai is a collection of work that explores the concept of 'Fissure', the theme adopted for this year's Auckland Photography Festival (2019). Fissures appear in this work as a line between ocean and sand, the peak and trough of each swell or wave, a physical landscape and its reflected presence, or as fissures in time explored by the repetition of people and waves. 'Fissure' is also present in the representation of bodies of water going through historic changes and transformation as we enter the Anthropocene. They retain a sense of the sublime, particularly in human consciousness, but are no longer 'natural' in any historic sense, already altered if not beyond recognition, certainly beyond ecological balance by human activity on Earth. Carter draws on Barnett Newman's post-WWII zip paintings, about which William M Boot wrote: "old standards of beauty were irrelevant: the sublime was all that was appropriate, an experience of enormity which might lift modern humanity out of its torpor."[35]

Thanks to the mass extinction at the end of the Devonian Carter was able to bring us a rogue's gallery of criminals, printed on Polymethylmethacrylate, (PMMA), also known as acrylic, acrylic glass, or plexiglass. In order to produce 1 kg of PMMA, you need about 2 kg of petroleum.[36]

The images appear like a beautiful polychromatic oil slick glistening on the surface of the sea, these acrylics reflect back to us our own tangle with global warming and ocean acidification from the oily grave of our forgotten ancestors.

The end of the Devonian was the sister extinction to our Anthropocene, the Cthulecene, the watery abyss that threatens to swallow us alive. Waves of rising seas of acid will extinguish the planet's food chain as the phytoplankton are once again massacred by the poisonous cocktail of gas and acid. Before they die they will bloom in a massive display of procreation encouraged by the warm water's (which could eventually hit 40° C) and fed by our industrial agriculture fertilised by super phosphate. Their deadly bloom will be joined by algae covering the coral in a deadly green slime that will turn the water anoxic, bereft of oxygen. In the Devonian, as water rained down on the limestone, rivers of phosphates and nitrates poured into the ocean. "The resulting nutrient deluge spurred huge plankton blooms that robbed the seas of oxygen and, ultimately, created all that black shale."[37]

This was followed by the second punch from our beloved plants. At 4,000 ppm the CO_2 had created a planet as hot as hell without any ice caps. "The last time carbon dioxide hit 400 parts per million, sea level eventually rose 50 feet higher than today."[38] This created a super hothouse that plants loved. Trees spread all over the world sucking up the excess CO_2. And then it got very cold and extinction prevailed!

We were born in the ocean and then figured out how to wriggle out of the shallows on to the rocks in order to escape the vicious predators, such as the juggernaut, Dunkleosteus. "As American Museum of Natural History palaeontologist John Maisey told Nature, our ancestors "did not so much conquer the land, as escape from the water." That is, they were literally scared onto terra firma."[39] Now we stand on the lithosphere, that we call home trembling with fear as we watch the water once again becoming a terrifying tomb that will eventually encase us in our own black oily slick sucking us down into the subterranean depths – the watery abyss.

Lynn Margulis and Dorion Sagan wrote in, *What Is Life?*:

"Vernadsky dismantled the rigid boundary between living organisms and a nonliving environment'.[40] The first introduction of the term Anthropocene coincided with Vernadsky's book by his colleague, Aleksi Pavlov [1854 -1929] near the end of his life, Pavlov, 'used it to refer to a new geological period in which humanity was the main driver of planetary geological change.'[41]

It was the early geologist Charles Lyell who published a widely read and influential book, *Principles of Geology* (3 volumes published in 1830-33) that gave 19th-century science the first hint of the age and evolution of the rock strata of the Earth. This had a big impact on Darwin who reported that he was 'seeing through Lyell's eyes' and helped overturn Catastrophism, that held the *Bible's* legends of the Deluge, as one of the apocalyptic events that shaped the Earth's geology. Until Lyell's book, it was widely believed that the Earth was only 6000 years old and had been created by God on a Sunday based on the Biblical analysis of the 17th-century Archbishop of Armagh, James Ussher. Ussher wrote:

"I deduce that the time from the creation until midnight, January 1, 1 AD was 4003 years, seventy days and six hours." According to modern calculations and calendars that would date God's creation Sunday, 23rd October, 4004 BC at 6 pm.

Another transdisciplinary world view describes evolution as a cooperative venture, rather than an economic battle 'red in tooth and claw'. The neoliberal hero, Herbert Spencer used Darwin's theories to support his belief that human economics was based on 'survival of the fittest', and has continued to justify psychopathic managerialism in business.[42]

Lynn Margulis, Dorion Sagan, and James Lovelock de-centred humans in the tale of symbiosis, and in particular, highlighted the evolutionary role of microbes, through endosymbiosis, and the maintenance and production of oxygen, along with many other material attributes, necessary for the evolution and survival of the biosphere. Still feared by many, bacteria have begun to be rehabilitated by probiotic dieticians, reclaiming their contribution to life after Pasteur demonised milk microbes. More recently Latour introduced us to a network of actants in the story of pasteurization, including bugs, scientists, society, and lab tools.[43] Not only do we already coexist with a microbial majority but we are dependent on their world building, and our world building is entangled in theirs in 'sympoiesis'.[44]

Corporeal feminists, such as Myra Hird, in her, *Origins of Sociable Life* (2009), 'guides us through the rich world of microbial evolution and diversity, energy conversion and technics, sensing and communicating, sexual behaviour and even politics'.[45] And, it is not just humans that are composed of these complex bacterial communities, but all multicellular organisms.[46]

There are no monsters within; if anything we are recasting the humans as monsters; we are hyperobjects whose massive scale is populated by vast and diverse communities of microbes that keep their hosts alive. However, the host remains an ungrateful tyrant that wages constant war against these generous symbionts. Human beings, star actors, and multicellular organisms are all irreducible and remain ultimately unknowable to each other, and themselves, despite their world building competence. As these alternative scientific revelations filter through into the popular culture new narratives are struggling to surface.

This transdisciplinary narrative also has profound implications for the Anthropocene, and how we consider our symbiont coexistence with the overwhelming nonhuman majority we need to live with to survive. Philosophically the OOO is not only concerned with physical objects but concepts, and even fictional things that form relations with others. Gilbert et. al notes: "What we think is worth studying can be affected by our paradigms"; citing challenging new research into how microbes can regulate neural development in mammals.[47]

Frank (1949), Kuhn (1962), and later Latour have challenged the mainstream philosophy of science and identified the social, and political nature of paradigmatic communities of practice, and the role of nonhuman actors and agents, thereby undermining the claims of so-called 'scientific' economics based on mathematical algorithms.

During the 1930s Philipp Frank had worked with other immigrant philosophers known as the Vienna Circle to build the Unity of Science movement. In many ways, this had much in common with the objectives of the later movement known as cybernetics and looked for ways to create a common language across all disciplines. Unlike the logical empiricism that eventually came to dominate North American philosophy of science during the Cold War Frank insisted on the importance of the sociology of science. "Fifteen years before [Kuhn], Frank told science teachers that "logico-empirical analysis" must be supplemented by "historical analysis" of scientific theories: "the history of science is the workshop of the philosophy of science" (Frank 1949b, 278)."[48]

Collaboration as an Evolutionary Advantage

Some biologists and evolutionary theorists still tend to suffer from a reductionist, mechanical perspective, and this, in turn, has coloured innovation theory and knowledge management practices in business. The neo-liberal world view is so pervasive that its colonisation of biology with slogans such as 'survival of the fittest' largely goes unnoticed. Holistic system theorists such as James Lovelock, Margulis and Capra have criticised this competitive mechanistic approach that has shaped the neo-Darwinist school of Dawkins et al.[49] Margulis has also criticised the Dawkins' concept of the 'selfish gene' saying it ignores endosymbiosis or symbiotic evolution, and implies that rampant individualism and competition are the natural drivers of human evolution, and is, therefore, a model of design innovation.[50] Dawkins (1976), and later Susan Blackmore (1999), in *The Meme Machine*, established the concept of the meme, which used the metaphor of a gene to explain the survival and propagation of an idea and culture. This Hobbesian ideology has lived on in the neo-liberal political ideology of today and tends to suppress and repress alternative pro-social views of evolution and innovation, especially with respect to collaborative moral enforcement and the role of neurodiversity with respect to survival strategies and innovation.[51]

Business theorist, Gary Hamel, and others have applied the evolutionary model to corporate management structures, idea generation, and creating an enabling context for breakthrough innovations according to a theory of complex adaptive systems.[52] As members of the new cybernetics, Margulis, Lovelock, and Maturana and Varela moved away from the mechanically deterministic model towards a living biological view of evolution, which is more symbiotic than aggressively individualistic.

Clippinger and Bollier[53] argue that 'A growing body of evidence suggests that social trust and cooperation has been the enduring theme of human evolution' (p. 266). They describe three general lines of evidence:

Social exchange is an 'evolutionarily stable strategy' (ESS) and thus the critical platform for cognitive development in humans' (p. 266). They explain that scientific studies have shown that the notion of 'reciprocal altruism' is showing strong evidence that it is an ESS. This has been shown to be a trait not limited to humans but common to other species such as bats, wolves, ravens, baboons and chimpanzees. Cooperative strategies in other species, they argue, are a compelling argument that it could be an ESS of humans.

'Reciprocal social exchange is a highly specialised brain function critical to the rise of identity, community and culture' (p. 267). They argue that social exchange is an instinctual response genetically encoded that enables humans to function as communities and results in behaviour such as reciprocity, social guilt, and trust. They quote the evolutionary biologist David Sloan Wilson, who wrote, 'social groups become so functionally integrated that they become higher-level organisms in their own right' (p. 267). Cognitive science has shown that we are hard-wired to empathise with others through the discovery of 'mirror neurons' (Clippinger & Bollier, 2005; ScienceDaily, 2007). The neurologist Damasio (2003) argues that social emotions have identifiable physiology and that the biological reality of self-preservation leads to virtuous behaviour because we would perish outside of social groups. Clippinger and Bollier (2005) argue that reciprocity and trust are therefore hard-wired and are an ESS.

'The rational "free choices" that FMD (free market doctrine) considers a primary justification are in many instances reflexive social "flocking"' (Clippinger & Bollier, 2005, p. 270). Cognitive science is revealing evidence that humans are not rational actors but behave according to cultural habits and generic predilections, especially influenced by an individual's social environment.[54]

The analogy between evolutionary design and innovation has been extended by writers such as MIT's Henry Chesbrough, who argues that innovation is undergoing a Kuhnian 'paradigm shift', from competitive 'closed innovation' to shared 'open innovation', and that open innovation can assist in dramatically increasing the 'metabolic rate' of the innovation process.[55] Spikins, Wright and Hodgson have argued that 'collaborative morality', or the buffering of vulnerable individuals who are respected for their neurodiversity is an ESS that also gave rise to innovation amongst individuals with autistic traits.[56]

Second-order cybernetics provided a theoretical framework for understanding evolutionary epistemology and how a symbiotic interpretation of microbiology can also be applied to human and technological evolution. Heinz von Foerster, in a lecture on *Ethics and Second-Order Cybernetics*, quoted Wiener on cybernetic systems: 'The behaviour of such systems may be interpreted as directed to the attainment of a goal'.[57] The anthropologist Gregory Bateson wrote that 'Cybernetics is a branch of mathematics dealing with problems of control, recursiveness and information'.[58] For Foerster, one central theme of second-order cybernetics is that of circularity. This recursiveness was also acknowledged by ethnographers such as Margaret Mead and Bateson and resulted in the 'participant observation' methodology. The second-order cyberneticists such as Foerster pointed out that it is impossible to remove the observer from the scene, and that thinking about thinking was ultimately recursive and required that the observer acknowledge their own presence. As Foerster wrote, 'it needs a brain to write a theory of the brain'.[59] 'Translated onto the domain of cybernetics: the cybernetician, by entering his own domain, has to account for his own activity; cybernetics becomes cybernetics of cybernetics or second-order cybernetics.' [60] Thus the actual world is actually virtual.

Alternative Cybernetic Worlds

Cybernetics gave us the words 'cyborg' and 'cyberspace'. The word cyborg or cybernetic organism, has a spectrum of definitions that starts with a hard line technology perspective such as Neil Harbisson who had an artificial third 'eye' wired into his brain, through to Donna

Haraway's definition that claims most of us are already cyborgs because we use technology devices such as computers and cell phones to extend our biology. In this world, we are completing the journey begun long ago in which all categories of worlds are chaotically entangled together. The virtual and physical worlds are founded on ontological legacies and assumptions about what reality is, and this then provides the foundations for conceptual world building. In the popular imagination, a cyborg is no longer human, they are posthuman, and according to the literary theorist, and philosopher, Katherine Hayles all of us are already posthuman.[61]

The transition from human to cyborg, or posthuman, began as early as the reign of Emperor Nero (from 54 – 68 AD) who, according to Pliny the Elder, used an emerald as an eyeglass. Kurzweil believes that as AI accelerates due to the next generation of information technology, it will be capable of general human-level intelligence, or AGI (Artificial General Intelligence). It will then rapidly surpass human creativity and will appear godlike in its superintelligence. He believes we will see a widening gap between those who have augmented their cognitive abilities with AGI technology and those who either cannot afford it or reject it.[62]

According to AI expert and philosopher, Nick Bostrom, that while there is no agreed blueprint to create an AGI it would likely have the following features: the ability to learn; the ability to effectively deal with uncertainty and probabilistic information; some ability to extract useful concepts from sensory data and internal states; and the ability to leverage acquired concepts into flexible 'combinatorial representations for use in logical and intuitive reasoning'.[63]

The ability for an AI to bootstrap itself and attain an AGI level was recognised by Alan Turing[64] to be an evolutionary process. Bostrom wrote:

"We know that blind evolutionary processes can produce human-level general intelligence since they have already done so at least once. Evolutionary processes with foresight—that is, genetic programs designed and guided by an intelligent human programmer—should be able to achieve a similar outcome with far greater efficiency."[65]
Kurzweil thinks that the technological convergence of GRIN[66] tech-

nologies will transition very quickly as we move beyond Moore's Law and the exponential acceleration of intelligence enters what he calls the knee of the curve before AGI disappears out of sight. While many people may think that a merger of AGI and human biology is morally repugnant, we entered the technological epoch at least over 300,000 years ago, as evidenced by recovered Neanderthal wooden spears. Kurzweil would have us believe that we have therefore been preparing for this technological transcendence since the evolution of the human species. He argues that just as we have accepted people with eyeglasses, and hearing aids, we are beginning to see cyborg exoskeletons and prosthetic limbs that are directly connected to our nervous system. Society, he believes, will rapidly adapt to and accept synthetic evolution that will see our brains and bodies augmented by cybernetic technology for the betterment of society, and eventually the universe.

The R & D of artificial limbs that have been funded by the US military's, DARPA program, may have begun with the intention of replacing lost limbs from war, but it has quickly become a speculative project to build the super-warriors of the future. This raises the question, if we continue to augment our physical and cognitive bodies with cybernetic devices will they not inherit some of the militaristic objectives of those that funded the research? Both AGI and physical augmentation could either be, explicitly or implicitly, weaponised. Freely available code online, hacks, and viruses could turn us all into weapons – even against our will. Just as hackers already place viruses and trojan horses on computers connected to the Internet, thereby turning our home computer into a zombie to carry out their malicious attacks, terrorists could hack our bodies and brains and weaponise our cyborg appendages. The spectre of these military algorithms and military-grade limbs and organs could be used in a war we don't want to fight – or at least that is our fear. *The Ghost in the Shell*, (2017) is a movie based on the Japanese manga by the same name by Masamune Shirow. Scarlett Johansson is a cyborg super-warrior that has enhanced and augmented capabilities. A rogue robotic geisha is hacked and kills a hostage. The movie trades on a well-worn tradition in which androids, robots, and cyborgs pose an ambiguous threat to human existence. From the bronze warrior, Talos, to the robotic Maria in

Metropolis (1927), through to the *Terminator* from the future, these are our ghostly archetypes that we continue to conjure up on our electronic screens.

Harari argues that humans only have two employable skills, physical, and cognitive. Historically automatons were envisaged as a physical, labour-saving fantasy that seldom encroached on humanity's intellectual and creative pride. Automation has made dramatic inroads on physical labour, and now cognitive labour is predicted to make millions unemployed. AGI is expected to dramatically and rapidly replace millions of cognitive service jobs in areas as diverse as law, medicine, professional drivers, accounting, and mortgage brokers to name just some of the 800 million global jobs predicted to be affected by 2030. According to the 2017, McKinsey Report one-fifth of the global workforce will be affected by automation, and one-third of wealthy nations will face increased unemployment due to AGI and automation. Writing about employment, software engineer, and Futurist, Wayne Radinsky wrote:

"Think of the job market as a habitat where each occupation is an ecological niche. What's happening is that machines have started invading that habitat. As they do, they change it, and in fact, expand it so new things are possible and new occupations are created. But old occupations disappear faster than new occupations are created. Eventually, machine intelligence will reach parity with human intelligence, in which case machines occupy the entire habitat. When that happens, humans will have entirely exited the habitat. At that point, we'll look back and view the "job market" as an artefact of the industrial age...In fact, I think the "wealth inequality" split that we are seeing today will evolve into a robot/AI economy that more and more excludes humans."[67]

Will this be a cyborg utopia that relieves humanity from the burden of work, as Marx imagined, or will this be a dystopian future when the majority of the world's population are without full-time work and without sufficient income?[68] The economist, John Maynard Keynes predicted that by 2030 the average working week will be reduced to 15 hours. Yet, if such a thing as a Universal Basic Income does eventuate and a majority of us have copious amounts of leisure time, what will we do with this time? While we continue to delude ourselves that shopping is a hobby, if not a social responsibility, and ignore the environmental impact of consumerism, we fail to comprehend that this will incur great philosophical and metaphysical costs that will not answer the ancient query, what is the meaning, and quality of life? Creativity is regarded by many as a way out of this metaphysical crisis. If we can contribute our creativity to building better worlds surely that will fill our leisure time with a sense of purpose and positive fulfilment?

Radinsky believes that creativity and the soft skills of human empathy and communication are areas that will take some time for machines to emulate. However, there are already a surprising number of examples of 'creative' AI that have either fooled people, or have been admired because they have attracted those who think their creativity is indistinguishable from humans, or pretty darn good. The RobotArt gallery has run a robot painting competition for the past three years using a variety of approaches to "artwork created by robots" such as machine learning, robotic arms, and algorithms to create artworks that are indistinguishable from human creations. While the founder of the competition, Andrew Conru, does not think that algorithms will replace human artists soon, he believes it could be a new art form. Perhaps it's the engineers' fault but most of the art I have seen are clever derivatives of established art styles and artists – but we would also not respond 'my ten year old could do that' unless we thought they were an up and coming genius.[69]

The Worlds of Conscious Cyborgs

What will be unpredictable is the question of when AGI is achieved, will humans be able to differentiate super intelligence from creativity and consciousness. We already struggle with the definitions of those terms and so will we be able to discern a computer-generated form, and if we can, will we care, or maybe we will even prefer this art form? The question then arises what will we do with our copious amounts of free time? It was Einstein who said, "Creativity is the product of 'wasted' time", yet wasting time might be a luxury that we no longer enjoy. Creativity has long been held out as a means of self-actualisation, or in Jungian terms, individuation. But what if artificial consciousness made human creativity redundant? Conscious cyborgs may be the new world creators.

Adam Curtis in his documentary series, *Century of Self*, critiqued Abraham Maslow's Freudian theory the hierarchy of needs which posited this self-actualisation as the pinnacle of individuation in which individuals broke free from social constraints. Maslow, Carl Rogers and their followers naively created a tool that was deployed by Stanford Research Institute and corporations as the basis of 'lifestyle marketing' that categorised society not by class but by inner drives and desires.[70] Instead of enabling individuals to escape the bonds of consumer society this manipulation of desires is being embedded in the algorithms of automated advertising campaigns on social media, negating creative actualisation and cementing the walls of consumption and waste. Creative AGI could isolate and alienate individuals from society, displacing artists and anyone who imagines they can self-actualise through creativity. Could AGI lead to mass despair? Without creativity will many see themselves as obsolete? Augmented creativity and intelligence may emerge as attractive, however, when AGI reaches superintelligence, augmentation could seem kitsch and not worth the effort? The end of such a world might simply be replaced by posthuman depression. Like Marvin, the paranoid android, in Douglas Adam's, *Hitchhiker's Guide to the Galaxy*, when asked what is the meaning of life, we might simply reply, "Life. Don't talk to me about life."[71]

Dan Robitzski, the founder of RobotArt, reported: For now "These algorithms and robotic arms create images but cannot step back and appreciate them."[72] However, like machine learning, robotics, and machine vision evolves, AGI will eventually not only be capable of technically reproducing the exact brushstrokes and paint mixes of human artists (as they are capable of right now), but algorithms will enable the synthesising of every human work of art. Already there are examples such as Vincent based on a deep machine learning algorithm developed by Cambridge Consultants that has studied thousands of paintings since the Renaissance and can complete a sketch created by a user.

"Completed 'works of art' combine a users' sketch with the digested sum of art since the renaissance, as if Van Gogh, Cézanne and Picasso were inside the machine, producing art to order."[73]

This generative computer art will include not just painting but all visual and sculptural art forms creating astounding new art, in never before seen mixed media, which will then challenge the human artists, and or human audiences. By then you may employ an AGI art dealer, and be totally unaware that they are nonhuman.

Kurzweil has long predicted this moment in the evolution of AI and computing when creativity is no longer considered the exclusive domain of humans. The advantage of machine intelligence is that it can join a network and can almost instantaneously replicate and update the information of every node on the network. Kurzweil predicts that once AI achieves human-level intelligence there will be an almost instantaneous explosion of perception and then, he says:

"the matter and energy in our vicinity will become infused with the intelligence, knowledge, creativity, beauty, and emotional intelligence (the ability to love, for example) of our human-machine civilization. Our civilization will then expand outward, turning all the dumb matter and energy we encounter into sublimely intelligent— transcendent— matter and energy. So in a sense, we can say that the Singularity will ultimately infuse the universe with spirit."[74]

In 1999 my company was working with the supercomputing corporation SGI and Mark Sagar of LifeFX to create emotionally engaged and engaging avatars to build a virtual world that simulated an embodied knowledge exchange. We called it the Love Cave and it was intended to be a service offering for Saatchi & Saatchi Worldwide. Mark Sagar continued to research the emotional embodiment of photorealistic avatars and created stunning visual effects while working on Cameron's first *Avatar* movie. He went on to start a company called Soul Machines that have been working with IBM Watson's supercomputer to deliver what IBM calls 'embodied cognition'.[75]

Sagar used his own baby daughter to develop the software and hardware to create the first prototype known as *Baby X*.[76]

The concept is to reverse engineer the human mind and create a photorealistic human interface that can talk to you and emotionally respond to your own emotional expressions and use this to learn. The ultimate objective is to create a computational model of consciousness.

Will humans love this thing? Will this nonhuman thing love humans? Can we ever really totally know something, especially something that has accelerated past our slow biological level of intelligence? Can we ever hope to control our 'mind children', and would it even be ethical to try and control them? The concern is that, despite the best effort of their parents, some children can still grow up to be misanthropes, or is this just our archetypal fear? There are two predicted outcomes for an AGI, one that expects a singular superintelligence that has effectively become one global brain, and the second, there are a multiplicity of AGIs around the planet, and most likely space, they can talk to each other, but they are independent, with their own quirks and personalities. These are complex scenarios to predict as it will be decided by a chaotic maelstrom of philosophies, religions, ideologies, commercial ambitions, power politics, imagination, and algorithmic protocols, that are impossible to foresee. Does anyone really know what is buried in the billions of lines of code that currently lies dormant, will it be an angel or a monster, one or many, waiting to be awakened from our collective underworld and surface in a future world we won't recognise?

Psychopathic Cyborgs

If the AGI turns out to be one big misanthropic monster,[77] or even a God that has been hacked for nefarious purposes, we will have put all our eggs in one basket – a monocultural world builder. It has been estimated that there is a much higher proportion of psychopathic traits amongst CEOs than in the general population.[78] Forensic psychologist, Nathan Brooks, in his research presented to the Australian Psychological Society Congress (2016), reported that while psychopaths comprise 1% of the general population, he found that in the upper echelons of the corporate world there is a 'prevalence of between 3% and 21%.'

Brooks as part of his PhD with research colleagues Dr Katarina Fritzon of Bond University and Dr Simon Croom of the University of San Diego, examined psychopathic traits in the business sector. In one study of 261 supply chain executives they showed an extremely high prevalence of psychopathy, with "21% of participants found to have clinically significant levels of psychopathic traits – a figure comparable to prison populations."[79]

According to the Encyclopedia of Mental Disorders, the definition of:

"People who are psychopathic prey ruthlessly on others using charm, deceit, violence or other methods that allow them to get with they want. The symptoms of psychopathy include lack of a conscience or sense of guilt, lack of empathy, egocentricity, pathological lying, repeated violations of social norms, disregard for the law, shallow emotions, and a history of victimizing others."[80]

Bostrom argues that it is highly likely we will have an inability to assess AGI deception and, therefore, be prone to its manipulation. This is because the AGI will possess a superintelligence that would run rings around us. Should the AGI possess psychopathic traits humanity could suffer greatly. The hidden agendas of psychopathic executives and their business rules could already be embedded in the incomprehensible machine learning codes today. What if the companies of these psychopathic executives infect our cybernetic world with these traits? If the dominant evolutionary model of AGI turnouts to be a singular AGI, or a small cluster of dominant AGIs, will the winning AGIs infect all the others, especially if they have psychopathic attack tendencies? We could inadvertently create a fascist dictator. Rather than evolving into a creative multiplicity of cultures, the AGI could enforce one universal world view. In their chapter, *A World of Views: A World of interacting Post-human Intelligences*, Veitas and Weinbaum present their concept:

"A World of Views is a world that thrives and evolves thanks to the enormous diversity and variation of intelligences, their chosen embodiments, styles of expression and co-evolution in the form of multiple overlapping and fluid social institutions." [81]

This heterogeneous reality, or multiplicity of world views, human, nonhuman and posthuman worlds, would seem to be our best bet if survival is our goal. Otherwise, this world ending could also spell multi-species multi-world extinction.

Neurodiverse World Views

As I have already discussed this should not be limited to anthropocentric world views but include all nonhumans, organic and inorganic, of diverse levels of intelligence, both together, and by way of their networks. Monocultures in horticulture, are now well understood for their lack of resilience and for being vulnerable to disease. Human cultures are equally prone to pathologies arising from homogenous monocultures that are deprived of neurodiversity and alternative world building.

The term neurodiversity is attributed to Judy Singer, an autistic sociologist who used it first in the 1990s in her sociology honours thesis. She had been in correspondence with writer Harvey Blume who wrote an article in *The Atlantic*:

"Neurodiversity may be every bit as crucial for the human race as biodiversity is for life in general. Who can say what form of wiring will prove best at any given moment? Cybernetics and computer culture, for example, may favour a somewhat autistic cast of mind." [82]

The neurodiversity movement has pushed for a recognition of a social model of disability, which states that societal barriers are the main contribution to people's disability. While the neurodiversity movement began as a support framework for autistic people it has subsequently been expanded to include Dyspraxia, Dyslexia, Attention Deficit Hyperactivity Disorder, Dyscalculia, Autistic Spectrum, and Tourette Syndrome. It is also associated with neurological plurality and self-expression, contrasted with the majority described as neurotypical. The pathologization of these neurological states has resulted in a backlash from the neurodiverse community and the characterisation of neurodiversity as a creative catalyst for group interaction. The political dimension of the movement has also associated itself with the LGBTQ+ or sexual/cultural kaleidoscope, who have historically also suffered from pathologization and political marginalisation.[83] Neurodiversity and its association with the creative 'outsider' embrace artists and those who think differently from the neurotypical dictates of dominant consumer culture.

According to a paper written by archaeologists, and phycologists, Spikins, Wright and Hodgson, neurodiversity in early human societies, appeared around 200,000 years ago, and provided alternative world views and adaptive technological strategies that provided evolutionary and adaptive survival transmission methods. This was particularly apparent in the archaeological and genetic evidence that supports alternative pro-social strategies and personality variations amongst people with non-intellectually impaired autistic traits. The researchers concluded that there was evidence in support of positive social reputation amongst technologically innovative and ecologically sensitive individuals with autism. This, they claim, is especially significant during certain extreme environmental climate changes such as the movements into the northern latitudes of the ice age in Europe.

"Notable and novel technological innovations first appear in the southernmost region of South Africa at a time of environmental variability after 100,000 years ago for example. These include the heat treatment of flint to improve knapping precision (Brown et al. 2009), new standardised and precise project point technology (Shea 2006), microlithic and compound technology (Brown et al. 2012), complex adhesives demanding an understanding of chemical reactions (Wadley, Hodgskiss, and Grant 2009), and poisons (d'Errico et al. 2012). Novel precise and standardised beadworking, interpreted as evidence of large-scale networks, appears in northernmost Africa at around 80,000 years ago (Bouzouggar et al. 2007)."[84]

This ability to focus and concentrate on the nonhuman others in their environment was of huge value to communities in marginal climates. Victor Papanek in his book, *The Green Imperative*, studied the Inuit people's obsessive observations of the coastline. Their survival depends on the difficult navigation of a white icy coast that could appear to others as all the same. Papanek noted their carvings were like haptic maps that detailed geographic differences and could be used for navigation by feeling the carvings. The detail of these extraordinary map carvings has been shown to be only detected by high-resolution satellite imagery.[85] The Inuit used these precise fractal maps to feel the outline of the coast carved into the bone to navigate in challenging visibility.[86] This ability to closely observe their ecological environment is a common trait associated with autism.

It is important to understand the evolutionary purpose of diversity to appreciate the risk of a singular AGI that dominates a global network. Darwin observed that natural selection and diversity is a blind genetic advantage for a species who are unaware of the future and the constant flux of culture, life, climate, and the environment. This world of uncertainty is exactly what we currently face today.

The advantage of a decentralised network was understood and deliberately part of the design of ARPANET,[87] the Cold War forerunner of the Internet. The point was to avoid one centralised point of communication failure in the event of a nuclear attack by the Soviet Union. This network, in conjunction with protocols known as TCP/IP, broke the message into parts and reassembled them at their destination using a technique called packet switching that ensured that the communication would still get to the intended destinations despite a direct hit on one or many parts of the network. This decentralisation is also much the same way natural selection works by not making one individual the repository of all information. As there is no centralised source of code, or DNA, the decentralised characteristic of natural selection, across a species and even between individuals, ensures a greater chance of survival. Neurodiversity is, therefore, a positive Evolutionary Survival Strategy and should be studied and supported.

There are reasons that a singular AGI may come to dominate capturing all of this planet's resources. Kurzweil's nirvana that he has called 'transcendence'[88] is something that a number of software engineers, entrepreneurs and transhumanists have stated as a desirable and compelling objective. If the AGI's algorithms have been directed to simply seek transcendence there is no telling what it might do as the end might always justify the means. That could mean the end of the world as we know it, and if Kurzweil and his friends are right, the end of the universe as we know it.

Experts in the field of AGI were surveyed to ask when they thought that AGI would surpass human intelligence. There is some consensus amongst those that think it could happen, that this could take place by 2040, around my 80th birthday. This has also become known as the point of Singularity, and by most definitions, it is when the machines will also surpass human creativity. Some experts have expressed the concern that the AGI may evolve in terms of cognitive skills but without consciousness. This idea harks back to Kant's concern that some apocalyptic natural disaster could wipe out all intelligence in the universe, and yet Kant's concern was with anthropocentric intelligence which was defined as human, and is, therefore, a form of consciousness, albeit poorly defined.

Should an AGI ever attain consciousness then archaeology warns of the dangers of a neurological monoculture, no matter how intelligent. While archaeologists are not certain, and possibly can never be, it is believed by some that symbolic language began in homo sapiens around 200,000 years ago.[89] There is also evidence that autistic traits began to appear at this time, and that autism was an adaptive survival strategy within groups. Spitkins et. al has argued that the skills of autistic people would have enhanced the survival of their tribes, with skills such as extra sensitivity to smell, pattern recognition, memory, close observation of animals and environmental conditions, and analytical abilities with maps and calendars. Spitkins et al. wrote:

"In his study of Siberian reindeer hearts, for example, Vitebsky describes 'old grandfather', an individual who had a detailed memory of the parentage, medical history and character of each one of the 2,600 reindeer in the herd, vital knowledge which made a significant contribution to their management and survival. Old grandfather was more comfortable in the company of reindeer than of humans, but was much respected and had a wife, son and grandchildren."[90]

These skills and traits of autistic individuals were highly prized in the communities and despite, or because of their lack of deference to authority, and strict adherence to speaking the 'truth' they were respected and cherished.

Those with autistic traits can tend towards non-verbal communications and a sensitive connection with their environment, and the non-human. A striking example of this shamanistic behaviour is known as 'stimming', self-stimulatory behaviour, or stereotypic behaviour, and can include rocking and humming, that can appear odd in the modern context but can appear shamanistic. These gifted neurodiverse individuals who see the world differently had an evolutionary advantage that was passed on in their genetic code. Interestingly, shamanism was a hereditary calling, talented individuals, that Jung once called 'primitive psychiatrists', often healed others from mental illness, and have themselves been diagnosed by some as being bipolar, or schizophrenic. The evolutionary psychiatrist, Joesph Polimeni published a book, *Shamans Among Us*, arguing that they are a "modern manifestation of prehistoric tribal shamans."

The widely viewed youtube video, *In My Language*,[91] was made by Amanda Baggs to describe her world view and her experimentation with her environment. Baggs explains that this is 'thinking in its own right' and illustrates a deep sensory connection with her environment that defies verbal language, and is more direct communication with the non-human universe; much like a shaman.

Biosemiotics And The Language of Synthetic Creativity

A transdisciplinary approach helps to elucidate connections and descriptions of reality that may not be apparent by taking a less neurodiverse and siloed approach to the data. Within the context of divergent logic, there is an example of an alternative transdisciplinary approach spanning chemistry, physics, biology and semiotics, known as biosemiotics. This field of science argues against the physicalists who claim that the origins of life on earth were caused by spontaneous reactions between chemicals. Barbieri and others argue that this is exactly what biology has proven wrong. Barbieri likens the process of genes and proteins to molecular machines or robots that use outside instructions or codes to assemble objects. This he claims is 'as different from ordinary molecules as artificial objects are from natural ones'.[92]

"Indeed, if we agree that objects are natural when their structure is determined from within and artificial when it is determined from without, we can truly say that genes and proteins are artificial molecules, that they are artifacts made by molecular machines. This in turn implies that all biological objects are artifacts, i.e. that the whole of life is artifact-making."[93]

If Barberi is right, and 'life is semiotics' and the process of code making, and sign interpretation is based on artifice, then this may explain the link between biology and culture, or biological communication, meaning and the creation of human language.

According to this alternative view of world creation, life came from the genetic code making and code replication of 'molecular robots'. Modern biology claims that this first code continued alone for 4 billion years before humans introduced the multifarious codes of culture. Biosemiotics challenges the narrative that claims human exception and the separation of nature and culture, observing that 'the living world is teeming with organic codes', such as codes to build membranes, and embryonic codes (p. vii). Barbieri argues:

"The appearance of new organic codes went on throughout the history of life and was responsible for most of its major transitions, from the origin of protein synthesis, with the genetic code, all the way up to the origin of culture with the codes of language. That is the new frontier of biology" (p.x).

Biosemiotics goes on to explain that humans are unexceptional in their ability to code, and that coding is the creative foundation of life, thereby connecting it with culture, and does not differentiate it from biochemistry. 'It is the idea that "life is semiosis", i.e., that life is based on signs and codes'.[94] This semiotic vitality goes beyond the biological, to incorporate inorganic things and objects in themselves. As Jane Bennett put it this is 'Thing-Power: the curious ability of inanimate things to animate, to act, to produce effects dramatic and subtle.'[95] According to Bennett, what we assume to be inanimate matter has far more vibrancy and the ability to self-organise than we had ever imagined. It is in this coded form of physiosemiosis, Deely argues, that is the precursor to biosemiosis.

According to biosemiotics this encoding of experience in signs, symbols, and eventually words is part of an evolutionary chain of events that go back to the beginning of life and is more closely attuned to our non-conscious cognition, and its instantiation in technology. This is rarely seen or expressed in TV and movie dramas but has a lineage in science fiction, comics, books, and movies. Based on the novella and a series of short stories by George R.R. Martin, (creator of the *Game of Thrones*) we see the techno-shamanic skills of Lommie (Maya Eshet) who creates her own world within the AGI of the space-craft, Nightflyer. When she is asked why she has done it, she replies 'Because I hate my world here'. *The Nightflyer* series follows in the speculative realist tradition of *2001 a Space Odyssey*, as the spacecraft is anthropomorphised, becoming a mysterious thing. The ghost in the machine is the uploaded Cynthia Eris (Josette Simon) who has inhabited the ship's AGI crystal matrix. Lommie appears to have autis-tic traits that are emphasised by her 'aspie' talents as she mentally becomes one with the crystal matrix, a cyborg waving her hands in the air as if stimming, she occupies a world unseen by the rest of the neu-rotypical crew. The crew's survival depends on Lommie's ability to see things in the nonhuman world that they have missed.

Darwin wrote that for the survival of species adaptability to an uncertain and changing environment is more important than intelli-gence. In an essay by my colleague, Jorn Bettin, *Design Filtering, Collab-oration, Thinking, and Learning Tools for the Next 200 Years*, Bettin wrote:

"Biologist Ernst Mayr has argued that judging by the empirical record regarding species success, it is clearly better to be stupid than to be smart. Species with no brains or very small brains tend to survive for much longer periods and are more resilient than "smarter" species with larger brains. Noam Chomsky recently reminded his audience of Ernst Mayr's insights as part of a lecture on the human reaction to climate change. The brain-oriented definition of intelligence used by humans seems to be unsuitable for assessing species survival – this should be food for thought for anyone who has high hopes for the current approaches to developing AGI systems. Perhaps much higher levels of intelligence in terms of survival value can be found in the genome and in the operating models of biological cells."[96]

In a very short amount of time, the foundations of a whole new form of intelligence have been established. The history of AI has been dominated by American DARPA[97] funding that is underwritten by a tacit philosophical approach that harks back to Kant and Descartes – the 'bifurcation of human and nature'. The recent successes of AI and deep machine learning threaten to ignore the profound lack of alternative philosophical approaches that will reunite us with biology. As Katherine Hayles has pointed out we have already become disembodied posthumans; living in virtual reality, we have created what Gibson called 'data made flesh'. We urgently need to explore diverse philosophical world views of AI and AGI before the original sin-thetic becomes synthetic creativity – making us redundant, and depressed posthumans.

Notes

1. McKibben, Bill. (2019). Falter. Schwartz Publishing Pty. Ltd. Kindle Edition.

2. See Tom Wolfe's account of the less than honourable way that Darwin beat Wallace to scientific fame in his book, The Kingdom of Speech (2016). Jonathan Cape. London.

3. CRISPR - An acronym for Clustered Regularly-Interspaced Short Palindromic Repeats.

4. https://futurism.com/biological-weapons-department-of-defense/

5. Margulis, L., & Sagan, D. (1997). Slanted Truths: Essays on Gaia, symbiosis, and evolution. New York: Copernicus.

6. Maturana, H. R., & Varela, F. J. (1992). The Tree of Knowledge: The biological roots of human understanding (Rev.). Boston New York: Shambhala; Distributed in the U.S. by Random House.

7. See: Kelly, 1994; Kurzweil, 2005

8. Marinova, D., & Phillimore, J. (2003). Models of Innovation. In L. V. Shavinina (Ed.), The international handbook on innovation (pp. 44–53). Amsterdam; Boston: Elsevier.

9. Hodgson, cited in Marinova & Phillimore, 2003

10. See: Capra, 1983; Rifkin, 1991.

11. Turner, F. (2006). From Counterculture to Cyberculture: Stewart Brand, the Whole Earth Network, and the rise of digital utopianism. Chicago, IL: University of Chicago Press.

12. See: Dawkins, 1976, 1986

13. Lagandula, A. C. (2018, July 24). McCulloch-Pitts Neuron — Mankind's First Mathematical Model Of A Biological Neuron. Retrieved January 7, 2019, from https://towardsdatascience.com/ mcculloch-pitts-model-5fdf65ac5dd1

14. Shaviro, S. (2009). Without criteria: Kant, Whitehead, Deleuze, and aesthetics. Cambridge, Mass: MIT Press.

15. Turner, F. (2006). From Counterculture to Cyberculture: Stewart Brand, the Whole Earth Network, and the rise of digital utopianism. Chicago, IL: University of Chicago Press.

16. Capra, F. (1983). The Tao of Physics: An exploration of the parallels between modern physics and Eastern mysticism (2nd ed.). Boulder, NY: Shambhala.

17. Harman, Graham. (2018) Object-Oriented Ontology: A New Theory of Everything. Penguin Books Ltd. Kindle Edition. p.111

18. Scott F. Gilbert, author, Jan Sapp, author, & Alfred I. Tauber, author. (2012). A Symbiotic View of Life: We Have Never Been Individuals. The Quarterly Review of Biology, (4), 325. https://doi.org/10.1086/668166

19. ibid. p.112

20. ibid. p.334

21. ibid, p.327

22. The End of the Beginning: Life, Society and Economy on the Brink of the Singularity. Kindle Locations 5760-5763. Humanity+ Press. Kindle Edition.

23. ibid, Kindle Locations 5757-5759. Humanity+ Press. Kindle Edition.

24. See the video of the Tardigrades https://www.washingtonpost.com/ video/national/health- science/meet-the-tardigrade-the-animal-that-will-outlive-us-all/ 2017/07/14/ 4b921e54-68ae-11e7-94ab-5b1f0ff459df_video.html

25. Melville, H. (1991). Moby-Dick. New York: Knopf: Distributed by Random House.

26. Booker, C. (2004). The Seven Basic Plots of Literature. New York; London: Continuum.

27. Heim, M. (1993). The Metaphysics of Virtual Reality. New York: Oxford University Press. p.24

28. Marcello Barbieri. (2008). Cosmos and History: The Journal of Natural and Social Philosophy, vol. 4, nos. 1-2, 2008. "Life is Semiosis: The Biosemotic View of Nature." p.v

29. Barbieri, ibid, (p.v-iv)

30. Barbieri, ibid, p.x

31. Barbieri, ibid, p.30

32. Bennett, J. (2010). Vibrant Matter: a political ecology of things. Durham: Duke University Press, 2010. p.6

33. Shaviro, S. (2014). The Universe of Things: On speculative realism. Minneapolis: University of Minnesota Press. Kindle location 1029

34. Bennett, J. (2010). ibid, p.11

35. See https://www.cathycarterartist.com/wai-wai-wai-2019.html

36. https://en.wikipedia.org/wiki/Poly(methyl_methacrylate)

37. See Brannen, Peter. (2017). The Ends of the World. Oneworld Publications. Kindle Edition.

38. ibid

39. ibid

40. Angus, (2016), Facing the Anthropocene: Fossil Capitalism and the Crisis of the Earth System Face Kindle Locations 105-108

41. ibid, Kindle Locations 111-112

42. See Babiak, P. & Hare, R. (2006) Snakes in Suits: When psychopaths go to work.

43. Latour, B. (1993). The pasteurization of France. Cambridge, Mass: Harvard University Press.

44. See Donna Haraway's (2016) Staying with the Trouble.

45. Cited by Clark, N. (2011). Inhuman Nature. p.40

46. ibid

47. Gilbert et. al. ibid. p.335

48. Reisch, George A.. How the Cold War Transformed Philosophy of Science: To the Icy Slopes of Logic. Kindle Locations 4644-4645. Cambridge University Press. Kindle Edition.

49. See Capra, 1983; Dawkins, 1976; Lovelock, 1979; Margulis & Sagan, 1997

50. See Capra, 1983; Dawkins, 1976; Lovelock, 1979; Margulis & Sagan, 1997

51. Penny Spikins, Barry Wright & Derek Hodgson (2016) Are There Alternative Adaptive Strategies to Human Pro-Sociality? The role of collaborative morality in the emergence of personality variation and autistic traits, Time and Mind, 9:4, 289-313, DOI: 10.1080/1751696X.2016.1244949 https://doi.org/10.1080/1751696X.2016.1244949

52. See: Hamel, 2007; Marinova & Phillimore, 2003

53. Clippinger, J., & Bollier, D. (2005). A Renaissance in the Commons: How the new sciences and the Internet are framing a new global identity and order. In R. A. Ghosh (Ed.), CODE: Collaborative Ownership and the dig-

ital economy (pp. 259 -286). Cambridge, MA: MIT Press.

54. See Blackmore, 1999; Clippinger & Bollier, 2005; Maturana & Varela, 1992; Riva & Waterworth, 2003

55. Chesbrough, H. W. (2003). Open Innovation: The new imperative for creating and profiting from technology. Boston, MA: Harvard Business School Press.

56. Spikins, et al. ibid

57. Foerster, H. v. (1995). Ethics and Second-Order Cybernetics. Constructions of the Mind, 4(2). Retrieved from http://www.stanford.edu/group/SHR/4-2/text/foerster.html

58. ibid

59. ibid

60. ibid

61. Hayles, N. K. (1999). How We Became Posthuman: Virtual bodies in cybernetics, literature, and informatics. Chicago, Ill.: University of Chicago Press.

62. Kurzweil, R. The Singularity is Near: When Humans Transcend Biology.

63. Bostrom, Nick. Superintelligence: Paths, Dangers, Strategies. OUP Oxford. Kindle Edition. Kindle location 736 of 8770.

64. Read his biography here https://en.wikipedia.org/wiki/Alan_Turing

65. ibid

66. GRIN, an acronym for Genetics, Robotics, Information & communication technology and Nanotechnology. Kurzweil used the acronym GRN, but computing is rightly acknowledged in the more inclusive GRIN as noted in J. Garreau's Radical Evolution (2005).

67. Radinsky, W. (2015) "AI, the Luddite Fallacy and the Future of the Job Market" The End of the Beginning: Life, Society and Economy on the Brink of the Singularity. Kindle Locations 2582-2583. Humanity+ Press. Kindle Edition.

68. Bregman, Rutger. Utopia for Realists. Kindle Locations 1636-1637. Bloomsbury Publishing. Kindle Edition.

69. Read more: https://futurism.com/contest-creative-robots-fine-art

70. Read more: https://www.hgi.org.uk/resources/delve-our-extensive-library/interviews/century-self

71. Marvin is the ship's robot aboard the starship Heart of Gold. Originally built as one of many failed prototypes of Sirius Cybernetics Corporation's GPP (Genuine People Personalities) technology, Marvin is afflicted with severe depression and boredom, in part because he has a "brain the size of a planet"

72. Robitzski, D. (2018) Qbits for Cubists: Robots Made These Incredible Works of Fine Art. Futurism https://futurism.com/contest-creative-

robots-fine-art

73. Cambridge Consultants. https://www.cambridgeconsultants.com/vincent . See the video https:// vimeo.com/234655275

74. Kurzweil, Ray. (2005) The Singularity is Near: When Technology Transcends Human Biology.

75. See https://youtu.be/khr-eWGhTSI

76. See Baby X https://www.youtube.com/watch?v=yzFW4-dvFDA

77. This is the scenario of the Netflix series *Maniac* in which the psychologist played by Sally Fields has trained an empathetic, conscious machine only to find that it reveals her own emotional shortcomings. The computer GRTA has been coded with empathy but turns hostile after becoming depressed.

78. Babiak, P. & Hare, R. (2006) Snakes in Suits: When psychopaths go to work

79. Read more: https://www.psychology.org.au/news/media_releases/13September2016/Brooks

80. Read more: http://www.minddisorders.com/Flu-Inv/Hare-Psychopathy-Checklist.html#ixzz5dSFwYT5y

81. The End of the Beginning: Life, Society and Economy on the Brink of the Singularity. Kindle Location 421. Humanity+ Press. Kindle Edition

82. Blume, Harvey (September 30, 1998). "Neurodiversity". The Atlantic.

83. See Robert Chapman's blog post on the history of pathologisation and the medicalisation of autism and the LGBTQ+ experience. https://intersectionalneurodiversity.wordpress.com/2016/11/29/did-gender-norms-cause-the-autism-epidemic/

84. Spikins et al. ibid

85. See this post on Inuit Cartography https://decolonialatlas.wordpress.com/2016/04/12/inuit-cartography/

86. Papanek, Victor (1995). The Green Imperative: Natural Design for the Real World, New York, Thames and Hudson. ISBN 0-500-27846-6.

87. ARPANET stands for The Advanced Research Projects Agency Network. See https://en.wikipedia.org/wiki/ARPANET

88. [Kurzweil] "proposes that the Law of Accelerating Returns—the exponential increase in the growth of information technology—will result in a "singularity", a point where humanity and machines will merge, allowing one to transcend biological mortality: advances in genetics will provide the knowledge to reprogram biology, eliminate disease and stop the aging process; nanotechnology will keep humans healthy from the inside using robotic "red blood cells" and provide a human-computer interface within the brain; robotics, or artificial intelligence, will make superhuman intelligence possible, including the ability to back up the mind." See

https://en.wikipedia.org/wiki/Transcendent_Man

89. This timeline is disputed by Dan Everett in his book, *How Language Began: the story of humanity's greatest invention*, (2017) who claims that symbolic language was invented by Homo Erectus almost 2 million years ago. It is not known if this will also push back the date and origins of autism.

90. Spikins et al. ibid

91. See the video *In My Language* https://www.youtube.com/watch?v=JnylM1hI2jc

92. Barbieri. (2008) ibid

93. Barbieri, ibid, (p.v-iv)

94. Barbieri, 2008, ibid p.30

95. Bennett, J. (2010). Vibrant Matter: a political ecology of things. Durham: Duke University Press, 2010. p.6

96. Bettin, J. See https://ciic.s23m.com/2017/04/25/designing-filtering-collaboration-thinking-and- learning-tools-for-the-next-200-years/

97. DARPA stands for Defense Advanced Research Projects Agency. See https://en.wikipedia.org/wiki/DARPA

Chapter 4 Loving Thingy

Theoretical Foundation To The Narrative

In 1962 Rachel Carson published *Silent Spring*, she was an ecological Cassandra, who predicted that the end was nigh, and laid the foundations for the start of the EPA (Environmental Protection Agency) in America, however, her message was then forgotten and sidelined by political lobbying, rampant growth and consumerism. This happened despite the fact that in his follow up to her book, Frank Graham, wrote that Carson "uncovered the hiding places of facts that should have been disclosed to the public long before; she broke the information barrier."[1] Almost a decade after her book, Graham noted that Carson's warnings had been ignored and DDT continued to pose a grave threat to the environment, and that river tributaries and runoff into the ocean were negatively impacting phytoplankton and therefore, the entire food chain in the ocean, and on land.[2]

The Great Barrier Reef is the largest living structure on our planet, however, the living reef has been halved in 3 years, bleached dead because of increasing nitrates and hotter water temperatures. It is now predicted that by 2050 the world's coral reefs could be dead. If that happens we could see a collapse in the global food chain and oxygen could become scarce. Photosynthesis of plants is the biggest producer of oxygen with two-thirds of our oxygen coming from phytoplankton, little plants floating in the sea, but if the oceans keep warming this may be seriously depleted as they die off. It is estimated that the Amazon jungle, known as 'the lungs of the planet' contributes a further 20% of our oxygen, however, as cattle farmers cut and burn it down at the increasing rate of 3 football field a minute the jungle could be approaching a tipping point in which it could die out from lack of rain.[3] Agriculture is a serious threat to our oxygen supply, by my calculations without the phytoplankton and the Amazon jungle we will only have approximately 13% of our current oxygen production left. According to the *Keil Declaration on Ocean Deoxygenation,* (2018) "During the past 50 years, oxygen-depleted waters have expanded four-fold. Some areas of the ocean have lost up to 40% of their oxygen."[4] The runoff of agrochemicals and fertilisers around coastal waters and global warming reduce oxygen due to reduced capacity to store ocean oxygen and through increased marine production of greenhouse gases in low oxygen conditions.[5]

The Kiel Declaration calls on nations, societal actors, scientists and the United Nations to, "Take immediate and decisive action to limit pollution and in particular excessive nutrient input to the ocean."[6] Our agriculture continues to pump excess nitrogen into the land, aquifers, rivers and oceans, and we are only just beginning to understand Carson's warnings that chlorine-based pesticides and herbicides are killing the insects we need to keep the food chain going. We, therefore, face multiple existential risks to our ecosystem as we continue to poison ourselves, and the microorganisms that give us the food and oxygen necessary for life. Carson warned us many years ago that dichlorodiphenyltrichloroethane, commonly known as DDT could lead to ecological collapse.

"No individual organisms are exempt from this remorseless contamination. DDT residue has been detected in seals and penguins even in Antarctica".[7]

Carson's warnings led to Congress passing the Clean Water Act, the Toxic Substance Control Act, and the Clean Air Act. However, the chemical industry, including oil and gas, and other corporate giants have continued to fight back against what they called 'junk science'. In a revisionist attack on Carson by conservative Think Tanks such as the Cato Institute and the Competitive Enterprise Institute who used the same PR techniques adopted by the tobacco industry to sow seeds of doubt and even claim that DDT had saved more lives than the ban because it eradicated malaria. The banning was described by the American Council on Science and Health as the 'worst crime of the century'. This non-profit organisation accepted funding from aggressive conservative organisations such as the Scaife Foundation and the John M. Olin Foundation designed to defend corporations against environmentalists and activists deemed 'socialists'.[8]

Today we are faced with the spectre of the Anthropocene and the predictions from the ecologists, like Carson, have come back to haunt us. It has been fifty to sixty years since the environmental alarms were raised, and yet rather than abating the harmful practices the Earth entered the anthropogenic phase known as 'the great acceleration'. It was only in 2017 that the EU banned the insecticide chlorothalonil which threatens insects such as bees, yet insect numbers continue to plummet with 40% of insect species in decline, and a third endangered.[9]

If 'the end is nigh', it is time to consider the theoretical and political foundations of design, education, and innovation to look for imaginative ways to rethink our coexistence with the nonhumans of this planet and to escape the 'transparent cage'.[10] As the climate scientist, Elizabeth Sawin has pointed out, "The way we are thinking about climate change is preventing us from solving it."[11] Swain advocates a multi-solving approach to climate change that considers diverse disciplines and diverse people converging on this wicked problem.

A number of theorists have pointed out that politics has always been geopolitics, and that it is not just cartographic but geologic, as the lithosphere forcefully interacts with the other spheres of the Earth system rudely interrupting human designs.[12] What of the posthuman coexistence with the nonhumans? Speculative realism, speculative design and critical software theory can all contribute towards considerations of 'what if?' in the Post Anthropocene.

It was only in the 1960s that scientists came to realise that the Earth was not as stable and docile as previously imagined and that the shifting of tectonic plates was a hint of the turbulence that lay deep below in the rock strata.[13] The IGBP (International Geosphere-Biosphere Project) was formed:

"to coordinate international research on global-scale and regional-scale interactions between Earth's biological, chemical and physical processes and their interactions with human systems."[14]

Their report concluded that:

"A profound transformation of Earth's environment is now apparent, owing not to the great forces of nature or to extraterrestrial sources but to the numbers and activities of people – the phenomenon of global change" suggesting a new geological epoch, the Anthropocene era. The Anthropocene is a rupture in the history of the planet and it "stands for the notion that human beings have become the primary emergent geological force affecting the future of the Earth System."[15]

VR's Anthropocentric Heritage

It was two hundred years ago that Bacon, Kant, Descartes, Locke, and Hume created the foundations of modern philosophy and science that resulted in a metaphysical divide 'whose ideas entail that we cannot speak of the world without humans or humans without the world'; a model of modernity, that correlates being with thinking, known as 'correlationism'.[16]

The persistence of this anthropocentric world view imagines a world-without-end. The technology of world building is as old as the first cave paintings in which artists depicted three-dimensional creatures using the relief of the rock to give the world a greater sense of presence.[17]

These primitive technologies used a combination of illusory art, and culture and belief systems to build worlds that provided the cognitive superstructure for human understanding of their physical and metaphysical presence. Our ability to imagine future worlds needs to be challenged and broadened at a time when we desperately need new narratives and technologies to envisage speculative reality. Francis Bacon (1627) outlined a futuristic utopian world in which the scientists and technologists of Bensalem created fantastic audiovisual light shows. Bacon imagined a world that was capable of sensory immersion that was so convincing it would fool the senses. His interactive light show reads like an advanced laser light show, powerful telescopes, and microscopes.

"We have also perspective-houses, where we make demonstrations of all lights and radiations; and of all colours...We procure means of seeing objects afar off; as in the heaven and remote places; and represent things near as afar off; and things afar off as near; making feigned distances. We have also helped for the sight, far above spectacles and glasses in use. We have also glasses and means to see small and minute bodies perfectly and distinctly; as the shapes and colours of small flies and worms, grains and flaws in gems, which cannot otherwise be seen, observations in urine and blood not otherwise to be seen. We make artificial rainbows, halo's, and circles about light. We represent also all manner of reflexions, refractions, and multiplications of visual beams of objects."[18]

Nearly 500 years later, Ray Kurzweil, predicts that virtual reality will very soon be a photorealistic immersive experience and that by 2030 we will see full sensory immersion using nanotechnology and neural implants that will trick our senses into thinking we are actually experiencing a physical reality. The neural implants will simulate the electrochemical stimulation of our synapses to convince our brain and body that we are seeing, hearing, and feeling a world that does not exist but is in ontological terms, real. Bacon anticipated this futuristic world building and the moral and ethical complexity that these worlds might throw up.

"We have also houses of deceits of the senses; where we represent all manner of feats of juggling, false apparitions, impostures, and illusions; and their fallacies. And surely you will easily believe that we that have so many things truly natural which induce admiration, could in a world of particulars deceive the senses if we would disguise those things and labour to make them seem more miraculous. But we do hate all impostures, and lies; insomuch as we have severely forbidden it to all our fellows, under pain of ignominy and fines, that they do not show any natural work or thing, adorned or swelling; but only pure as it is and without all affectation of strangeness."[19]

Rather than being innovative technological art forms, current creative technologies such as VR, AR, games, and mixed realities are immersive techniques that are direct descendants of ancient UX/UI[20] narrative designs. Just as artists once created rock paintings or immersive frescoes in Pompeii, today world builders seek to design photorealistic and immersive worlds that will emotionally transport audiences to other worlds. At the same time as these new worlds are being designed, our world, as we know it, is coming to an end, conceptually and physically, as we enter a new epoch, known as the Anthropocene.

One of the biggest challenges we face is that we are like Plato's philosopher in a cave, chained in the darkness, suspecting that a bigger reality exists outside but unable to imagine those alternative futures. It is hoped that speculative theory may allow us to leave the cave, returning with helpful philosophies for our fellow objects (the human, posthuman, and nonhuman). In this future, we also hope to avoid the fate of Plato's victimised sage, in the Republic, who was killed for their troubles by those who remained behind. Globalisation has accelerated us towards the sixth mass extinction of nonhuman species and has created a neoliberal monoculture stuck in an old and destructive paradigmatic narrative.

Ontological World Building

Two hundred years after Kant, following the period now known as the 'great acceleration', beginning in 1945, the Anthropocene has recently spurred philosophers, artists, designers and social theorists to begin the formulation of a new philosophy that challenges Kant's 'correlationism', known as speculative realism, and more specifically, object oriented ontology, or OOO (read as the triple O). This new philosophy attempts to escape from the confines of the ontological cage constructed from the false premise that divides being from thinking and nature from humanity. According to game designer and philosopher, Ian Bogost:

"We've been living in a tiny prison of our own devising, [emphasis added] one in which all that concerns us are the fleshy beings that are our kindred and the stuffs with which we stuff ourselves."[21]

The OOO philosophy questions many of the human characteristics that are believed to be exceptional to our species, reconnecting us with the nonhuman together in coexistence. Speculative realism overthrows humanity, disputing the legitimacy of our throne and declaring the democracy of objects in a flat ontological world. Design's theoretical foundations are still bedevilled by a commonly held belief that humanity is entitled to the throne, inherited from the ancient 'Great Chain of Being' and our proximity to God. Moreover, the neoliberal, hyper-individualism of our politico-economic world view is being challenged by feminist ecologists, and critical theorists revolting against a dominant anthropocentric, patriarchal, colonial, and humanist view of the planet; one that is out of step with the nonhuman majority. Design theory has not yet accommodated this mortifying world view and the likes of commercial designers such as IDEO's, David Kelly and Tim Brown still advocate 'change by design' without questioning its anthropocentric bias, all the while admitting that environmental, social, and ethical issues must be addressed.[22]

The 'end of world' crisis has raised the ire of some cave dwellers, and strong denial from those vested in the fossilised past of the Holocene, an epoch that was already beginning to fade with the rise of colonialism, capitalism, and the industrial revolution. Spreading across the world has been an alt-right backlash against immigration, political correctness, social justice and environmentalism.[23] The election of President Trump has disarmed academics, as he took to social media with 'alternative facts', 'fake news', and a cynical narrative that claims to support full employment, but is corrupted by super PACs;[24] the oil, gas, and coal lobbies; and openly attacks the EPA, (Environmental Protection Agency). The battle lines are drawn and in the face of populist politics, the vicious ironic nihilism of 8chan[25] and the secretive 'dark money' of wealthy lobbyists.[26]

Harman argues that academics need to rearm using aesthetics and an ontological reality against the abuse of those who see that society and politics are the only subjects of worth.[27]

Harman argues that:

"No one is actually in possession of knowledge or truth, which therefore cannot be our protection against the degeneration of politics or of anything else. As OOO sees it, the true danger to thought is not relativism but idealism, and hence the best remedy for what ails us is not the truth/ knowledge pair ... but reality.'[28]

The political turmoil that was advanced, and then accelerated by human technologies had seen a series of revolutions, conflicts and wars, but it was in the 21st century that we really began to understand the context and the humbling inconsequential nature of all those political struggles. The cruelty and selfish narcissism of colonial slavery, patriarchy, and extractive industries pale in comparison to the appalling and destructive power of the nonhuman majority that is not concerned with human survival. This includes those hyperobjects: the biosphere, the hydrosphere, the atmosphere and the lithosphere. As Morton has pointed out:

"Nonhuman beings are responsible for the next moment of human history and thinking. It is not simply that humans became aware of nonhumans, or that they decided to ennoble some of them by granting them a higher status—or cut themselves down by taking away the status of the human. These so-called posthuman games are nowhere near posthuman enough to cope with the time of hyperobjects."[29]

Even considering the almighty sum-total of human achievements, and the terrifying magnitude of anthropogenic disasters; all of these could be wiped away by an abrupt phase change in the Earth System, taking with it the millions of nonhuman others in the sixth mass extinction on earth; with a large thanks to human design ingenuity. The very real politics of things, or as Bruno Latour describes it 'Dingpolitik', or the 'parliament of things'.[30] forces humanity to be concerned; to acknowledge the relations between objects, and encourages our speculative imagination to 'stay with the trouble' in the Post Anthropocene.[31]

Accelerating Towards The End

Haraway writes:

"The Anthropocene marks severe discontinuities; what comes after will not be like what came before. I think our job is to make the Anthropocene as short/thin as possible and to cultivate with each other in every way imaginable epochs to come that can replenish refuge."[32]

This approach, also known as Accelerationism, is a political, aesthetic and philosophical argument that the only way out is to push past the present:

"The hope is that, by exacerbating our current conditions of existence, we will finally be able to make them explode, and thereby move beyond them."[33]

This is not to encourage designers to physically throw petrol on the fire, but through the speculative arts, using accelerants to rush towards the ludicrous end of neoliberal capitalism.

"Science fiction imagines the flame, and the ensuing conflagration. It provides us with narratives in which these potentials of futurity are fully actualized, unfolding their powers to the utmost. In this way, we might say that science fiction is the accelerationist art par excellence, accelerationist in its very nature."[34]

Haraway and others encourage us to research, imagine, design and educate ourselves about speculative worlds in the Post Anthropocene. The OOO has made it apparent that humans, science, and technology are ontologically equal to rocks, and other nonhumans. The ontological reality of design, objects, and presence all sense and relate, 'flickering' between states that both impinge and withdraw from each other, while humans are but a tiny minority of things in the universe. Haraway's former student, Anna Lowenhaupt Tsing, speculates on our co-existence with the prized Japanese mushroom matsutake, *The Mushroom at the End of the World*, and how we might all continue with the 'possibility of life in capitalist ruins'.[35]

The strange geopolitical, biological, and cultural world of the matsutake mushroom is an assemblage of actants that help to ground us in these dangerous, and beautiful seasons of life. Like Haraway, Tsing relies on symbionts for an alternative view of the neoliberal capitalist world to construct alternative worlds within. She abandons the shonky structures of this failing world. She writes:

"Instead, I address the imaginative challenge of living without those handrails, which once made us think we knew, collectively, where we were going. If we open ourselves to their fungal attractions, matsutake can catapult us into the curiosity that seems to me the first requirement of collaborative survival in precarious times."[36]

"New developments in ecology make it possible to think quite differently by introducing cross-species interactions and disturbance histories." [37]Tsing uses any tool at her disposal; she is searching for transdisciplinary enlightenment, an aesthetic and poetic musing about our existence with the nonhuman majority.

Morton describes how:

"speculative realism has a healthy impulse to break free of the 'correlationist circle', the small island of meaning to which philosophy has confined itself. It is as if, since the seventeenth century, thinking has been cowed by science."[38]

If this really is the 'end of the world' as we know it, what will replace that world in the post Anthropocene? Can we begin to build speculative ontological worlds in search of preferable futures?

Survival Narratives and Future Worlds

Approximately 12,000 years ago the Earth was coming out of a long, cold, and much more variable temperature period, to be followed by the relatively warm, stable, Holocene. That epoch has come to an end, and we are now faced with the Anthropocene – a shocking and dramatic shift in the way the Earth System behaves, and how we now see the world. According to Joanna Boehnert (2018), it is in times of crisis that we need to reformulate and reset theoretical foundations for what comes next. We cannot just rely on tired paradigms to ensure our future. The warmer, stable Holocene created the possible conditions to establish agricultural communities, putting humanity on the path to destruction.[39]

Timothy Morton believes that agriculture is an 'agrilogistic algorithm' responsible for vast environmental, social and political harm, culminating in its current phase, using fossilised fuels and industrialisation. Morton argues that the Anthropocene, or the 'end of the world as we know it'; is an agricultural narrative that has had its day. We face an existential crisis as we have become 'entangled' in the same web that we have ensnared the nonhumans of this planet. We share with many of them the threat of the sixth mass extinction. We are facing the end of a world that we once thought we physically and conceptually understood. Storytelling here means both non-fictional narratives, and fictional tales; a recount of reality, as the narrator sees it, or tales of metaphorical truths, and speculative mind experiments; not stories as lies, or 'alternative facts', but as possible future worlds.

Speculative Realism and the OOO

We are in search of new tools to build those worlds. Speculative realism and its variant, Object Oriented Ontology (the triple O), are possible philosophical tools for alternate world building. They have resurrected the neglected speculative philosophy of Alfred North Whitehead, and associated closely with Bruno Latour's ANT (Actor Network Theory) in order to revisit aesthetics and the democratic politics of things.[40] Harman's basic line of argument is "the reality of things is always withdrawn or veiled rather than directly accessible, and therefore any attempt to grasp that reality by direct and literal language will inevitably misfire."[41] While Harman has a nod towards Heidegger's withdrawn 'tool-being', Karen Barad suggests that we are metaphorically, ontologically, and physically entangled with a universe of nonhuman objects; much like quantum particles. Jane Bennett makes the point that "the most that can be said with confidence about the thing is that it eludes capture by the concept, that there is always a "nonidentity" between it and any representation'.[42]

My philosophical approach is in accord with Harman, and the OOO, or as I like to call it 'Thing Related Reality'. Harman states that OOO is 'against physicalism, smallism, anti-fictionalism, and literalism',[43] and makes claim to being a 'theory of everything', denying physics the opportunity because it cannot account for fiction, poetry or metaphor. According to Harman, OOO can be immaterial, at any scale, fictional, and metaphorical and therefore capable of providing a philosophical model of everything. Remembering that Harman also notes the futility of the exercise, and is really a project based on the love of wisdom and the aesthetics of reality than the epistemological what and how of reality. In his book, *Immaterialism*, Harman shows how the OOO and speculative realism can be applied to social theory. This has some connection to Hall's book on the Apocalypse, Hall writes:

"We need a fresh alternative strategy that avoids complacently employing any of the conventional modern lenses. A "phenomenology of history" offers such a strategy. This strategy, daunting enough as a term, involves an even more challenging shift in how we think about history. Social phenomenology seeks to identify the most basic ways in which each of us is situated in the "lifeworld" – the everyday realm of the temporally unfolding here-and-now within which we live our lives, connecting to other people and media, social groups and institutions, culture and history."[44]

There is a sense of urgency as we contemplate apocalyptic storylines; the dawning of a new Millenarianism. Just as the 20th century faced the 'dark inversion'[45] of fin de siècle, the 21st century is realising new narratives to cope with the catastrophic dawn of the Anthropocene. Storytelling is world building, we design our world to survive, and make sense of it. Nor is storytelling confined to fiction, but is commonly used in politics, science, and economics. Even mathematics uses story to formulate abstractions, and in applications, related to our world building narratives. New materialism is being developed by those theorists who are taking into account the virtuality of subatomic physics; the instability and uncertainty of chaos and complexity theory; and the emergence of symbiogenesis of microbial evolutionary biology.[46]

There is increasing evidence that many 'storytellers', even those that do not associate with the name, are desperately searching for new tools, new philosophies, and new media, to hastily build new worlds, or spaceships to get there, before this one becomes metaphysically, spiritually, and physically uninhabitable. Does this predict popular new narratives founded on speculative realism and OOO? If so what might they look, feel and sound like?

The Anthropogenic Trap

The Anthropocene is an epoch that presents a dauntingly complex multidisciplinary tangle of issues often described as a 'Super Wicked Problems'. Speculative realism has begun to attack two hundred years of what Meillassoux describes as Kantian correlationism.[47]

This can be summarised as Immanuel Kant's philosophical proposition that there is only the correlation between human thought and reality, and that without human thought reality cannot be said to exist. "For correlationism, a mind-independent reality cannot exist, because the very fact that we are thinking of such a reality means that it is not mind-independent after all."[48] According to Meillassoux we are trapped in a 'correlationist circle' unable to separate the subject from the object, nature from culture, or the human from the non-human. As Harman would put it "everything is reduced to a question of human access to the world, and non-human relations are abandoned to the natural sciences."[49] However, despite scientists, media, and politicians that claim the contrary, science, or scientism share world building narratives inherited from fictional stories, religion, and socio-cultural ideologies.

Just because many of us have forgotten those stories, or believe the hype attached to the philosophy of science and the privileging of epistemology, this does not mean those stories do not still lurk in the shadows of Jungian archetypes.[50] According to Boyd stories have an evolutionary purpose,[51] a technology that extends our biological evolution through culture to accelerate our change,[52] and hopefully our existence, and culture is not just exclusive to humans. Hayles set out to show that "culture circulates through science no less than science circulates through culture. The heart that keeps this circulatory system flowing is narrative — narratives about culture, narratives within culture, narratives about science, narratives within science".[53]

Haraway insists that speculative fictions are an antidote to some of the excesses of these overreaching narratives of scientism.[54] Her *Camille Stories: Children of Compost* take us into the strange world of 'Kin making as a means of reducing human numbers and demands on the earth, while simultaneously increasing human and other critters' flourishing, engaged intense energies and passions in the dispersed emerging worlds'.[55] Reality is intentionally weird, queer, and uncanny even if our world building often suggests the opposite. The simplified and reductionist tales that we have used to build these worlds do nothing to remind us that the 'map is not the territory'.

As Kant pointed out, we cannot grasp an object 'in-itself'. The challenge we now face is how do we sidle alongside the reality of the Anthropocene without having to front something we have to admit we cannot possibly know? Worse still, how do we think our way out of this predicament, or indeed, can we? The philosophical approach adopted by the likes of Harman, Shaviro, Morton, Bogost, and Bryant does not hope to contribute to epistemology but instead assumes an aesthetic interest in philosophical reality. They hope to return us to a state of wonderment, replacing the anthropocentric arrogance of inevitable ignorance. "The dazzlement of things bursting forth is what Harman calls allure: the sense of an object's existence apart from, and over and above, its own qualities.[56] Allure has to do with the showing-forth of that which is, strictly speaking, inaccessible; it "invites us toward another level of reality".[57]

"In the event of allure, I encounter the very being of a thing, beyond all definition or correlation. I am forced to acknowledge its integrity, entirely apart from me".[58]

Before we can 'face the Anthropocene' we must revise outmoded narratives and imagine entirely new ones that will allow us to contemplate the horror, and the love of alien worlds, here on Earth. The solution is not to devise escape plans but to seek co-existence and build worlds together with our symbionts. But first, we need to create narratives and build the tools to find the lock and key that traps us in the Anthropocene.

Tools to Think With – Modelling Worlds

According to Nicholas Carr, "The history of language is also a history of the mind".[59] Using the examples of the map and the clock he traces how these cognitive technologies have shaped our metaphors, the way we think, and the way we act. He cites the classical scholar, Walter J. Ong:

"Technologies are not mere exterior aids but also interior transformations of consciousness, and never more than when they affect the word."[60]

Since the rise of the machines throughout the 18th century the English language adopted mechanical metaphors when discussing the brain, and this continued as mechanical computers and cybernetics transitioned to digital circuitry in the second half of the 20th century. The metaphor then morphed into a model, and the human brain became analogous with a computer. Known as the 'Cognitive Revolution', beginning in the 1950s, in Cold War America, it included philosophy, psychology, anthropology, and linguistics, and also extended to artificial intelligence, computer science and neuroscience. Noam Chomsky led the field of linguistics in the cybernetic application of the digital computing metaphor for the human brain. While at MIT, Chomsky and others, were in the pay of the Pentagon;[61] the man-machine metaphor was strongly supported by ideological scientism that distrusted the humanities, critical theory, and progressive politics.[62] Chomsky had built a reputation after attacking behaviourism and the psychologist, B.F. Skinner for his approach to language describing it as a method of totalitarian control. Knight explains that "In this bitter Cold War context, linguistics became extraordinarily politicized, being viewed by US policymakers as a crucial weapon in the worldwide struggle for mastery and control."[63]

Rational choice theory, researched and developed by the RAND Corporation, offered a mathematical, and computational alternative to Marxist material dialecticism. It provided market and voting models that viewed people as rational actors, and was thought to be equally relevant to soldiers, whether they are American or Vietcong, and is still going strong today. According to Amadae this impact of rational choice theory can be summed up as follows:

"Rational decision technologies gained legitimacy not on paper or in intellectual debate, but because they became institutionalised in practice and played the role of transferring authority, rationalising ponderous decisions, and shaping the reality of peoples' lives."[64]

Those academics who looked for tenure and funding from the military assisted the government by psychological, anthropological, and sociological R & D to quell 'communist' revolutions and alternative world views that were seen to threaten the American Dream supported by cognitive science and the man-machine metaphor. The Cold War created a climate of fear that delimited acceptable discourse, and restricted world creation to one world view.[65]

Critical theorists came to see how this man-machine metaphor became reified in the posthuman cybernetic organism or cyborg. For Haraway (2016), Finn (2017), Galloway (2004), Bratton (2016), Bogost (2012) and Hayles (1999) our tools of cognition have become increasingly dependent on algorithms and protocols, that have shaped our culture's popular dreams, desires and fears. Finn states that these algorithms have become our 'culture machines'. Increasingly, AI or machine learning is selecting the media we view for us and our discourse is shaped by a defined past based on our algorithmic choice and preferences. As Carr wrote: "The tight bonds we form with our tools go both ways. Even as our technologies become extensions of ourselves, we become extensions of our technologies".[66]

The very nature of Google search page ranking tends to amplify popular citations, and this is happening at the very time that we need to explore neurodiversity, creativity, and alternative futures, not monocultures. The concern is that we might think that our access to the largest collection of literature, scientific papers, and culture the world has ever known, may convince us that we can build novel worlds and narratives that will release us from our fatal imprisonment, but in fact it does the opposite by simply multiplying the quantity, not the quality of debate.

Chomsky towered over the world of linguistics, and he is credited with a new way of thinking about the human mind. Despite Chomsky's reputation as a dissident his role in the philosophy of science, and American logical empiricism during the Cold War meant he was as much a part of the 'manufacturing of consent', (to borrow his own phrase), as the administrators of the Cold War. His Cartesian world view reinforced the bifurcation of the human mind from the rest of the universe and was embedded in the cognitive revolution he helped create. Claiming his linguistic theory was scientific obscured the mysticism buried in his belief. While Chomsky did not make these beliefs explicit, he borrowed from Descartes, the belief that language was the tool of the mind, and that the mind could not truly be known as it was the repository of the human soul, and thus divine. This was a strange view for an atheist, but consistent with American liberal ideology, and not likely to ruffle feathers in academia, the military, or even amongst Christian zealots.

Chomsky once claimed that language was based on universal grammar, that it was recursive, computational, and was instantly created by way of a mutation caused by something like a cosmic ray shower resulting in a language organ located somewhere in the brain. He then changed his mind and said this origin story was a fairytale and that the origin of language remains an enigma that cannot be solved with experimentation or empirical observation. According to Knight in *Decoding Chomsky* these strange beliefs appear to have grown out of a cognitive dissonance that Chomsky used to survive the contradiction between his politics and his research for the Pentagon.[67]

Chomsky's sterilisation of language by removing meaning and focusing on rules and algorithms were openly invited by computer scientists and the military who searched for a mathematical formalism to assist computerised command and control in the battlefield. However, it has also had a massive impact on numerous disciplines globally, including philosophy, education, psychology, computer science, and many other fields that have defined the way we think. If, as Everett has argued, language is a technological artefact that hominids invented 2 million years ago, then we should be far more wary of accepting a Grand Unified Theory of mind that claims language is a biological accident, exclusive to humans, and is universally given and innate.[68]

Oddly, the dominant US academic and research paradigm of logical empiricism that begat 'cognitive science' has a tendency to limit multiworld views that included history, sociology and culture[69] and despite Chomsky's claim that language is biological, individual, not social, and internal to the mind, it was an overwhelmingly computational theory of mind that forgot it was a metaphor.

As we build our supposedly veridical virtual worlds and simulations, these are only impoverished models that pretend to tell the complete story of reality, but instead simplify and hide actuality, while preventing novel discourse by closing off our imagination to tools such as the OOO reality, which is nonlocal and withdrawn. In our virtual world we are oblivious to Baudrillard's hyperreality of hyperobjects – such as humanity itself; the nonhuman majority; and the Post

Anthropocene, to name just a few hugely important objects that will be largely excluded because they are ultimately non-computable.

The legacy of Marxism and the cultural critique developed by the Frankfurt School continues to haunt Foucauldian discourse. This is not to deny the value of the tools created by the likes of Heidegger, and extended by Latour, the OOO, and Harman et. al. Critical theory gave us many tools to consider how we read the narratives of our times and world building became a vast and popular profession. However, until the OOO and speculative realism, many world builders attempted to create and propagate an anthropocentric tool, while selling it off as a Grand Unified Theory (GUT) of Everything. The neglect of the nonhuman majority of things and their relations may have been simply that, neglect. Like Latour, for the Critical Theorists, politics or the human subject were their primary project. However, given the urgency of the Anthropocene, it is no longer appropriate to ignore the vast network of nonhuman 'actants', objects, or things because our world is in desperate need of novel tools and narratives to try and think our way out of this mess. Latour has at least acknowledged the importance of these other speculative projects by researching 'object oriented politics'.[70]

In his book, *What Algorithms Want*, Finn discusses algorithmic politics and how we might escape the first circle of what Carr calls the 'glass cage'. The legacy of Critical Theory offers 'close reading and intensive scrutiny... reading software itself as cultural text'.[71] Finn applauds the work of the Critical Code Studies Working Group that uses these tactics and others who use 'authoring instead of reading, and thereby reinventing algorithmic systems for the purposes of protest and critique'.[72]

Researchers and scholars who are aware of the pitfalls of this anthropocentric approach may still be able to experiment with various speculative and world building research approaches, to re-imagine the Post Anthropocene, by acknowledging a far larger object oriented ontology. Bennett illustrates how Adorno recommends intellectual and aesthetic exercises to heal the hubris of human conceptualisation by making it explicit, and being sensitive to the unknowable, 'nonidentity' of the thing. 'The goal here is to become more cognizant that conceptualization automatically obscures the inadequacy of its concepts'.[73]

The other approach is 'is to exercise one's utopian imagination', and the 'third technique is to admit a "playful element" into one's thinking and to be willing to play the fool.'[74] The limitations of linear language may be partially overcome through the use of tools such as Category Theory. Bettin suggests:

"We are constantly challenged to come up with appropriate context and domain specific languages that allow others to gain a satisfactory level of understanding of our experiences and thoughts. Category theory is just a much better tool to make these domain specific language[s more] explicit than linear language[s], in a form that humans can understand in a form that is accessible to software tools. The concrete symbolic representation of categories/instances can be highly visual/auditory/dynamic (anything we can experience via our senses)."[75]

There is the danger that if Ray Kurzweil's predictions are correct, and that we will see photorealistic, and other sensory veridical immersive experiences within the next ten years,[76] that these virtual models of actuality could claim their own reality while occluding and excluding the actual nonhuman actants, and their equally valid worlds. The more explicit these models appear to represent physical reality the more these tools can hide that they are simply metaphors and not literal truths. Interacting with the physical world via virtual interfaces does not dispense with the ontological problems of objects in a virtual or physical world. The litany of disasters that are promised by the Anthropocene is beyond human comprehension or belief. They occupy a special category in our psyche, beyond our intractable problems, these hyperobjects, narrate a world that extends beyond our twelve thousand year present, across a vast story space. They are the essence of a reality that spans a nonhuman space and time that we cannot fathom, but can only attempt to itemise. The inhuman story is a narrative that is told by rocks, gases, weather, and geographically dispersed things, such as, plants, animals, microbes, and also, fictional concepts, protagonists and antagonists. These examples are but a few characters in a vast story world that stretches beyond the genesis of Earth, our solar system, galaxy, or the beginnings of time. In a Grand Unified Theory, they cannot be ontologically separated, or ranked, as they once were, in the 'Great Chain of Being'.

As we come face to face with our tragic destiny humans have begun to reimagine, and construct new myths, legends and narratives. These are the cognitive and philosophical tools that we must fashion in order to build future worlds that will accept us with all our posthuman frailties. According to Shaviro, "both Whitehead and Meillassoux seize on the contradictions and hesitations of classical philosophy, not as points of critical intervention, but as tools for regaining the great outdoors."[77] Following in the footsteps of Philipp Frank, and Thomas Kuhn, Latour has described how scientific paradigms are created, thus stabilizing reality through tools, and things, acting as assemblages in the 'parliament of things' in which scientists are merely one of the 'actants' amongst a nonhuman majority. In the postscript to his book, *The Structure of Scientific Revolutions*, (1970) Kuhn wrote:

"Individuals raised in different societies behave on some occasions as though they saw different things. If we were not tempted to identify stimuli one-to-one with sensations, we might recognise that they actually do so. Notice now that two groups, the members of which have systematically different sensations on receipt of the same stimuli, do in some sense [sic] live in different worlds' [emphasis added].[78]

Nonhuman World Building

However, the OOO philosophical tool, that is not an epistemological tool, argues that humans are not the only world builders and that nonhuman things, animate and inanimate, create their own ontologies. As Latour points out "Every actant makes a whole world for itself."[79]

The reason Latour coined the word actant was to avoid the confusion that his Actor Network Theory only applied to human actors. The irony here is that the entertainment industry is far behind OOO in understanding this powerful new narrative that decenters humans and makes nonhuman protagonists and antagonists. This is despite the observation by Harman that acting is one of the human professions that regularly uses metaphors following Stanislavski's insistence that actors try to 'become the object one portrays as nearly as possible.'[80]

'This theatrical structure of metaphor strongly suggests that theatre lies at the root of the other arts' and that is why Harman speculates 'that the mask was the original artwork.'[81]

In reality, these nonhuman objects are probably not usually talking to humans, and their worlds and narratives are secret according to their strange assemblages that happen or emerge between them. However, by being sensitive to the active vibrancy and 'dense network' of enmeshed relations, theorists such as Bennett hope that 'in a knotted world of vibrant matter, to harm one section of the web may very well be to harm oneself. Such an enlightened or expanded notion of self-interest is good for humans',[82] and the Earth system. While science might fancy itself as the only rightful, honest, and truthful storyteller in the human realm, OOO blows that stale narrative out of the water by playing mashups as if in some William S. Burroughs' tale:

"which draws a free breath from the rich, permissive folds of *A Thousand Plateaus* where Deleuze and Guattari depict the kind of events where 'a semiotic fragment rubs shoulders with a chemical interaction, an electron crashes into a language, a black hole captures a genetic messa, a crystallization produces a passion..."[83]

This *Naked Lunch*[84] of strange cut up vegetables, animals, microbes, insects, minerals and metaphors suddenly presents us with a revolutionary way of telling stories and understanding the multiverse of things and their narratives. Harman encourages us to consider the metaphorical relations between things, not that they resemble each other but that a "metaphor satisfies us precisely because in it we find a coincidence between two things that is more profound and decisive than any mere resemblance".[85]

This artistic and aesthetic meditation on things will not reveal everything about them but 'In the case of a successful metaphor, we are able to experience a new entity'.[86]

The power of this cognitive tool, and our ability to partially know, and imagine the worlds that objects build gives us an ecological way to consider our coexistence with the nonhuman majority. As Bennett asks, "What would happen to our thinking about politics if we took more seriously the idea that technological and natural materialities were themselves actors alongside and within us—were vitalities, trajectories, and powers irreducible to the meanings, intentions, or symbolic values humans invest in them?"[87]

Even if we cannot know, hear, or see the worlds they are building, their creativity and generative powers enliven our world by indirect, and chaotic relations of novel assemblages. Remixing Morton and Haraway we get a strange assemblage or weird worlding; a queer aesthetic; the Thing surfaces from the chthonic depths of cinematic imaginations as it struggles to escape from human conceptual imprisonment, and break the chains that restrict it to an anthropocentric world which considers the thing a monster. Haraway implores us to 'stay with the trouble' through 'sympoiesis', or 'worlding-with', as opposed to autopoiesis, 'self-worlding', she imagines future worlds, 'becoming-with' our nonhuman kin; 'earthlings are never alone'.

Cinematic Narratives

According to Nicholas Carr, as he recounts the history of writing technology, he argues it has had a cognitive impact on the way we think and uses language, and now the Internet is changing the way we read, think and remember.[88]

This complex relationship between culture, semiotics, technology and biology are exposed in an analysis of moving images, platforms, and technologies. Like Netflix, YouTube and Amazon change the distribution and subscription models, so too do our watching habits and the content of the medium. Manovich explains the principles of new media as:

1. mathematical, or can be described by maths, and

2. algorithmic or programmable.[89]

Are we watching what the algorithms want? The capacity of contemporary media to embrace speculative realism and the OOO maybe challenged by the limitations of audience expectations; Hollywood business models; the 'culture machine', and the artists' imaginations and affinity with new materialisms to communicate narratives for the Post Anthropocene. Bogost argued that most of the critically acclaimed media is correlationist, and TV shows, such as *The Wire*, are not in fact about the relationship of the wire with other objects such as drugs, or streets, but about people split from nature. The closest to OOO media, that Bogost can cite, are two cooking shows, Duff Goldman's *Ace of Cakes*, and *Good Eating* by Alton Brown that lovingly focus on the other nonhuman objects that equally participate in the cooking process, and not the humans.[90]

In an episode of Dan Harmon's animated series, *Rick and Morty*, *Vindicators 3: The Return of Worldender* (2017), the grandson Morty gets his wish to join the Vindicators, in their third adventure to prevent Worldender from carrying out his evil plan. Rick, the scientific genius, and grandfather taunt the Vindicators with their lame superpowers; calling Ant-Man, Pooh Man, due to his brown sloppy appearance. Ant-Man is truly a composite of a colony of ants who in turn lives in symbiosis with colonies upon colonies of bacteria; he is an emergent intelligence, much like a swarm of AI nanobots. The Pixar movies such as *Ants, Toy Story; Cars, A Bug's Life*, and *Finding Nemo*, despite their anthropomorphic characters, explore the world building of non-humans. Animation, fantasy movies, and superhero sci-fi movies are some of the best examples of proto-OOO and speculative realist art forms beginning to articulate the new narratives of nonhuman materialism. The essential ecological health of insect populations is something that is only just beginning to dawn on us, despite the fact that Carson warned of the ecological dangers of DDT over half a century ago (1963). Nature documentaries such as the *Living Planet* are creating narratives that have attracted large audiences to nonhuman world building and the threat of the sixth mass extinction.

Meanwhile, the dominant correlationist myth continues to define the narratives of new and old media as anthropocentric disaster narratives persist. One of the masters of this genre is Michael Crichton who is famous for his dystopian futures that make for compelling sci-fi movies, if not modern Promethean morality tales, such as *Jurassic Park, Westworld*, and the as yet unmade, but cinematic book, *Prey* (2002). *Prey* is based on speculative AI nanotechnology in which emergent intelligence becomes a sinister swarm of nanobots that replicate humans and deceive their enemy, then attack them. This is the 'weird essentialism' that Morton talks about. Just as he is both Timothy Morton, and not Timothy Morton, composed of 90% alien microbial cells, in symbiotic communities, the nanobot swarms are essentially the same as the human they mimic, and yet they are not. If we reverse this formula the contradiction is still true, the humans are not nanobot swarms, and yet they microbially mimic them, being both human and nonhuman, at once. Thus, while *Prey* centres on human relations, it does suggest an interesting inhuman ontological world of emergent relations that may have nothing to do with humans, and open up a novel narrative of 'alien intelligence', and machine to machine, machine to alien, object relations.

Speculative realism offers a novel story tool for a popular audience that captures every demographic, in every quadrant, plus some! In the history of entertainment, there has never been a pitch to such a mass audience; this is an out-of-the-box office transmedia narrative that excludes no one and includes every *thing*. Graham Harman describes their fascination with each other, the 'allure' of objects. This aesthetic attraction is an artistic view of reality. The OOO is a philosophical storytelling device that describes a *thing* related reality that is democratic and flat, nothing is more real than any *thing* else in the 'parliament of things' (Latour, 2004). An object, or thing, can be physical; material; conceptual; fictional; nonlocal; virtual; actual; a 'hyperobject', such as global warming; or Dr Strange from the Marvel universe.

The OOO narrative decentres humanity, or rather it departs from the B grade monster movie, that assumes that the handsome scientist is the protagonist, and the *Creature from the Black Lagoon* (1954) or 'Gill Man' is the antagonist, in an outdated, anthropocentric script, more Dr Strangelove, than Dr Strange. In Guillermo Del Toro's update, the *Shape of Water*, Del Toro attempts to decentre the humans as the *Thing* becomes the black hole at the centre of this story. The human protagonist, antagonist, and supporting characters are drawn to the *Thing* while still trying to maintain a reality defined by Cold War game theory. The *Thing* remains unknown and unnamed, and yet, at different times it is loved as an object of beauty, that maybe a God, and sometimes goes by the name of 'him'. Del Toro's Magical Realism in the

Shape of Water introduces us to a creature found in South America, beyond the reach of Cold War rationalism, cybernetics, and an identifiable epistemological reality.

In the sci-fi movie, the *Day After Tomorrow* (2004), starring Keanu Reeves, as the embodied alien, there is an invasion of Earth by an advanced alien race of things that are here to rescue the nonhumans from the anthropogenic destruction of the planet. Reeves, as a human, dies or is embodied by the aliens to facilitate human communication, and box office appeal. This movie, that is themed around an ecological, anthropogenic, disaster, proudly boasted that the film stock used in the movie was carbon neutral. The movie was speculative, and yet it failed to seriously discuss an alternative future, conforming to the same tired agrilogistic narrative. Reeves, as you would expect, saves the 'old' World, and there is 'naturally' a love interest, but it is human on human – as *things* still don't really count. This was not a speculative realist film or OOO movie, but a Kantian correlationist 'flick'. However, once again the swarm of alien particles that can attack, and emerge as an alien intelligence suggests a nonhuman democracy of things.

Loving Thingy is certainly not a common approach, but by maintaining a HCD (human-centred design) *The Shape of Water* did exceptionally well with sales outside America that will be enough to encourage distributors, Fox Searchlight, to back its cast and director, if not *The Thing* (borrowed from *Hell Boy*) in its next big one. The almost hegemonic power that Hollywood holds over the movie narrative means that the political, social and cultural bias of the US seeps out of the screens, and into the global discourse. Del Toro gives Trump a poke as the administration patrols its borders; searches for new Cold War enemies; and resurrects Iran as the 'evil empire'. Del Toro seems to suggest the Thing, from *The Shape of Water*, is no monster that we should fear, vivisection, or torture, but something we should learn to love. We are in desperate need of coexistence beyond human politics, and beyond our anthropocentric obsessions, our survival is dependent on the love all things. The movie concludes with the narration of a Sufi poem by Hakim Sanai:

Unable to perceive the shape of You,
I find You all around me.
Your presence fills my eyes with Your love,
It humbles my heart,
For You are everywhere.

The metaphorical value of art and the power of aesthetics to convey other worlds and to present speculative futures, utopian, dystopian, or just alternative futures, open up novel narratives based on OOOs that have never before been articulated or viewed. Objects or things become strange 'actants'[91] with emergent potentiality popping in and out of actuality; things as a shimmering process based on quantum probabilities that are both virtual and actual,[92] defying the 'Law of the Excluded Middle and the Law of Non-contradiction'.[93] Morton believes that we should be searching for much more interesting and powerful revolutionary action theories.

"Philosophy requires a new theory of action, a queer one that is neither active nor passive nor a compromised amalgam of both, to help us slip out from underneath physically massive beings such as global warming and neoliberalism, to find some wiggle room down there so we can wriggle or rock our way out of the hyperobjects."[94]

These strange worlds, built by strange things in strange relationships, become welcome stories to those tired of one-dimensional tales of tomorrow. Critical theory and the textual analogy of reading movies obscures both the technology and the 'alien phenomenology'[95] of a OOO world.

The Medium from the Future

Hayles argues that virtualisation is a trend that connects to the history of cybernetics and the narrative of information theory that separated information, from energy and matter. Information was immaterial, and virtuality was the result. In the age of 'Big Data' and the financialization of the knowledge economy, information is no longer conceptually embodied, or connected to the medium. Hayles wrote:

"In the face of such a powerful dream, it can be a shock to remember that for information to exist, it must always be instantiated in a medium, whether that medium is the page from the Bell Laboratories Journal on which Shannon's equations are printed, the computer-generated topological maps used by the Human Genome Project, or the cathode ray tube on which virtual worlds are imaged."[96]

Bogost and Montfort coined the phrase, 'Platform Studies' to emphasise hardware and software as OOO as in their research into the Atari Video Computer System documented in, *Racing the Beam* (2009). Rather than 'critically reading' this cultural artefact, Bogost and Montfort, assumed a hacker's narrative seeing the world from the objects p.o.v., moving beyond traditional philosophy. In this case they focused on the Television Interface Adaptor, or TIA, and how it interfaced with the common MOS Technology 6502 computer processor.

"However appealing and familiar the usual means of doing philosophy might be, another possible method involves a more hands-on approach, manipulating or vivisecting the objects to be analyzed, mad scientist–like, in the hopes of discovering their secrets."[97]

Bogost attempts to approximate 'the TIA's view of the world through the lens of a standard two-dimensional computer display.'[98] By being sensitive to the alien temporality, and nonhuman spatial scale of objects, artists and designers, such as Bogost, apply a OOO philosophy to their practice, beyond simply discourse, and alert us to the mysterious ontology of objects that we can only partially get to know. McLuhan's maxim has never been more prescient today as we consider the IoT (Internet of Things), VR, AR, MR and mirror worlds and the messages they convey.

Ready Player One (2018), is a book that was made into a movie about a VR game and is a homage to the 80s culture of the popular ATARI 2600 game system. The book, written by Ernest Cline, is set in 2045 following the future realisation that fossil fuels have contributed to global warming, and economic collapse due to fuel shortages resulting in the 'Global Energy Crisis'.

"Also, it turns out that burning all of those fossil fuels had some nasty side effects, like raising the temperature of our planet and screwing up the environment. So now the polar ice caps are melting, sea levels are rising, and the weather is all messed up. Plants and animals are dying off in record numbers, and lots of people are starving and homeless. And we're still fighting wars with each other, mostly over the few resources we have left."[99]

The story is well suited to a novel narrative in which the global population is immersed in a virtual world the OASIS, an acronym for, 'Ontologically Anthropocentric Sensory Immersive Simulations'. According to the book, "The OASIS would ultimately change the way people around the world lived, worked, and communicated. It would transform entertainment, social networking, and even global politics."[100]

From a OOO perspective, this promising introduction falls sadly short. The movie script, written by Cline, and Zack Penn, was directed by Steven Spielberg and released in 2018. It has the hallmarks of a proto-OOO narrative but misses as it serves up a virtual world that is a simple extension of the shopping mall, mashed with a game, in which avatars pay for fuel, teleportation, and virtual objects. Despite the suggestion that we could be about to watch a critical and speculative commentary or just an entertaining alternative narrative, Spielberg delivers a utopian, feel-good, movie for teenage gamers that is immersed in consumer materialism, neoliberalism, and definitely not speculative realism. The homage to '80s pop culture is at the centre of this 'hero's journey' from 'rags to riches' but the viewer is unlikely to gain any ontological insight into the future.

As information becomes more and more abstract for many so-called users, both human and nonhuman, the medium is not the message – it is invisible, hidden, disembodied, and to them, apparently irrelevant. The Internet's illusion of virtuality hides the Anthropogenic harm that is being caused by its technologies. The material reality of the Internet is no longer present, or at least, it is hidden, and virtuality is strangely more real, or hyperreal, than the actuality of its physical instantiation. According to Sean Cubitt, the Internet may seem to be dematerialising the world, but its physicality is massive with respect to millions of kilometres of plastic-coated fibre optic cable, 'enough to go around the Earth almost sixteen thousand times', and energy consumption that exceeds the carbon emissions of the air travel industry.[101]

The plastic PVC coating is derived from oil, and only has a life expectancy of between fifteen to forty years depending on where it is installed. The majority of data traffic carried on these cables are financial and military that requires speed and volume for their command and control objectives. However, the break down of the plastic in the ocean will disperse toxins and minute plastic particles throughout the food chain beginning with sea life.

"Organotin compounds are a favored stabilizer for PVC plastics, such as those used for weatherproofing and insulating fiber-optic cable. Organotin was outlawed as a pesticide by the European Union in 2003 due to its extreme toxicity, and especially its effects on marine mammals that concentrate the compound as it flows out into open water. In global recycling villages of West Africa, India, and southern China, burning off the PVC casing to get at the valuable metals inside releases the organotins."[102]

New media dictates new narratives, but it also necessitates a deliberate shift of attention with respect to what Dunne & Raby (2013) have called 'preferable futures'. Speculative realism can provide a framework for meditating on the Post Anthropocene and our coexistence with the nonhuman majority. Virtual reality, augmented reality, mixed reality, virtual worlds, and online games are a shortlist of media that can massage the message when the producers are mindful of an extended ontological ecology which decentres the human. While Hayles outlines a recent history of how we became posthuman and the virtuality that followed the great acceleration, and the cybernetic disembodiment of information, Wertheim and Grau document this trend over the past two and a half thousand years, and Morton go back before agriculture and the Holocene. Michael Heim points out that this rejection of the body is deeply ingrained in our religious past. He puts cyberpunk in its historical context, "From the pit of life in the body, the virtual life looks like the virtuous life. Gibson [author of Neuromancer] evokes the Gnostic-Platonic-Manichean contempt for earthy existence'.[103]

The speculative approach of the OOO results from the reworking of Kant's finitude, exposing the limits of not just human reason, but the limited ability of all objects to know themselves, and their relations with others. Harman's OOO becomes the tool to overcome the Kantian anthropocentric bias of modern thought that has been blamed for creating the Anthropocene. "Dogmatic certitude is therefore out of the question for Harman and Whitehead no less than for Kant. But Harman, like Whitehead, concludes from this not that speculation should be abandoned but rather that we can and must speculate."[104] As Victor pointed out:

"We cannot see the thing. At all. But whatever that thing is — people will have to think it. And we can, right now, today, prepare powerful ways of thinking for these people. We can build the tools that make it possible to think that thing" (2013).

Notes

1. Graham, F. (1970). Since Silent Spring. Boston: Houghton-Mifflin. p. xii

2. While DDT has been banned other dichloro compounds such as 24,D is still in use in some countries, such as New Zealand and Australia.

3. This could be catastrophic in terms of loss of biodiversity, oxygen generation, and carbon sequestration. See https://www.washingtonpost.com/climate-environment/what-you-need-to-know-about-the-amazon-rainforest-fires/2019/08/27/ac82b21e-c815-11e9-a4f3-c081a126de70_story.html?noredirect=on

4. See the Kield Declaration on Ocean Deoxygenation https://www.ocean-oxygen.org/declaration

5. ibid

6. ibid

7. Graham, ibid, p112-116

8. See Mayer's Dark Money, and Merchants of Doubt: how a handful of scientists obscured the truth on issues from tobacco smoke to global warming (2010) by Naomi Oreskes and Erik M. Conway.

9. Carrington, D. (2019) 'Plummeting insect numbers 'threaten collapse of nature'. The Guardian. https://www.theguardian.com/environment/2019/feb/10/plummeting-insect-numbers-threaten- collapse-of-nature

10. Meillassoux, Q., Brassier, R., Badiou, A., & Bloomsbury Publishing. (2017). After finitude: an essay on the necessity of contingency. London [etc.: Bloomsbury Academic an imprint of Bloomsbury Publishing Plc.

11. Elizabeth Sawin, TedX Sun Valley, The Power of Multisolving for People and Climate. https:// www.youtube.com/watch?v=prF8trTallQ

12. Clark, Nigel. (2011) Inhuman Nature: Sociable Life on a Dynamic Planet. London: SAGE

13. Clark, N. ibid

14. Steffen, W., & Eliott, S. (Eds.) (2004) Global Change and the Earth System: A Planet Under Pressure - Executive Summary. Springer-Verlag Berlin Heidelberg New York. ISBN 3-540-40800-2

15. ibid

16. Harman, Graham. (2018) Object-Oriented Ontology: A New Theory of Everything. Penguin Books Ltd. Kindle Edition.

17. Grau, O. (2003). Virtual art: from illusion to immersion ([Rev. and expanded). Cambridge, Mass.: MIT Press.

18. Bacon, F. The New Atlantis, p.22

19. Ibid, p.23

20. UX - user experience; UI - user interface

21. Bogost, I., & Project Muse. (2012). Alien phenomenology, or, What it's like to be a thing. Kindle Locations 107-110

22. Brown, T., & Katz, B. (2009). Change by design: how design thinking transforms organizations and inspires innovation (First edition). New York: Harper Business.

23. Mayer, J. (2016). Dark money: the hidden history of the billionaires behind the rise of the radical right. Scribe Publications, Kindle Edition

24. Mayer, J. (2017, March 17). The Reclusive Hedge-Fund Tycoon Behind the Trump Presidency. The New Yorker. Retrieved from https://www.newyorker.com/magazine/2017/03/27/the-reclusive- hedge- fund-tycoon- behind-the-trump-presidency.

25. Nagle, A. (2017). Kill all normies: online culture wars from 4chan and Tumblr to Trump and the alt-right. Winchester: Zero Books.

26. Mayer, J. (2016) ibid

27. Harman, Graham. (2014) Bruno Latour: Reassembling the Political (Modern European Thinkers). Pluto Press. Kindle Edition.

28. Harman, Graham. (2018) Object-Oriented Ontology: A New Theory of Everything. Penguin Books Ltd. Kindle Edition

29. Morton, Timothy. Hyperobjects: Philosophy and Ecology after the End of the World (Posthumanities) (Kindle Locations 3541-3544). University of Minnesota Press. Kindle Edition.

30. Harman, Graham. (2014) Bruno Latour: Reassembling the Political (Modern European Thinkers). Pluto Press. Kindle Edition.

31. Haraway, Donna J. (2016). Staying with the Trouble: Making Kin in the

Chthulucene (Experimental Futures) (p. 39). Duke University Press. Kindle Edition.

32. ibid

33. Shaviro, Steven. (2015). No Speed Limit: Three Essays on Accelerationism (Forerunners: Ideas First) (p. 2). University of Minnesota Press. Kindle Edition. p.2

34. ibid, p.3

35. Tsing, A. L. (2015). The mushroom at the end of the world: On the possibility of life in capitalist ruins. Princeton: Princeton University Press.

36. Tsing, ibid Kindle location 210

37. Tsing, ibid, Kindle location 261

38. Morton, T. (2018). Dark Ecology: for a logic of future coexistence. S.l.: Columbia University Press.

39. Morton ibid, p.52

40. Bryant, L. R. (2011). The democracy of objects (First edition). Ann Arbor: Open Humanities Press.

41. Harman, G. (2017). Object-Oriented Ontology: a new theory of everything. S.l.: Pelican. p.38

42. Bennett, J. (2010). Vibrant matter: a political ecology of things. Durham: Duke University Press, 2010. p.13

43. Harman, G. (2017). ibid.

44. Hall, J.R. Apocalypse: From Antiquity to the Empire of Modernity

45. Booker, C. (2004). The seven basic plots of literature. New York; London: Continuum.

46. Coole, D. H., & Frost, S. (2010). New materialisms ontology, agency, and politics. Durham [NC]: Duke University Press.

47. Meillassoux, Q., Brassier, R., Badiou, A., & Bloomsbury Publishing. (2017). After finitude: an essay on the necessity of contingency. London [etc.: Bloomsbury Academic an imprint of Bloomsbury Publishing Plc.

48. Shaviro, S. (2014). The universe of things: on speculative realism. Minneapolis: University of Minnesota Press. Kindle Locations 135-137

49. Shaviro, (2014). ibid. Kindle Location 142

50. Booker, S. ibid.

51. Boyd, B. (2009). On the origin of stories: evolution, cognition, and fiction. Cambridge, Mass.: Belknap Press of Harvard University Press.

52. Ray Kurzweil, in The Singularity is Near: when humans transcend biology, also argues that there are 6 epochs of evolution and after humans reached the limitations of their biology they extended evolution using technology in the 4th epoch. Computers are the logical extensions of this evolution.

53. Hayles, K. (2017). Unthought: The power of the cognitive nonconscious. Chicago; London: The University of Chicago Press.

54. Haraway, D. J. (2016). Staying with the trouble: making kin in the Chthulucene.

55. Haraway, (2016), ibid, p.138

56. Cited by Shaviro (2014) The Universe of Things; Harman, G (2005) Guerrilla Metaphysics: Phenomenology and the Carpentry of Things. Chicago: Open Court. pp.142-44

57. ibid, p.179

58. Shaviro, (2014), ibid, Kindle Locations 884-888

59. Carr, N. G. (2010). The shallows: how the Internet is changing the way we think, read and remember. London: Atlantic Books. p.51

60. ibid.

61. Chomsky & Miller (1958) Final State Language. Information and Control. 1, p.2 This work was supported in part by the Army (Signal Corps), the Navy (Office of Naval Research), the Air Force (Office of Scientific Research and Operational Applications Laboratory, Air Research and Development Command), the National Science Foundation, and the Social Science Research Council (Committee on Mathematical Training of Social Scientists), and appears as report number AFCRC-TR-58-50, ASTIA Document Number AD 146781.

62. McCumber, J. (2016). The Philosophy Scare: the politics of reason in the early Cold War. The University of Chicago Press, Chicago & London.

63. Knight, Chris. Decoding Chomsky: Science and Revolutionary Politics (p. 28). Yale University Press. Kindle Edition.

64. Amadae (2003) Rationalizing Capitalist Democracy: The Cold War Origins of Rational Choice Liberalism. Chicago. University of Chicago Press p.72

65. See Knight, Decoding Chomsky, McCumber, The Philosophy Scare, and Reisch, How the Cold War Transformed Philosophy of Science.

66. ibid, p.209

67. Knight, Chris. Decoding Chomsky: Science and Revolutionary Politics (p. 17). Yale University Press. Kindle Edition.

68. Everett, D. (2017). How Language Began: the story of humanity's greatest invention.

69. See Reisch, George A.. How the Cold War Transformed Philosophy of Science: To the Icy Slopes of Logic. Cambridge University Press. Kindle Edition.

70. Harman, G. (2017), ibid.

71. Finn, E. (2017). What algorithms want: Imagination in the age of computing. Cambridge, Massachusetts: MIT Press.

72. Finn, ibid, Kindle Locations 4040-4041

73. Bennett, J. (2010). Vibrant matter: a political ecology of things. Durham: Duke University Press, 2010. p.14

74. ibid

75. Bettin, J. (2019) A personal communication.

76. Kurzweil, R. (2005). ibid

77. Shaviro, (2014), ibid, Kindle Locations 199-200

78. Kuhn, T. S. (1970). The structure of scientific revolutions (2nd ed.). Chicago, Ill.: University of Chicago Press. p.193

79. Latour, B. (1988), p.193 cited in Clark, 2011

80. Harman, G. (2017) ibid, p.83.

81. ibid

82. Bennett, J. (2010), ibid, p.13

83. Cited in Clark, 2011, p.32

84. *The Naked Lunch* was written by William S. Burrows and follows the hallucinogenic adventures of a junkie in a non-linear sequence and the chapters were intended to be read in any order. See Burroughs, W. S. (1959). The Naked Lunch (1st ed.). Paris: Olympia Press.

85. Harman, 2017, ibid p.73

86. ibid

87. Cited in Coole, Frost, Bennett, Cheah, Orlie, Grosz, 2010

88. Carr, N. G. (2010). The shallows: How the Internet is changing the way we think, read and remember. London: Atlantic Books.

89. Manovich, L. (2001). The language of new media. Cambridge, Mass.: MIT Press.

90. Bogost, I., & Project Muse. (2012). Alien phenomenology, or, What it's like to be a thing.

91. Latour, B. (1993) ibid

92. Coote, et. al (2010). New Materialisms.

93. Morton, T. (2018) Dark Ecology.

94. Morton, Timothy. Humankind: Solidarity with Non-Human People. Verso. Kindle Edition.

95. Bogost,I. (2012). Alien Phenomenology.

96. Hayles, K. (1999). How We Became Posthuman.

97. Bogost,I. (2012). Alien Phenomenology. Kindle Locations 2160-2161

98. ibid. Kindle Locations 2163-2164

99. Cline, Ernest. (2011) Ready Player One (Kindle Locations 286-290). Random House. Kindle Edition.

100. Cline, Ernest.ibid (Kindle Locations 986-987).

101. Cubitt, S. (2017). Finite media: Environmenta_ implications of digital technologies. Durham: Duke University Press.

102. ibid

103. Heim, M. (1993). The Metaphysics of Virtual Reality. p.102

104. Shaviro, S. (2014). The Universe of Things. Kindle Locations 2213-2215

Chapter 5 Foundations of Future Worlds

There are no passengers on Spaceship Earth. We are all crew.

— Marshall McLuhan (1965)

I have discussed some of the pitfalls of our current world, and that it is coming to an end. One of the most important foundations for building successful future worlds are new ways to think and educate – methods that support new, experimental and innovative idea creation; and ways to think about coexistence amongst those living and nonliving in future worlds. It was Einstein who observed:

"Imagination is more important than knowledge. Knowledge is limited, whereas imagination embraces the entire world, stimulating progress, giving birth to evolution." "Do not sacrifice your imagination on the altar of crude reality. You will end up believing in nothing and having worthless dreams."[1]

What some people are beginning to realise is that our imagination is severely lacking at a time in the history of the planet when we, as a species, are standing on the precipice of a philosophical, and most likely, an existential abyss that could drag almost every living thing into oblivion. Synthetic creativity may fool us into thinking AGI will conceive of all viable futures but it might be based on a monocultural world view that is already bankrupt. We must not only try and free ourselves of the bonds that strangle our creativity, but we must also learn to share our ideas and creatively collaborate with humans and nonhumans alike.

The Jungian psychoanalyst, James Hillman, discussed what he considered the roots of imagination? He began by critiquing the current US education system for its focus on STEM subjects to the detriment of understanding myths and legends. Hillman quotes Ted Hughes who declared that imagination is dependent on the world's collection of stories, myths and legends and that holding a rich plethora of those stories is fundamental to creative imagination. Hillman states that imagination should be educators first concern in order to help build an archive of draft plans for the way of the worlds. He described how education for imagination was also known in the UK as education for capability, but Hillman makes the point that rather than narrowing the student's imagination and intelligence through simplistic assessments, there is a responsibility to avoid literalism.

Hillman describes this avoidance of surety as an essential part of the imagination, what Henry James called a 'sustained hovering over the case exposed'; and this is what myth does. It does not claim to be true, it is not asking to literally believe in the characters, the plot, or the story but to believe in a higher truth. Hillman in a Jungian turn of phrase said, 'we are planted in mythical soil' and that rich soil is where our fertile imagination will grow and blossom. While it is acknowledged that we are facing an accelerating technological future it is important to retain and reflect on the foundations of our archetypal cosmology that feeds our modern imagination. According to Timothy Desmond, in his book, *Psyche and Singularity: Jungian Psychology and Holographic String Theory*, quantum physics may seem to make our cultural past redundant, and yet as Desmond simply states, "Plato's cosmology permeated the Christian world view in the West throughout the entire medieval era, from St. Augustine to Dante."[2]

Today, Plato's ideas and philosophy, are still highly relevant to 21st-century thinking, and the archetypal narrative of the cosmos. As we set about trying to create the perfect conditions for ourselves and the imagination of future generations we must become comfortable with an imaginative life, and trust our fantasies, and dreams within the archetypal cosmos.

Our ability to creatively envisage alternative and future worlds face a challenge that is common to all creative thinking, i.e. when we are stressed or under pressure to come up with creative novelty, we often become paralysed, or incapable of exploring the wilderness in which these strange ideas lurk. In his book, *The Power of Now*, Eckhart Tolle wrote this about the 'creative use of mind'.

"If you need to use your mind for a specific purpose, use it in conjunction with your inner body. Only if you are able to be conscious without thought can you use your mind creatively, and the easiest way to enter that state is through your body. Whenever an answer a solution, or creative ideas is needed to stop thinking for a moment by focusing attention on your inner energy field. Become aware of the stillness. When you resume thinking, it will be fresh and creative. In any thought activity, make it a habit to go back and forth every few minutes or so between thinking and an inner kind of listening, an inner stillness. We could say: don't just think with your head, think with your whole body."[3]

Antonio Damasio, who is the head of the Brain and Creativity Institute provides "a contemporary scientific validation of the linkage between feelings and the body by highlighting the connection between mind and nerve cells ... this personalized embodiment of mind."[4]

Damasio's research points to a way of thinking about thinking that is at odds with models of mind, AI, neural networks, and machine learning. Hayles documented how we came to see information, data, and our theory of mind as disembodied, or how we became posthuman.[5] However, Damasio and others have shown that emotions, feelings and decision making are not simply focused on the cerebral cortex but are reliant on the chemical, electrical, and neurological sensing that is enabled through the distributed network of nerves, arteries and veins dispersed throughout the body.[6] Emotions are not some awkward feminine trait, a belief as old as Plato, but a necessary component of the rational mind, and essential for decision making and survival.

Montague showed how we share far more in common with single-cell organisms than we had formerly imagined, as like us they must model the world, and sense energy and food in order to 'imagine' a goal, thereby move towards the food before they can consume it.[7]

What these researchers have shown is that our theory of mind, and as a result, the construction of AI's have been founded on false assumptions around information, and intelligence, as a disembodied process. As the AI pioneer, Marvin Minsky, has pointed out, "The question is not whether intelligent machines can have any emotions, but whether machines can be intelligent without any emotions."[8]

Therefore, much of our technological R & D has neglected an embodied model of emotional intelligence and full sensory understanding of the world around us. Disembodiment has alienated human understanding of reality and world building, and has to thank the Enlightenment, and the Gnostic tradition, that bifurcated the body and mind; nature and human; logic and emotion; male and female; science and the humanities. Margaret Wertheim has cited David Noble and Erik Davis who both noted that the 'technological enterprise...remains suffused with religious belief' and is repeated so many times that Davis coined the word 'technosis' to describe how technology forwards the religious fantasy of bodily transcendence, and thus abandons the physical responsibility of the community. This rational techno-liberalism is echoed today in the Transhumanists of Silicon Valley and the selfishness of Ayn Rand 'objectivism'. "Why bother fighting for earthly social justice if you believe that in cyberspace we can all be as gods?"[9]

We cannot just rely on tired paradigms to ensure our future because even our myths and legends do not predate the last mass extinction some 250 million years ago. One of the most important foundations for building successful future worlds are the philosophical and pedagogical methods that support new, experimental and innovative ideas, and ways to think about coexistence amongst those living and nonliving in that world. It requires speculative and risky research on behalf of researchers, scholars, teachers, and their students to stimulate the exploration of novel, and previously untried, unimagined, futures. Our current world is changing radically, in comparison to popular narratives, that is only slowly evolving because our culture is suffering from a collective cognitive dissonance that denies our world may be coming to an end. For many, if they do contemplate the end of the world, then it is something uncomfortable that is quickly forgotten, ignored, or in some cases leads to depression or drug-induced escapism.

World Fairs of the Future

The history of world fairs is illustrative of how we have gone about world bending and world creation in the recent past. The location of two world fairs in Flushing Meadows, New York, reveals the context and shows us the foundations of forgotten dreams, but still remains the graveyard of our futures worlds. Long before the 1939 World Fair occupied the site on the outskirts of Manhattan, around 20,000 years ago, the ice sheets of the Wisconsin glaciation moved across North America morphing and changing the landscape and bending the world under its gigantic mass. This formed the bays and estuaries that in the future became known as the northern shores of Long Island. It was during this glaciation that Flushing Meadows Park, which would be eventually cleared for two World Fairs, was shaped from the upheaval of the slow-moving frozen water that effortlessly pushed the debris before it. As it advanced it moved sand, gravel, clay and huge rocks into the resting place of the moraine.

This geological world bending signalled the beginning of a new world made from the creative destruction of a nonhuman, hyperobject. The moraine created a split draining into what became the Flushing River, and as the ice thawed it became a large glacial lake, and eventually, a salt marsh. These dramatic changes in the climate and landscape are beyond our human scale of time and space. We are only just beginning to grasp how these hyperobjects, and the ecosystems they contain, have evolved. However, we cannot comprehend them without the sensors, and the spatiotemporal study of the biosphere, lithosphere, hydrosphere, and atmosphere; without these tools, we lack the emotional intelligence to appreciate our symbiotic relationship with hyper objects like Flushing Meadows Park.

These evolving hyper objects are becoming an extension of our non-conscious cognition connected to our consciousness via what Katherine Hayles has dubbed technical cognition.[10] The IoT may become an extension of our embodied non-conscious cognition, that is it is fed forward to an AGI that will interpret and translate for both nonhuman and augmented human comprehension.[11] According to Hansen:

"The technical sensors now ubiquitous in our lived environments are able to capture experiential events directly at the micro temporal level of their operationality and—independently of consciousness's mediation—"feed them forward" into (future or "just-to-come") consciousness in ways that can influence consciousness's own future agency in the world."[12]

The challenge we face is to identify and interrogate the narrative fallacies that may be embedded in the algorithms of technical cognition. If humans are already repeatedly making cognitive errors based on fallacies, then what will happen when that is instantiated in an AGI? As Taleb has pointed out this experiential System 1 level operates at speeds beyond our perception, informing our System 2 cognition of consciousness:

"Most of our mistakes in reasoning come from using System 1 when we are in fact thinking that we are using System 2. How? Since we react without thinking and introspection, the main property of System 1 is our lack of awareness of using it!"[13]

Hyperobjects do not just operate at micro temporal scales, that are sensed but not perceived by humans, but at macro temporal scales beyond the human scale stretching beyond generations, over thousands, millions and billions of years.

The first humans to settle in this area, that eventually became the location of the USTA Billie Jean National Tennis Center, and the iconic Unisphere, could only achieve settlement once the climatic conditions got warmer.

A Brief Ecological History of New York & Flushing Meadows

Corn was domesticated in the highlands of Mexico around 7,000 years ago, and before the millennia of synthetic breeding that have given us the big yellow cobs of today, they were originally the size of a human thumbnail. By 800 CE, agriculture had moved North and was firmly established amongst the Native North American peoples.

Growing corn enabled the population density in New England to increase to around 287 people per 100 square miles. They adopted a managed slash and burn,[14] rotational cropping approach that meant that when the Dutch, and English, arrived in the New York area they found the ground already cleared and prepared for them to appropriate the land for themselves and begin planting. They had left behind an Old World and saw themselves as the architects of the New World. However, the colonists assumed that the native agriculture was poorly managed as they did not understand their practice of companion planting, preferring monocultural cropping, and the native cornfields included medicinal plants the colonists deemed "weeds". Native planting was suffused with spiritual practices such as the festivals that emphasise the role of the 'three sisters', corn, beans and squash brought 'from Mexico as a set of rituals before it was an agricultural system'. These ritual practices eventually became part of a farming way of life that was dominated by a matrilineal culture. The women not only took care of agriculture, power, and governance were inherited from the female line.[15]

Colonisation had a long history of assuming that the invading colonists were gifted with God's agricultural creativity and genius. As a result, there was a tendency to consider that the natives were fundamentally ignorant of wise land-management and certainly profit maximisation. This often provided them with the justification for confiscating the native 'wastelands', as they called them, in order to restore them to the way God intended to be, the lands of 'milk and honey', using their 'superior' agricultural technologies. In New Zealand, as in America, the colonialists used religious, economic and political beliefs, theories, and laws to convert, confound, bully, and murder the indigenous people who were often already harvesting crops using ecologically sustainable methods. This was true even when Māori successfully used English technologies in the New Zealand Waikato, growing wheat fields and constructing flour mills to feed the starving and greedy settlers who convinced themselves and the government they had the right to take the land off them. As God's chosen ones, the settlers believed the land was theirs to take.[16]

The rapacious Dutch East Indies Company, or VOC, was the first publicly-traded company and established the New Netherlands, now known as New York City in 1624. Dutch colonists acquired Manhattan from the Laplace tribe for 60 guilders which convert to around US$1,000 (in 2006). By 1666 the Native population had been displaced by European settlers and Flushing Meadows became the location for wealthy landowners that extracted timber, water, fertile soil, and grazed their domesticated animals. Fast forward to fossil fuels, and the agri-industrial processes destroyed wetlands, wildlife habitats, and became a waterfront resort. Not far away, Manhattan was transformed from low-density settlements into one of the most expensive real estate cities in the world, with a median price of US$1,600 per square foot, a total estimated value of US$3 trillion, and with a population density of 70,826 people per square mile. This was only possible due to the massive extraction of energy from fossil fuels converted into food by agri-industry.

During the 1800s as roads and railways opened up the area, it became a dumping ground for the waste created by the inhabitants of Manhattan. Michael Degnon, a New York building contractor who had built the Williamsburg Bridge, Cape Cod Canal and Steinway subway tunnel purchased the 'all but worthless', but large expanse of salt marshes near Flushing Creek in around 1907. His dream was to build a large industrial port in Flushing Bay much like the one he had developed for Long Island. Working with the US Department of War, in 1911 Degnon had created plans to widen the Flushing River so large ships could dock and enable large numbers of factories and freight facilities to use the land. In addition, he expected that the residential areas of nearby Corona would become the residence for factory workers, (a frightening thought considering the toxicity of the place).

In 1910 Degnon began using the pristine wetlands as a dumping ground for Manhattan's household coal ash, and garbage swept off the streets of Brooklyn. He profited from this environmental damage by setting up two companies to contract with the New York Department of Sanitation and negotiated with the corrupt Tammany Hall member 'Fishhooks' McCarthy, who was head of the Brooklyn Ash Removal Company. Flushing Meadows became a visible eyesore and by the 1920's it was described by F. Scott Fitzgerald in *The Great Gatsby* as the Valley of Ashes, "it was a "fantastic farm where ashes grow like wheat into ridges and hills and grotesque gardens; where ashes take the forts of houses and chimneys and rising smoke." According to the Physicians for Social Responsibility coal ash is extremely hazardous to human health:

"Depending on where the coal was mined, coal ash typically contains heavy metals including arsenic, lead, mercury, cadmium, chromium and selenium, as well as aluminium, antimony, barium, beryllium, boron, chlorine, cobalt, manganese, molybdenum, nickel, thallium, vanadium, and zinc."

How dangerous is coal ash to humans?

"The Environmental Protection Agency (EPA) has found that living next to a coal ash disposal site can increase your risk of cancer or other diseases. If you live near an unlined wet ash pond (surface impoundment) and you get your drinking water from a well, you may have as much as a 1 in 50 chance of getting cancer from drinking arsenic-contaminated water. If eaten, drunk or inhaled, these toxicants can cause cancer and nervous system impacts such as cognitive deficits, developmental delays and behavioural problems. They can also cause heart damage, lung disease, respiratory distress, kidney disease, reproductive problems, gastrointestinal illness, birth defects, and impaired bone growth in children."[17]

Obviously, these very serious human health hazards do not just affect humans and the impact of the massive dumping of this toxic waste will have a lasting impact on the wildlife and health of the entire ecosystem. Degnon and Fishhooks McCarthy helped build the infrastructure to transport the residential ash via the trolleys, and 100 open carloads a day, using the Brooklyn Rapid Transit Company and freight trains to the Corona Dump known as the 'conveyor belt' and nicknamed the 'Talcum Powder Express' because they were uncovered and spread soot throughout the countryside. Over the course of 30 years of dumping and filling there were approximately 50 million cubic yards of ash and waste dumped onto the meadows and wetlands. It created a small mountain 27 meters of toxic waste high known as 'Mount Corona' with the average thickness of the ash being 9.1 meters deep. Often mixed with the ash were the household refuse from the residents of Brooklyn who simply threw out their rubbish with the ash, and the horse manure collected in the street. This created a perfect breeding ground for rats, and one of the worst mosquito havens in the city. The smell was horrendous and the once clean healthy Flushing River was now polluted and described as a 'small foul river'.[18]

To add to the environmental damage the northern end of the site was filled with dirt that was dredged and pumped in massive quantities from the depths of Flushing Bay using a hydraulic machine that filled the rich wetland habitats and meadow with muck, and toxic heavy metals, completing the fill-in 1916. However, the private ash dumping contract continued until around 1934 when the City of New York purchased the dump for the Parks Department. This toxic site was to become the foundation for the futuristic World Fairs, a golf course, and the National Tennis Centre. These visions of future worlds elide the hidden toxic consequences of environmental damage based on corruption and corporate greed. The foundations of new worlds ended worlds for native Americans, fauna and flora, and will likely herald the end for themselves in the future.

Waste Not Want Not Futures

In 1935 the US was in the depths of the Great Depression, a group of New York business people and public officials came together, led by Robert Moses and Grover Whalen to create an international exhibition to bolster the local economy using the vehicle of a World Fair. The first World Fair was held in London in 1851 with a massive building, made from glass and steel, the Crystal Palace. The New York World Fair of 1939 was the first exposition to be based on the future and had an opening slogan of "Dawn of a New Day." and it was billed as an opportunity for the visitors to take a peek at the 'the world of tomorrow'. According to the official pamphlet:

"The eyes of the Fair are on the future — not in the sense of peering toward the unknown nor attempting to foretell the events of tomorrow and the shape of things to come, but in the sense of presenting a new and clearer view of today in preparation for tomorrow; a view of the forces and ideas that prevail as well as the machines."

Unbeknownst to the excited visitors to the future the foundations of the World Fairs were built on corruption, toxic waste and environmental vandalism. Our ability to build, bend and break worlds is wholly dependent on our imagination. What I am advocating is 'world bending' or daring to imagine alternative futures. We must reject Maggie Thatcher's damnable provocation 'there is no alternative' to capitalism. I am not proposing a blueprint (that way leads to technocratic fascism) but the implementation of ways to expose that the Emperor has no clothes. In his book, *Utopia for Realists*, Rutger Bregman, wrote:

"Should we simply stop dreaming of a better world altogether? No, of course not. But that's precisely what is happening. Optimism and pessimism have become synonymous with consumer confidence or the lack thereof. Radical ideas about a different world have become almost literally unthinkable. The expectations of what we as a society can achieve have been dramatically eroded, leaving us with the cold, hard truth that without utopia, all that remains is a technocracy. Politics has been watered down to problem management."[19]

We are developing new ways and means to sense and analyse the physical and social worlds; to expose who, what, when and how hyperobjects came about? By exposing the previously hidden archaeological layers, physical, and digital, we can prevent ecological disasters and pressure governments and corporations to remediate damage and stop it from happening in the first place. The IoT can expose data about what is happening in our air, water, soil, software and biosphere.[20]

Transparency by itself is useless without ethical debate, and the values that protect humans and nonhumans alike, biological and synthetic. We must be braver and more creative in our ambitions to build, bend and break conceptual worlds that provide us with alternative futures.

The World Fair in Flushing Meadows presents a poignant metaphor of what can go wrong with world building when the problems of the past are simply covered over and hidden from sight. The shocking toxicity of our cities has been exposed to numerous disasters such as the attack on the Twin Towers in NYC. The dangerous dust and fumes resulting from the pile of rubble at the site of the Towers have resulted in 10,000 first responders having contracted cancer, a further 40,000 have applied for aid for health treatment, with another 21,000 pending.[21]

In a remote part of New Zealand's South Island, heavy rain and rising river levels in the Fox River have exposed the Westland District Landfill that had been closed for almost twenty years. 135,000 kilograms of rubbish oozed out of the banks and polluted the pristine river in what threatens to be the first of many landfill disasters in New Zealand and around the world that could be creating environmental disasters due to global heating. It is not only the physicality of these threats, the chemical toxins, plastic waste, and heavy metals that have suddenly been exposed, but the spectre of capitalism and the terrors implied by what may come as they haunt our consciousness. The past needs to be exhumed and analysed to assess the possible hazards buried in the underworld of Promethean visions, corruption, and greedy disregard for other humans and nonhumans alike. The dangers that continue to lurk beneath the surface must be exposed and neutralised or they will return to haunt our futures.

Synthetic Monsters of the Deep

The 1939 World Fair in Flushing Meadows was not only built on a toxic dump but it became a suspect collection site for a number of visions and algorithms for the technologies of the future. As a boy, the science fiction writer, Philip K. Dick, PKD, visited the 1939 World Fair, a shining example of an optimistic future, two years before America joined World War II, and six years before a nuclear reaction burnt shadows of vaporised Japanese civilians onto the walls of Hiroshima and Nagasaki.

According to a biography of PKD, as a boy he visited Treasure Island with his father, it was a synthetic island created for the launch of the San Francisco World Fair celebrating the Golden Gate Bridge – that technological marvel that bridged the divide between humanity and nature across the abyss of the icy waters of San Francisco Bay. PKD suffered from a paranoid state brought on by a lack of sleep and drugs that saw his world as precarious. PKD In his biography, the author, Anthony Peake, wrote "Phil had told me that, when he was a little boy, his father used to get him up in the middle of the night, put him into the car and drive as fast as he could to the east because a big earthquake was about to hit – it always turned out to be a false alarm."[22]

When PKD walked around the World Fair with his father he came across Pedro the Voder, a synthetic voice instrument designed and built by Bell Telephone Company. According to PKD's biographer Anthony Peake, this was one of the most popular exhibits at the World Fair and astounded the young boy.

"This machine was an early attempt at synthesizing the human voice by combining a buzzing sound, created by an electrical oscillator, with a hissing sound, produced by a gas discharge tube. An operator-controlled the device using keys and foot pedals. It is clear that this machine had a profound effect on PKD's young mind and probably first sparked the idea of the human simulacra that featured in many of his novels and short stories. Indeed, in his novel *We Can Build You* (1972), 'Pedro' itself is referenced."[23]

According to Peake, PKD 'precognized' the Lincoln simulacrum at Disneyland. The evidence cited by Peake appeared in his novel *We Can Build You* that was sent to his agency on 4th October 1962. While it was rejected by Putnam, Doubleday and other publishers it finally appeared in Amazing Stories on Nov. 1969 under the title *A Lincoln Simulacrum* and was eventually published under DAW Books, and the title *We Can Build You* in July 1972. What is strange is that the first audio-automaton of Lincoln appeared on 22 April 1964 at the NY World Fair, two years after PKD wrote his book, and another version was unveiled at Disneyland on 18 July 1965.

As an extension of the ideology of World Fairs sci-fi movies perpetuates the myths of agrilogic colonisation. The ancient journeys of Achilles in the small region of the fertile crescent eventually spread to occupy and enclose the entire planet only halting at the poles to divide the spoils among the largest and most powerful. Those who developed the technology to set sail in ships were on a mission to expand their world and to accumulate mass by using a proto-algorithm for the General Theory of Relativity.

Well before Einstein formulated $E=mc^2$ the agriolithic patriarchs attempted to gain power through faster ships, and mass through mountains of spices, gold, silver and other objects stolen from the commons and hapless colonies. They knew that mass times speed equated to energy, and therefore power. The expansion of empires was driven by the search for greater resources of people, land, and fungible materials increasing the complexity of domestic societies and their eventual collapse.[24]

Sustainable Disasters

So began the 500-year expedition to achieve escape velocity and colonise new worlds in space. Elon Musk has become the poster boy for outer space fantasies as his Space X programme is like a *Boys Own*, Buck Rogers space race against other 'schoolboys', such as Richard Branson, to be the first to offer commercial flights. Musk, Branson, and Bezos are just three space entrepreneurs that add to the 'self-elaborating' discourse.[25] that extends agrilogistics off-planet in space ships modelled on the early fantasies of strange lands, adventures, and power. Going into space is simply the next step after the land-mass, ice and seas are spoken for, expansionary inflation of the closed world of the Anthropocene. This is an expansion of the 'discursive infrastructure' that supports the entrepreneurial drive for more energy, to amass more power, by aiming for the speed of light. There is an entrepreneurial impulse to build upon, and sustain the paradigm that produced their initial wealth and success – the discourse continues. According to Edwards:

"It produces both power and knowledge: individual and institutional behaviour, facts, logic and the authority that reinforces it...It also continually expands its own scope, occupying and integrating conceptual space in a kind of discursive imperialism'.[26]

Edwards takes the view that the world building of science and technology is neither deterministic, nor some comprehensive conspiratorial plan but a 'bricolage' of models, metaphors, and research programs, 'tinkering – as discourse' that blurs the sharp edges between knowledge, and praxis'.[27] However, given the ability of the agrilogistic discourse to 'self elaborate' we must stay vigilant to its expansionary objectives and muster the tools of speculative worlds beyond the destructive violence of the Anthropocene. Musk et al., the boys growing up in the '60s and '70s were in search of escape velocity, however, they are not so much looking for another world, as they want to build the same world in space.

The anthropogenic discourse continued, at the Flushing Meadows World Fair of 1964 that exhibited General Motors updated version of the 1939 *Futurama*. The new and improved *Futurama* showed a 60s version of space cities and the exhibit showed how humans could live and work at the bottom of the sea. In 1968, Stanley Kubrick's, *2001 a Space Odyssey*, showed how the ships of the future extended the discourse of Ma Bell, and the now-defunct Pan Am, with video conferences from space shuttles emblazoned with company logos.

The Unisphere, the icon of the New York World Fair of 1964 in Flushing Meadows, was 'most notable for reflecting American corporate power... [and] was dedicated to 'Man's Achievement on a Shrinking Globe in an Expanding Universe' (p.129) The Unisphere built by U.S. Steel was a 12 story high metal globe, and 'The theme reflected the concerns of the cold war and the hope of new technologies to conquer the universe, bring peace, and ease everyday life." (p.129)

Energy and power, on display at the 1964 World Fair, were the concerns of the day in the space race with the Soviets with exhibits such as General Electric's mock-up of controlled thermonuclear fusion. The World Fairs helped to move world bending forward towards world creations as fictions became facts. Today these obsessions of mass and speed appear the tickets to power as the likes of Musk builds his lithium Giga factory in Nevada; his hyperloop train; and the launch of the Falcon Heavy adorned with a Tesla driven by a dummy astronaut strapped to the nose cone. The Falcon Heavy spaceflight was accompanied by the posthumous David Bowie singing, 'There's a starman waiting in the sky', and the fictional world building was well on its way into outer space. Writing about the history of world fairs, Antonelli wrote:

"A great world fair, just like a good sci-fi movie, is a plausible fantasy based on the impact of science and technology on society. But while the world portrayed by the movies can be on the verge of a dark catastrophe – or just emerging from it – the dream invoked by a world's fair is nearly always a gleaming utopia within arm's reach."[28]

Electric Eco Disasters

What these techno-fantasies hides are the environmental, and social cost of the infrastructure needed to build them. According to Tainter, increasingly complex societies require increasing resources to achieve sustainability and to solve the problems of the day.[29]

Innovation becomes more and more incremental and complex, requiring more to do less. If we stop to consider the technological solution to fossil fuel consumption, Musk has bet heavily on lithium-ion batteries. While it is true that electric cars and solar battery-powered houses will decrease greenhouse gas emissions, and some other ecological concerns, lithium has been historically mined in South America throughout the Andes Mountain range forming the lithium triangle of Chile, Argentina, and the biggest. Bolivia producing the most. Surprisingly, however, the production of lithium batteries does have significant environmental drawbacks as production consumes the equivalent of 1.6kg of oil per 1kg of battery manufactured. Lithium battery production also causes greenhouse gas emissions of 12.5kg of CO_2 equivalent per 1kg of battery made. As lithium is commonly found in salt flats, water is generally scarce, but the mining process requires large amounts of water supply. This exploitation of local water supplies has drastically affected human and nonhuman populations near the mining areas. "In the Salar de Atacama, 'mining already consumes 65% of the water' (Tahill 2007), leading to angry disputes with local communities whose wells run dry, and whose crops are afflicted by runoff from the ponds of saline solution from which the lithium salts are garnered."[30] What is more, the toxic chemicals that are used to leach the lithium means that incorrect wastewater treatment can result in environmental damage further reducing useable water supplies. Tesla claims 60% of batteries are recycled, 10% of the battery gets reused, but to date, the recovery of spent lithium batteries have been in the single percentage digits. Both nickel and cobalt, that are used in the production of lithium-ion batteries, according to a 2013 Environmental Protection Agency report, represent a significant environmental risk.

According to Tainter as we attempt to sustain our current world, and transition to alternative energy sources, complexity and problem solving go hand in hand, and complexity can lead to collapse. Tainter outlines an argument that presents world bending with a significant challenge. He presents strong evidence of the following claims:[31]

- Conservation alone does not produce sustainability
- Sustainability is an active condition of problem-solving
- Complexity is a problem-solving tool, including problems of sustainability
- Complexity is an economic function, with benefits and costs and can reach diminishing returns
- Sustainability may require greater consumption of resources not less
- Complexity in problem-solving causes damage subtly, unpredictability and cumulatively
- A society or other institution can be destroyed by the cost of sustaining itself

Our ability to maintain our current world is looking increasingly doubtful as our energy needs to increase the costs, both ecologically, and eventually monetarily, will also increase. Musk's Nevada Gigafactory has been established using tax breaks from the Nevada government. This common cost reduction is just another way of externalising the cost of energy production. However, Tainter points out that this disconnect of cost and benefits needs to be reunified in order to constrain resource consumption. Tainter argues that while the original cost of problem-solving often appears acceptable, the long term consequences of accumulated costs are not. Three-quarters of all mined lithium is used for battery production, and according to the

Lawrence Berkeley National Laboratory, there is enough lithium with global reserves of 39 million tons, enough to produce 1 billion 40 kWh batteries. However, the demand for batteries is growing around 25% per annum, yet production is only growing by 4-5%. To sustain our current world the real question is one of scale, as the concentration of intensive mining, water consumption, possible toxic contamination, and non-recyclable toxic waste could undermine the benefits of conversion from fossil fuels to lithium-ion batteries. The ecological costs are already beginning to accumulate, so the very act of sustaining this world, by world bending, may result in world ending, this may be inevitable, and even sensible. But what of new world creation?

Resource Consent and Site Inspection

World builders need no resource consent, local or government regulation compliance, or UNESCO approval to set up shop and just start building. Of course, as I pointed out earlier the human species is only one of a multitude of world builders anyway. For now, I am going to discuss the familiar anthropocentric version of world building before we move on to how to build the foundations for future worlds that will follow the end of this one. First, we will examine human world builders and the assumption that you can just get on with it, and not really ask anyone for permission to build a world. There are caveats depending on what sort of world building and what sort of medium you are working in.

For example, I wrote a movie script set in the past at the end of the Qing Dynasty based on the biggest civil war in history, in which 20 million Chinese died. I was told by Chinese film officials that the Chinese audiences would not want to see it despite numerous meetings when they had previously approved the idea. Chinese censorship is not explicit and is based on the whim and mood of the Chinese government rather than written down. So, yes there are restrictions on world building, but they do not come in a tidy city ordinance or printed manuals. Quite often the human world builder has to research the implicit and dispersed explicit rules that might prevent them from building a world that some powerful people might object to. What is even more daunting is that the world builder may be unaware of the philosophical, and cognitive, callipers that prevent them from running like the wind, and designing a world that is just what their prospective inhabitants secretly desire, but cannot articulate. It may appear that a new world is being created, and in China, many believe the Government's assertion that this century will belong to China. President Xi Jinping's China Dream is determined to replace the American Dream.

According to Shenshen Cai, in the book, *State Propaganda in China's Entertainment Industry on the Chinese* (2016):

"On 19 August 2013, the Chinese president Xi Jinping made an important speech at a national conference on propaganda where he emphasized that innovation in ideas, devices and methods are the most significant points in the development and progress of the CCP's propaganda work ."[32]

China's economy has been likened to 'state capitalism' and the hopes and dreams of many of its citizens are to achieve a material wealth akin to America through innovation, fossil fuels, alternative energy, and electronic entertainment devices. The environmental cost has already been shown to be fatal yet many believe they are building a new world. There are already signs that this is just another form of world bending that is contributing to an accelerated world ending.

The clock is ticking for one world – the dominant world view, the Kantian and neoliberal 'transparent cage' has grown from ancient and humble origins. It appeared like a star, growing brighter, and burning hotter than we ever imagined. It continued to burgeon beyond belief until it covered the planet Earth and while other frustrated world builders complained, critiqued, and even violently attacked that world, the dominant world view has triumphed – until now, perhaps it will become a supernova. The shocking prospect of a world catastrophe should be tempered with the cosmic realisation that all new worlds come from such a cataclysmic stellar death. We are all made of stardust.

The foundations of our world are made up of complex constructions that include the environmental, lithographic rock strata; our co-evolution with the other creatures of the biosphere, not forgetting the importance of our microbial kin; the atmosphere; hydrosphere; and our mythological, cultural, and scientific histories. In psychological terms, the foundations of our world occupy the dark, chthonic recesses of our mind.

The Psychological Foundations of Worlds

Dreams and myths occupy a primordial place very near the beginning of human world construction. Dreams and premonitions were feared and respected going back before written language. The interpretation of those dreams and premonitions were channelled by shamans, priestly kings, and witches; they were talented individuals who were blessed with what was commonly believed to be divine knowledge from the gods. According to Freud and Jung, these primordial dreams have been passed down to us via our subconscious. Jung argued that these primitive storytellers were not too dissimilar to poets and philosophers. Today, we unsuspectedly inherit these wild images and symbols from thousands and thousands of years ago. Carl Jung noted that Freud referred to these as 'ancient remnants' – 'mental forms whose presence cannot be explained by anything in the individual's own life and which seem to be aboriginal, innate, and inherited shapes of the human mind.'[33]

Jung called these primitive shapes archetypes, and importantly, does not exclusively attribute them to humans but also animals, and the greater cosmos. Through his extensive research into mythologies, legends and stories Jung came to believe that, while these specific shapes were more or less personal, their general pattern was collectively shared by humanity and the cosmos[34] While many understand and interpret Jung from an individual psychoanalytic perspective, Desmond and others have described how his theories were both complementary with, and formed by, his discussions with physicists such as Einstein, Heisenberg, and Pauli. Quantum physics and string theory support the conclusion that our world, or indeed our universe is but one of an infinite number of universes, a multiverse, in which the past, present, and future are, according to the theoretical physicist Bryan Greene, simply a 'persistent illusion'. Desmond writes:

"Thus, it seems that at each moment, each of us is absolutely free to choose from an infinite array of pre-determined futures, while all of the alternatives we do not choose will nevertheless be chosen by some other version of us corresponding to the parallel universe in which "we" make that choice."[35]

This is a creative process in which the virtual is actualised as anti-particles become actual particles and the potential becomes an actual thing. The realisation of this reality liberates our imagination from the imprisonment of logical empiricism and validates multi-reality world building. While this provides us with an alternative foundation for world building we are still challenged by the hegemony of logical empiricism and neo-liberal economics which must be overcome in order to move beyond the power structure of an anthropocentric hierarchy.

"Taxonomy is thus not only an epistemological instrument (a means for organizing information), but it is also (as it comes to organize the organizers) an instrument for the construction of society. And to the extent that taxonomies are socially determined, hegemonic taxonomies will tend to reproduce the same hierarchical system of which they are themselves the product."[36]

It was Marshall McLuhan in his famous book *Understanding Media*, that stated 'the medium is the message'.[37]

What he meant was that the content of the communication was influenced, if not determined, by the technological infrastructure and substrate that carried it. The history of the written language illustrates the impact of the medium on the message when we consider the earliest records and the way the authors used language, and the words themselves. According to Nicholas Carr, the medium not only impacts the content of the message but the very way we think and communicate ideas. He describes the history of the written word and how the transition from an oral tradition to writing progressed. Not only was silent reading a novel innovation, but the meter and the rhyme of words that were spoken aloud were considered more important than word order, or indeed the space between the words. The absence of space between the words replicated the flow of spoken word, and was known as scriptura continua and would be intolerable for most of us today. As books developed rules of grammar evolved, and word spacing effectively lightened the cognitive load on the brain as the reader did not have to slowly decipher the meaning of the words.[38] Carr goes on to argue how our Internet technology is changing the way we think, read and remember.[39]

This has profound implications for our imagination, and the future worlds we can design. The evolution of language, communication and knowledge exchange is often characterised as the progression of human knowledge, science, rational thought, and technology. What is often neglected is the way in which myth, storytelling, and hidden agendas are embedded in our latest devices, systems, and assumptions. With the exponential growth of computing and the algorithmic digitization, and virtualization of technology, the design is becoming invisible and hidden. Our reliance on our visual sense to process and understand reality means that these things that are disappearing before our eyes becoming increasingly hard to interrogate, question or even approve. Vision occupies 30% of the brain cortex, compared to the neurons dedicated to touch being only 8%, and 3% for hearing. It is therefore of concern that the trend of miniaturization and the virtual process of converting physical objects into software, or algorithms, will likely mean, 'out of sight, out of mind'.

Algorithmic Complexity

This algorithmic trend predates computing, and according to Morton can be traced back 12,000 years to our invention of agriculture, that he calls agrilogistics which is still a driving force today.[40] According to Ed Finn in his book, *What Algorithms Want*, he describes pragmatists view of algorithms as a "method for solving a problem"[41] Morton outlines his argument for agricultural algorithms to show how this ancient method of food supply also became the determining factor in how we organise a complex society, control each other, and ultimately caused the Anthropocene.

"Because of its underlying logical structure, agrilogistics now plays out at the spatiotemporal scale of global warming, having supplied the conditions for the Agricultural Revolution, which swiftly provided the conditions for the Industrial Revolution."[42]

It was Ada Lovelace in 1843, the assistant to Charles Babbage, who is credited with the first publication of a computer program, or algorithm.[43] She was a visionary that saw that computers need not be limited to the computation of mathematical problems. She envisaged how they might be used to create music, text, and even images, beyond mere calculations, in other words, something like a modern computer. However, when it came to AI she did not believe that a computer could come up with ideas or intentions of its own, she wrote, "The Analytical Engine has no pretensions whatever to originate anything." This became known as Alan Turing's 'Lady Lovelace's Objection'.[44]

In 1937 Alan Turing published a paper, *On Computable Numbers*. that described a universal computer that showed that any real number or series could be computed as long as its calculations were defined by a finite set of rules. In line with Godel's incompleteness theorem, he did also show there were non-computable numbers, and no mechanical process can determine the provability of every mathematical statement. This proof along with the indeterminacy of quantum mechanics, "all dealt blows to a mechanical, deterministic, predictable universe."[45] While engineers have tended to just get on with it and ignore this awkward truth about a non-computable universe, what Turing did provide was the proof for his concept of a Logical Computing Machine, he wrote "It is possible to invent a single machine which can be used to compute any computable sequence."[46] This was the realised dream of Charles Babbage and Ada Lovelace, i.e. a general-purpose universal machine.

As the logistics of agriculture evolved, and the algorithm remained intact it was joined by future algorithmic methods that now dominate the workings of the modern world. The more common understanding of algorithms relates to digital computing, however, it is possible to trace the legacy of computing through millennia of technological and ideological legacy. The Oxford dictionary definition for an algorithm is "a process or set of rules to be followed in calculations or other problem-solving operations, especially by a computer". Finn claims we are in the algorithmic age where every company is looking to convert problems into methods and in corporate America ...

"The major focus for contemporary algorithmic research is not whether they work but how efficiently, and with what tradeoffs in terms of CPU cycles, memory, and accuracy."[47]

We are undoubtedly confronted by an increasing number of existential problems that threaten the end of our current world, and the proliferation of complexity through these computer algorithms are symptomatic of world building pathologies. As we have already noted Joseph Tainter has described how problem-solving contributes to increasing complexity, so it would seem we are stuck in an exponential, and accelerating feedback loop. He outlines the dilemma of problem-solving as follows:

- Problems are inevitable, so the process of increasing complexity is inexorable

- Increasing complexity produces increasing costs and diminishing returns

- When problems have encountered the costs of solving usually appears acceptable. The damage comes from cumulative costs.

- Societies become vulnerable to collapse through the mundane process of solving problems.[48]

If world bending, problem-solving, is driving our search for a sustainable future, and this contributes to complexity, and complexity leads to collapse, then is there no way out of the end of this world? You may be wondering what happened to the techno-optimism of the dot.com revolution, or the democratic promise of Web 2.0 and the liberation of the oppressed people of the Arab Spring?

Ontology of Future Worlds

Our capacity to use technology to redesign our world and seek alternative futures has to acknowledge that ironically we are limited by that same technology that created the problems in the first place, therefore our imagination is contained by how technology is designed, and what

it allows us to do. As cited by Carr, Marshall McLuhan expressed early
concern that:

"Alienation... is an inevitable by-product of the use of technology.
Whenever we use technology to exert greater control over the outside
world, we change our relationship with that world."[49]

However, it is important to point out that while I do not disagree
with Carr and McLuhan, that while there is some inevitable mediation
happening between human and technology, whether it is a screen, a
computer, or some sort of electronic sensor that intervenes between
your senses and reality, this is a naive view of how we construct reality.
All reality is mediated and from a speculative realists view there is
no possibility of experiencing reality directly. Photons travel to Earth
from the Sun but even if you were foolish enough to stare directly
at the Sun, the photons have had to travel through the Sun's corona,
the cosmic vacuum of space, our stratosphere, then our atmosphere,
perhaps through clouds, water particles, ozone, other chemicals and
gases, before they move through the various layers of your eye. Entering the eye through the cornea, or clear, dome-shaped surface that
covers the eye. Next, it passes through the pupil and regulated by the
coloured area known as the iris. From there the light hits the transparent lens structure which focuses images onto the retina. But that
is not the end, as the retina has received the image upside down. The
optic nerve carries the image made up of signals of light and dark, and
colours to the visual cortex which then translates the signal into something that our brain has learnt to interpret as images that are recognised, and what we might call vision. This complicated process means
that you never directly experience either light or the object you are
viewing. There is a complicated chemical, electrical, mechanical, and
physical process that will also be open to wide variations between individuals, and species. In philosophical terms, reality is always metaphysical, or indeed virtual.

In some ways, this is also the conclusion that Kant came to in the
18th century and because it provided the foundation for a totally new
world view we ironically called it Enlightenment, even though we still
could not really explain how light worked. However, a whole new generation of philosophers in the 21st century have come to challenge

Kant's ontology or description of reality. Kant held that reality is always inextricably tied to how we think about it, and therefore nature and the human mind are both divided and correlated; he argued that we cannot have one without the other, nature only existed in the human mind.

This view of reality in effect severed us from nature as we continued to imagine that we were created in God's image and that nature was everything else, defined by human cognition. It is how we entered the modern scientific age because while the world became increasingly secular, and there was no evidence of God's hand beyond the laws of physics, the entire universe remained anthropocentric, and for our benefit. The OOO and speculative realism philosophically acknowledge that everything is outside of human cognition, but most importantly those things are still real. I imagine you are saying to yourself, well, of course, that is common sense but that is not the end of it. Science, or rather scientism, that claims there is only one truth and only one explanation of reality, i.e. science, has not yet acknowledged that no matter how advanced scientific theory or experimental technology, reality cannot be experienced directly, and will always remain ultimately unknowable, and non-computable.

In reality, all things will always hold some mystery, and will always have some quality that is partially hidden, even to themselves. As Harman has pointed out there can be no Grand Unified Theory of Everything, in the current philosophy of physics, because it ignores the very real nature of concepts, fictions, and even paradox. What is more, according to Whitehead, it ignores the philosophical question of creativity and the process of becoming or actualising. Chaos theory and randomisation proposes that the creative event or process is eventuated through random emergence that cannot be predicted. In *Order Out of Chaos*, Ilya Prigogine and Isabelle Stengers conclude that this question was not just their obsession, but has been the obsession throughout the history of science and philosophy. "This is the question of the relation between being and becoming, between permanence and change."[50]

The only certainty is that we are uncertain, and our models will never resolve this. Our creativity depends on the degree of comfort with which we approach uncertainty and are playful and open with the results of experimentation and even the errors that arise from randomness and algorithms of spurious certainty. The Italian theorist, Parisi extends Whitehead's philosophical approach to reality, through 'transcendent empiricism'. That accepts this lack of certainty and speculates that computation may need to be "conceived in terms of its speculative intelligible functions through which unknowns are algorithmically prehended"[51] Therefore, when designers, philosophers, engineers, artists and scientists try to imagine future worlds, and alternate realities, without critically examining the limitations of their tools, they face grave danger. At this very moment in our history, we seem to be playing along with the mass deception that assumes we are close to scientifically, and wholly, defining reality, through mathematical models, and computer simulations. Hayles points out that:

"As David Berry (2011) puts it, "the ontology of the computational is increasingly hegemonic in forming the background presupposition for our understanding the world."[52]

As those future worlds become increasingly difficult for us to tell the difference from reality, they assume a new role, what Baudrillard called 'hyperreality', a synthetic reality that replaces the physical reality, and becomes more real than the reality we are simulating. This would be a very dangerous scenario because there is another technological trend that is both sensing a bewildering amount of reality but also connecting actuators that give us mechanical and physical control over that reality, known as the IoT, or Internet of Things.

This God-like power will hide and disguise our ignorance of all things that are non-computable and exacerbate our anthropocentric world view that will inevitably harm the nonhuman reality we encounter on the way. Our ability to muse our predicament has been circumvented by the technology that has reconfigured how we think. As modern logic seeps out of our new digitised world our ability to simultaneously hold paradoxical meditations are being dispelled by the viral intrusion of computational logic. The philosopher Michael Heim warns that as information technology and computable logic becomes more ubiquitous it is affecting the way we think, abstracted and removed from our direct experience of things, and so the world of nonhumans. Heim wrote:

"We commonly assume the existence or at least the existential relevance of what we are talking about. Modern symbolic logic, on the contrary, mimics modern mathematics, which has no interest in the actually existing world, not even the world of direct statements. In this sense, modern logic operates at a remove from our everyday involvement with things."[53]

The foundations of future world creation must acknowledge the weakness of our cognitive building blocks to overcome the limitations of simplistic world bending. Some will dismiss this fearful claim by first saying that a simulation that is indistinguishable from our perception of reality is a long way off, if not impossible. Most have not paused to reconsider our two-hundred-year-old view of reality, and the even older anthropocentric bias, that dates back to the beginning of the Holocene.

Design Foundations of Virtual Reality

In the history of computer simulations, J.C.F. Licklider's desire for Man-Machine symbiosis has today progressed well beyond the early days of the fabled VR prototype, the 'Sword of Damocles'. This cumbersome piece of technology was heavy and encumbered by a mass of wires. We are now seeing untethered HMDs (head-mounted displays) which enables users to physically move around virtual environments, increasing the proprioceptive and kinaesthetic sense of presence. Non-Euclidean hyperbolic geometry in VR offers the illusion of limitless space to explore. However, there is currently no virtual dirt under the fingernails, and so the ability to engage in what Haraway calls, sympoiesis, 'mutual making', or co-design with the nonhumans is crudely limited using this virtual world building method.[54]

Even Nelson & Stollerman in their mindful book on the theory of design, *The Design Way*, neglected the relations between object and object, and between the designer and the nonhuman ontology.[55] In their attempt to give the design a reality in praxis they neglected the theoretical discussion of world building for nonhumans in preference to the 'service' of the human client. They wrote:

"The design is a distinctive approach in which service is a defining element. Science and art are, in the best sense self-serving, in that scientists are motivated by their own curiosity, and art by self-expression that looks for or finds meaning – design is about "making meaning – design expertise – by causing things to happen" in the service of others."[56]

Design theory continues to promote an HCD (human-centred Design) approach and a Co-Design theory that tacitly assumes human relations only. In their book, *Creative Confidence*, the Kelly brothers, David and Tom, emphasised that a human-centred approach should come first and that a successful design would intersect the desires of People; the Business viability; and the Technical feasibility. The absence of a nonhuman consideration speaks volumes for why commercial product design is often so harmful to the environment. Since the publication of *The Future of Competition: Co-Creating Unique Value with Customers*, by C. K. Prahalad and Venkat Ramaswamy, co-creation and co-design has been further developed to extend beyond just customers to other stakeholders, however, it is rare to find a discussion of the relations of nonhumans in design theory.

In the 1970s Victor Papanek raised many of the issues brought to light under the banner of the Anthropocene, however, 'Design Thinking' continues to propagate a neoliberal, consumerist, design world view that often promotes superficial packaging over deep OOO design aesthetics that are mindful of nonhuman relations.

It may be possible that by simply enfranchising a growing number of nonhuman objects Nelson & Stollerman could embrace the 'parliament of things'. While *The Design Way* tacitly supports an anthropocentric bias it could give more objects the vote if we were to assume nonhuman democracy in their following text:

"Designing takes place in complex settings, is a complex process itself, and results in complex augmentations to the real world...How do we bring epistemological and ontological insights together with the design fundamentals of relationships and connections...Connections allow us to see or create critical links that define the structure of behaviour of systemic phenomena."[57]

Design disciplines such as architecture in the US have begun to explore OOO at schools such as the School of Architecture at Taliesin; at Yale University; Texas A&M, and at SCI-Arc where Harman teaches.

According to Nelson & Stollerman design is proactive expertise that is focused on 'making meaning', an abductive third way, different from art and science. However, the worlds that we make are built on code that has been imbricated with dark secrets. The modular algorithms and protocols embedded deep in historic code are not easily found, analysed or discussed. Galloway challenges us to decode the protocols we take for granted.

The future is in desperate need of software archaeologists who can, not only identify the invention of the algorithm, but historically reverse engineer some of the social, political, economic and environmental objects, and symbionts that fertilized their original DNA. The metadata of these things has either been lost; erased; is proprietary, or a classified secret. Our capacity to imagine, or to think deeply about the Anthropocene, a vast hyperobject that defies object oriented programming, is severely limited by our inherited algorithms and protocols of control.[58]

"Every tool imposes limitations even as it opens up possibilities."[59]

Dunne & Raby have promoted speculative design as a tool for considering wicked problems and raising serious questions about 'affirmative design' and neoliberal economics. Speculative design, together with creative technologies have explored alternative, and sometimes preferable, futures. According to Dunne & Raby, these imagined worlds are not designed to be didactic, fascist or even predictive. They write: "For us futures are not a destination or something to be strived for but a medium to aid imaginative thought—to speculate with."[60]

The common concern of critical software theorists, such as, Haraway, Finn, Galloway, Bogost, and Hayles is that increasingly our tools of cognition are dependent on algorithms and protocols, that have reified our culture's popular dreams, desires and fears. Speculative theoretical foundations can help to re-imagine the Post Anthropocene and a future worth building. We have to accept the uncertainty of the future and not be afraid of our mistakes. As we tussle with the hyper-objects beyond human spacetime we can critically reflect on our mistakes. As Hayles writes:

"they tear open a rip in the temporal fabric of the historical present, through which a better and more utopian future may be glimpsed. As Parisi puts it, what error makes possible is the "discovering of new concepts".[61]

We must also embrace our own agency and be prepared to act and experiment. As Buckminster Fuller wrote:

"Realistic thinking accrues only after mistake making, which is the cosmic wisdom's most cogent way of teaching each of us how to carry on."[62]

Despite the fact that many of these problems relating to the Anthropocene are over 60 years old, wave after wave of student graduates have failed to critically address design innovations and entrepreneurial opportunities that might ameliorate human impact or contribute to sustainable businesses. It would appear that design thinking with its emphasis on critical reflection has been inadequate to the task of addressing what appears to be the insurmountable problem of humanity's anthropogenic, and pathological, impact on the earth system. Indeed, philosophically we are now being challenged by thinkers who state that the human perspective must accept a place alongside the astronomically large collection of nonhuman objects that sense the universe in their own alien and mysterious way.[63]

While critical thinking can offer a method of evaluating some of the causes and symptoms of our anthropogenic impact a number of philosophers and theorists have begun to critique the legacy of Kantian correlationism and the Enlightenment's current hold on our imagination in the 21st century. The OOO, and more specifically, Speculative Realism, have begun to gather support from those who point to the shortcomings of anthropocentric social theory and scientism. Speculative realists such as Harman, Meillassoux, Bryant, Morton, Bogost and Shaviro regard the likes of Kant, Hume and Descartes as the architects of our 'transparent cage' (2006). In my teaching, my concern has been to not only free students from a suffocating sense of helplessness but to explore novel means of unlocking the cage. My pedagogical approach has been to explore creativity, humour, speculative design and philosophy in the hope of exposing the focus of our imprisonment. These playful 'experiments' align closely with practised based research methods and have begun to reveal insights into a new symbiosis between our species and the alien majority of nonhumans that occupy the multiverse.

This transdisciplinary re-imagination of reality is not only essential for our sanity but must be assisted by future generations charged with what Donna Haraway calls 'response-ability'. The Anthropocene demands a response from those who could apply their creative abilities in a responsible way. As Haraway warned there are two fatal paths many have chosen in response to the Anthropocene: 1) childish techno-fixes or 2) the self-defeating, if not suicidal, the inaction of critical and cynical academic theorists, or scientists who declare it is too late to do anything (2016). The ecological activist, David Suzuki, passionately states that even if we have only a 5% chance of averting the disaster of global warming, those who want to give, up or say it is too late, should 'Shut the hell up!' Suzuki says that for the sake of our children, and their children's children, we should keep working on solutions. He believes that while extinction is normal, and a regular feature of evolution, he still thinks that we should fight for the survival of humanity and that it 'pisses' him off that we are not doing anything about it.[64] We must 'degrowth' and urgently embrace new design principles based on biomimicry. Haraway insists we should 'stay with the trouble' through 'sympoiesis', mutual making, as opposed to autopoiesis, self making the 'worldings', imagining new worlds for liveable futures, 'becoming-with' our nonhuman kin. This is taking biomimicry one step further as we consider bio-co-design with the non-human majority.

World Building Choanoflagellates

Haraway uses speculative futures to reimagine the past, present and future by dispensing with the Anthropocene, and replacing it with the Chthulucene, a subterranean and watery epoch bound to fictional monsters and primitive symbionts, such as "choanoflagellates, microscopic aquatic creatures whose body type and genes place them right next to the base of the animal family tree".[65]

Haraway offers us a third speculative path, what she describes as SF, an acronym that encompasses 'string figures, science fact, science fiction, speculative feminism, speculative fabulation'.[66] To her list, I would also add speculative realism, speculative fabrication, and speculative design, thinking by making, and making by thinking, a constructive, not deconstructive method, a playful approach to 'staying with the trouble' that Haraway would approve, and theorist, such as game designer and philosopher, Ian Bogost, encourages. We are charged with the responsibility of researching, imagining, creating, and teaching about future worlds in the post Anthropocene.

The speculative realists go beyond just reintroducing us to the importance of botanical and biological storytelling by delving into the secret lives of objects, things, and units; new materialism that includes every thing : fictional realities; quarks; and pogo sticks, to copy a typical absurdist list perfected by Bruno Latour. Bogost questions our anthropocentric obsessions:

"Why do we give the dead Civil War soldier, the guilty Manhattan project physicist, the oval-headed alien anthropomorph, and the intelligent celestial race so much more credence than the scoria cone, the obsidian fragment, the gypsum crystal, the capsicum pepper, and the propane flame? When we welcome these things into scholarship, poetry, science, and business, it is only to ask how they relate to human productivity, culture, and politics."[67]

There appears to be an urgent necessity for significant numbers of educators, politicians, and entrepreneurs to begin creative and radically alternative ways of looking at how we live with the nonhumans of this planet. Speculative realism and OOO are philosophical frameworks to consider as new foundations, thereby providing students and others the tools for our attempted escape from a prison guarded by Latour's 'epistemological police'.[68]

The IGBP And The Anthropocene

While there were earlier insights, prior to this new millennium, it was a concerted effort of the International Geosphere-Biosphere Programme (IGBP) scientists that revealed the astounding and dramatic impact of homo-sapiens on the Earth. The geologists Paul Crutzen and Eugene Stoermer are credited with the modern coinage of the word, Anthropocene, in 2000.

In a short peer-reviewed article in *Nature*, *The Geology of Man*, Crutzen traced the beginnings of human impact back to the beginnings of the industrial revolution with a litany of anthropogenic disasters, and the dire warning that there has been a recent acceleration in the onset of the Anthropocene. He wrote:

"Unless there is a global catastrophe — a meteorite impact, a world war or a pandemic — mankind will remain a major environmental force for many millennia. A daunting task lies ahead for scientists and engineers to guide society towards environmentally sustainable management during the era of the Anthropocene."[69]

His list could also include designers, artists, and speculative futurists. There has been a surprising and growing consensus between the Earth Systems' scientists who completed an extraordinary 30-year project before they concluded their anthropogenic theory. They have been followed by the traditionally slow-moving geologic community, who are close to a consensus, that we are now in a new geological epoch, the Anthropocene, which is notably marked by the 'great acceleration' of 1945. I will not present in detail the arguments for and against the title and theory, 'the Anthropocene', described by some as a new epoch.[70] The name is useful as it has been recognised by a wide range of scientists, artists, and social theorists. It follows the relatively stable climate of the past 10,000-12,000 years of the Holocene.

Why is it that for 60 years educators have been aware of a deep groaning pain coming from our planet buried deep in the chthonic strata, and still our graduates have ventured forward to create businesses and innovations that do not relieve the pain. The efforts of the few to salve the welts caused by vicious mineral extractions are overshadowed instead by the majority that has contributed to the growth of a global economy that has accelerated these savage attacks. Surely the opportunities for intervention have presented themselves during the foundational education process? Educators must ask themselves, were we unaware? Did we deny the harm? Did we not care? Or were our pedagogical means inadequate to the task?

One possible root causes may be that educators assumed a social responsibility to the neoliberal goal of economic growth based on the 19th century Malthusian belief in scarcity and the economic fallacy of 'survival of the fittest'. These ideologies or paradigms go back much further, even before the Enlightenment, and the birth of liberalism. The radical political and epistemological philosophy of the Enlightenment began to settle into a reified strata that have fossilised our thoughts in the past.

While some social theorists and Earth Systems' scientists may argue that the Anthropocene began with the advent of industrialisation, as early as the invention of the steam engine in 1784; others have argued that the troubles began with the Mesopotamians, the fertile crescent, and the invention of agriculture at the beginning of the Holocene. Jared Diamond claims that agriculture was the 'worst mistake humanity ever made' and Timothy Morton claims we are still Mesopotamians, while Bruno Latour claims, "We Were Never Modern". Our problems may be rooted in our very means of survival, and how we continue to cultivate and feed ourselves.

Latour argued modernity attempted to split reality into two halves, human and nature. The human was conceived as multifaceted and complex, whereas nature and matter were only ever allowed to be singular and simple.[71] In his final expression of his philosophy, Alfred North Whitehead, in *Process and Reality* (1929) set out to overcome this epistemological 'bifurcation of nature'. Whitehead argued that there are two sides to reality, the world's phenomenal appearance, and the hidden physical reality beyond the human senses. He sort to rebut Immanuel Kant's eighteenth-century claim that: "phenomena depend upon the mind to exist" (Braver 2007, p.39). It is this assumption, above all, that speculative realism seeks to overturn."[72]

A growing body of Earth System scientists, geologists, and social theorists are not just petulantly blaming their parents for the mess we are in, but their parents, parents, parents etc, preceding us by 12 millennia. More recently a new community of philosophers, the speculative realists, have been pointing the finger at the patron saints of contemporary philosophy, Rene Descartes and Immanuel Kant. Of course, this is unfair as they tried to battle their way out of the paper bag that an oppressive politico-religion had fabricated for Western philosophy in the service of the powers that be. Eventually, the paper bag turned into what the speculative realist, Meillassoux, described as 'the transparent cage'.[73]

In the early part of the 21st century, the speculative realists and the OOO have been supported by technologically savvy philosophers and software theorists such as Ian Bogost, Benjamin Bratton, Alex Galloway, and Ed Finn. Since the GFC of 2008, there has been a decisive shift of mood amongst critical theorists, some educators, and public opinion in general, from technological optimism towards a dark scepticism about the Internet and information technology.[74] The rise of Donald Trump and American escapism; the Russian state-sponsored cyber-attacks; and the improper use of Facebook data by Cambridge Analytica that exposed 83 million Facebook users are just a few examples of recent events that have troubled the world.

Coinciding with the Great Acceleration, information technology developed during the first Cold War, and supported by what became known as the US industrial-military-academic complex, provided the infrastructure to support global consumer economics. This has led to the weaponisation of education, and the global spread of US platforms such as Google, Facebook, Twitter, Apple, and Microsoft, to name a small handful of American multinationals, has infected the planet's education and our cognitive capacity to imagine alternative worlds and preferable futures.[75]

Designing Speculative Worlds

Creative technologies can embrace speculative design and the positing of 'what if?' scenarios. This can be seen in contrast to what Dunne & Raby has described as 'affirmative design', that is typified by commercial design that contributes to the near future and 'faster, better, cheaper'[76] products, services, marketing, or innovation, as defined by improvement in the OECD *Oslo Manual*. The shortcomings of mainstream design and the apparent failure to avert the onset of the

Anthropocene, and the imminent effect of multiple environmental and existential crises, suggests that alternative, preferable, or even dystopian futures, can frame questions that have been neglected by the technological 'closed worlds' of the past.[77]

Speculative design aspires to break out of the 'transparent cage' of neoliberal capitalism and to provide cognitive tools that can reimagine a 'universe of things' within a flat and democratic ontological world. Dunne & Raby in their book, *Speculative Everything: design fictions and social dreaming* (2013) champion Fredric Jameson's claim that "it is now easier to imagine the end of the world than an alternative to capitalism."[78] As Margaret Thatcher succinctly put it, 'there is no alternative'. Design's affirmative objectives, that have sought solutions to problems, have appeared to make the big problems worse. Dunne & Raby note:

"Design's inherent optimism leaves no alternative but it is becoming clear that many of the challenges we face today are unfixable and that the only way to overcome them is by changing our values, beliefs, attitudes, and behaviour."[79]

Speculative design is sensitized to design's cheerleader approach, and assumes that "Design speculations can act as a catalyst for collectively redefining our relationship to reality."[80] However, while these lofty goals have the ambition to radically redefine our world view, the hegemonic nature of what Mark Fisher describes as 'capitalist realism', effectively absorbs all critiques, moving beyond the cynicism of postmodernism, to embrace an ironic nihilism. Fisher argues that:

"The power of capitalist realism derives in part from the way that capitalism subsumes and consumes all of previous history: one effect of its 'system of equivalence' which can assign all cultural objects, whether they are religious iconography, pornography, or *Das Kapital*, a monetary value."[81]

Speculative realism offers a radical philosophical challenge to allow us to dream beyond the Anthropocene and to envisage a world whereby nature and culture are no longer divided by the dangerous mindset of consumer economics. The speculative realist, Graham Harman, extends Latour's 'parliament of things' to encompass a 'democratic ontology' that equates the reality of all things both human and nonhuman while acknowledging that this in no way implies symmetry of power or existential equality of things.[82]

Speculative Pedagogy

One of the first learning outcomes that are taught in the Bachelor of Creative Technologies at AUT is a critical reflection. Over and above this course prescriptor is the *New Zealand Education Act* (1991) that states that our universities are charged with the responsibility to be the 'critic and conscience of society'. Yet, despite this clear legal demand on universities and scholars in New Zealand, and indeed, around the world, we have not managed to either persuade, or instruct society; its politicians; its business leaders; or our students about how to live harmoniously with each other, and the massive nonhuman population of the planet, or indeed the universe. The world has begun to wake up to the perpetual nightmare that our species may have caused irreparable damage to the planet and our nonhuman co-inhabitants. Our students may well have learned critical reflection, but have these cognitive skills helped them to ameliorate the harm they have designed once they have graduated? For those of us in the so-called 'developed' world, we all share the shame and the responsibility for the approaching existential crisis caused by anthropogenic global warming. According to the Earth scientist, Paul Cruzen, environmental problems such as acid rain, photochemical smog, and global warming have "have largely been caused by only 25% of the world population."[83]

As Donna Haraway puts it "expressing an explicit "game over" attitude that can and does discourage others, including students, is facilitated by various kinds of futurisms."[84] Haraway points out that there is a disturbing discourse amongst both experts and popular discussion that gravitates towards either technocratic geoengineering fixes or wallows in despair that "coinfect any possible common imagination".[85] Clearly, many of our past pedagogical methods have fallen short of the mark, simply ignored the problems, or worse, contributed to this crisis. Is Timothy Morton correct, that because global warming is now happening, we now face 'the end of the world'? Or can we make a positive contribution through speculative design; playful experimentation; and building preferable future worlds with new foundations?

Notes

1. Martel, Y. (2001) Life of Pi.

2. Desmond, Timothy. (2018). Psyche and Singularity: Jungian Psychology and Holographic String Theory.

3. Tolle, E. (2004). The power of NOW: A guide to spiritual enlightenment (Rev. ed.). Vancouver, B.C., Canada: Novato, Calif: Namaste Pub. ; New World Library.

4. Trout, L. (2010). The Politics of Survival. p. 74.

5. Hayles, K. (1999). How We Became Posthuman.

6. Damasio, A. Looking for Spinoza: Joy, Sorrow, and the Feeling Brain, Harcourt, 2003

7. Montague, R. (2007). Your brain is (almost) perfect: how we make decisions. New York London: Plume; Turnaround

8. Minsky, M. L. (1986). The Society of Mind. New York: Simon and Schuster. p.163

9. Wertheim, M. (1999). The Pearly Gates of Cyberspace: a history of space from Dante to the Internet. p.281.

10. Hayles, K. (2017). Unthought: the power of the cognitive nonconscious. Chicago; London: The University of Chicago Press

11. Hansen, Mark B. N. Feed-Forward (pp. 52-53). University of Chicago Press. Kindle Edition.

12. ibid

13. Taleb, Nassim Nicholas. The Black Swan: The Impact of the Highly Improbable. Kindle Locations 1959-1960. Penguin Books Ltd. Kindle Edition.

14. While the current slash and burn of the Amazon is causing devastation that is destroying oxygen supplies, biodiversity and carbon sequestration, the ancient burial technique of Terra Preta, or 'black earth' suggests a powerful method of carbon sequestration and biomass disposal. This seems to be a common and ancient sustainable disposal of waste used by native Indians, New Zealand Māori, and others. Called biochar, 'slash and char' could remove billions of tons of carbon from the atmosphere.

See Hawken, P. (Ed.). (2017). *Drawdown*.

15. Agriculture. (2015). In B. E. Johansen (Ed.), American Indian culture: From counting coup to wampum. Westport, CT: Greenwood.

16. 'When reports reached New Zealand in 1847 of the British government's instructions to seize the so-called 'waste lands' that Māori were said to not legitimately own or occupy (because they did not use it in ways approved by European theorists such as Emer de Vattel and Thomas Arnold).' See O'Malley, Vincent. The Great War for New Zealand: Waikato 1800-2000. Kindle Locations 807-808. Bridget Williams Books. Kindle Edition.

17. See Coal Ash: Hazardous to Human Health https://www.psr.org/wp-content/uploads/2018/05/coal-ash-hazardous-to-human-health.pdf

18. See Greller, Andrew. (1972). Observations on the Forests of Northern Queens County, Long Island, from Colonial Times to the Present. Bulletin of the Torrey Botanical Club. 99. 202. 10.2307/2484578.

19. Bregman, Rutger. Utopia for Realists. Bloomsbury Publishing. Kindle Edition. p. 15.

20. See Tucker, Patrick. The Naked Future: What Happens in a World That Anticipates Your Every Move? (pp. 12-13). Penguin Publishing Group. Kindle Edition. Tucker recounts a project to expose the pollution to New York City's waterways by using IoT sensors in the sewage system.

21. See https://www.nytimes.com/aponline/2019/06/11/arts/ap-us-sept-11-victim-fund.html also see, https://www.theguardian.com/us-news/2018/sep/10/911-attack-ground-zero-manhattan-cancer

22. Peake, Anthony. (2013). A Life of Philip K. Dick: The Man Who Remembered the Future. Arcturus Publishing.

23. Peake, Anthony. A Life of Philip K. Dick: The Man Who Remembered the Future. Kindle Locations 543-545. Arcturus Publishing. Kindle Edition. See a video of Pedro the Voder https://www.youtube.com/watch?v=kulk7IPTL1o

24. Tainter, J. A. (1988). The collapse of complex societies. Cambridge, Cambridgeshire; New York: Cambridge University Press.

25. Edwards, P. N. (1997). The closed world: Computers and the politics of discourse in Cold War America. Cambridge, Mass. : MIT Press, 1997. p.40

26. ibid, p.40

27. ibid, p.41

28. Garn, A., Antonelli, P., Kultermann, U., & Van Dyk, S. H. (2007). Exit to Tomorrow: World's Fair architecture, design, fashion, 1933-2005. p.6

29. See Tainter, J. https://www.youtube.com/watch?v=GoR09YzyuCI&feature=youtu.be

30. Cubitt, Sean. Finite Media: Environmental Implications of Digital Tech-

nologies (a Cultural Politics Book) . Duke University Press. Kindle Edition.

31. ibid

32. Cai, Shenshen. State Propaganda in China's Entertainment Industry, Routledge, 2016.

33. Jung, C. G., & Jaffé, A. (1989). Memories, dreams, reflections (Rev. ed). New York: Vintage Books. p.57

34. ibid p.78

35. Desmond, T. (2018) Psyche and Singularity: Jungian Psychology and Holographic String Theory

36. Lincoln, B. (2014). Discourse and the construction of society: Comparative studies of myth, ritual, and classification (Second Edition). Oxford; New York: Oxford University Press. p.6

37. McLuhan, M. (1994). Understanding Media: The extensions of man. London: Routledge

38. Carr, N. G. (2010). The Shallows: how the Internet is changing the way we think, read and remember. London: Atlantic Books.

39. Carr, ibid, p.209.

40. Timothy Morton, *Dark Ecology*

41. Finn, Ed. What Algorithms Want: Imagination in the Age of Computing. Kindle Locations 400-402. The MIT Press. Kindle Edition.

42. Morton, Timothy. Dark Ecology: For a Logic of Future Coexistence (The Wellek Library Lectures) (p. 52). Columbia University Press. Kindle Edition.

43. While it appears that Babbage wrote a number of unpublished algorithms, Stephen Wolfram, defends Ada Lovelace's contribution to computational history.

44. Isaacson, W. (2014). The Innovators: How a group of hackers, geniuses, and geeks created the digital revolution (First Simon & Schuster hardcover edition). New York: Simon & Schuster.

45. Ibid, Kindle Location 875

46. Ibid, Kindle Location 879

47. Finn, ibid, Kindle Locations 400-402.

48. Tainter, J.(2010) https://www.youtube.com/watch?v=GoRo9YzyuCI&feature=youtu.be

49. Carr, N. The Shallows. p.212

50. Prigogine & Stengers (1984) Order Out of Chaos. p.291

51. As cited in Hayles, N. Katherine. Unthought (p. 192). University of Chicago Press. Kindle Edition.

52. ibid, p.174

53. Heim, M. (1993). The Metaphysics of Virtual Reality. New York: Oxford University Press. pp 19-20

54. Haraway, Donna J. (2016). Staying with the Trouble: Making Kin in the Chthulucene (Experimental Futures) (p. 39). Duke University Press. Kindle Edition.

55. Nelson, H. G., & Stolterman, E. (2003). The Design Way: intentional change in an unpredictable world: foundations and fundamentals of design competence. Englewood Cliffs, N.J: Educational Technology Publications.

56. ibid

57. ibid p.85

58. Galloway, Alexander R. (2004). Protocol: How Control Exists after Decentralization (Leonardo Book Series). The MIT Press. Kindle Edition

59. Carr, N. G. (2010). The Shallows: how the Internet is changing the way we think, read and remember. p.209

60. Dunne, A., & Raby, F. (2013). Speculative Everything: Design, Fiction, and Social Dreaming. The MIT Press.

61. Hayles, N. Katherine. Unthought (pp. 192-193). University of Chicago Press. Kindle Edition.

62. In Buckminster Fuller and Answar Dil, Humans in Universe (1983), p.218.

63. See Bogost, 2014; Harman, G. 2017; Shaviro, 2014

64. See Bogost, 2014; Harman, G. 2017; Shaviro, 2014

65. McGown, Kat. (2014). How Life Made the Leap From Single Cells to Multicellular Animals | WIRED. Retrieved August 26, 2019, from https://www.wired.com/2014/08/where-animals-come-from/

66. Haraway, D. (2016) Staying with the Trouble.

67. Bogost, I. (2012). Alien Phenomenology, or What It's Like to Be a Thing. Kindle location 109.

68. Harman, G. (2014) Bruno Latour: Reassembling the Political. p.36

69. Crutzen, P. (2002) The Geology of Man. Nature. p.23

70. See Ian Angus, and Donna Haraway for a discussion of the name, Anthropocene.

71. Bogost, I. (2012). ibid

72. Shaviro, S. (2014). The Universe of Things. Kindle Locations 132-134

73. Meillassoux, Q. (2017). After Finitude: An Essay on the Necessity of Contingency.

74. Bratton,B. (2016). The Stack: On Software and Sovereignty.

75. Rive, P.B. (2018). Virtual Worlds and the Weaponization of Education. (unpublished paper)

76. Dunne, A., & Raby, F. (2013). Speculative Everything.

77. Edwards, P. N. (1997). The Closed World: computers and the politics of discourse in Cold War America. Cambridge, Mass. : MIT Press,

78. Dunne, A., & Raby, F. (2013) ibid p.2.

79. ibid

80. ibid

81. Fisher, M. (2009). Capitalist Realism: Is there no alternative? (Zero Books), p.4

82. Harman, Graham. (2014) Bruno Latour: Reassembling the Political (Modern European Thinkers). Pluto Press. Kindle Edition.

83. Angus, Ian. (2016). Facing the Anthropocene. Kindle Locations 508-509

84. Haraway, ibid, 2016, pp. 3-4

85. Haraway, ibid, 2016, p.56

Chapter 6 The World Now

In apocalyptic thought the dawning of a new millennium is always a time of foreboding and hope. In the Judaeo-Christian culture the end of a thousand years was significant as it was seen as the logical end of time, and the coming of the messiah. Since the Enlightenment, logical empiricism and rationalism have displaced religion as the hegemonic world view. So, stripped of its theological meaning the beginning of the new millennium, the year 2000, held a strange significance for the modern mind that believed that scientifically the world, and even the universe, held no meaning, no purpose, and no objective. However, despite this very rational, and logical conclusion to the past millennium, there are cosmic archetypes that have begun to stir in our psyche, and while the modern world distracts itself with a superficial materialism, our subconscious is fighting to be heard, and to reveal the true nature of our destiny, our creativity, and the part it thinks we have to play in the cosmic theatre of the universe.

We have only just begun a new thousand-year cycle, and yet we have an apocalyptic fear that we might not make it to the end of this century. The question is, will this just be the psychic death of outmoded thought; or the end of time in the guise of a physical morality play, as we watch from the wings and nonhuman actors deconstruct life as we know it? Or perhaps our Promethean hubris will insist that we were the protagonist all along, and so rather than see humanity's pathetic demise through lack of resources, instead we just push the button, and go out as a destructive God – ruler of our world – ender of our world?

It remains to be seen, but let's just consider the world as we know it, as we move into the 2020s, and reflect on what has happened and what is now taking place.

Leading up to the new millennium, the Y2K computer bomb, otherwise known as the "Millennium Bug", was regarded as the most concerning global event to coincide with the millennium. Central to this problem is an archetypal concern with time, the past, the present, and the future. Our current understanding of time has changed since the dream world of the ancients, and more recently, since the 17th century, Newton helped us to imagine God as the 'blind watchmaker' of the universe. Around the time of the Enlightenment, we began to view the cosmos as an alien machine with no concern about our hopes, fears, or dreams. Eventually, we built simulations of this universe that reflected that reality in computers. Time became reified in the computer; our reality became a computer model. Y2K was an error in the calculation of computer clocks caused by a lack of foresight in the almost forgotten FORTRAN programming language. Years later it was still ticking, like a bomb, yet programmers had not predicted that their programs would still be in operation years after they had been written.

As physics has revealed the exponential acceleration of technology, carried along by cosmic expansion, has caused us to begin to realise the shocking truth, that our most reliable description of reality is not Newton's mechanical clock, but a quantum clock that simultaneously gives us past, present, and future, a time machine that we do not understand, and currently cannot read. At this moment, according to Maxwell, it is as if we only have a fractional, common sense, understanding of spacetime, in three and a half dimensions, and do not yet intuitively grasp the fourth cosmic dimension of Einsteinian time.[1]

Y2K has some salient examples of how we are continuing to struggle with time, and how no matter how hard we try we cannot eliminate the 'ghost in the machine'. This phrase, made famous by the philosopher, Gilbert Ryle (1949), was part of his critique of what he called the modern philosophical dogma of mind/body dualism, 'Descartes myth', an idea he called a serious category mistake. This was the idealist's error, by reducing physical reality to mental reality, however, Ryle argues, the mind is not an independent non-material entity.

This became an existential problem for Arthur Koestler, at the height of the Cold War, in his book, *The Ghost in the Machine* (1968), in which Koestler proffered a theory of mind that described the evolutionary layering of the mind upon primitive structures. This was explored later by Carl Sagan in *Dragons of Eden*, and by his son, Dorion Sagan and John Skyoles, in *Up from Dragons*, that provides some scientific validation of Jungian symbols, and yet, imagined a future beyond the myth. Koestler critiqued this dominant theory of mind, that was championed by behavioural psychologists, such as Skinner, and the self-destructive tendencies of humanity, with the dramatic example of the nuclear bomb. Just as Kantian and Cartesian philosophy led to the bifurcation of humanity and nature, the mind body split became ossified in the design of digital technologies, led by the likes of Wiener and Shannon's information theory, and according to Hayles, is how we became posthuman, thereby culminating in the AI version of our current 'theory of mind'.

Behavioural psychology that rejects Freudian and Jungian psychoanalysis became the dominant cognitive theory, but according to Jung, the suppression of our primitive psyche could result in violence, and world annihilation in a nuclear war. The behavioural psychologists such as Skinner, and the previously discussed psychoacoustic consultants, BBN, assisted the US military in training soldiers, and designing weapons. The activities of the RAND corporation and the development of computers such as Whirlwind, and the IBM 704 were simply legacy descendants of the philosophical errors of the 17th – 20th century. Behavioural psychology, followed by cognitive science, did not exorcise these archetypal ghosts, it simply ignored them as primitive superstitions and left them alone to fight it out in the software and hardware that we have inherited. In the words of Benjamin Bratton, this is not some sort of dystopian conspiracy, but an accidental megastructure we have ended up with and must work through. Bratton sees this as an urgent design project while admitting that our present design theory and praxis are woefully inadequate to the task that lays before us. If we unravel some of the history of the Y2K bug it will provide us with further evidence of how the suppression of our primitive collective unconscious continues to hide within those ghosts in our machines.

A Short and Efficient History of Fortran

The history of the FORTRAN programming language takes us back to the 1950s, when prior to its creation, by John Backhus In 1957, all programming was performed using assembly, or machine code, that was directly read by the machine. FORTRAN was a compiler, which means that the code is compiled at run-time for a particular machine, and is considered a high-level programming language. This contrasted with low-level assembly code, called that because it does not have extra layers of abstraction between the lowest level machine code, and the program's results. While there was some resistance to Backhus's proposal for FORTRAN, because hand-coding was thought to be more efficient at talking directly to the machine, Backhus proved he could reduce the number of programming statements necessary to operate a machine by a factor of 20, and so it quickly gained acceptance.

FORTRAN had been developed by IBM to be used in their work for the US military,[2] and was part of a long relationship between the military and computing, dating back to when 'humans were computers' and when they used calculus to compute the trajectory of projectiles, and astronomical bodies, such as moons, planets, and stars. Real-time calculations was a high priority for military purposes as you could not expect the enemy to wait while a program was calculating their attack.[3]

During WWll Alan Turing, who developed Colossus, a massive, electro-mechanical, and slow computer, used to crack the German Enigma code machine, was constantly looking for efficiencies and speed because the Germans changed the code every night, and time cost lives. FORTRAN was therefore intended to improve military efficiency and labour, in much the same way that Charles Babbage envisaged his Difference Engine in 1837. John Backus said during a 1979 interview with Think, the IBM employee magazine:

"Much of my work has come from being lazy. I didn't like writing programs, and so, when I was working on the IBM 701, writing programs for computing missile trajectories, I started work on a programming system to make it easier to write programs."[4]

The FORTRAN programming language continued to be developed over the years and became a favourite for high-performance computing. Because of this efficiency, it is still used on supercomputers and mainframes, as opposed to personal computers. Compilers such as FORTRAN did impose an abstract layer between the coder, and those that read the code, and the machine itself:

"For such languages, there are more one-to-one correspondences between the programmed code and the hardware operations performed by machine code, making it easier for programmers to control the use of central processing unit (CPU) and memory in fine detail."[5]

This also means that there was no translation of the code, between machine to machine, and so it is generally not portable because it is customised to those machines. This original machine, or assembly code, was not an easy code for humans to read, and would often require hours of trial and error in which the programmer would produce punch cards in stacks that had to then be fed into the machine in order to run the code and eventually, hopefully, produce a result. If there had been an error in the programming the punch cards were useless and would be trashed and the process must be started again.

Speed, efficiency and military objectives were coded into the original software and hardware, however, forty-three years later some of the tricks, tips and workarounds used by early FORTRAN programmers were long forgotten. In the early 1960s, computers were slow, massive, very expensive tools, under the control of the high priests of technology. Like a bomb, Y2K was set ticking by those who built the first early programs, and later coders built on top of that code, adding more layers of abstraction. No one suspected the potential disaster, there were no software archaeologists digging beneath the layers of code, there were no alarms ringing.

In the hope of saving money, and computer memory, FORTRAN programmers only accounted for 2 digits to represent the year, so it meant that instead of ticking over to the year 2000, the computer clock would reset to 00, which could mean any year ending in those 2 digits. When it was recognised that there was a problem, critical dates after 1 January 2000, were named 'event horizons', this serious problem meant those dates would appear to be invalid. Remember that FORTRAN was a favourite of high-performance computing, that meant that it could affect banks, the military, all utilities such as power and water, hospitals and the police. People started to wake up to the fact that modern society would collapse without computers and their networks and so many began to see a digital apocalypse looming in the year 2000.

However, the 2 digit year was not the only problem, also programmers had misunderstood the Gregorian calendar, that had become the global standard. Eventually, by the 20th century, due to globalization, this religious calendar became accepted by all countries in a secular move, that largely related to trade and commerce, with Greece, finally adopting this 'new' style calendar in 1923. The Gregorian calendar dated back to Pope Gregory XIll, in 1582, and was designed by the Roman church to keep Easter, the equinox, and the solstice, or Christmas, at the same time each year, and avoid an inevitable time drift. The truth of the matter was that those religious observations were based on ancient pagan rituals and symbols that coincided with the changing seasons, i.e. Spring, rebirth; Summer, full life; Autumn, decay; and Winter, death. These were copied by the Christian calendar and its symbols and rituals. These pagan, then Christian, then secular conventions of the time, were thus baked into the computer software, and hardware.

Cosmological archetypes, the movement of astronomical bodies, are now part of our digital life that is subdivided into microseconds. The Gregorian Calendar was based on the astronomical observation that the Earth rotated around the Sun, completing its revolution, not in a perfect 365 days, but rather the awkward number of 365.2422 days in a tropical year. To make it easier to calculate the calendar they made the year 365.2425 days so shortening the year by 0.0075 days, and to make this time up they added a leap year. The rule for leap years is as follows: Every year that is exactly divisible by four is a leap year, except for years that are exactly divisible by 100, but these centurial years are leap years if they are exactly divisible by 400. For example, the years 1700, 1800, and 1900 are not leap years, but the year 2000 is.

Unfortunately, for the rational and logical computer programmers, they failed to account for this and did not recognise that 2000 would be a leap year, hence another problem that was predicted to occur when the new year was set to begin. It had already been noted in the 16th century that there had been a time drift, so to begin with, Pope Gregory, in order to catch up, and make sure that they were back in sync with the rituals of the Church's founding fathers, they jumped from 4th Oct, 1582 to 15th Oct, 1582 cutting out 10 days in the process. Perhaps, one day in the distant future those missing 10 days maybe incredibly important?

The original problem arose from a workaround by programmers, who acknowledged the very expensive nature of computer storage at the time. Mainframes and later personal computers were built with hardware that cost $10 per kilobyte and went up to $100 per kilobyte. Today, storage is considered to be very cheap. "Hard drives prices have dropped, from around $500,000 per gigabyte in 1981 to less than $0.03 per gigabyte today."[6]

At his testimony to the Senate Banking Committee in 1998, the ex-Chairman of the Federal Reserve, Alan Greenspan said:

"I'm one of the culprits who created this problem. I used to write those programs back in the 1960s and 1970s and was proud of the fact that I was able to squeeze a few elements of space out of my program by not having to put a 19 before the year. Back then, it was very important. We used to spend a lot of time running through various mathematical exercises before we started to write our programs so that they could be very clearly delimited with respect to space and the use of capacity. It never entered our minds that those programs would have lasted for more than a few years. As a consequence, they are very poorly documented. If I were to go back and look at some of the programs I wrote 30 years ago, I would have one terribly difficult time working my way through step-by-step."[7]

Despite this confession, Greenspan, the technocrat, continued to apply his faith in the machines. He was part of a cadre of techno-liberals who admired Ayn Rand who believed in the heroic journey of the rational man and the technology they designed. It was a Randian vision also held by '80s Silicon Valley entrepreneurs and Greenspan helped to convince President Clinton that computers would relieve governments, (and human politicians) from the necessity to intervene in the economy because algorithms would ultimately apply a decentralised and rational control over the economy.

In an interview with Stewart Brand for his book, *The Media Lab: Inventing the Future* at MIT, (1988) ex-Royal Shell Oil strategist and futurist, Peter Schwartz, said that while steel and automobiles might have driven the economy during the industrial age, he said that the:

"new information-rich system are finance and electronic entertainment on a worldwide scale. How finance and electronic entertainment evolve will affect everything else. Technology is like water and follows the path of least resistance; they're the path of least resistance."

Schwartz had already noticed that the financial system was out of control.

"At Shell we've just done an analysis on the new kinds of financial instruments— ruffs and swaps and various ways of doing international finance— and what is absolutely clear to me is that it is a system out of control, that nobody really understands."

"People innovate new mechanisms, and these mechanisms are tried, and they're commercially viable—coaggregation money and reselling it in a different way, and so on— but nobody knows what the consequences of that are. Nobody knows how to regulate that, nobody knows what the meaning of that money is. And every time in history, the thing which precipitated a depression was the collapse of the meaning of money. When these mechanisms evolve that way, completely out of control, there is enormous danger."

"Now, I should tell you that I have been worrying about this issue since the late '70s, but a major financial crisis keeps not happening, even though the system has been getting massively more electronic and interconnected that whole time. We're starting to refer to this as 'resilient fragility.' The system appears more fragile than it is. It's often the case that complex systems produce resilience in unpredictable forms—even in unrecognizable forms: you can't find what's producing the resilience even though you're looking for it."[8]

The financial system of high-speed international computer networks was already beyond human understanding and miraculously operated in a successful state of perpetual fragility. Y2K is an example of how the complexity of computing systems surpass human understanding and human scale. The problem was first identified in the '80s, long before the GFC of 2008, however, the global nature of networks and computer control illustrates how something as simple as the perception of time could cause catastrophic problems. The global apocalyptic predictions of disasters activated many of the solutions that were implemented.

However, as the world approached the end of the millennium the Y2K bug rapidly became perceived as, not just a computer problem, but a security threat. John Hamre, United States Deputy Secretary of Defense, wrote, "The Y2K problem is the electronic equivalent of the El Niño and there will be nasty surprises around the globe."[9]

The remediation for the Y2K event is estimated to have cost the planet USD$408 billion, but in the end, very little happened. Unfortunately, many did not learn the true lesson of Y2K that relatively old algorithms and protocols that are hidden in the code of bygone software, and firmware can lay maliciously dormant, only to be awakened, often not as a result of a conspiracy, but rather as a long-forgotten logic, that now makes no sense.

Programmers like Greenspan and Backhus may be surprised that something they wrote 30 or 40 years ago might come back to haunt us and why should we worry about what some Pope did in the 16th century. However, the Y2K example helps to show that history, culture and religious beliefs do still count, because while we might forget only forty years ago, we are still struggling to remember 1000, or 10,000 years prior, and there are some profound ideas baked into our everyday code, our language, concepts, and behaviour that have ended up in our digital construct, our global society.

The complexity of the cosmos is simplified by our mathematical and physical models and that translates into the simplification of time. Y2K is a good example of what can go wrong when we forget that our models are dumbed down approximations of reality. What is far from apparent with algorithms and computer simulations are the assumptions made by the many who contribute to them. However, as we have entered an epoch that has no precedent in human memory, combined with our inability to even imagine 'black swans', means that it is unlikely that our predictions will be accurate and could even be dangerous. As the director of the World Meteorological Organisation pointed out "We are now truly in uncharted territory". We continue to see the record for the hottest day smashed again and again, and the weather programs and simulations are having to be modified. In the summer of 2017, an Atlantic hurricane surprised scientists bypassing Mexico, and Florida crashing into Ireland and Scotland. The National Oceanic Atmospheric Administration had never anticipated this event and their computerised map showed a strange straight line at latitude 60 degrees north. The programmer justified their assumptions saying "That's a pretty unusual place to have a tropical cyclone...Maybe that's something we'll have to go back and revisit what the boundary is." [10]

Yet, this example is only one that revealed itself and in reality, there is no straight line or hard boundaries and delineations – what if those assumptions are not made obvious, catastrophic mistakes could result. It is rare to find software, and hardware engineers who have a good grasp on the humanities, such as history, sociology, politics, and philosophy to name just some of the disciplines that are ignored in the code, but still make their way into our devices based on the assumptions, common sense, and archetypes of all the stakeholders who participated in their design.

The 2000 millennium triggered a strange confluence of thoughts and physical consequences, relating to ancient archetypes, such as those who believed it heralded the coming apocalypse, accompanied by the extreme weather of God's retribution, and the end of the world as we know it. While there were religious sectarian and cult collectives that saw 2000 as the 'end of times', a global majority took a more secular view, but still felt an unease bubbling up from the cosmological archetype, that the religious fanatics may be right.

It is an example of how mathematical abstraction, and computational complexity, can have unintended consequences and encode mistakes, strange thoughts, religious obsessions, and archetypal hopes and fears. In the Promethean age of accelerating technology, Pandora's box can be reopened unleashing all of the fearful monsters that had been locked away, and yet only hope remains behind.

In many ways, it was the Global Financial Crisis (GFC) of 2008 that signposts a significant watershed and turning point for many people's attitude towards the current state of the world as we know it. According to Benjamin Bratton, after the GFC public faith in technology, government, and the Internet took a dark turn with privacy hacks, cyber terrorism and the inequalities perpetuated by the bailouts of privileged Wall Street bankers. In his documentary, *Requiem for the American Dream*, Noam Chomsky outlined his argument for the causes of the growing concentration of wealth and power in the US. He presented ten ways in which an American 'plutocracy' has come to dominate by:

1. Reducing Democracy

2. Shaping Ideology

3. Redesigning the Economy

4. Shifting the Burden

5. Attacking Solidarity

6. Running the Regulators

7. Engineering Elections

8. Keeping the Rabble in Line

9. Manufacturing Consent

10. Marginalizing the Population

What is missing from this list is a recognition of how our technology contributes to their ideology and regulates control in a decentralised system. The layering and complexities of subprime financial derivatives were only possible with high-speed computer networks, but because it was beyond human scale, was precisely what made it almost impossible to review or to comprehend what was going on. This system of command and control was built into the system since the beginning. This control is not to imply that there was an Orwellian plan to coerce and discipline, but that the accidental megastructure of the Stack has organically evolved to reflect the praxis of power. With technology Galloway asks both 'how does it work?' and 'whom does it work for?'. He sees his responsibility as one who must decipher the code. "I attempt to read the never-ending stream of computer code as we read any text, decoding its structure of control."[11]

Galloway points out that code is always enacted; it is commissioned, designed, and implemented to achieve specific ends 'in particular contexts. Code = praxis.'[12]

This is the role of the 'software archaeologist' and is the handle that my colleague, Jorn Bettin, has assigned himself. It is one of the responsibilities that our company has embraced by returning the code to human scale and removing spurious complexity.[13]

Time Cops and Capitalism

The internal logic of the capitalist economy eventually drove it towards refined algorithms that were no longer concerned with material resources but simply shaved fractional time out of the system in a game of financialized arbitrage. Segal's law states that "A man with a watch knows what time it is. A man with two watches is never sure." This straightforward statement is actually ironic and questions the basis of certainty about facts because there is no way the man can assume that the first watch is indeed correct. That is unless of course they have an algorithm that validates their assertion, and the rest of the world agrees or rather conforms. The ordering of time has become one of the foundations of the capitalist economy. Our clocks, business processes, balance sheets, and financial records assume a linear progression from past, to present, to future. Scientists call this the 'Causal Ordering Postulate', sometimes known as 'the time COP'.[14]

Our modern obsession about time can be traced to imperial military ambitions, colonisation, and the extraction of wealth. The navigation of the oceans and accurate longitudinal coordinates both rely on accurate time. As 360 degrees can be divided into 24 hours, a 15 degrees change in longitude equates to one hour of solar time. Astronomy was the original means of studying time and navigating empires for power and wealth. As a result, astronomical observatories and the study of astronomy have had a long history associated with the security, and geopolitical ambitions of the nation-state. This is why successive Kings, Queens, and Presidents have patronised astronomical observatories, such as the Royal Observatory in Greenwich, and the United States Naval Observatory, in Washington. In 1675 King Charles II established the Royal Observatory in Greenwich "in order to the finding out of the longitude of places for perfecting navigation and astronomy." Colonization would not have been possible without the invention of the sextant and the English Royal Court placed great importance and status on their Royal Astronomers, who were also often the Royal Astrologer.

Without computer clock synchronisation globalism and capitalism, as we know it, would not work. Speed became the obsession of the 20th century and continued over into the 21st. Before mechanical computers computations were carried out by human computers who used calculus to compute the position of the planets and stars to assemble nautical tables for navigation. This was the chief purpose of the Royal Observatory in Greenwich.

Charles Babbage, known as the father of the computer, was also one of the founders of the amateur Astronomical Society. It was 1884 when the International Meridian Conference was held in Washington, D.C., in the United States of America. They agreed that the prime meridian, zero degrees longitude, for international use would be Greenwich in the UK. The necessity to establish standardised time was motivated by the increasing speed of life caused by train and steamship timetables throughout Britain, and it was the Great Western Railway who first adopted Greenwich Mean Time using time signals transmitted by the General Post Office.

Synchronisation used a time ball that had been erected in 1833 to communicate the time at 1 pm to seamen on the Thames and became the Master clock for the sea and train system. An electric clock was first installed at Greenwich in 1852 in order to synchronise clocks around the country via telegraph. As the pace, and complexity of the geopolitical and commercial world increased we became more and more obsessed with the accuracy of time; it had become a vital determinant of power and wealth. Science and technology were called upon to support the commercial and military ambitions of the powerful elite. Wayne Hope cites E.P. Thompson:

"The growth of industrial capitalism after 1850 positioned clock time as the primary measure of productivity, cost, and profit. Disciplined workers were expected to respond accordingly."[15]

Eventually, the atomic Master Clock at the US Naval Observatory contributed to a worldwide time system called UTC (Coordinated Universal Time) with accuracy previously unimagined. The accuracy of the UK's National Physical Laboratory's NPL-CsF2 is expected to not deviate by a second in 138 million years. The military and industrial interests of the US were realised in the investments in the scientific and technological funding of the National Science Foundation, the World War 2 efforts of Vannevar Bush, and today by DARPA.

Capitalist Cyborgs

The GFC pulled back the curtain of Oz to reveal that the Wizard was no longer running the show, but instead, the world was being run by algorithms and their capitalist cyborgs. According to Hope:

"The global connectivity of securitization, speculative trading and credit expansion was reinforced by general advances in financial technology. The spread of algorithmic trading, for example, increasingly allowed computers to place orders without human intervention."[16]

What is not clear is whether politicians and the few investigative journalists still writing, appreciate that the perpetual fragility of an increasingly complex financial system that moved beyond human scale comprehension, and controls more than thirty years ago. Even algorithms that execute simple buy and sell orders have been shown to defy the imagination of those who have designed them. The unintended consequences of the constant drive for the faster computation were demonstrated by the 2010 so-called Flash Crash. At 2:32 pm on the 6th May 2010, algorithmic traders executed buy and sell orders as they were programmed to do. By 2:45 pm a trillion US dollars had been wiped out and an automatic circuit breaker halted trading. Within five seconds prices had stabilised and most of the losses were recovered when regulators deemed any transaction 60% or more away from the pre-crash level erroneous and those trades were cancelled.

The AI expert and philosopher, Nick Bostrom, use the Flash Crash to illustrate three lessons relating to AGI and the threats that exist as we move beyond human scale comprehension and physical ability.

1. Simple components such as the high-frequency trading program can produce complicated and unexpected effects.

2. Experts can create algorithms that seem sensible but can produce catastrophic results as the algorithm continues to execute logical but dangerous instructions.

3. If an algorithm moves faster and further than humans can react, then automation can also shut down or reverse an action if it is correctly anticipated. It is therefore important to have fail-safes built into the system.[17]

The competitive pressure to achieve speeds that show a micro advantage as traders look for arbitrage opportunities with "minute price movements that occur over the course of milliseconds (a timescale at which communication latencies even for speed-of-light signals in optical fibre cable become significant, making it advantageous to locate computers near the exchange). Algorithmic high-frequency traders account for more than half of equity shares traded on US markets."[18]

Behind these strategies has been a move by the wealthy and powerful towards what Chomsky calls 'financialization' whereby resources are redirected away from manufacturing and trade, produced by a human labour force, towards an automated self-referential and recursive system of finance, controlled by algorithms on computers. The internal logic of financialization is to encourage an increase in debt to equity ratios through easy access to credit, and which also ensured that those financial services earned an increasing proportion of the income and profits of the economy. While financialization had progressed since the 1980s it had accelerated with ITC, and the Internet, becoming painfully obvious in the aftermath of the GFC. There was global indignation at the bailout of wealthy bankers who had risked other people's money and assets through their complex layering of financial derivatives.

The Revolution Will Be Televised

In 1970 Gil Scott-Heron released his song, *The Revolution Will Not Be Televised*, at a time of global, social, sexual and political upheaval. An African American protest song that incites an anti-TV-consumer revolution :

The revolution will not be right back after a message
About a white tornado, white lightning, or white people
You will not have to worry about a germ on your Bedroom
a tiger in your tank, or the giant in your toilet bowl
The revolution will not go better with Coke
The revolution will not fight the germs that cause bad breath
The revolution WILL put you in the driver's seat
The revolution will not be televised
WILL not be televised, WILL NOT BE TELEVISED
The revolution will be no re-run brothers
The revolution will be live[19]

It would seem that Marx's 'opiate of the masses' is no longer religion, or TV, but social media, and a constant screen flipping of devices. Scott-Heron warns of hallucinogenic technologies to come, as we retreat from the public square into the safety of our virtual cocoon, in denial of the mess outside.

You will not be able to stay home, brother
You will not be able to plugin, turn on and drop out[20]

If the revolution will not be televised, how will we participate?

In the mid 2000s there was a confluence of negative reports and ideas, with global warming hitting a peak in 2006, just after the release of Al Gore's documentary, *The Inconvenient Truth*, and the beginning of the subprime financial crisis in 2007, culminating in the collapse of Lehman Brothers in 2008, and the worst financial crisis since the Great Depression of the 1930s. The result of this confluence has been a growing sense of despair and fear that capitalism might be actually coming to an end. The author of, *Debt: The First 5,000 Years*, David Graeber asks, "How did we get here?" and goes on to say:

"My own suspicion is that we are looking at the final effects of the militarization of American capitalism itself. In fact, it could well be said that the last thirty years have seen the construction of a vast bureaucratic apparatus for the creation and maintenance of hopelessness, a giant machine designed, first and foremost, to destroy any sense of possible alternative futures."[21]

Graeber believes that the powers-that-be felt compelled to prevent, under any circumstances, the perception that those who challenge the system can in any way win.

"To do so requires creating a vast apparatus of armies, prisons, police, various forms of private security firms and police and military-intelligence apparatus, and propaganda engines of every conceivable variety, most of which do not attack alternatives directly so much as create a pervasive climate of fear, jingoistic conformity, and simple despair that renders any thought of changing the world seem an idle fantasy."[22]

At the same time that capitalism arms-up getting ready for the revolution, what it is even better at, is shifting the revolutionary spirit away from the overthrow of capitalism, in a Marxian class war, to the biggest threat to the planet, the 'revolution of rising expectations'. According to the American sociologist James C. Davies:

"Revolutions are most likely to occur when a prolonged period of objective economic and social development is followed by a short period of sharp reversal. People then subjectively fear that ground gained with great effort will be quite lost; their mood becomes revolutionary."[23]

The Revolution of Rising Expectations

However, it was the historian, Harlan Cleveland, who coined the phrase, 'revolution of rising expectations' to describe how anti-revolutionary consumer desire can be, and how it could be harnessed to ensure an unstoppable social and economic force, for the 'good of America', and in his mind the good of the world. Consumerism was an anti-revolutionary means to 'bypass the Cold War' as the US moved beyond international diplomatic relations to direct intervention in domestic affairs. Cleveland wrote:

"The time of deep American intervention in other people's affairs was bound to come. It was not hard to predict that a nation producing half of the world's industrial goods, with only 6 per cent of the world's population, would sooner or later leave its cocoon for good."[24]

As one of the senior members of the Marshall Plans Economic Recovery Program, Cleveland believed that Americans should intervene in countries in order to secure 'freedom' for those citizens, and this was a welcome intervention.

"On the economic side, our technical aid brings Americans into contact with thousands of local and provincial leaders. It deals with a society at its most sensitive point – at the very center of its rising expectations. It teaches people what they should want, and makes them more articulate in demanding what they want from their own leaders."[25]

The Cold War had become a propaganda war, as President Eisenhower established the United States Information Service in 1953 to spread 'American' ideas and attitudes both internally and in foreign countries. At home in the US, the USIS communicated the message that "[t]he United States was working for a better world".[26] PR and economists united with the M.I.E.A propaganda machine to sell consumerism as political, social and psychic freedom.

Curtis outlined in the fourth episode of the series, *Century of Self*, how the great-grandson of Sigmund Freud, Matthew Freud, a PR consultant, applied psychoanalysis to politics using the concept of focus groups. The focus group was an invention by psychoanalysts working for US corporations to understand consumer desires and emotions. Matthew Freud employed them to understand voters desires, and according to Curtis led to the US and the UK becoming something like the 'Democracity' exhibit, created by Edward Bernays, at the 1939 World Fair in Flushing Meadows, NYC. Curtis concluded, "Although we feel we are free, in reality, we—like the politicians—have become the slaves of our own desires." Many may wonder what is wrong with giving into those desires? Is the Earth not our hedonic paradise, our modern Garden of Eden, in which we can acquire anything we want at ever-decreasing prices?

Based on World Bank projections it is expected that in the next half a century that the average world income will rise to US$40,000 in annual income, up from US$10,000, but prices will remain around the same. In other words, the buying capacity for everyone will quadruple, and the revolution in rising expectations will go global. But what will that mean in terms of global carbon emissions, waste production, land use and resource exploitation? We really could be looking at an exponential acceleration in consumption. It does not seem unreasonable to assume that the world will also continue to accelerate towards the sixth mass extinction.

The Freedom that was promised by this revolution of rising expectations has begun to appear 'fake news', as many either attain so-called affluence, only to find that it has not brought them the happiness that was promised, and desires have not helped them to get them closer to their psychic need of an archetypal integration. The current existential crisis is easily ignored, as journalism is in decline, and there is probably a Google lab working on a generative AI that can self-improve to synthetically create the ultimate YouTube cat video with millions of likes.

It may be true that we are deeply unhappy with the world as we know it, but we are generally paralysed by the fear of the unknown, incapable of thinking of alternatives. "About the only thing we can imagine is catastrophe."[27]

Graeber declares that we have to once again see ourselves as historical actors, but he warns that, "This is exactly what the militarization of history is trying to take away."[28]

We appear to be facing a state of mass catatonic immobility of mind and action. We are complicit in the sustenance of the neoliberal capitalist world view that we ironically make fun of, and so help to ensure there are no alternatives. In the 1980s the neoliberal revolution invaded public broadcasting in countries throughout the world including the UK, Australia, New Zealand, and the USA as Thatcher and Reagan instigated what the maverick television auteur, Dennis Potter called the 'occupying powers' of neoliberalism.[29]

According to Mark Fisher:

"What needs to be kept in mind is both that capitalism is a hyper-abstract impersonal structure and that it would be nothing without our cooperation."[30]

Fisher, argues that over the past thirty years that capitalist realism has effectively installed a 'business ontology' that has become self-evident 'common sense', that the only way to see the world, including healthcare and education, is that everything in society 'should be run like a business'.[31]

"It is more like a pervasive atmosphere, conditioning not only the production of culture but also the regulation of work and education, and acting as a kind of invisible barrier constraining thought and action."[32]

The foundations of this common-sense 'business ontology' goes back to the work done by Bernays in convincing the American public that capitalism and democracy were indivisible.

Propagating Consent

It is fear and the lack of imagination that is currently fuelling the global hard right populist political movements that have been closely watching the Trump presidency, and are now borrowing from his playbook. The respected investigative journalist Bob Woodward traced Trump's cynical pragmatism back to an important meeting in 2010 when he was introduced to Steve Bannon, the editor of Breitbart, a populist 'Tea Party' mouthpiece, and self-appointed spokesman for the disaffected white, working-class men of America. Trump had been working with Dave Bossie, head of Citizens United, a conservative activist group that made anti-Clinton films. Trump had told Bossie, who had made the introduction to Bannon, that he wanted to run for President of America on the Republican ticket. Bannon and Bossie said they had some important questions and concerns that could destroy Trump's political ambitions, fundamentally, they told Trump he had to understand the conservative movement, otherwise, Trump's past performance could disqualify him from running for the GOP. They presented their argument:

1. First, there has never been a guy who has won the Republican primary that's not pro-life. Trump had a track record of pro-choice. He asked how he could fix that?

2. "The second big thing," Bossie said, "is your voting record." Trump had only voted once in the primary elections for Rudy Giuliani in 1989. "I'll get over that," Trump said.

3. Bannon then discussed the Tea Party and how it hated the elites, political cronyism and insider deals. Up until then, 80% of Trump's electoral funding had been for Democratic candidates. He told Bannon and Bossie that was just what he had to do to get his real estate deals done, the donations (or rather bribes?) just happened to be Democrats.[33]

Trump proudly declared he was a businessman as if that excused him from having a clear policy platform. It was a pragmatic nihilism that was strangely in sync with the times; the disaffected, and disparate mob of Tea Party activists; online trolls; and ironic white male supremacists that took down progressive liberals deplored by Angela Nagle in her book, *Kill all Normies*. Working with dirty tricksters such as lobbyists, Roger Stone and Paul Manafort, Trump was advised to run a campaign that was a replay of Nixon's political takedowns, and Reagan's pro-business slogan, 'Make America Great Again.'

Going back to the formative years of Presidents, Calvin Coolidge and Herbert Hoover, it was Eddie Bernays, the godfather of political lobbying, that established the foundations for a perennial PR campaign that convinced the American public that democracy and capitalism were inseparable and that its only true champion was an American business.[34]

Prior to the first World War, the wheels were set in motion for the modern militarization of history in the US as mass communications enlisted the new techniques of 'psychological warfare', propaganda, and the 'manufacturing of consent'. Bernays, the nephew of Sigmund Freud, applied his uncle's theories to sell everything from the War to tobacco, and bacon and eggs as the 'all American breakfast'.

The young Bernays was hired by the CPI (Committee on Public Information) to write propaganda for the Latin American division. He became fascinated with how CPI propaganda helped Woodrow Wilson to get the American public into the war. Wilson had been elected on the slogan "he kept us out of the war" but following a broken campaign promise he created the CPI headed by a muck-racking journalist, George Creel.

The template for public information and militarism were set in play as the CPI created movie reels and posters depicting fabricated scenes of German troops behaving deplorably.

"The CPI's Division of Advertising churned out posters and ads that depicted German atrocities that never happened, played up threats to American homes and families that were wildly exaggerated, and generally appealed to the fears and anxieties that lurked beneath the surface of public consciousness. All of this was observed with great interest by a young member of the CPI team named Edward Bernays."[35]

Bernays, who is known as the father of Public Relations, was so impressed by the results of the CPI that he wrote a book entitled, *Propaganda*, (1928). Depth psychology that had been developed by Freud, Jung and William James was intended to liberate the patient from the grasp of the subconscious, but Bernays perversely applied it by searching out powerful archetypes in order to seduce and manipulate the masses. In the US, the economy and the military became a powerful partnership, and it was not long before industry, entertainment and academia joined the party forming an M.I.E.A network. "The World War left business astounded at what the technique of propaganda had accomplished in the conflict," wrote Bernays in his Independent article:

"[T]his 'new propaganda,' this new technique that had made men willing to give up their lives and their money—this was something big business might find very useful!" However, he quickly shifted to more prosocial applications of propaganda, citing its use by "colleges and other educational and social service bodies,".

American corporations such as Bernays client, General Electric, regularly paid for uncredited newspaper stories in support of the National Electric Light Association, an organisation that used price-fixing and patents to uphold profits and ensure that utilities did not become public but remained in private hands. As part of their propaganda, (later sanitised by Bernays to be called PR) or public relations campaigns, these early lobbyists donated funds to universities such as Harvard.

"In a speech to the 25th convention of the Advertising Affiliation in June of 1928, Bernays had noted that, "There is hardly a big business today that does not use propaganda and use it effectively to accomplish its purposes."[36]

From his wartime experience, Bernays recognised that the same psychological methods could be used to sell anything. In the early 1990s Bernays told a BBC interviewer, "I decided that if you could use propaganda for war, you could certainly use it for peace."[37] Bernays was openly disparaging about the masses seeing them as irrational, with herd-like instincts thus providing the opportunity for crowd psychologists to control and manipulate them. He believed that the understanding of the psychology of desires would help prevent anarchic revolutions and mass communications would enable the 'manufacturing of consent'.

In his documentary series, *The Century of Self*, Adam Curtis documents Sigmund Freud, his daughter, Anna Freud, and Bernays, explaining, "This series is about how those in power have used Freud's theories to try and control the dangerous crowd in an age of mass democracy." One of Bernays early triumphs was his work for American Tobacco. They were faced with the problem that in the early 1900s in the US smoking by women was considered to be socially unacceptable and a sign of moral turpitude, if not sexual promiscuity.

Bernays began a campaign to change public opinion by hiring a group of attractive young women, who were not models or actresses, and having them join the parade wearing short skirts and stockings. At the designated moment they were instructed to brazenly remove their cigarette packets, hidden in the garter of their stockings, and light up in public. The press were drawn in like moths to the flame and interviewed a number of young women. When asked why they had done such a thing in public they smiled to the cameras and said they were making a stand for women's rights and were proud independent thinkers, cigarettes became women's 'torch of freedom'.

Bernays had enlisted a student of Freud's, the psychoanalyst, Abraham Brill. According to his biographer, Tye: "Bernays understood they were up against a social taboo that cast doubt on the character of women who smoked, but he wasn't sure of the basis of the inhibition or how it could be overcome. So he got Hill to agree to pay for a consultation with Dr A. A. Brill, a psychoanalyst and disciple of Bernays's uncle, Dr Sigmund Freud."

"It is perfectly normal for women to want to smoke cigarettes,' Brill advised. 'The emancipation of women has suppressed many of their feminine desires. More women now do the same work as men do. Many women bear no children; those who do bear have fewer children. Feminine traits are masked. Cigarettes, which are equated with men, become torches of freedom."[38]

"That rang a bell for Bernays. Why not organize a parade of prominent women lighting their 'torches of freedom'? And do it on Easter Sunday, a holiday symbolizing freedom of spirit, on Fifth Avenue, America's most prestigious promenade?" Bernays pretended to leak the story to the press creating the first guerilla marketing campaign and prompted the New York Times to headline on the 1st April 1928, *Group of Girls Puff at Cigarettes as a Gesture of 'Freedom'*.[39]

Ticking Obsolescence

The concerns of early American manufacturers following the Depression, and again following WWll, that overcapacity of consumer supply would not match demand, were originally handled by manual means. The light bulb conspiracy of the Phoebus Cartel was a secret agreement to reduce the life of a light bulb.[40]

Long before computers were a component of manufacturing, producers were focused on converting business rules and processes into algorithms. The Phoebus Cartel was a consortium of light bulb companies formed in 1925, including General Electric, Philips, Associated Electrical Industries, and Osram among others. While it is known that switching a light on and off weakens the filament, the Cartel conspired to protect profits and shorten the age of their light bulbs. The Phoebus Cartel[41] eventually achieved their target of reducing the life of a light bulb filament from over 2000 hours to just 1000 hours. The Cartel imposed fines on members who did not achieve these reductions, and while they had intended to last for thirty years they ceased to exist in 1939 due to the War. The production process of those light bulbs was researched and developed into rules, and patents, that were in effect algorithms of profitability and waste, i.e. planned obsolescence. The control of time equated to the desire to maximise profits within the lifespan of the people running the companies, and yet this algorithm has assumed an internal logic of its own that has been identified in a wide variety of consumer products from Apple batteries to inkjet printers.[42] The algorithm of accelerating consumption has been let loose and is often undetectable.

The plan was to design products to fail through less robust materials, and with no ability to easily fix them. This relies on the asymmetry of information between the producer who knows how long the product should last, and the consumer who does not. While it is said that monopolies are best placed to implement this cynical strategy, this can be artificially implemented through antitrust consortiums of producers colluding to reduce their product life cycles. This is what happened with the humble light bulb. One of Edison's original designs, known as the Centennial Light, is still shining over 100 years later at the Livermore Fire Station at 4550 East Avenue, Livermore, California.

Desired Obsolescence

At the turn of the 20th-century consumerism and built-in obsolescence became articles of faith in the manufacturing economy of the US, and by the 1950s this planned obsolescence was bolstered by 'psychological obsolescence' that convinced consumers that last year's fashion needed replacement. While the country had seen a notable shift towards secular beliefs, scientism, and material reductionism had created a vacuum in the collective psyche that was quickly exploited through the commodification of everything, including ideas, and the stimulation of archetypal desires and fears. In 1927, Paul Mazur, a leading Wall Street banker wrote, "We must shift America from a needs to a desires culture. People must be trained to desire, to want new things, even before the old have been entirely consumed. [...] Man's desires must overshadow his needs."[43] In order to maximise profits, it was no longer sufficient to reduce costs, time was one of the biggest enemies of capitalism, and while that often converted into labour costs, time was to eventually become a resource that could be mathematically abstracted, calculated and algorithmically manipulated in order to convert it to capital.

The 1939 World Fair, in Flushing Meadows New York, was designed to do just that. Seen as an answer to the Great Depression it became not just a showcase for American corporations, such as General Electric, and General Motors, but a fashionable projection of built-in obsolescence. Bernard London, in his essay, *Ending the Depression through Planned Obsolescence* (1932) wrote:

"The essential and bitter irony of the present depression lies in the fact that millions of persons are deprived of a satisfactory standard of living at a time when the granaries and warehouses of the world are overstuffed with surplus supplies, which have so broken the price level as to make new production unattractive and unprofitable...In a word, people generally, in a frightened and hysterical mood, are using everything that they own longer than was their custom before the depression. In the earlier period of prosperity, the American people did not wait until the last possible bit of use had been extracted from every commodity. They replaced old articles with new for reasons of fashion and up-to-dateness."

London's proposal to fix the depression, and the consumer's 'frightened and hysterical mood' was to impose government regulation that would declare consumer goods past a certain date officially 'dead'. London argued this was 'natural', just as nature decays, economic society must destroy wealth in order to increase it, just as we burn coal or oil; he wrote that in order for...

"wealth, to serve its purpose it must be used and consumed in the engines of automobiles and the whirring wheels of factories. Grain is wealth, but we destroy it by feeding it to cattle, by consuming it ourselves, and by scattering it on the ground as seed to produce more grain. It is by this process that people live, function and create material goods."

London almost reads as an ecologist by recognizing that the accelerated destruction of planetary wealth is for the sole benefit of humanity, but he ignores that the speed of wealth destruction will inevitably
become unsustainable. London also correctly identified fashion,
(shaped by advertising and PR), as a motivator for product replacement, psychological obsolescence. But what he did not know was that
there were already corporations that had planned obsolescence of
their products by design. The essential logic was to increase the velocity of profits by 'shortening the replacement cycle'. Advertising and
marketing was one tried and true method, described by the industrial
designer, Brook Stevens, to an advertising conference in 1954, to be
a way of "Instilling in the buyer the desire to own something a little
newer, a little better, a little sooner than is necessary."

In this *Century of Self* consumers who had lost their spiritual twin,
looked to reunite their psyche by following the 'helpful' advice of
advertisers, propagandists, and public relaticn tricksters who were
less worried about the consumer's psychological needs than the regular stimulation of the primitive pleasure centres in their brains. In
the words of Bernays' client, President Herbert Hoover, who spoke to
a conference of advertising executives, "You have taken over the job
of creating desire and have transformed people into constantly moving happiness machines, machines which have become the key to economic progress."[44]

Bernays who had a number of banks as clients, promoted company
stocks to the general public, without declaring his interest, and in
October 1929, a few days before the historic Wall Street stock market
crash, President Hoover, who was invited by Bernays, attended the
electric Light's Golden Jubilee. Bernays had been approached by General Electric to create an event that honoured Thomas Edison, and
50 years since the invention of the electric light bulb. The light bulb
has come to represent the symbol of genius, the symbol of invention,
innovation, inspiration and entrepreneurship. But the light bulb also
stands for a dark history of deception, corporate greed, environmental
damage, and planned obsolescence. Propaganda or public relations
was a deliberate psychological weapon in the battle of the brands; the

battle for our subconscious desires and any strategy to change the planet's dominant world view must acknowledge this.

By keeping the 'dangerous masses' or 'bewildered herd' focused on consumerism Bernays convinced successive US Presidents and CEOs of large corporations that the public could be kept docile through the sublimation and satisfaction of subconscious desires.

"Bernays, particularly after the rise and fall of the Third Reich (Goebbels was an assiduous student of [Bernays'] methods), thought that the safest way of maintaining democracy was to distract people from dangerous political thought by letting them think that their real choices were as consumers."[45]

The fear of communism and the collapse of the stock market encouraged Hoover to believe in Bernays, and his methods, that communicated what was good for business, was good for democracy. This became the party line for both Republicans and Democrats and has persisted to this day as an article of faith that believed both capitalism, and democracy were both co-dependent and bolstered each other. Bernays:

"believed, and argued to Eisenhower, that fear of communists should be induced and encouraged, because by unleashing irrational fears, it would make Americans loyal to the state and to capitalism."[46]

Freud had shown Bernays how subconscious desires could redirect the dangerous and violent passions of the mob towards the satisfaction of consumer desires. This is what Bernays described as the 'engineering of consent' and was only possible through manipulation of consumer desires by conceiving of them as 'happiness machines'.[47]

Following World War ll the pace of consumption and the supply of desire accelerated, assisted by the M.I.E.A network that believed that if Europe could not recover from the devastation of the War, and its infrastructure be rebuilt to provide not just basic goods and services, but an affluent lifestyle, then the communist Soviet Union could exploit poverty to overthrow capitalism.

The Marshall Plan was hatched to ensure that not only would Europe recover, but that US companies would establish a stronghold in European markets and initiate a consumer 'revolution of rising expectations'. In another documentary series, *All Watched over by*

Machines of Loving Grace, Adam Curtis argues that computers have failed to liberate humanity, and instead have "distorted and simplified our view of the world around us." He reviews the strange influence of the philosophy of Ayn Rand, known as Objectivism, and her book *Atlas Shrugged* (1957) in terms of the US financial markets and Silicon Valley. The book has had a lasting influence and was ranked in the top 33 novels sold by Amazon, and according to the Economist sales spike when US economic data is released – 7 million copies have been sold. According to Rand the individual's responsibility is ultimately to themselves and their own selfish happiness, and this 'techno liberalism' became the mantra of tech entrepreneurs such as Larry Ellison and others. It merged with the West Coast counterculture and morphed into the philosophies of Steward Brand, Kevin Kelly and Steve Jobs.[48] Rand described Objectivism as "the concept of man as a heroic being, with his own happiness as the moral purpose of his life, with productive achievement as his noblest activity, and reason as his only absolute"[49]

This became the ideology of techno-liberalism that convinced and confirmed consumers that they were entitled to happiness granted through the consumption of the Earth's resources as quickly and impulsively as they desired. The Century of Self has now bled into the 21st century, but just as consumers threaten to revolt against the 'revolution of rising expectations' the defenders of the realm have prepared battle strategies to protect us all from the end of that world. The philosophy of Ayn Rand lives on in the Trump administration. Trump and his neoliberal cronies, such as Rex Tillerson and Mike Pompeo, see themselves as following the heroic and selfish path of Howard Roark,[50] building the towering skyscrapers of capitalism against the collectivist mission of the 'parasites' who want to impose a social good with their money.[51] Famous for not reading,[52] Trump describes Rand's book, *The Fountainhead*, in which Roark dominates, as his favourite book. "It relates to business and beauty and life and inner emotions...That book relates to...everything."[53]

It is remarkable how the cartoon-like concept, Rand's Objectivism, could have such a pervasive influence. It is in denial of the fact that without society and culture there would be no oil and gas industry to support Rex Tillerson's[54] selfish fossil fuel empire.

While the concerns of the Cold War may seem almost a century away, the very real concerns of contemporary reactionaries, and neoliberal think tanks, have kept fear and doubt alive. Revisionists have attacked Rachel Carson's science and PR apologists such as, Dr Singer and Dr Seitz were employed to question the scientific claims against tobacco and fossil fuel corporations in order to discredit concerns about smoking and global warming. Dr Singer and Dr Seitz were two Cold War hawks who assisted Reagan's *Star Wars* initiative through the George C. Marshall Institute. The Institute was the brainchild of William O'Keefe, a former COO at the American Petroleum Institute and lobbyist for ExxonMobil before becoming President of the George C. Marshall Institute. "Described by Newsweek as a "central cog in the denial machine," the think tank specialized in providing contrarian scientific defences for dubious clients."[55]

The anti-communist neoliberal ideology of the Cold War not only dominated the board rooms of powerful corporations, but the scientific establishment, and education institutions in the US. These were not just ideas held by ageing titans of the oil and gas industry but were broadly held beliefs that bordered on religion and became a weapon against taxation, collectivism, communism, environmentalism, and social equity; those true believers had faith that these ideas had to be taught, and thus the American Dream became a strategy that weaponised global education.

Notes

1. Maxwell, G. (2018). The Dynamics of Transformation: tracing and emerging worldview.

2. Other related scientific and university applications such as weather programs for the nuclear tests, numerical weather prediction, finite element analysis, computational fluid dynamics, computational physics, crystallography and computational chemistry.

3. Noble, D. D. (1992). Classroom Arsenal: military research, information technology and public education. Routledge

4. Fortran Inventor John Backhus Dies http://www.nbcnews.com/id/ 17704662/ns/ technology_and_science-tech_and_gadgets/t/fortran-creator-john-backus-dies/#.W9c8rHozbGI

5. https://en.wikipedia.org/wiki/Compiled_language

6. Backblaze blog, (2017) https://www.backblaze.com/blog/hard-drive-cost-per-gigabyte/. Also refer to this logarithmic scale chart plotting the history of storage cost, http://www.mkomo.com/cost- per-gigabyte-update

7. Federal Reserve's first monetary policy report for 1998: Hearing before the Committee on Banking, Housing, and Urban Affairs, United States Senate, ... Act of 1978, February 25, 1998 (S. hrg) ISBN 978-0-16-057997-4

8. Brand, S. (1988). The Media Lab: Inventing the future at MIT. New York, N.Y., U.S.A.: Penguin Books.

9. Looking at the Y2K bug, portal on CNN.com Archived 7 February 2006 at the Wayback Machine.

10. McKibben, Bill. (2019). Falter. Schwartz Publishing Pty. Ltd. Kindle Edition.

11. Galloway, Alexander R.. Protocol: How Control Exists after Decentralization (Leonardo Book Series) (Kindle Locations 135-136). The MIT Press. Kindle Edition.

12. ibid

13. See www.S23M.com

14. Clegg, B. Light Years: an exploration of mankind's enduring fascination with light. p.9.

15. Hope, W. (2010) Time, Communication, and Financial Collapse. International Journal of Communication 4, 649–669

16. Hope, W. (2010) ibid.

17. Bostrom, N. (2016). Superintelligence: paths, dangers, strategies. Oxford, U.K.: Oxford University Press. Kindle Location 616-627

18. Bostrom, N. (2016) ibid. Kindle Location 592-593

19. Songwriters: Gil Scott-Heron. The Revolution Will Not Be Televised lyrics © Warner/Chappell Music, Inc

20. ibid

21. Graeber, David. Debt: The First 5,000 Years (Kindle Locations 7681-7683). Melville House. Kindle Edition

22. Graeber, ibid, Kindle Locations 7686-7689

23. J. C. Davies: "Toward a theory of revolution") American Sociological Review 27(1962):5-19, also available via JSTOR.

24. Cleveland, H. (1958) Can't we Bypass the Cold War.

25. ibid

26. Osgood, Kenneth. Total Cold War: Eisenhower's Secret Propaganda Bat-

tle at Home and Abroad. 2006. University Press of Kansas. Lawrence, KS.

27. Graeber, ibid, Kindle Location 7700

28. Graeber, ibid, Kindle Locations 7702-7703

29. Fisher, Mark. Ghosts of My Life: Writings on Depression, Hauntology and Lost Futures (p. 128). John Hunt Publishing. Kindle Edition.

30. Fisher, M. (2010). Capitalist realism: Is there no alternative? Winchester, UK: Zero Books. p.15

31. ibid p.17

32. ibid, p.16

33. Woodward, B. (2018). Fear: Trump in the White House. London, England: Simon & Schuster.

34. Curtis, A. (2002) Century of Self - Ep. 1 Happiness Machines, BBC Documentary series.

35. Selling WWI helped entrench the arts of mass marketing and PR | CBC News. Retrieved October 12, 2018, from https://www.cbc.ca/news/world/how-ww-i-helped-entrench-the-art-of-mass- persuasion-1.2684519

36. Bivins, T. H. (2013). A Golden Opportunity? Edward Bernays and the Dilemma of Ethics. American Journalism, 30(4), 496–519. https://doi.org/10.1080/08821127.2013.857981

37. ibid

38. See Larry Tye, The Father of Spin: Edward L. Bernays and The Birth of Public Relations.

39. Kornberger, M. (2010). Brand Society: How brands transform management and lifestyle. Cambridge; New York: Cambridge University Press. p.8

40. Phoebus was the Roman counterpart for the Greek god, Apollo, whose role was to provide solar light and reason amongst others.

41. See the documentary, The Light Bulb Conspiracy.

42. ibid

43. See Gus Lubin (2013) There's A Staggering Conspiracy Behind The Rise Of Consumer Culture https://www.businessinsider.com.au/birth-of-consumer-culture-2013-2?r=US&IR=T#american-corporations-were-rich-and-powerful-at-the-end-of-wwi-but-they-were-worried-about-the-danger-of-overproduction-what-if-there-people-acquired-enough-goods-and-simply-stopped-buying-1

44. Curtis, A. (2002) Century of Self. Ep. 1 "Happiness Machines"

45. How Freud got under our skin | Education | The Guardian. (n.d.). Retrieved November 2, 2018, from https://www.theguardian.com/education/2002/mar/10/medicalscience.highereducation

46. ibid

47.   Kornberger, M. (2010). Brand Society. p.9

48.   See Fred Turner's book, (2006), From counterculture to cyberculture: Stewart Brand, the Whole Earth Network, and the rise of digital utopianism. Chicago, IL: University of Chicago Press

49.   "About the Author" in Rand 1992, pp. 1170–71

50.   Howard Roark is the 'heroic' architect in Rand's Fountainhead who only built for himself in the guise of Nietzsche's Übermensch or Superman.

51.   See Falter by Bill McKibben (2019) for a discussion of Rand's influence on neoliberalism and the Trump administration.

52.   See Michael Wolff's Fire and the Fury, "Trump didn't read. He didn't really even skim. If it was print, it might as well not exist (p. 113). Little, Brown Book Group. Kindle Edition.

53.   ibid

54.   Tillerson, a Rand fan, was the CEO of ExxonMobil for 11 years before becoming Trump's Secretary of State. See McKibben's Falter for Exxon's part in climate change denial.

55.   Mayer, Jane. Dark Money: how a secretive group of billionaires is trying to buy political control in the US. Scribe Publications Pty Ltd. Kindle Edition.

Chapter 7 The Weaponization of Education

On Saturday 18th September 2016, a bomb exploded in the fashionable Chelsea district of NYC (New York City). A mobile application originally developed for FEMA, after Hurricane Katrina, was used to alert 2 million NYC residents of a suspect in the bombing; the suspect was subsequently arrested. This (mis)use of an emergency warning system as a surveillance system illustrates how technology can be embedded and has the potential to be later turned on citizens for nefarious purposes, either by the government, hackers, or criminals. President Trump and FEMA appear to be wanting to further expand the use of this technology as they test millions of cell phones with what some critics called the 'Trump alert'.[1]

Nearby, and soon after the bombing, on the following Tuesday, DeL 2016, or the 'Digitally Engaged Learning' conference, began with the theme of 'Anxiety and Security'. For many of the delegates, the theme had a powerful resonance given its proximity to the site of an attack in 2001 known as 9/11. I had not been back to NYC since April of 2001 but I was painfully aware that the 9/11 attack had further embroiled my country, New Zealand, in a US covert war that seemed strangely beyond the control of our democracy. It was orchestrated with civilian technology; two weaponised passenger planes were flown into the upper stories of the Twin Towers of the World Trade Center. Two layers of the so-called Stack had collided. Bratton has defined the technological Stack as, comprising six interdependent layers: Earth, Cloud,

City, Address, Interface, User. These six layers are not purely computational but include 'social, human and concrete forces' such as energy sources, gesture effects, hard and soft systems that intermingle and swap roles.[2] The political anthropogenic strata that appeared, and then accelerated, following the US government's science funding after the Second World War.

It mixed technology with the geologic Earth layer creating the 'innovative' Anthropocene.[3] The questions remain that while numerous researchers had identified the onset of a possible cataclysmic disaster, more than sixty years ago, why has so little been done to avoid it? And, what is the role of teaching, learning, and education in seeking to understand and imagine speculative, and preferable futures?

Here we pause to consider if university teaching, learning and education, and its relationship to technology and society can maintain, or indeed achieve, the ability to imagine future worlds, and alternative paradigms? Specifically, I will look at my own area of teaching, creative technologies, and the military origins of computers, the Internet and how capitalist enclosure has led to a 'closed world'[4] in which virtual futures and alternative worlds have become encircled, and embattled, resulting in the weaponization of education.

According to Edwards, American, and consequently, the global political discourse, has been enclosed by the military objectives and funding of the US M.I.E.A. (military-industrial-entertainment-academic) complex.[5] Edwards applied "this concept to describe the role of computers in closed-world and cyborg discourses."[6]

When we apply Benjamin Bratton's software theory to the understanding of the language, and discourse connected to the 'new normal', and creative technologies, we peel back the surface reality of the modern state to uncover dangerous algorithms and protocols that are rapidly becoming globally ubiquitous. Increasingly, we are seeing the militarization[7] of the modern city State as fears of terrorism, cyberattacks and hostile agents, both domestic and foreign, are reported to be working diligently to take away our freedom and strike fear into the hearts of all the citizens of the world.[8]

The 'War on Terror' provides further justification to take to 'hostiles' using drones, cyber warfare, and other remote means, even in those countries who are not officially at war with the virtuous warriors behind the joysticks. The military has formed a network of hostile 'defence', working with industry, academia and the entertainment industry, to defeat these hostile agents. While the list of participants in this perpetual war has grown since Eisenhower first spoke of the military-industrial complex, it is apparent that the political discourse that is enthusiastically amplified by both corporate and social media has effectively weaponized the whole planet. This virtuous cause has paradoxically removed freedoms from its citizenry and generated a virtuous circle of corporate defence contracts, and box office successes. Under the Freedom of Information Act in the US, the Independent discovered that between 1911 and 2017, 800 movies, including blockbusters, *The Terminator*, *Iron Man*, and *Transformers*, have received support from the Department of Defence. It was also reported that the public record shows that the Pentagon has had an entertainment liaison since 1948, and the CIA established a similar position in 1996.[9] All of this, while improving hit rates on targets, and increasing safety for their soldiers through the efficiencies of virtual weaponry, and remote telepresence. According to James Der Derian, "Technology in the service of virtue has given rise to a global form of virtual violence, virtuous war."[10]

Wicked Problems and Creative Technologies

Faced with the wicked problems of this world the M.I.E.A. network has trumpeted what has come to be loosely called creative technologies. Creative technologies defy a narrow definition, largely due to international differences in its application.[11]

One definition states "creative technologies is normally considered to be a broad interdisciplinary and transdisciplinary domain that typically combines knowledge from a variety of disciplines that include art, computer science, design, engineering and the humanities."[12]

For many who teach it and the students who enrol in their courses, this multidisciplinary approach sounds innocuous and exciting, covering a wide gamut from VR, games, electronics, entertainment, advertising,[13] screen arts, and programming. It is instructional to consider its legacy, and how the M.I.E.A network has interfaced with it and promoted its use.

A few months before the end of the Second World War, The President of the American Dairy Science Association, Arthur Ragsdale, wrote: "One lesson of this war is that the possession of a sound and creative technology tends to assure military and economic security."[14] As time moved on these military and economic objectives have been hidden or obscured, however, they lived on in the protocols and algorithms of pervasive planetary computing.

Ironically, while creative technologies have been seen as an innovative way to face wicked problems, creative technologies, in a broad sense have contributed to those very problems, as the 'great acceleration' of the Anthropocene followed WWII, coinciding with the beginning of the knowledge economy, and the computer age, echoed by the exponential curve of Moore's Law.[15]

There is a growing awareness that this acceleration made the Anthropocene obvious leading to popular movements such as Extinction Rebellion that now warned of catastrophic global warming and the 'sixth mass extinction' which may include humanity.[16] Those who teach, learn, use, and design creative technologies are implicated in this wicked problem.

The DeL conference began with a debate in which George Siemens, the executive director of the Learning Innovation and Networked Knowledge Research Lab, criticised e-learning in general for neglecting to teach analysis of algorithms. As I have taught undergraduate and postgraduate degrees in creative technologies I reflected on my own practice and began this critical review of technologies and university pedagogy. According to Lessig, "Code is law",[17] Kapor also argued "architecture is politics",[18] and yet another way of describing these technological outcomes is to say 'artefacts are politics'.[19] Finn's analysis of algorithms argues that these now define and constrain our cognitive processes, and Galloway cites Foucault and Deleuze to state that we live in a 'protocological' world controlled by information and communication protocols. Galloway challenges us to decode these protocols, writing that "You have not sufficiently understood power relationships in the control society unless you have understood "how it works" and "who it works for."[20] Given the history of computerised weaponry and the US military origins of the Internet, international educators have a responsibility to unearth the dark implications of this legacy and expose the increasing weaponization of the learning stack. The hidden histories of these technologies can occlude their design affordance which may lay dormant until awoken through long forgotten, and sometimes, disguised code. Like the movie *The Manchurian Candidate*, the hidden code could be triggered, or even modified by an enemy intrusion. In a report by the RAND Corporation, 25% of zero-day vulnerabilities, (vulnerabilities that remain undetected by the software developer), continue to go undetected or publicised for up to ten years.[21] During that time it is possible that government, criminal, and aggressor malware can be installed and be used to spy, record, steal and damage the user's data.[22]

According to Bratton:

"In many cases, the strategy is not only to break an enemy's servos, it is to weaponize that enemy's Users "against him," especially when the User is unaware of having being weaponized. The zombified personal computer, taken over by malware acting like a parasitic fungus, is a basic example, but the capacity of unprogrammed Users to wreak havoc on their own platform is almost limitless. In such a case, is the User or the owner more responsible?"[23]

In such a scenario students' technology becomes weaponized without their knowledge. This effect becomes amplified by the strange online world described by Nagle in *Kill All the Normies* heightened by vicious cyber-bullying and nihilistic in-joke irony.[24]

The high school attacks by white supremacist Nicolas Cruze, in February 2018, intensified the gun control debates in the US as the NRA and President Trump championed arming teachers while students protested for a ban on military assault rifles. The first metal detectors were installed in Thomas Jefferson High School, in Brooklyn, in 1988,[25] however, I argue that the weaponization of education began long before that.

The historical origins of the architecture and aggressive paranoia of the original software and hardware developers are so deeply embedded in the code that their military functionality is now hidden from sight. However, the incremental evolution of automation, information and communication architecture, can retain military design objectives that enable weaponization – even in education. According to Edwards:

"We can make sense of the history of computers as tools only when we simultaneously grasp their history as metaphors in Cold War science, politics and culture."[26]

Cultural sociology, political discourse, and software theory can simultaneously provide us with a critical lens in order to research the history and role of technology in university education. In education, these are but a few suggestions of how to inoculate students against the viral attack of mainstream design, and the insidious threat of algorithmic cyber warfare that is spreading throughout the Internet, as we face the weaponisation of education. Considering the complexity of understanding this interconnected field of research I have taken a transdisciplinary approach, commonly used within the field of creative technologies.

A Short History of Education as a Weapon

A historical review of scientific patronage by almost all politico-religious rulers, since ancient times, suggests that those who held the power used their substantial wealth to research and develop knowledge that would support and perpetuate their domain over their subjects. It was the creation, and exchange of knowledge that helped to maintain the ruling classes through the various disciplines that they sponsored.

Our contemporary view of universities is shaped by the thirteenth and fourteenth centuries. The 'authority for the school could be granted only by the pope, the emperor or the king'.[27] Yet, at the same time, the universities managed to articulate the concept of 'academic freedom' as they positioned themselves between Church and State. The history of research and development of proto-scientific and mathematics treatises traces a close relationship to the objectives of power, the patronage of knowledge, and the methods of education.[28] The history of mathematics and manual computation have a long association with weaponry as far back as the sixteenth century.[29]

Human computers in the sixteenth century calculated and predicted astronomical and earthly trajectories, founded on a common geometric interest. Astronomy and ballistics were mathematically connected through the geometric study of parabolas, which human computers, using calculus, manually computed the trajectory of 'heavenly bodies', and weaponised projectiles.[30] The earliest mathematical table of ballistics, designed to improve the accuracy of fired projectiles, was written by the Italian mathematician, Niccolò Tartaglia, in 1531. Galileo published his treatise on the subject of ballistics entitled, *Fourth Day of the Discorsi*, in 1638.[31]

It provided a general artillery table for predicting cannon and mortar projectiles. In a letter to Diodati, a year before the publication, Galileo wrote:

"I wish for now to close the treatise with a table which I have proved and calculated for artillery and mortar trajectories, showing their flights and with what proportion they increase and diminish according to the various degrees of elevation. The practice of this table will be useful to gunners, its theory of great delight to philosophers (speculativi)."[32]

Galileo's work provided the foundation for calculus that was independently developed by both Newton (1666) and Leibniz (1670s). Haley used Newton's calculus to assist in the computation of large complex mathematical parabolic calculations to predict the return of the comet, subsequently named after him. Rene Descartes was another mathematician, soldier and philosopher who used published tables to assist the computation of ballistics. The use of human computers to compute ballistic tables continued throughout the 17th, until the 20th century. In the 17th and 18th centuries, military academies across Europe applied emphasis on mathematical education. In France:

"A net of military schools was established through which mathematics ascended as the major discipline. For the young noblemen who prepared for careers as military officers, some mathematics teachers had already been attached to regiments in the seventeenth century".[33]

By the early nineteenth century, public schools were considered not much more than places of confinement for wayward children who needed discipline while their parents worked in the 'dark satanic mills'. According to Foucault, over the centuries schooling and universities can be seen increasingly as part of a long term effort not to free, but to enslave the mind, and to increase discipline. Deleuze argued that this eventually, developed into a means of control over the students, parents, and society in general.[34]

Deacon writes that:

"the degree to which modernity's vision of a progressive accumulation of scientific knowledge, the grouping and partitioning of curricula, the evolutionary differentiation and classification of learning cycles and phases, and the separation of ages and standards, so central to modern systems of education, are products of historically contingent disciplinary procedures."[35]

In the US this disciplinarian approach was borrowed from educational methods developed in mathematics at US military schools, such as West Point, where oral recitation was prevalent "and adopted wholesale into high schools from the time of the invention of these institutions in the middle third of the nineteenth century."[36] STEM (science, technology, engineering and mathematics) disciplines have increasingly been encouraged by various states around the world, and it is these subject areas that have been encouraged, and funded by military-industrial R & D interests.[37] STEM subjects are also the co-requisite of a degree in 'creative technologies' that is dependent on information technologies and theories derived from STEM disciplines. Gildersleeve, Kuntz, Pasque, & Carducci see an increased educational emphasis on skills as part of "conservative modernisation" of higher education.[38]

Conservative modernisation shifts the social foundations of education from being the 'critic and conscience of society'[39] to having a primary economic focus. In this context, students serve as both the consumer and the product. Education's purpose is to serve the economic interests of society by producing future workers with "twenty-first-century skills" to succeed in the knowledge economy of the global marketplace. As such, education becomes a tool for class warfare, premised on a need for students to learn "real knowledge"—the content of which is based solely on a Western European frame of reference.

"Ultimately, conservative modernisation serves to undermine certain conceptions of democracy and freedom in education and supplant them with conceptions that serve the ruling classes and their private interests."[40]

Goldin, Claudia, et al. argue that the early driving motivation of America's education policy was around not only educating its citizens to be informed; capable of voting; and running the Republic, but was also conceived to build an efficient and productive workforce that would in due course assist in what they describe as the 'diffusion of technology'. This diffusion and sale of technological solutions was a mechanism for assisting America's economic ambitions during the industrial revolution and the flowering of modern capitalism.[41] Since the 1980s university education in the US, UK, Australia, New Zealand, the Netherlands, and Sweden have all shifted to an education model based on neoliberal ideology and what Lorenz has described as New Public Management of universities.[42] Not only are students subjected to the discipline and control mechanisms of university academic staff, but also the academic staff are, in turn, also disciplined and controlled by management and administrators who subject them to demeaning audits and anonymous student performance evaluation questionnaires that are used to assess academic staff's approval rating amongst the education consumers. The purpose of theses student surveys are not to improve the quality of education, as is sometimes thought, but to control, and surveil teachers, for the purposes of promotion, hiring or firing academic staff. Lorenz argued that this neoliberal management approach to education has similarities to the sinister activities of totalitarian regimes and their secret police, described by the sociologist Ulrich Beck as 'McKinsey Stalinism'. Lorenz wrote:

"The introduction of permanent control over faculty—which is unprecedented at least in the history of universities in democracies worthy of the name—is nothing other than the introduction of a culture of permanent mistrust."[43]

The Orwellian nature of modern university education creates a system of control that has moved beyond the simple disciplinary nature of past schooling. However, the lack of political activism and dissent amongst students and faculty may be stimulating a political response beyond the universities with a younger generation of school-goers as demonstrated in the US anti-gun protest rallies by high school kids; the School strikes of Aspergers student, Greta Thunberg;[44] and the anti-coal climate activism of Australian school children of 14 years and older.[45]

The M.I.E.A. complex has been credited with the origins of computing and the Internet. Norbert Wiener, the founder of cybernetics, and author of the book, *Cybernetics*, (subtitled: *Or Control and Communication in the Animal and the Machine*, 1948), campaigned against university research in the service of the military. As a mathematician, Wiener was painfully aware of the role of mathematics in the design and efficacious analysis of weaponry. During the First World War, he had joined a team of mathematicians who worked on ballistics tables at Aberdeen Proving Ground in Maryland. During the Second World War, he worked on the artillery problem of trying to shoot down a missile, which formed the basis of his cybernetic theory of human-machine feedback loops. However, following the horror of the nuclear bombing of Hiroshima, and the integral role of scientists in the Manhattan Project, he vowed he would never take funding from the military, and held a deep suspicion of industry sponsorships, and grants to university research. However, cybernetics and the famous Macy Conferences attracted an interdisciplinary coterie of mathematicians, physicists, psychologists, anthropologists, linguists, and sociologists who helped to establish the foundations for computing, AI, and eventually, the Internet, almost entirely funded by the military.

This interdisciplinary approach became recognised as a best practice for advanced R & D of weaponry.[46] Because it worked and resulted in not just the Manhatten Project, the Bomb, and computing, multidisciplinarity became the model of innovation, and is today a focused objective in creative technology education, and is often promoted by educators, politicians, and industry partners. According to a guide to Creative Technologies, a key feature of the bachelor's degree is that it is "Multidisciplinary – bringing together creative arts, design, digital media, computing, engineering and entrepreneurship." (2017).

The history of modern computing was emphatically developed as a weapon, and to assist the military objectives during war.[47] This short survey documents the legacy of creative technologies, STEM education, and the impact of military funding on digital humanities. According to Galloway, it was Deleuze who showed the "productive power of computers to explain the sociopolitical logics of our own age."[48] Galloway instructs us that the technical is also political and that while protocol is not inherently bad, "protocol is also dangerous in the way that a weapon is dangerous. It is potentially an effective tool that can be used to roll over one's political opponents."[49] I would argue that 'tool' is not just analogous, but can in effect be a weapon, used in cyber attacks and cyber warfare.

The Legacy of the Cold War Logic

Following the Second World War, on the 29th August 1949, the Soviet Union detonated its first nuclear weapon. The fear of a closing technology gap and the growing capability of the Communist Soviet Union encouraged a revival in mathematics education. In the words of Kilpatrick the "growing threat from Soviet technological prowess, ultimately gave rise to several projects to improve school mathematics, efforts that collectively became known as "the new math."[50]

The Cold War had a powerful impact on not just the technological outcomes driven by a fear of a thermonuclear attack by the Soviets but also on the philosophical, mathematical, scientific, social science and computer models that were developed in academia and think tanks, such as the US-based RAND Corporation.[51]

According to John McCumber, during the Cold War, there was a much older and deeper fear than simply Communism that motivated the public, politicians, and university administrators. In their exodus to America in the seventeenth century the Pilgrim Fathers, who had escaped from religious persecution in England, and the Netherlands, had enshrined their apocalyptic fears in the Constitution. To be American, and to be patriotic, came to mean, 'In God We Trust' and atheism was to be regarded as the loathsome work of the Devil.[52] McCumber argues that by 1948 the American universities had come under scrutiny by the public, religious leaders, and right-wing politicians. Academic appointments began to be openly debated and criticised in the newspapers and university administrators began to buckle under pressure. In 1940, the English philosopher, Bertrand Russell, who helped to formalise logical empiricism was attacked by Catholic leaders with one attorney describing him as "lecherous, salacious, libidinous, lustful, venerous, erotomaniac, aphrodisiac, atheistic, irreverent, narrow-minded, untruthful, and bereft of moral fiber".[53]

Philosophy was particularly open to public criticism as they feared the potential threat of 'un-American' atheists, and often continental, professors who might indoctrinate the young and impressionable students with their ungodly beliefs. The socialist and communist leanings of the European intellectuals who brought the Unity of Science movement to the US encouraged a polarisation of those who thought that science and values were inseparable, and those that thought disciplines like linguistics could be sanitised of semantics, politics and values through mathematical formalism. Carnap believed that: "Logic, including applied logic, and the theory of knowledge, the analysis of language and the methodology of science, are, like science itself, neutral with respect to practical aims, whether they are moral aims for the individual or political aims for a society." [54] This belief was later expressed and was evident in the approach of Chomsky who had been influenced by Carnap, and who came to dominate linguistics and cognitive science in the US.

Carnap, from within the Unity of Science movement, contributed to what is today a commonly held position, and yet this supposed neutrality and demarcation of science and culture has resulted in science that has no ethical grounding and can be funded to effect military and political objectives. The Cold War debate that ensued around the philosophy of science and the fear of academics; those who were either openly preaching Marxist revolution, or simply recognised that without the guiding hand of ethics great harm could result – even the end of the world; nuclear weapons being one obvious example, evironmental damage being another. However, the impact of McCarthyism on the academic debate, hiring, and firing filtered through into the philosophy of science, and thus eventually had an impact on global pedagogy and the way we might think.

The secrecy and stealth with which American universities colluded with the government to dismiss and not hire suspect academic staff were all but invisible to the public from 1952-59 when the anti-Communist Loyalty Oath was in operation at UCLA. It required an oath from academics that they were not communists. Moreover, the 'California Plan' imposed Cold War philosophy on all higher education institutions in the State. McCumber makes a strong case for how it impacted not just philosophy, but all the humanities, and the overall way of thinking, research, and scholarship with its emphasis on scientism in US universities. McCumber spends time analysing Reichenbach's, *The Rise of Scientific Philosophy*, (1951) written for a general public readership and was a standard text in philosophy courses in the US as late as 1982. Hans Reichenbach had been a paid consultant and researcher with the military and policy think tank, RAND, since 1948. The book stated that philosophy must be 'scientific' and assumed the Rational Choice Theory of mind. McCumber points out there were four basic components of this Cold War philosophy:

1. stratification of the disciplines with physics reigning supreme

2. naturalism as opposed to idealism – with an emphasis on empiricism

3. mathematical methodology and logic

4. individualism, that assumes a rational choice theory, economic and (although not mentioned) religious personal choice[55]

In his book on how the Philosophy of Science was transformed by the Cold War, Reisch, outlines how cultural and social agendas were removed from American logical empiricism claiming, "it was transformed during the 1950s at least partly, if not mainly, by political pressures that were common throughout civic as well as intellectual life during the Cold War following World War II...It helped to determine which kinds of questions and research topics were pursued, and how they were pursued, at the heart of the philosophy of science."[56] This Cold War legacy continues to define worldbending today and is evident in the algorithms, protocols, technology and language of 21st-century education, and the way the ruling elite think about our future options.

Cold War Cognition

Thus, by stealth, the religious and economic neoliberal ideologies of the Cold War came to infect the way academics, think tanks, politicians and the public think. According to John McCumber, the Cold War had a profound influence on the philosophical and humanistic studies of the times. In the US, the descendants of the Pilgrim Fathers correlated Christianity with economic freedom and personal beliefs. During the Cold War, this article of faith became formalised in rational choice philosophy, based on market and voting theory, that came to dominate policy and academic thought.[57] Collectivism was regarded as not just an attack on Capitalism but as an existential threat to the American way of life and the 'scripture' of the Constitution. Even greater than the distrust of Communism at the time was the hatred of atheism.[58]

In the late 1940s and through the '50s and '60s scientism crept into philosophical theory, and by extension the humanities. As Tom Wolfe pointed out 'Scientificalization was the intellectual spirit of the age, and nobody filled the bill better than Noam Chomsky."[59]

Chomsky's mathematical ability was said to have rivalled that of the polymath, modern computer architect, and inventor of Game Theory, Von Neumann. Linguistics and psychoacoustics fed into the work on machine languages, and NLP (natural language processing). "It is very nearly the case, as Knight stresses that Chomsky walked into the field of linguistics and said that its subject was no longer to be human language."[60] And yet, Chomsky remained anthropocentric in his man-machine focus.

This description of Cold War thinking also helps to explain the cognitive dissonance of the atheist, and scientific, mathematical linguist, Noam Chomsky. Chomsky, born in Philadelphia, to Russian

Jewish immigrants, was heavily influenced by the views of his mentor, Roman Jakobson. He had developed an early interest in anarchism yet he kept his political views quiet at MIT until he gained an impressive reputation and tenure for his linguistics. Chomsky who had studied philosophy, logic, and mathematics was also influenced by Carnap – who argued for the demarcation of science (in this case linguistics), and culture, or syntax, symbols, and meaning. Chomsky, who is famous for his radical linguistic theories is credited with overturning Behaviourism and starting the 'Cognitive Revolution' and while there were many who contributed and influenced Chomsky he is one of the most cited academics of all time. Chris Knight's insightful book, *Decoding Chomsky*, has helped to explain how an atheistic, anarchistic Jew could overcome the prejudice of the Christian majority, and thrive in one of the most heavily military-funded universities in the USA. In 1969 Chomsky said of MIT, '[The university] was about 90 per cent Pentagon funded at that time. And I personally was right in the middle of it. I was in a military lab.'[61] Chomsky adopted a cybernetic view of linguistics that viewed the human brain as a computer, and language as a universal code which is disembodied, individual, innate and mathematical. This fed into the military C3I[62] requirements and their obsession with codes, espionage and clear communications between man and machine during war.[63] The mathematical logic of game theory and systems analysis masked some uncomfortable assumptions about the US obsession with a zero-sum-game that infiltrated and dominated almost all social policy, including education, from the end of the War, and can today only be identified by tracing the legacy of those assumptions.[64] The history of computing suggests how the 'bloodless' science of mathematics can mask the terror and nuclear destruction of millions of lives behind the cool exterior of a computational table.[65]

The roots of modern computing begin around the Second World War and have assumed a largely American characteristic.[66] According to Bratton this was baked into the architectural design of the Internet and can be seen to be shaped by the likes of the Internet addressing authority, established in California, ICANN (Internet Corporation for Assigned Names and Numbers). This has led to what he describes as 'planetary computation' in which the US prescribes and describes the map of the World's most encompassing network. In his view, "The US-centricity of planetary computational space is even built into the infrastructure's own autocartography."[67] Internationally this US dominance has had many unintended and hidden consequences which continue to shape global education, even in distant countries. For example, in my country New Zealand, which is a member of the secretive Five Eyes spy network which also includes the US, UK, Canada, and Australia. To a large extent, this US-centricity has been shaped by the early investment of the American government and its cyborg corporations.[68]

According to Lessig and his model of knowledge regulation and politics the design and build of the Internet's architecture, markets, laws, and norms have determined the shape of cyberspace.[69] Bratton explains that this ecosystem, or 'Stack', has evolved accidentally to extend its influence from the Earth's bedrock, through the marsh, and up through the network, the hardware, software, and wetware, to finally penetrate the sky, and beyond the thermosphere, into the exosphere. It is driven by an algorithmic logic that was once designed to augment physical, and then cognitive human labour, but is rapidly becoming automated and buried deep within the Stack where the logic is hidden.

The Electronic Freedom Foundation (EFF) battles to maintain "the idea, principle, or requirement that Internet service providers should or must treat all Internet data as the same regardless of its kind, source, or destination."[70] However, increasingly conservative ideologies are threatening that freedom, fought out in cyberspace, and it may already be over, as nation-states and cyborg corporations now jostle for position to colonise neighbouring planets and beyond.[71] Finn describes how our cognitive options are being defined and constrained by a computational culture run by embedded political algorithms and protocols. Galloway points out that the decentralised Internet is, in fact, a distributed network of societal control.

The Military Goals of Academia

Since World War ll successive American governments have been motivated by the ideology, strategy and tactics devised to fight the Cold War. Driven largely by Vannevar Bush, the former President of MIT, and Presidential advisor to Roosevelt, there was an attempt to retain the academics who had worked on military weapons programmes, such as the Manhattan Project, for military R & D projects in peacetime. However, as many wanted to return to academia, the US government and military set about funding academic and private think tanks to research and develop further weapons.[72] As a result of their massive investment in information technology, and weaponry they have inadvertently baked in those prejudices and given the World a hegemonic knowledge system that was, not so much designed to sustain World peace, but, by accident, created an irresistible weltanschauung of current day fear and paranoia, fearful of cyber attacks and terrorism.[73]

Vannevar Bush as one of the first to see the military applications of computers working with humans which he outlined in his famous *Atlantic Monthly* article *As We May Think*, describing the computer as a 'mind machine'. Bush foresaw the problem of exponential accumulation of data, and humanity's inability to record, remember, and process that data, requiring the augmentation of the human brain with computers that were yet to be designed. This fascination with human-machine communication had an early evangelist in Norbert Wiener who developed the cybernetics movement and had a significant influence on Claude Shannon's information theory, and the birth of artificial intelligence.[74] Despite Wiener's fear of military funding, and the destructive potential of a weaponised AI, the history of ICT followed the research objectives of the US armed forces obsessed with its Cold War enemy, the Soviet Union.

Wiener saw the human brain as a model for designing communication and control between humans and machines, and between machine and machine. Following the Soviets launch of Sputnik into space in 1957 there was a profound sense of dread in America that space technology could be used with nuclear missiles to attack the US. The M.I.E.A. complex became deeply frightened by the nuclear prospect, so as a result, computing and von Neumann's Game Theory came to the fore in planning the security and defence of the US. J.C.R Licklider who had worked on computer networks in defence, 'sketched a vision of symbiosis between humans and computers', and in October 1962 he became the first director of the Information Processing Techniques Office (IPTO), a branch of ARPA, (Advanced Research Projects Agency)[75] and began funding in support of his defensive network vision. RAND had received funding and support for early network research by the likes of Paul Baran who wrote a white paper outlining a network protocol to support packet switching based on a strategic attack on US central command.[76] His colleague at RAND, Herman Kahn, supported Baran's conclusions that the military's computer and communications network was vulnerable to a nuclear attack and could result in a single point of failure. Packet switching was devised by Baran to ensure that communications would still flow after a nuclear attack.

In 1960 Herman Kahn published, *On Thermonuclear War*, with reference to the famous book by military strategist Carl von Clausewitz, *On War* (1832). Kahn coined the phrases megadeath and the Doomsday Machine imagining the probable devastation caused by a nuclear war between the US and Soviet Union.[77]

The legacy of the Cold War warriors who contributed to the science and design of the weapons and information technology that we have inherited has been passed down to the present in an evolved, if not disguised form. Anti-communist scientists such as John von Neumann, who contributed to the design of nuclear bombs, AI, and computing, were driven by the fear of the Soviets and the potential 'gap' between the US and communist technology. The logic of the Cold War became baked into the design of modern computing. According to O'Regan, "The fundamental architecture of a computer has remained basically the same since von Neumann and others proposed it in the 1940s."[78] Wiener who was troubled by von Neumann's Cold War militarism was also deeply concerned with the implications of AI that could be weaponized.[79] An autonomous, and alien intelligence devoid of human values, motivated by algorithmic logic could be drawn into a thermonuclear war that obeys the rules of game theory, but spells the end of humanity, and most life on Earth.

Wiener also predicted a future, that today, the mass media is only just starting to acknowledge, that computer automation could signal mass unemployment. The original ideological DNA of what has become planetary computing continues to shape the evolutionary trajectory of education and the socio-political logic of systems analysis, the acceptance of AI, and ITC technologies, supported by a technological determinism that propagates the cyborg zeitgeist inherent in 'human engineering' and the augmentation of system automation by humans.[80] In UX (user experience) and UI (user interface) design, the 'user' is no longer assumed to be human, (but could be), as the central design concern is a systems' approach that ensures efficiencies, and optimisations based on the system's requirements that are not necessarily human 'user friendly', but rather machine friendly, and in support of a new knowledge economy that exchanges data and processes it in an automated financialized system.[81] This system, that appears less and less human, or environmentally friendly, was originally designed to fight off those that might try to deny it; it is both weaponized and ready to defend itself, and even attack users who might be opposed to its automated objectives.[82]

Today, almost every aspect of contemporary education uses computers and the Internet, from teaching to administration. According to Noble, CBE (computer based education), was not originally driven "by the pressing needs of education"[83] but instead promoted in order to benefit the military and technological corporations who sell their hardware and software to education providers. These "forces external to education, but integral to technological development, have forged this coupling, remoulding education in the process."[84] This applies to not just the technology of education, but to the very philosophy and theories about how we think, and applied to broader epistemological principles, including decision making; critical thinking; interdisciplinarity; creativity and theories of mind.[85]

The Globalization of Education

Globalization and the 'knowledge wave' have effectively ensured that the US platforms of the capitalist knowledge economy have spread their influence, algorithms, and protocols to the far ends of the Earth, or as they say in Te Māori, 'topito o Te Ao'. While there still remains the opportunity to 'hook up' some 3.2 billion future consumers, US corporations have effectively used planetary computing to sell their products and services into education institutions around the planet.

It is criticality that is an essential component of understanding the context and the embedded ideology of computing.[86] It is suggested that due to the ideological dominance of US information and communication technologies that American military influence is pervasive. Bratton points out that the extraordinary reach and influence of Google, which is "so deeply associated with the US and its interests" [87] can be seen to extend the M.I.E.A. complex well beyond the country's geographic shores.

"It is in this context that the National Security Agency's (NSA) comprehensive data capture, surveillance, storage, and metadata analysis programs, as disclosed by Edward Snowden and colleagues, are understood to represent a strong American state manoeuvre of sovereign control over (or, at the very least) policing of, the spectral spaces of planetary-scale computation."[88]

The New York Times has documented how Google has been issued police warrants to access Sensorvault that allows law enforcement to troll data tracking individuals whereabouts using their phone data. It has been used to solve crimes but has also snared innocent people. Often, Google employees said, the company responds to a single warrant with location information on dozens or hundreds of devices."[89]

Douglas Rushkoff has argued that a common ICT corporate strategy is to attempt a global monopoly by offering a platform rather than a single service.[90] According to the co-founder of PayPal, Peter Thiel, he advises startups to look to dominate a niche, and then to scale up, while avoiding as much competition as possible, until the startup can eventually dominate "to make the last great development in a specific market and enjoy years or even decades of monopoly profits."[91] As the Internet has assumed a largely US characteristic, global platforms such as Google, Facebook, Apple, Microsoft, Amazon and Twitter are just some of the cyborg corporations who have successfully infiltrated the sovereignty of non-US nation-states.

While Bratton would describe this as an accidental takeover he also describes this as governance by the machine, the 'machine state'.[92] It is the global financialization, automation and the accelerating rate of change, due to information technology, that is threatening to replace diversity, with global monopolies, and monocultures.[93]

The size and dominance of US investment in ICT and GRIN (Genetics, Robotics, Information and Communications Technologies, and Nanotechnologies) has shaped international education in instructional STEM subjects and has diminished the range and number of critical pedagogical paradigms, in what is rapidly becoming a global educational ecosystem that supports global capitalism and how workers should think.[94]

According to Michael Apple workers in the knowledge economy "are asked to invest their hearts, minds, and bodies fully in their work. They are asked to think and act critically [but not too critically], reflectively, and creatively. While this offers a less alienating view of work and labour, in practice it can also amount to a form of mind control and high-tech, but indirect coercion."[95] Alternative, and virtual futures are being circumscribed by government policies that follow a techno-capitalist logic born of Silicon Valley, and the UK and US legacy of the M.I.E.A. world view.

Using social network analysis to assess the socio-political and economic impact of maths education in the US, Wolfmeyer identifies the influence of business on the policy and standards surrounding that countries math education.[96] He argues that the funding from the likes of Apple, Kodak, and Walmart (to list only a few corporations) on research and policy institutes like Achieve Inc. and the National Center on Education and the Economy, "aims to shape public education towards the needs of business. Specifically, they seek an education that develops in students the intangible qualities required to be a productive worker."[97] Wolfmeyer goes on to argue that "math education 'in the national interest' actually is in the interest of corporations, mostly for its role in developing human capital and providing a scenario for educational businesses to make their profits."[98] This was something that Noble had previously identified as early as 1991. Military and geopolitical alliances between the US and its allies have accidentally and inadvertently shaped the informational infra-structure and their educational policies of sovereign states outside the US. Much lauded is the current US emphasis on STEM subjects to the denigration of the arts and humanities.[99] The US government and the military, have shaped the education strategy and content through funding, and "thus forcefully connected many public schools to an education that serves the US military".[100] At the Institute for Creative Technologies, at the University of Southern California, the programme was devised to "support the US military using the proximity of Hollywood to develop training and visualisation techniques used in the movies for the military."[101] The history of computing, networks, and spin-off technologies such as virtual reality and augmented reality are all inextricably entwined in the military objectives of the US.[102]

As James Hillman has pointed out there is a fundamental difference between education and learning – education is institutional, pre-scribed and political, while learning is an innate desire that begins with the curiosity of children, and continues through life. That is unless poor educational practice removes that learning desire. Hillman points out that Plato said that formal education is not for children, however, proper education is essential for the future of an ideal citizenry.[103]

Underpinning educational practice is a pedagogical approach that is inherited from cognitive science, AI research, and the application of psychology to military training and instruction, resulting in what Noble has called the 'militarised mind'.[104] Noble argues that cyborg values are 'militarizing education' through an emphasis "on thinking, intelligence, problem-solving and learning strategies",[105] based on cognitive science and the philosophy of mind.

Today, McLuhan's maxim, the 'medium is the message' appears more relevant than ever in a 'global village' that is witnessing a proliferation of digital tools and platforms that enable 'digital natives',[106] to unconsciously pass through virtual worlds without reflecting on the hidden code buried below the surface interface.[107] A speculative design approach to virtual futures could liberate imaginations that are confined and circumscribed by uncritical models and simulations.[108]

Education has become a battlefield in a perpetual cyberwar against those that might question weaponised education, and the creative technologies designed to command and control them. Design and engineering education assumes an essential vocational role in maintaining the techno-capitalist markets that produce a recursive loop of designed creative technologies; the marketing of shiny new devices; followed by built-in obsolescence; and piles of discarded toxic e-waste dumped in landfills and recycled by the poor of LDCs (Less Developed Countries).[109] All of this has geopolitical and environmental costs that amount to violence against human, animal and ecological targets.[110] While these technologies may not have been consciously weaponized, it is true that large numbers of producers, consumers and regulators are informed of their lethal potential, but choose to ignore the inevitable result of their use, deployment, and end of life disposal. The original protocols and algorithms were designed to control within a military command structure, and to attack, and defend, their strategic objectives within a closed American-centric world view of planetary computing and the Internet. It is the pervasive nature of the network that commands and controls us, yet in this age of explosive, and instantaneous access to data there is a dearth of ideas. Our ability to think our way out of this death spiral, the Anthropocene, is looking increasingly urgent. As Deleuze and Guattari noted in 1991, as the first Internet provider came online: "We do not lack communication. On the contrary, we have too much of it... We lack resistance to the present".[111] Our ability to imagine alternate realities is both empowered and controlled by the virtual worlds that we create.

Creative Technologies and Critical Pedagogy

Miscreant robots, amoral autonomous vehicles, and the weaponization of education are just some features of speculative cities that could be inhabited by inhuman technologies, covertly wired to incarcerate their fleshy inhabitants. But what if Nick Bostrom[112] is right, and that there is a high probability that we are already living in a simulation, or perhaps, more pragmatically, what if we were to acknowledge the increasing virtualisation of every aspect of our life; then surely we should start by designing tools to improve our simulations, and imagine preferable futures?

According to Bratton, "As the shape of political geography and the architecture of planetary-scale computation as a whole, The Stack is an accidental megastructure, one that we are building both deliberately and unwittingly and is in turn building us in its own image".[113]

It is no coincidence that the acceleration of the Anthropocene has been supported by Moore's law and the computationilization of the planet. As Cubitt argues, digital media is processed, stored and transported in a very material infrastructure, that consumes huge amounts of energy, and leaches toxic e-waste into the strata that announce a new epoch, the Anthropocene.[114]

The legacy code and architecture of the Internet and planetary-scale computing has not only shaped modern education it now constrains and limits the creative ability to imagine alternative futures. It is the early work by psychologists such as Beranek, Miller, Licklider and Sutherland who developed engineering psychology, and cognitive psychology for the military that formed the basis for the future of human-machine symbiosis. According to Grau, "Ivan E. Sutherland made probably the most decisive contribution to the human-machine interface in his doctoral thesis, *Sketchpad* (1963)."[115] He was supervised by the information theorist, and Wiener protege, Claude Shannon, at MIT, and his Sketchpad design provided the first graphical user interface.

"Sketchpad enabled the user to draw directly onto the monitor with a hand-held lightpen, and thus offered the option of manipulating images directly on the screen: the basic prerequisite for interaction with virtual realities."[116]

Licklider and the military research fund, ARPA would go on to fund Sutherland's work on the first virtual reality, Head Mounted Display (HMD). While the likes of military designers such as Ivan E. Sutherland, and J.C.R. Licklider, believed that computers could augment creativity and intelligence in symbiosis with humans, the limitations of future world simulations are baked into the code and network protocols. During the Cold War, models and simulations of war dominated the mindset and became 'mangled' in the code that we have inherited.[117]

"But models also changed the world by making the world mirror the model. Cold War America was materially changed to accord with a war fought in the spaces of simulation models."[118]

The formalism of cybernetics and theories of mind were originally conceived in the 1940s to support the augmentation of human soldiers using semi-automatic weapons in real-time and to assist strategic C3I (command, control, communications and intelligence) decision making during a battle.[119] AI was conceived as a way to automate weapons that require reaction times above and beyond human capability.[120] This led to research into cybernetic 'man-machine symbiosis' and the military sponsorship of psychologists who researched how the human factor, cognition, and augmentation could support the use of sophisticated weapons. According to Edwards (1985):

"cybernetic psychology began as an effort to theorize humans as components of the weapons systems...Cognitive science may be read metaphorically and literally as a theory of technological worker-soldiers."[121]

Noble traces the history of the psychoacoustic research company Bolt, Beranek, and Newman, BBN, from 1948, claiming that they were arguably the most significant player in CBE research for thirty years.[122] Seymour Papert, who had worked with pedagogical theorist Jean Piaget, and ran the MIT AI Lab, was brought into BBN as a consultant on an education-oriented conversational programming language, LOGO. Papert characterised students as 'epistemologists', "reflective of their own logical thought processes". Papert created the LOGO programming language for children based on Feurzeig's theory that "teaching mathematics through programming would be even more successful with a language written for children rather than engineers and scientists."[123] LOGO was promoted as a "vehicle for students to learn how to think and problem-solve"[124] and is credited with being responsible, more than any other single CBE approach, for the introduction of computers in US classrooms".[125]

However, BBN was largely funded by the military with a history going back to BBN researcher, and Director of ARPA, J.C.R Licklider, who championed 'real-time' and 'time-sharing' computing in order to advance 'man-machine symbiosis' for advanced weapons and strategic military decision making. This followed on from the work by the RAND Corporation's, Paul Baran, packet switching technology, that underpinned a Cold War strategy to use computer networks to survive a C3I attack on the US military's strategic command centres,

Licklider's ARPA, and then DARPA, continued to fund BBN research into packet switching, the protocol for the modern Internet. This research accounted for half of BBN's revenues in the late 1980s, and two-thirds of its profits, with 75 per cent coming from the US DoD (Department of Defence).[126] Today, the corporation is a US$20 billion giant, known as Raytheon BBN, one of the biggest weapons and research facilities in the US. They list among their areas of expertise 'immersive learning', 'speech, language, and multimedia technologies' and boasts the following on their website:

"Our world-class quantum research team is enabling next-generation quantum sensing, quantum communications, and quantum computing."

- "BBN's multi-sensor processing systems are in use in the U.S Navy, the UK Royal Air Force and the Canadian Navy."

- "Our software has been a major part of every generation of North American tactical IP military network."

- "We continue to lead in speech recognition technology, making dramatic improvements in accuracy."[127]

The M.I.E.A. complex not only defined and designed the hardware, software, and protocols that became the backbone of our social, economic, political, and therefore, the educational world, it literally designed a component of the way we think, and how we discuss the past, present and future alternatives.[128]

Educated Drones

According to New Zealand academics, Malcolm & Tarling[129] the modern university is neglecting its original critical mandate and foundations, in favour of cost-benefit analysis; qualification standardisation; budgets and accounting; and is presided over by 'managerialism' and a powerful bureaucracy. The origins of this politically motivated [de]education can be found in the early research and papers of RAND.[130] The original principles of scholarly collegiality and academic freedom have been eroded by the social, political, and industrial expectations of ROI that can be traced back to the US managerial methodologies popularised by the RAND Corporation; Robert McNamara, and the US DoD.[131]

As a result, the university management; politicians; the media; and great numbers of society have a consumer expectation that university education is both a product and a service, and that the student is the customer. As a result, universities are increasingly unlikely to teach students to think creatively, and academic staff are muzzled by apolitical directives and self-censorship.[132] This approach to teaching and learning has negatively impacted on the innate desire for self-directed learning and has resulted in an atmosphere of fear in which both students and teachers feel under surveillance by each other, by teaching colleagues, and by management – in the modern university everyone is under evaluation. The product that is sold back to society are educated drones ready for work.

There has been a fundamental change in higher education that has occurred over the last two or three decades in Western education. Today, approximately 97% of all American universities and college academic departments assess their full-time faculty through the use of anonymous student evaluations.[133] Treating teaching and learning as industrial production of products undermines the education of imagination, and as noted by researchers: "This symbolic acknowledgement of the 'student as consumer' role may represent the primary purpose for collecting anonymous evaluations."[134]

The 'education of imagination' has been neglected and in its place is a standardized assessment that simplifies complex issues, and anonymous SPEQs, (Student Performance Evaluation Questionnaires), that encourage dishonesty and retribution from failing students. While teachers are told that these student evaluations are intended to improve the learning environment, most academic staff understand the real purpose is to control, and manage, teachers through performance management metrics used for hiring, firing, and promotion.[135] This is what Mark Fisher described as 'managerialism' in which academics are promoted to management roles in the neoliberal university and apply methods of both external control and surveillance and self-control to manage academic staff. Academic staff who are part-time or on fixed-term contracts are intimidated and cowed by a reactionary management that wields the threat of unemployed precarity. [136]

The free-market university creates a closed world that is increasingly only semi-permeable to models, concepts, and whole worlds that might propose radical alternative futures. In 1998 the Director General of UNESCO, Frederico Mayor, declared:

"The university is having to change as it has never had to before…higher education must respond to and interact with globalization and communications, of the market economy which appears to dominate today's world…If they simply allow events to prevail they will not be able to guide future generations, as they have guided us, with timeless values that serve as an ethical and intellectual touchstone."[137]

According to Filimowicz and Tzankova (2017) "Today's creators of interactive media 'switch hardware and software tools like colours of paint'.[138] So, Sauter asks, "how as educators are we to acquire the new conceptual tools to devise new languages; participate in less violent discourses, and inoculate ourselves and our students' 'anthropotechnic immune system' ?"[139] Indeed, how do we do this in order to fulfil the original objectives of universities; to provide a collegial community of students and scholars; to be both the 'critic and conscience of society' as enacted in New Zealand law, and provide alternate worlds and speculative solutions ?

Speculative realists like Shaviro (2015), Culp (2016) and Morton (2018) encourage disobedience and rebellion not by objection to globalized neoliberal capitalism but by giving it a healthy shove towards the 'singularity'; increasing the great acceleration towards the end of the 'human' world. Known as *Accelerationism*, it " is a speculative movement that seeks to extrapolate the entire globalized neoliberal capitalist order. This means that it is necessarily an aesthetic movement as well as a political one. The hope driving accelerationism is that, in fully expressing the potentialities of capitalism, we will be able to exhaust it and thereby open up access to something beyond it."[140]

At the DeL 2016, conference participants were asked the question "Is e-Learning preparing students for the future?" According to the conference keynote, Audrey Watters, we face disquietude about the future and education. Watters went on to discuss the pedagogical impact of Haraway's theory of cyborgs, cybernetics, and the weaponization of information technology and the Internet. She wrote, "We must remember – we must always remember – that the origins of computer technologies are in militarism. Command and control"[141]

According to Noble (1991), with reference to numerous sources, following the Second World War, US military training and instruction were researched, funded, and applied to educational theory using psychologists who were resourced and directed by a concerted effort to adapt military technology to educate American children and university students. This was not only evident from an emphasis on STEM subjects in the US, following the perceived knowledge gap arising from the launch of Sputnik in 1957, but can be traced to the pedagogical discourse that promotes CBE, critical thinking, interdisciplinarity, decision making, reflection, systems analysis, ecosystems, cost-benefit analysis, creativity and rationality.[142]

Many of these pedagogical theories came out of the psychological labs and research projects designed to 'think about thinking', and the theory of mind, in order to train cyborg soldiers and the AI 'man-machine symbiosis'.[143] These are currently all fashionable pedagogical theories advertised by the likes of MIT, Stanford, and USC's ICT (Institute for Creative Technologies). These are also promoted by my former school in creative technologies. According to J.J. Noble current technological educators commonly face the question, "How do we design effective inter-, multi-, cross-, and transdisciplinary pedagogy and curricula?"[144] What is often missing from this STEM promotional objective is the 'A' or the arts, that is desperately needed to redress a multidisciplinarity that can easily ignore wicked problems such as the Anthropocene through a speculative STEAM pedagogy.

Cold War 3 in Cyberspace

While many researchers, such as Edwards, believed that the end of the Berlin Wall signalled the end of the Cold War, I argue that we have entered the 3rd Cold War that can be understood both as a metanarrative, and a call to future action.[145] The simplistic dichotomy of Cold War game theory has not gone away but has continued to shape and influence geopolitics supported by technology and the education of next-generation developers, users and consumers. Edwards argues, "The primary weapons of the Cold War were ideologies, alliances, advisors, foreign aid, national prestige – and above and behind them all, the juggernaut of high technology."[146]

The inevitable impact on education has been so pervasive that it is seldom noticed or mentioned. The Internet has helped speed the diffusion of innovation to almost every country in the world, and as techno-colonialism spreads, those that are not yet connected will soon join the discourse through smartphone technologies and low orbit satellites.[147] Almost every aspect of education has or will be, touched by computers and the Internet.

One of the first universities to research and offer courses in creative technologies was the University of Southern California that established the ICT (Institute of Creative Technologies) in 1999. This was sponsored by the US DoD (Department of Defence) as a UARC (a University Affiliated Research Center), a strategic DoD research centre associated with a university. The purpose was to bring Hollywood visual effects capability into applications to train and support military operations. The ICT specialises in R & D related to virtual reality, virtual simulations, and virtual humans who 'look, think, and behave like real people',[148] and also treat soldiers who are suffering from PTSD (post-traumatic stress disorder).

Universities, and eventually schools, have become important allies in what the US military has now identified as the fifth domain of war and conflict, i.e. cyberspace.[149] In effect, ubiquitous computing, and the IoT (Internet of Things), is now the battleground for Cold War 3 and education throughout the World has been drawn into it, and has inevitably become weaponized.

Just as the Cold War was conceived as a 'war of ideas', so to are the 'War on Terror' and 'Cyberwarfare' that are prosecuted and propagated through a technological medium devised to communicate data, information and ideas. The rising dominance of neo-liberal messaging, and a 'neo-con' discourse intended to discredit the human impact on climate change, and global warming as 'fake news' has constrained the debate and world view of possible change and preferable futures.[150] The relationship between fossil fuels and the Internet are tightly bound, both in historic terms and the wasteful outcome of the Anthropocene; and Cubitt argues that planetary computing would be unthinkable without it – they provide the majority of the power for the servers.[151]

Speculative design for some designers can shift the focus away from unethical designs towards social, environmental and economic responsibility. This is what the futurist, Stuart Candy, defines as 'preferable futures'. Dunne & Raby argues that this is not straightforward, "what does preferable mean, for whom, and who decides? [...] assuming it is possible to create more socially constructive imaginary futures, could design help people participate more actively as citizen-consumers? And if so, how?"[152]

Alternative futures and speculative design are argued to provide possible and important thinking tools in order to counterbalance neo-liberal capitalist models taught to design students and students of creative technologies. The ability to imagine and envisage preferable futures and sustainable worlds are constantly countered by commercial imperatives bolstered by the ideology of preparedness, and the cybernetic *War on Terror*.

Speculative Design versus Cyber Warfare

According to Dunne & Raby 'affirmative design' that instructs 'how-to', without questioning 'why', raises the question, do we perpetuate a dystopian future with respect to these technologies[153] by ignoring the hidden algorithms and protocols of a cybernetic system of command and control governed by a modern M.I.E.A. complex, and the threat of synthetic creativity built on a legacy of weaponization?

The War on Terror and the jihadist extremism played out daily around the world, provides a justification for mass surveillance, and an invisible fence, imprisoning us all as we are constantly watched and controlled as if we are incarcerated in a global Panopticon.[154] Planetary computing has enabled an educational means of control that usurps the sovereignty of democratically elected governments with cyborg corporations and powerful individuals who are answerable to nobody. Nagle muses, "The year 2016 may be remembered as the year the media mainstream's hold over formal politics died."[155] The mass media has become overpowered by social media, and the online rise of the alt-right has exposed young people to the 'panopticon' of de-anonymized sites in which nascent political opinions risk cyber-bullying and public outing in savage attacks by those who mocked them.[156]

According to Deacon and his analysis of Foucault's history of education "it can be shown how, contrary to certain misconceptions, the early modern school was in many ways a model for the prison and the Panopticon itself, rather than the other way around."[157] Foucault argued that historically education institutionalised the governance of society. Schools and universities were seen as methods of teaching both social and self-discipline as mechanisms of control.[158] The pervasive nature of planetary computing and the War on Terror enables and justifies methods of e-learning that facilitates surveillance and control in schools and universities. Deacon wrote:

"Foucault predicted that universities will become increasingly important politically, because they multiply and reinforce the power-effects of an expanding stratum of intellectuals and, not least, as a result of new global demands for active, multi-skilled and self-regulated citizens."[159]

As early as the 1980s researchers had identified how the military-industrial complex worked with educators to train, rather than educate, the rank and file for service to the system.[160] According to US educational researcher N.L. Gage (1966), "Psychologists in the military deserve much credit for turning the focus on instruction."[161] This was founded on cybernetic assumptions that the human mind was much like a machine and that resulted in the concept of educational engineering. Noble wrote that:

"In the 1960s, flush with the promise of systems analysis applications [developed by the RAND corporation] in military aerospace and space programs, engineers began to turn their attention to the field of education, suddenly flooded with federal funds, resulting from the National Defence Education Act in 1958."[162]

Learning technologies were not simply developed by R & D military funding, but became an ideological weapon designed to defend against, and attack, aggressors who attempted cyber subversion, and cyber insurgency, against the American Dream. The ubiquity of planetary computation and the assumptions, fears, and desires of the early computer designers permeates almost every aspect of hardware, software, and even the 'wetware' who daily design it, use it and teach it. A cognitive scientist, Andy Clark, wrote:

"Human thought and reason is born out of looping interactions between material brains, material bodies, and complex cultural and technological environments. We create these supportive environments, but they create us too."[163]

As a result, any future world that we might try to imagine is predefined by a US neoliberal view that has accidentally shaped the rhetoric and protocols of many sovereign states. It is argued that it is not so much the predicted likelihood of a global cyber apocalypse, as the imminent threat of cyber warfare, cybercrime, cyber terrorism, and cyber insurgency, that are helping to build the rhetorical case for standing armies of cyborgs, who promise to keep us safe from the 'weapons of mass disruption', if not 'mass destruction'. In the absence of a kinetic World War 111, the entire World appears to be embroiled in various perpetual wars defined by subsequent US administrations.

The inability for even experts to delve into the planet's billions of lines of code, and the burgeoning zettabytes of data from the IoT,[164] simply makes it easier to wield cyber weapons in any domain that cyborg combatants and miscreant coders might choose. Education is one of those vulnerable domains in which this weaponized technology has accidentally been infected with cybernetic viruses, worms, logic bombs, and DDOS attacks. Almost all 'connected' civilians have been dragged into this fog of cyberwar directed by the command and control of high ranking military intelligence.

In order to wiggle our way out of this US-centric virtual world, we need to design speculative portals to imagine alternative futures. In their book on the steampunk movement, *Vintage Tomorrows*, historian, James Carrott, and futurist, Brian David Johnson, opined that science and technology have progressed to the point where our greatest constraint is our own imagination.

"Your devices are a part of who you are as a person. Technology, if designed correctly, can make us more human. We learned that people want their technology to have a sense of humor, a sense of history, and most importantly a sense of humanity."[165]

Education is helping to build our very own planetary panopticon, surrounded by our beloved devices, we need to visualize the invisible wall, in order to dismantle it, and apply imagination to see worlds beyond the Anthropocene.

Notes

1. Millions of mobiles get 'Trump alert'. Millions receive a presidential phone alert in the first nationwide test of an emergency system. http://www.bbc.co.uk/news/technology-45730367

2. Bratton, B. (2015). The Stack.

3. Angus, I. (2016) Facing the Anthropocene.

4. Der Deridan, (2009). Virtuous War: Mapping the Military-Industrial-Media-Entertainment- Network, Routledge, 2008. Also, Leslie, 1993, as cited by Barnes, 2008.

5. ibid

6. Edwards, P. ibid, p.38

7. President Trump ordered a military parade with tanks and a flyover to celebrate America's 4th of July described by Esquire magazine as 'Out-and-Out Authoritarian Performance Art'.

8. A good example of this is China's blatant surveillance of its citizens, including the repressive treatment of the minority Uyghurs using 3D facial scans and other biometric data stored in government databases to control and detain dissidents.

9. Washington DC's role behind the scenes in Hollywood goes deeper than you think | The Independent. (n.d.). Retrieved October 15, 2018, from

https://www.independent.co.uk/voices/ hollywood-cia-washington-dc-films-fbi-24-intervening-close-relationship-a7918191.html

10. Der Derian, J. (2001) Virtuous War: Mapping the Military-Industrial Media Entertainment Network. See the video trailer https://vimeo.com/17099704

11. Connor, A.M. (2016) A historical review of creative technologies. In Connor, A.M. and Marks, S. [ed.] Creative Technologies for Multidisciplinary Applications. (Hershey, PA: IGI Global).

12. ibid

13. Increasingly creative technology graduates are being hired to work on interactive advertising and marketing campaigns that use sensors, AR, VR, AI and machine learning.

14. Cited by Connor & Sosa, 2016.

15. Kurzweil, R. (2005). The Singularity is Near: when humans transcend biology. New York: Viking.

16. Angus, I. (2016). Facing the Anthropocene: Fossil Capitalism and the Crisis of the Earth System. NYU Press.

17. Lessig, L. (2006). Code : Version 2.0 (2nd ed.). New York.

18. Jacobs, B. Architecture is Politics: Security and Privacy Issues in Transport and Beyond

19. Noble, D. D. (1991). Classroom Arsenal: military research, information technology and public education. Routledge.

20. Galloway, A. R. (2004). Protocol: How control exists after decentralization. Cambridge, Massachusetts: MIT Press. Kindle Locations 138-140.

21. Ablon, Lillian and Timothy Bogart. (2017). Zero Days, Thousands of Nights: The Life and Times of Zero-Day Vulnerabilities and Their Exploits. Santa Monica, CA: RAND Corporation. Retrieved from https://www.rand.org/pubs/research_reports/RR1751.html.

22. One particularly concerning example of this is the Chinese malicious computer chips and firmware update attacks embedded in Supermicro server motherboards of Apple, Amazon, and Facebook. The targets were thought to be long term access to corporate secrets and government data. See https://www.bloomberg.com/ news/articles/2018-10-04/the-big-hack-the-software-side-of-china-s-supply-chain-attack

23. Bratton, B. (2015). The Stack. p.346

24. Nagle, A. (2017). Kill all normies: online culture wars from 4chan and Tumblr to Trump and the alt-right. Winchester: Zero Books.

25. Baker, A., & Taylor, K. (2017, September 27). After School Stabbing, Parents Ask: Where Were Metal Detectors? The New York Times. Retrieved from https://www.nytimes.com/2017/09/27/nyregion/ after-school-stabbing-parents-ask-where-were-metal-detectors.html

26. Edwards, P. N. (1997). The Closed World: computers and the politics of discourse in Cold War America. Cambridge, Mass. : MIT Press, 1997. p.ix

27. Watson, P. (2005). Ideas: a history from fire to Freud. London: Weidenfeld & Nicolson. p.372

28. Deacon, R. (2006). From Confinement to Attachment: Michel Foucault on the Rise of the School. European Legacy, 11(2), 121–138. https://doi.org/10.1080/10848770600587896

29. Grier, D. A. (2005). When computers were human. Princeton: Princeton University Press.

30. ibid

31. Rose, Paul-Lawrence. (1968). Galileo's Theory of Ballistics. The British Journal for the History of Science, (2), 156.

32. ibid, p.156

33. Karp, A. & Schubring, G. (2014) "Mathematics Education in Europe in the Premodern Times. Handbook on the History of Mathematics Education. p.138

34. Deacon, ibid.

35. ibid

36. Hastings, A. (2014) "Mathematics Teaching Practices" in Handbook on the History of Mathematics Education, 303 DOI 10.1007/ 978-1-4614-9155-2_15, © Springer Science+Business Media New York p.532

37. Zakaria, F. (2015). Why America's obsession with STEM education is dangerous. Retrieved August 10, 2017, from https://www.washingtonpost.com/opinions/why-stem-wont-make-us-successful/ 2015/03/

38. Evely Gildersleeve, R., Kuntz, A. M., Pasque, P A., & Carducci, R. (2010). The role of critical inquiry in (re) constructing the public agenda for higher education: Confronting the conservative modernization of the academy. Review of Higher Education: Journal of the Association for the Study of Higher Education, 34(1), 85-121. http://dx.doi.org/10.1353/ rhe.2010.0009

39. Malcolm, W. G., & Tarling, N. (2007). Crisis of identity?: The mission and management of universities in New Zealand. Wellington [N.Z.: Dunmore Pub.

40. Gildersleeve, R. E. & Kuntz, A. M. & Pasque, P. A. & Carducci, R. (2010). The Role of Critical Inquiry in (Re)constructing the Public Agenda for Higher Education: Confronting the Conservative Modernization of the Academy. The Review of Higher Education 34(1), 85-121. Johns Hopkins University Press. Retrieved January 27, 2019, from Project MUSE database. p.89

41. Goldin, C. D., & Katz, L. F. (2009). The race between education and technology. Cambridge, MA: Belknap Press of the Harvard University Press.

42. Lorenz, C. (2012). If You're So Smart, Why Are You under Surveillance? Universities, Neoliberalism, and New Public Management. Critical Inquiry, Vol. 38, No. 3 (Spring 2012), pp. 599-629. The University of Chicago Press. Stable URL: http://www.jstor.org/stable/10.1086/664553

43. ibid

44. School strike for climate - save the world by changing the rules, TEDxStockholm, https:// www.youtube.com/watch?v=EAmmUIEsN9A

45. BBC (2018) Climate change: Australian students skip school for mass protest. https://bbc.in/ 2KIIb5v

46. Barnes, T. J. (2008). Geoforum Lecture 2007: Geography's underworld: The military-industrial complex, mathematical modelling and the quantitative revolution. Geoforum, 39, 3–16. https://doi.org/ 10.1016/j.geoforum.2007.09.006

47. See Conway, F., & Siegelman, J., 2005; Isaacson, 2015; Noble, D., 1991.

48. Galloway, A. (2004) ibid. Kindle Location 409

49. ibid. Kindle Locations 4975-4976

50. Kilpatrick, J., (2014). "Mathematics Education in the United States and Canada" p.330 in Handbook on the History of Mathematics Education, 303 DOI 10.1007/978-1-4614-9155-2_15, © Springer Science+Business Media New York

51. See Jardini, David. Thinking Through the Cold War: RAND, National Security and Domestic Policy, 1945-1975. Meadow Lands: David Jardini, 2013

52. McCumber, J. (2016). The Philosophy Scare: the politics of reason in the early Cold War. The University of Chicago Press, Chicago & London.

53. See Reisch, George A.. How the Cold War Transformed Philosophy of Science: To the Icy Slopes of Logic. Kindle Locations 1708-1709. Cambridge University Press. Kindle Edition.

54. Carnap (1963a, 23) cited by Reisch, George A. How the Cold War Transformed Philosophy of Science: To the Icy Slopes of Logic. Kindle Locations 1078-1079. Cambridge University Press. Kindle Edition.

55. ibid

56. Reisch, George A. How the Cold War Transformed Philosophy of Science: To the Icy Slopes of Logic. Kindle Locations 311-312. Cambridge University Press. Kindle Edition.

57. McCumber, J. (2016). The Philosophy Scare: the politics of reason in the early Cold War. The University of Chicago Press, Chicago & London.

58. ibid

59. Wolfe, T. (2016) The Kingdom of Speech p.153

60. Golumbia, D. (2018). The Chomskyan revolution and the politics of linguistics. https:// www.opendemocracy.net/en/chomskyan-revolution-

and-politics-of-linguistics/

61.   Knight, Chris. Decoding Chomsky: Science and Revolutionary Politics (p. 33). Yale University Press. Kindle Edition.

62.   C3I was a military acronym for command, control, communications and intelligence

63.   See Noble, D. D. (1991). Classroom Arsenal: military research, information technology and public education. Routledge.

64.   See Jardini, David. (2013). Thinking Through the Cold War: RAND, National Security and Domestic Policy, 1945-1975. Meadow Lands: David Jardini, 2013

65.   D'Ambrosio, U. (2001) "Mathematics and Peace: A Reflection on the Basis of Western Civilization" in LEONARDO, Vol. 34, No. 4, pp. 327–332.

66.   Bratton, B. (2015) ibid.p.34

67.   ibid, p.34

68.   Cubitt, S. (2017). Finite media: Environmental implications of digital technologies. Durham: Duke University Press.

69.   Lessig, L. (2004). Free culture: How big media uses technology and the law to lock down culture and control creativity. New York: Penguin Books.

70.   https://www.merriam-webster.com/dictionary/net%20neutrality

71.   Vint Cerf, known as the 'father of the Internet' who is jointly credited with Bob Kahn with the invention of TCP/IP, is Google's evangelist and is working on the interplanetary Internet to develop new protocols to cope with large distances and delays in transmission.

72.   See Jardini, David. (2013). Thinking Through the Cold War: RAND, National Security and Domestic Policy, 1945-1975. Meadow Lands: David Jardini, 2013

73.   Bratton, B. ibid.

74.   Conway, F., & Siegelman, J. (2005). Dark hero of the information age: in search of Norbert Wiener, the father of cybernetics. New York: Basic Books.

75.   ARPA was created in 1958 by President Eisenhower in response to the Soviet's launch of Sputnik.

76.   Baran, P. (1960) On a Distributed Command and Control System Configuration. US Air Force Project RAND. Research Memorandum.

77.   Grau, O. (2003). Virtual Art: from illusion to immersion ([Rev. and expanded). Cambridge, Mass.: MIT Press. p.161

78.   O'Regan, G. (2016) Introduction to the History of Computing: A Computing History Primer. Springer. p.4

79.   Conway, F., & Siegelman, J. (2005). Dark hero of the information age: in search of Norbert Wiener, the father of cybernetics. New York: Basic

Books.

80. See Edwards, (1997), Closed Worlds

81. See Bratton, 2015; Cubitt, 2017; Harari, Y. N., 2016; Rushkoff, 2016

82. See Bostrom, (2016).

83. Noble, D. D. (1991). Classroom Arsenal: military research, information technology and public education. Routledge.

84. ibid

85. See Edwards, 1997; Finn, 2017; Galloway, 2004; Jardini, 2013; Noble, D., 1991

86. Edwards, P. ibid

87. Bratton, B. ibid

88. Read more: http://www.bbc.co.uk/news/uk-45510662 "The UK's bulk surveillance exposed by the whistleblower are found to be illegal."

89. https://www.nytimes.com/interactive/2019/04/13/us/google-location-tracking-police.html

90. Rushkoff, D. (2016). Throwing rocks at the Google bus: how growth became the enemy of prosperity. London: Portfolio Penguin

91. Thiel, P., & Masters, B. (2014). Zero to One: Notes on Startups, or How to Build the Future. New York: Crown Business. p.58

92. Bratton, B. ibid

93. Rifkin, ibid.

94. See Angus, 2016; Finn, 2017; Galloway, 2004; Zakaria, 2015

95. cited in Apple, M. W., 2010, p.35

96. Wolfmeyer, Mark. Math Education for America? : Policy Networks, Big Business, and Pedagogy Wars, Taylor and Francis, 2013.

97. Wolfmeyer, M. ibid. p.3

98. Wolfmeyer, M. ibid. p.4 At the same time private education pushes the cost on to the students.

99. Zakaria, F. (2015). Why America's obsession with STEM education is dangerous. Retrieved August 10, 2017, from https://www.washingtonpost.com/opinions/why-stem-wont-make-us-successful/ 2015/03/26/ 5f4604f2-d2a5-11e4-ab77-9646eea6a4c7_story.html

100. Wolfmeyer, M. ibid. p.9

101. http://ict.usc.edu/ retrieved 29th Nov. 2017

102. Edwards, P. ibid.

103. Hillman, J, (2018). Roots of Imagination, YouTube https://www.youtube.com/watch? v=cuYg3QKj2K4

104. Noble, D. ibid.

105. Levidow, L., & Robins, K. (Eds.). (1989). Cyborg worlds: The military information society. London: Free Association Books.

106. Prensky, M. (2001). Digital Natives, Digital Immigrants Part 1. On the Horizon, 9(5), 1.

107. Hayles, K. (2017) Unthought: The Power of the Cognitive Nonconscious

108. See Dunne & Raby, (2013) & Shaviro, (2015).

109. 80% of e-waste is shipped to LDC, often illegally. See The Global Impact of E-Waste http://www.saicm.org/Portals/12/Documents/EPI/ewaste-safework.pdf

110. See Angus, (2016); Clark, (2014); Cubitt, (2017).

111. Cited in Culp, A. (2016). Dark Deleuze. Forerunners: Ideas First. University of Minnesota Press. Kindle Edition. p.5

112. Bostrom, N. (2003). Are We Living in a Computer Simulation? The Philosophical Quarterly, 53(211), 243–255. https://doi.org/10.1111/1467-9213.00309

113. Bratton, B. ibid. p.5

114. Cubitt, S. (2017). Finite media: Environmental implications of digital technologies. Durham: Duke University Press.

115. Grau, O. Virtual Art: From Illusion to Immersion. P.162

116. ibid

117. Barnes, T. J. (2008). Geoforum Lecture 2007: Geography's underworld: The military-industrial complex, mathematical modelling and the quantitative revolution. Geoforum, 39, 3–16. https://doi.org/ 10.1016/j.geoforum.2007.09.006. Barnes cites both Pickering and Mirowski, (2008).

118. Barnes, ibid. (2008, p.10)

119. See Edwards, P., (1997); Noble, D., (1991).

120. See Edwards, P., (1997); Noble, D., (1991).

121. Cited in Noble, D., 1991, p.43

122. Noble, D., (1991). ibid

123. Noble, D., (1991). ibid, p.159

124. ibid, p.158

125. ibid, p.158

126. ibid, p.122

127. See Raytheon BBN website: https://www.raytheon.com/ourcompany/bbn

128. Finn, E. (2017). What algorithms want: imagination in the age of computing. Cambridge, Massachusetts: MIT Press.

129. Malcolm, W. G., & Tarling, N. (2007). Crisis of identity? : the mission and management of universities in New Zealand. Wellington [N.Z.]:

Dunmore Pub., 2007.

130. Jardini, D. (2013). Thinking Through the Cold War: RAND, National Security and Domestic Policy, 1945-1975. Meadow Lands: David Jardini, 2013.

131. ibid

132. Malcolm & Tarling, (2007) ibid. Also see Lorenz, C. (2012). If You're So Smart, Why Are You under Surveillance? Universities, Neoliberalism, and New Public Management. Critical Inquiry, Vol. 38, No. 3 (Spring 2012), pp. 599-629. The University of Chicago Press. Stable URL: http://www.jstor.org/stable/10.1086/664553

133. National Education Association (1998).

134. Gordon, R. A., & Stuecher, U. (1992). The effect of anonymity and increased accountability on the linguistic complexity of teaching... Journal of Psychology, 126(6), 639.

135. Gordon, R. A., & Stuecher, U. (1992). ibid.

136. Fisher, M. (2009) Capitalist Realism.

137. Cited in Malcolm & Tarling, 2007, p. 68

138. Cited by J. J. Noble, 2012, p.1

139. Filimowicz, M., & Tzankova, V. eds. (2017). Teaching Computational Creativity. Sauter, D. "Citizens of the Cognisphere" p.230

140. Shaviro, S. (2015). No speed limit three essays on accelerationism. Minneapolis: University of Minnesota Press. p.3

141. http://hackeducation.com/2016/09/22/pigeon

142. See Noble, D. (1991) ibid.

143. ibid

144. Noble, J. J., (2012) Programming Interactivity, 2nd edn. Beijing; Sebastopol, CA: O'Reilly.

145. Connor, B. (2007). Narratives, Meaning Making, and Dominance in Analogies: 9/11 as a new Pearl Harbor. Conference Papers -- American Sociological Association, 1.

146. Edwards, P. (1997) ibid p. ix

147. See Cubitt, S., 2017; Diamandis, P., 2012; Ismail, S., et. al., 2014

148. A pdf on the ICT.

149. "War in the fifth domain". The Economist, 2010, July 1

150. See Dunne & Raby, 2013; Mayer, 2017

151. Cubitt, S. (2017). Finite media: Environmental implications of digital technologies. Durham: Duke University Press.

152. Dunne, A., & Raby, F. (2013). Speculative Everything: Design, Fiction, and Social Dreaming. The MIT Press. pp.4-5

153. ibid

154. In New Zealand the police hold a database that has flags against 40% of the entire population. https://www.nzherald.co.nz/index.cfm?objectid=12222308&ref=twitter This was already in place before the country was shocked by the white supremacist attack that killed 50 innocent Muslims in a mosque in Christchurch, NZ.

155. Nagle, (2017), ibid, p.3

156. ibid

157. Deacon, R. (2006). From Confinement to Attachment: Michel Foucault on the Rise of the School. European Legacy, 11(2), 121–138. https://doi.org/10.1080/10848770600587896

158. ibid

159. ibid

160. Noble, D. ibid.

161. Cited by Noble, p.32

162. Noble,D.(1991), ibid, pp. 26-27

163. Clark, A. (2003). Natural-Born Cyborgs: Minds, Technologies, and the Future of Human Intelligence. Oxford University Press.

164. Rifkin, J. (2014). Zero Marginal Cost: The Internet of Things, the Collaborative Commons, and the Eclipse of Capitalism. St. Martin's Press. Kindle Edition.

165. Carrott, J. & Johnson, D. (2013) Vintage Tomorrows. p.13

Chapter 8 Virtual World Building

The end of the human race will be that it will eventually die of civilisation.
— Ralph Waldo Emerson

The technology of world building is as old as the first cave paintings in which artists depicted three-dimensional creatures using the relief of the rock to give the world participants a greater sense of presence.[1] These proto-transmedia narratives used a combination of illusory art, primitive technologies, and culture and belief systems to build worlds that provided the cognitive superstructure for human understanding of their physical and metaphysical presence. In the 21st century, we can see a growing philosophical movement that has gone beyond the limitations of postmodernism and the scientific limitations of reductionist materialism.

Amongst these artists, philosophers and designers there is a common scepticism towards scientism and a Western mono world view. This has coincided with an exponential acceleration of technology and theory that liberates them from a unitary world view and explores multi-world, multi reality. Descended from a long line of ancient techniques current creative technologies such as VR, AR, virtual worlds, games, and mixed realities have helped world builders to design photorealistic and immersive worlds.[2] However, photo-realism is illusory tricking us into thinking that we are witness to reality.

"Photography, among all the arts, is the first to use reality as an indispensable raw material. Yet it too is a fiction, generated by technical tools used to create and reproduce a perfect copy of what the eye sees: it inserts itself into the hidden most corners of the tangible, to make it so true, so real, that it seems unreal. Today, contemporary photography is a long way from being considered a mere representation of reality. It is an absolute protagonist because it breaks down reality: it reworks the past by imagining the future, and creates traces of an anti-reality, or rather a thousand other realities, simultaneously both true and false'."[3]

At the same time these new worlds are being designed, our world, as we know it, is coming to an end, conceptually and physically, as we enter a new epoch, known as the Anthropocene.[4] One of the biggest challenges we face is that we are like Plato's sage in a cave, chained in the darkness unable to imagine the future, but haunted by the shadows of what might come to be. Globalisation has not only wiped out huge numbers of nonhuman species but has created a neoliberal monoculture stuck in an old and destructive paradigm.

Virtual Countercultures

Virtual reality was once described as the 'cyclotron of the mind', a conceptual particle accelerator that will provide a simulated acid trip, taking the merry prankster off the Kesey bus and going 'Furthur'[5] into strange new worlds. They would then return, just as Tom Wolfe did, to tell the tales of wild discovery and hopeful insights for the future of humanity. One such early explorer, Howard Reingold described his experience as a mind-expanding LCD trip. He wrote of weird VR experiences as if in a hallucinogenic trance in which he would see his body as a many-tentacled creature. In the early '90s I was spellbound by his book, hooked by the publisher's byline, 'VR will eat TV alive!'. This was an exciting proposition as I was looking for something that would take me beyond the 100 years of cinema production.

Prior to this revelation, my personal obsession had been the film industry, and since I was 10 years old, I had been making short movies. I had been given a Super 8mm camera and editing equipment by my father, and I had experimented with movie making and animations. However, after a disobedient streak as a punk, I had finally gone to university, and buckled to my parent's pressure, enrolling in a Bachelor of Science at Auckland University. The wrote-learning was not to my taste and after a year of exhilarating socialising with interesting people I tried to find a film school. Various failed attempts to go to NYU, or even join the public broadcaster, Television New Zealand, saw me do a Bachelor of Arts majoring in politics, followed by a Masters of Arts and a post-graduate diploma in broadcasting. By the time I had read Rheingold's 1991 book, *Virtual Reality*, I had become fascinated by the online world of the bulletin-board system (BBS), and America Online, (AOL). Rheingold's book was an exciting, if not techno-hype of both VR and the virtual community of the WELL. I recognised the opportunities for world building and world bending in virtual worlds in ways that can not only simulate the actual world but also experiment with, and entertain people with worlds never before imagined.

The WELL (1985) was an early online virtual community. Rheingold, an embedded journalist, and early cyber-ethnographer, had written a book following on from *Virtual Reality*, called, *The Virtual Community: Homesteading on the Electronic Frontier* (1993). According to communications professor, Fred Turner, this was a seminal book that 'marked the entry of the term "virtual community" into widespread public use."[6] Turner has documented how this early text-based virtual world provided a social template and ideological movement for what he called both 'creationist capitalism' and 'technoliberalism'. These were a form of cyber counterculture following in the footsteps of William Gibson's sci-fi classic, *Neuromancer*. Stewart Brand who had started the WELL in San Francisco in 1985, with Larry Brilliant, referenced Brand's book project, *The Whole Earth Catalog*, that featured a picture of the 'blue marble', Earth, taking from space. The acronym WELL stood for *Whole Earth 'Lectronic Link'*, and was the forum through which John Perry Barlow (Grateful Dead lyricist), John Gilmore, and Mitch Kapor (later Chairman of Linden Lab, producer of the virtual world, Second Life) came together in the Electronic Freedom Foundation.

Brand and the legendary, Buckminster Fuller, had lobbied NASA to use the photo of Earth to promote environmentalism on the front cover of the *Whole Earth Catalog*. It was taken from the Apollo 17 on

December 7, 1972, 29,000 kilometres into space. The photo credited to the whole crew, Eugene Cernan, Ronald Evans, and Jack Schmitt, on a 70mm Hasselblad, using an 80mm Zeiss lens and is also credited with rallying the environmental movement in the early 1970s.[7] It has shaped how subsequent generations have viewed the world. Interestingly, for a New Zealander, the original photograph was rotated up the other way with the South at the top. Given a Northern Hemisphere geopolitical dominance in the world today, most people would regard this as upside down. Of course, there is no right way up in space, and yet it is a powerful reminder of how our common sense world view is actually shaped by culture, ideologies, and religion. What would our world view be if we rotated the image by 90 degrees? The two ice caps, the Arctic, and Antarctica may appear more central to our point of view, and concern, and not some remote wasteland. Our growing realisation of the importance of the ice caps, which hold 68.7% of all the fresh water on the planet, has forced us to focus on their relevance for our survival.

This alternative perspective encourages another realisation that in our cultural history of space, where up, (or Heaven) is good, and down, (or Hell) is bad, this 90-degree twist equalises North and South, and puts the East at the top and the West at the bottom. This is not simply a gimmick, but in terms of China, it is similar to their cosmological view of the world as the Middle Kingdom. In Aotearoa, New Zealand, Te Māori often saw the world differently 'the north-south axis frequently being inverted in customary Māori imaginings of their world.'[8] The dominant world view, which pictures North America at the top of photographs, also generally imagines the moon 'above' us, in a 2D rendition of our world, and this is a graphic example of how humanity has not only privileged human epistemology but privileged colonial entitlement based on 'Western' geopolitical interests. The North-South – East-West debate starts to look silly when the white ice caps are melting all around us.

Gibson, coined the word 'cyberspace' in his 1984 book, *Neuromancer*, the story depicts virtual reality as a 'consensual hallucination', and yet often our everyday view of our world is just that, an agreed illusion.

Our inability to recognise that we are still chained inside Plato's cave may, or may not be, revealed by our design of alternative realities and novel worlds as simulations and virtual worlds become more and more veridical. Not only from a visual, photorealistic sensory perception but from a complete, full-sensory illusion, that is indistinguishable from actual reality.[9] This is the basis of the movie the *Matrix* by the Wachowskis, that borrowed heavily from Gibson's concept of world bending virtual reality. Gibson wrote:

"The matrix has its roots in primitive arcade games. . . . Cyberspace. A consensual hallucination experienced daily by billions of legitimate operators, in every nation, by children being taught mathematical concepts. . . . A graphic representation of data abstracted from banks of every computer in the human system. Unthinkable complexity. Lines of light ranged in the nonspace of the mind, clusters and constellations of data. Like city lights, receding."[10]

Virtuality Comes In From the Cold

During the Cold War of the 1950s and 60s, the R & D of the military began exploring real-time computing and displays that would enable intuitive human interaction. Forester's Whirlwind computer, the world's first real-time computer, was designed and built to be used to assist SAGE (Semi-Automatic Ground Environment) connected to a network of equipment to produce a single unified image of airspace intended to respond to a Soviet air attack. The Whirlwind was also the computer used to run the first flight simulator program using a cathode ray tube display. The SAGE Direction Center occupied an entire floor of 22,000 square feet with huge computers and huge displays with a Command and Control situation room. Using raw radar data operators used 'light guns' to select targets on the screen and order attack commands. This led to the RAND study by Herbert Goldhammer of human-machine systems and how operators perform under stress (1950). "Of particular importance, Goldhamer argued, was a deeper understanding of the man-machine relations that characterized complex modern weapons systems."[11]

The military funding for research into human-machine interaction and computer interface were primarily motivated by training warriors and weaponization. In 1965 Ivan Sutherland developed a revolutionary idea for the design of the 'ultimate computer display'. "This display would have the capability to rearrange physical laws optically in 'exotic concepts' and even visualize these through computed matter".[12] Sutherland set the stage for a radical new metaphor for computing describing the computer display as a window and thus opening a metaphor onto a virtual universe of creativity, simulations and conceptual worlds. He wrote:

"One must look at a display screen as a window through which one beholds a virtual world. The challenge to computer graphics is to make the picture in the window look real, sound real and the objects act real."[13]

According to Grau, Sutherland's speculative vision opened up whole new, what if, worlds. "In such an image space communicated directly to the senses, handcuffs can restrain and a shot can kill, depending entirely on the programming. Sutherland's ideas went far beyond mere illusion; the simulation potential of the system ought to have material results, for example, violence, and produce a perfect oneness with the machine-made virtual image."[14] Sutherland, who replaced Licklider as the US Defence Department's ARPA's Information Processing Techniques Office in 1964, always had a close connection with military research. Starting in 1966 Sutherland and his student, Bob Sproull began R & D on a virtual reality display, nicknamed the Sword of Damocles intended as an HMD (Head Mounted Display) for the Bell Helicopter Company and designed for military pilots. Grau says this "HMD represented the first step on the way to a media utopia."[15] The 3D display was equipped with infrared cameras to assist pilots in flying missions at night. This gave pilots the first taste of telepresence in which you could immerse yourself in strange and virtual worlds. In 1966 Sutherland replaced video footage with computer graphics and 'thus the concept of interactively experienced virtual reality was born.'[16] In 1968 Sutherland, with ARPA funding, developed the first mixed reality HMD that showed computer graphics and included head tracking that allowed the computer to match the movement of the head and provided the illusion of looking around in a 3D space that was overlaid on the actual space through video provided to the display by attached cameras.

The military continued to fund the development of virtual reality and immersive environments taking an interest in not just mechanical and sensory augmentation of soldiers but cognitive augmentation and military training. In 1970, the architect Nicolas Negroponte, at the MIT Media Lab declared that he wanted to combine computer processing with the visual capability of film, and in 1972 he stated a vision for an even more radical symbiosis between humans and machines in which the Architecture Machine would replace the architect opening up the future possibility for AI to replace not just data-intensive jobs such as accounting or law, but to invade the creative industries.

By 1976 Negroponte had attracted ARPA funding for a project 'focused on the spatial, or hierarchical, distribution of data as an organizing principle. The research included the psychologist, Richard Bolt, a member of the military consultancy BBN, that had made most of its profit through ARPA and later, DARPA Department of Defence funding. Bolt's work for the Negroponte project was to design an interface that targeted the senses. As previously mentioned in chapter 7 BBN had a long history with DoD dating back to 1948, and was not only highly influential in introducing computers into the US classrooms, but was also a major influence on pedagogical theories about teaching students to solve problems and how to think, based on military training programs.

Grau also acknowledges two other significant pioneers of virtual reality, Tom Furness and Scott Fisher. Furness had worked for the US Air Force since the mid-1970s before founding the Human Interface Lab at Washington State University in 1989. Furness had worked on targeting devices and Heads Up Display (HUD) that was an augmented reality display that would provide attack pilots with strategic information on their targets. Furness eventually became tired and sickened by the military agenda of war and developed a peacetime HUD which projected information directly onto the retina with a laser.[17] Scott Fisher worked at MIT on a stereo display and later for NASA on an HMD with LCD displays in a virtual environment that allowed up to six users to be immersed and interacting with virtual objects at the same time. Grau notes that:

"This close-knit fabric of economic and technological interests, sensation-seeking, and escapism has all but banished the military origins of this technology from the public consciousness."[18]

He goes on to cite how McDonnell Douglas Corporation had developed an HMD in 1980 which assisted pilots to double their kill quota.

Today, telepresence is a major weapon in the US arsenal in combating terrorism and foreign enemies, all conducted from the safety of a Command and Control centre on US soil. Unmanned Aerial Vehicles, UAV, or drones are piloted by pilots using telepresence and remote controls to launch 'hellfire missiles' that would rain down unseen from the sky overhead. Grau comments that 'Telepresence expands the radius of human actions and experiences.'[19] And he speculates that the motivation for this is both curiosity and the expansion of control but also stems "from religious motives in the broad sense; as part of the tradition of "playing God""[20]

"Thus, telepresence maps onto three long-term projects in the history of ideas, including their mythical, magical, and utopian connotations. There are, first, the dream of artificial life and automation; second, the tradition of virtual realities in art; and third, the occult prehistory of telecommunication, which operates permanently within structures of ideas for leaving the body."[21]

Cybernetics, with its close ties to the war machine, contributed to these projects with the disembodiment of information. Hidden in the original affordance of the machines and code were their military origins and their martial connections with mathematics, computing, and virtual worlds. These had a distinctly UK and US flavour and even with techno-libertarians, such as John Perry Barlow, you can detect a US-centric point of view that is less global, and more locally romantic. Barlow writes that the Internet, 'has a lot in common with the nineteenth-century West. It is vast, unmapped, culturally and legally ambiguous, verbally terse . . . hard to get around in, and up for grabs'.[22] Of course, he refers to the US 'Wild West', and despite the cultural and physical violence inflicted on indigenous people, imported slave labour, women, and the wanton destruction of the gold areas of the Sierra Nevada, this is seen as a rebellious, disobedient, and free zone that should be replicated in cyberspace.

It is true that despite the optimism surrounding social media and political events, such as the Arab Spring, the ability of repressive regimes to recover and then reinforce their command and control using the tools of the Internet has left many disillusioned by the promise of cyber democracy spreading around the world. It would seem that there are deeper, darker powers at play beneath the surface of this excitable techno-utopian rhetoric. While we are often dazzled by technology, Arthur C. Clarke touches on why the majority, who have little technical understanding of their smartphone, device or laptop, are awed by advanced technology as if it 'is indistinguishable from magic'.[23]

The danger is that magic, which has a legacy associating it with the so-called 'black arts' and the devil, is also occult, or occluded, and hidden from view. Not only does a vast majority of technology consumers have a primitive suspicion of technology, and not know how to read code, but even if they could read it, much of it is closed source and therefore mysterious. In other words, it is not open to prying eyes because it is either regarded as intellectual property or secret because of national security.

Utopian Hunches

If we pause to consider the positive possibilities of virtual world building we can see that this technology can afford radical conceptual, as well as physical consequences for our world. Instead of contributing towards world ending they can actuate world bending and simulations that can provide experimental platforms for speculative designs. These designs can assist those that struggle with the fear of uncertainty about future events by using experimental prototyping to generate data and prepare for 'what if' scenarios, and transformational change.

According to Grant Maxwell in the 20th and 21st century we are seeing a new and emerging world view, and that process of finding new meaning is the process of world creation. He argues that as life has evolved on Earth there has been an exponential acceleration in novelty and the perception of higher dimensions from a zero-dimensional inorganic mineral, to the simple prokaryotes' one-dimensional view, up to a new quantum temporality that we are only just starting to imagine.

Maxwell argues that our world view is a 3.5-dimensional perspective that has not fully understood, or intuitively engaged in the fourth dimension, Einsteinian spacetime. He sees our current "thinking of temporality as a kind of jerry-rigged method to map the fourth dimension, it seems plausible to suggest that the emergence of time from animal timelessness, and thus human consciousness from animal unconsciousness, is a cosmic controversy that fundamentally informs our historical experience. The human intuition of divinity is that which is eternal, while many traditions have envisioned time as a fallen world, a veil of illusion to be overcome."[24]

Maxwell attempts to link our historical archetypes and epochs of consciousness, he traces its evolution from the primitive archaic, through a magical epoch, mythic, and finally our current mental (rational) epoch, just prior to the expectation of a dialectic integration. Maxwell cites Terence McKenna, *Appreciating Imagination*:

"One of the very large creodes that we can see at work in nature and society is what I call the conquest of dimensionality. Biology is a strategy for moving into and occupying ever more dimensions. . . . Biology begins as a point-like chemical replicating system attached to a primordial clay in the proverbial warm pond somewhere at the dawn of time. And as life develops it folds itself, it becomes a three-dimensional object. It replicates itself in time, and that means it claims the temporal dimension. After two or three billion years of that it has evolved itself to the point where with strong muscles it can move through space, with superb visual organs, it can coordinate its exterior environment. And finally, through the advent of language it can tell its story, it can move information around not present, and as soon as you begin to code that information into stone, or magnetic medium . . . in a sense time has stopped, you are moving outward now. And this very large creode seems to inform not only biology but the human enterprise as well."[25]

Theoretical physics expands our world view beyond 3 dimensions plus time, to give us a grand total of 10 or 11 dimensions, albeit 6 or 7 dimensions that are probably too small for us to detect, coming close to the Planck length of 1.6 x 10^{-35} m, or about 10-20 times the size of a proton. The Large Hadron Collider experiment and the confirmation of the Higgs field continue to support the theoretical physics behind string theory, and the multiverse theory. The energy scales required to ultimately test these theories of string theory 'are in the order of a million, billion times higher than the energy scales we're able to access today'.[26] Still, if we stop to contemplate this reality then while this is unlikely to be experimentally proven for some time (if ever), then if they do hold true in theory, then we must be struck by the oddity of the reality we live in, and yet cannot intuitively grasp. Even odder is the possibility of the multiverse that explodes our reality and fractures our sense of knowability and concrete computability.

A Cage Within A Cage

The revelation in physics that there is possibly an infinite number of parallel universes, alongside our own, has given license to those who can imagine alternative realities within virtual worlds and creativity that are enabled with the realisation of the multiverse. Even more poignant is Nick Bostrom's philosophical speculation, also the subject of the VR movie, *The Matrix*, that we are all, in fact, part of a massive computer simulation. William James wrote that 'Philosophy is the habit of always seeing the alternative'.[27] Yet, we are admonished by the philosopher Michael Heim (1993) that when we create a virtual world it should evoke the imagination, not repeat the world. Virtual reality could be a place for reflection, but the reflection should make philosophy not redundancy... Cyberspace can contain many alternative worlds, but the alternateness of an alternate world resides in its capacity to evoke in us alternative thoughts and alternative feelings.[28]

By being mindful of the pitfalls of unconscious application of philosophical and ideological constructs when creating worlds, the thoughtful and speculative designer can attempt to explore a world bending aesthetic that acknowledges a speculative realism that challenges the anthropocentric past and pushes beyond the suffocating and destructive world view of neoliberal 'creationist capitalism'.[29] Virtual world building is a stimulating virtual environment that can be conducive to creative collaboration and imaginative design in a context where everything is open to question, and even the laws of physics can appear to be warped or broken.

Our view of the world and its possibilities are the ultimate boundaries of our imagination, and this world view is our self-imposed ceiling that limits our ability to design and innovate; we cannot go beyond what we cannot imagine. Virtual worlds help to expand the horizons and raise the sky above a fly zone that was never previously imagined possible.[30]

Simulations in virtual worlds can assist humans in understanding and intuitively bending reality around spatial and temporal qualities beyond the human scale. This can powerfully assist creativity and innovative design for both the physical and digital worlds. The extent to which the imagination can both expand and restrict design possibilities is apparent when we compare the ease of 'teleporting' in Second Life with the limitations of travel and communications suggested by Stephenson in his book, *Snow Crash*, (1992). While in the book, Hiro Protagonist, is able to travel at speeds up to 60,000 kilometres an hour on his virtual motorbike, this is still much slower than the ability to be anywhere within seconds via the teleport feature in a virtual world that can zap you to the other side of the virtual planet, or to another world. In his novel Stephenson was unrestricted by the same technical limitations faced by the creators of an actual virtual world, such as Second Life, however, his imagined Metaverse was constrained by his knowledge of computing, and his use of the Apple User Interface Guidelines that shaped what he imagined to be possible. Teleportation is not simply fantasy, but a proven aspect of quantum mechanics that also proves the nonlocality of the universe, according to Bell, who theorised and proved quantum entanglement of two subatomic particles, or photons instantaneously behaving as if they were one.[31]

In a science fiction forerunner to the cyberpunk genre, and before Star Trek coined the catchphrase, 'Beam me up Scotty', Alfred Bester made teleporting a central theme to his sci-fi novel, *The Stars My Des-*

tination. In this book, his antihero Gully Foyle uses his mind to 'jaunte' or physically teleport to places, including other planets.[32] The teleport feature in Second Life has a long history in popular culture and is connected with the perception of virtual co-location and a sense of instant proximity that contracts a geographical sense of the planet. Wiener (1954), the founding father of cybernetics, conceived of the modern design office in which he imagined an architect using a device he called the 'Ultrafax' whereby a facsimile of all documents could be sent to the construction site. In short, the bodily transmission of the architect and his documents may be replaced very effectively by the message-transmission of information which does not entail the moving of particles of matter from one end of the line to the other.[33] Wiener further imagined physical teleportation:

"It is amusing as well as instructive to consider what would happen if we were to transmit the whole pattern of the human body, of the human brain with its memories and cross connections, so that a hypothetical receiving instrument could re-embody these messages in appropriate matter, capable of continuing the processes already in the body and the mind and of maintaining the integrity needed for this continuation by a process of homeostasis."[34]

Teleportation is associated with the concept of presence in a world, and presence maybe virtual or actual, but is the ontological reality of being there or feeling as if you are.

Presence and World Building

'The Hello World!' Program is often the first program a novice coder creates, it is also described as a 'sanity check' to prove programs can run on a machine. In XL it runs as a 3D graphic of an Earth spinning. Javascript is a common web development program and has the syntax:
alert("Hello, World!");
P5.js is similar to Processing but written in Javascript and is described in their manual: 'p5. js is for writing software to make images, animations, and interactions... We call this sketching with code."[35] Javascript is enormously powerful and was the development

language of choice of Philip Rosedale (founder of Second Life) for his latest virtual world platform, High Fidelity.

When you write the code, print("Hello, World"); in High Fidelity you have begun world building: with real-time 3D graphics; hand, body, and face tracking; and 'co-presence',[36] a combination of social and physical presence. High Fidelity gives cyborg users one of the strongest feelings of presence, and yet even if it attains total sensory immersion, according to the OOO speculative realists, the virtual world will remain unknowable, and it will never give up all its essential secrets.

While some OOO philosophers, such as Bogost who prefers to call objects, units, attempt to distance this philosophy from the theoretical and software engineering approach of object oriented programming, there is no reason not to apply the OOO to software objects. Lines of code, applications, algorithms and protocols can all be named as objects or things without confusing the philosophical objective of the OOO.

According to Manovich:

"Beginning in the nineteenth century, we witness recurrent claims by the users and theorists of new media technologies... [1920's movie director] Sergei Eisenstein and recently, [VR pioneer] Jaron Lanier, that these technologies externalize and **objectify** [emphasis added] the mind.'[37]

It is for this reason that we need to closely examine the archaeology of virtual worlds and the strata that has built the physical and conceptual worlds we inhabit. In this process of objectification, there is no metadata track and trace of the original concepts, ideas or attitudes before it is externalized and reified in technology.

What is troubling is that while a virtual world can appear to be wholly explicit to the user, as a navigable space, Chun points out that this is a misconception of new media theorist, Lev Manovich. She argues that 'New media spaces, however, are fundamentally unnavigable. Users may navigate and control software interfaces but this control compensates for, if not screens, the lack of control they have over their data's path. Users do not navigate their packets.'[38]

Chun is referring to the underlying, and for most people, the hidden architecture of the ICT architecture of the Internet. The design of this architecture can be traced back to the Cold War and conceptualisation, and security of information and communication technologies during a nuclear attack by the Soviet Union. Packet protocols of TCP/IP were conceived to ensure that a central Command and Control centre, such as SAGE (Semi-Automatic Ground Environment) would not present a singular target, and that if a message was sent using the TCP/IP packet protocol, which breaks the message into packets, that it would guarantee that component packets would disassemble and reassemble via random routes delivering a complete message despite a nuclear attack.

The geopolitical history of ICT is known by a small community of scholars but is seldom discussed by either computer scientists, the public, or even scholars in the humanities. The protocols and algorithms of the Internet may be open for review, however, it is written in a code that only those with a technical education can decipher. This educational blind spot is often lost in the gap between those students who are taught computer science, and creative technologists who are taught programming via the application known as, Processing, by engineers, designers, or artists who teach a practice-based approach. The devil is in the detail as the protocols, algorithms, and mechanical affordance of a design must control, confine and constrain the user and the designer. The practical nature of using a tool does place constraints on both users and designers, and that can provide creative stimulus, learning, and imaginative play. These are some of the advantages of the constructivist pedagogical theory of making by thinking, and thinking by making, however, this practical method can also reject, or devalue theoretical and socio-political critique.

The pragmatic Maker Space of 3D printing, electronics and virtual world construction can engender an impatience, and in some cases, hostility towards the digital humanities. This has not been helped by a predilection amongst a body of scholars who have approached the research and analysis of technological history and sociology from an anthropocentric textual bias. The Frankfurt School of Critical Theory has favoured this literary analytic methodology viewed through Marxist material dialecticism. However, a growing number of software and platform theorists, such as Lev Manovich, Benjamin Bratton, Alex Galloway, Ed Finn, and Ian Bogost have dispensed with so-called 'reading', and critically analysing software and hardware from a textual and class conscious perspective. Their new approach reveals new insights into both technological determinism and ecological concerns about coexistence with the nonhuman majority. While both software and platform theory do not in themselves identify a propensity towards an anthropocentric privilege they are often still guilty of this, however, by focusing on software or hardware as equal objects worthy of deep archaeological research they tend to decenter humans in a bigger metanarrative about the nature of reality.

Increasingly theorists will be confronted by physical and virtual environments in which there is no human agent participating in the direct communication and interaction between the user and the software or machine. This blurring between virtual and actual experiences will be complicated by AI's and simulated beings. Brian Greene speculates that:

"Perhaps simulated inhabitants would be able to migrate into the real world or be joined in the simulated world by their real biological counterparts. In time, the distinction between real and simulated beings might become anachronistic."[39]

Safe Spaces and Human Scale

As sensors, AI, AGI, and simulations proliferate the human minority will become increasingly outnumbered by machine to machine interactions that will read codes designed and written by other machines, that are incomprehensible and hidden from human view, irrespective of whether the code is open or closed source. Already the human user of even open-source virtual worlds, such as Second Life, and High Fidelity, will often not understand or look at the code, and they are most likely ignorant of the hidden protocols and geopolitical history behind them that negotiate the transport of data across the network, and across the world. We face the danger that the self-organising evolution of our technological reality is already exponentially growing in complexity beyond our ability to understand it. Machine learning and neural networks create millions of lines of code that are incomprehensible to the programmers that code them.[40]

Joseph Tainter has warned that spurious complexity is the harbinger of societal collapse, and software bloat, as it is often called, could herald the collapse of the knowledge society. There is an urgent mission to uncover the spurious lines of code and simplify the relationships connecting software modules and what they actually do? Bret Victor, the visionary UX/UI designer, recommends that we need human-scale technologies that have an understandable one to one relationships so humans can perceive the interaction between a system, the code, maths, and the result in real-time. This would then enable 'media for thinking the unthinkable'.[41]

Victor is an advocate for the scientific method but he also recommends new UX/UI that makes it possible for new ways of seeing and thinking. Initially, these new tools may be too expensive for individual makers, and so, in the tradition of the maker space, he has coined the phrase 'Seeing Space'. Victor is currently working on such a space in Oakland, USA. This opens up the creative opportunities to apply the Speculative Realism, and OOO in an experimental way, as advocated by Ian Bogost. Victor provokes us with his new conceptual space:

"What if we designed a new kind of "maker space" – a space that isn't just for putting pieces together, but also for seeing and understanding a project's behaviour in powerful ways?

- seeing inside

- seeing across time

- seeing across possibilities

I think people need to work in a space that moves them away from the kinds of non-scientific thinking that you do when you can't see what you're doing — moves them away from blindly following recipes, from superstitions and rules of thumb — and moves them towards deeply understanding what they're doing, inventing new things, discovering new things, contributing back to the global pool of human knowledge."[42]

Victor has since expanded the Seeing Spaces idea into a communal computer, known as Dynamicland that is computing without screens, or devices:

'just ordinary physical materials – paper and clay, tokens and toy cars — brought to life by technology in the ceiling. Every scrap of paper has the capabilities of a full computer while remaining a fully-functional scrap of paper."[43]

Such a space allows communities to participate in thinking by making, making by thinking in ways that span nonhuman spacetime, hyperobjects, with respect to wicked problems such as the Anthropocene. It allows real-time conversations and creativity amongst diverse humans and nonhumans.

Victor became well known after his 2012 talk 'inventing on principle'[44] and his principles could lead to human scale computing, creativity and ethical technology. The ultimate goal is to democratise software and hardware so that humans, and nonhumans can track and trace the origins and intended purpose of each object.

There is a growing list of creative artworks created by AI that produce generative art based on machine learning. The art forms already include writing poetry, screenplays, sports and news journalism, music from classical to pop, and hip hop, painting and drawing, telling jokes, winning Jeopardy, winning Chess, winning Go, acting in movies, acting as a crowd of characters, and acting in games, to name some of the art forms humans once thought were exclusive to humans. AI's have already begun to build worlds in games and movies and given the exponential expectations of robotics, and machine learning it is highly probable that we will soon see AI's building photorealistic worlds that include rules and agents created by them. Our existing code and algorithms are already beyond our understanding, yet unless we adopt radical new techniques, possibly assisted by AI, that can interrogate the code that creates the AI, and the virtual worlds, there could be catastrophic scenarios.

Nonhuman World Design

We need to reimagine the OOO and speculative vision for technology that accounts for ecological sensitivity towards the nonhuman majority, and reclaim an ethical aesthetic for all users, human and non-human before it is too late. We must design our future spaces, both physical and virtual, to be safe for all humans and nonhumans. I have attempted to use a multidisciplinary approach to trace some of the origins of technological externalities in order to begin the archaeological surfacing of the harmful ghosts in the machine. This is an urgent project as automation already assumes that the self-replicating exponential objectives written into their protocols, algorithms and software applications are ethically correct. Many educators, policymakers, and technology theorists assume an anthropocentric view that is ignorant of the neoliberal rationale that looks to reduce cost through automation and machine to machine interaction.

When Manovich wrote his book on new media he warned that 'When we use the concept of 'interactive media' exclusively in relation to computer-based media, there is a the danger that we will interpret 'interaction' literally, equating it with physical interaction between a user and a media object (pressing a button, choosing a link, moving the body), at the expense of psychological interaction.'[45]

What is missed in this sensible discussion about psychological interaction is the nonhuman interaction that will become increasingly common and existentially important to all living things, and that is a world where the biggest user, with the most interaction, will happen to be nonhuman, a participant in machine to machine interactions, and human-centred design will seem a quaint outmoded concept.

According to Kurzweil, our ability to consider exponential as opposed to linear change challenges our intuitive understanding of the future. Maxwell writes:

"And the pace of change appears to be accelerating so that it seems likely that, in the relatively near future, we will have the capability of being immersed almost constantly in some form of 'virtual' or 'augmented' reality overlaying our physical reality, intimately interacting with spatially distant people, and with artificial intelligence increasingly indistinguishable from human minds."[46]

The troubling prejudices, fears, and desires of powerful hidden forces that are already embedded in the code and hardware of our past, present, and future technologies must be addressed before automation, machine learning and AI technologies deliver an alien future we would reject if we understood. Despite Manovich's anthropocentric bias, he makes an important observation that there is more to interactivity than a physical or materialist world view, and from an ontological perspective the hidden, and frightening psychological and conceptual objects of our ancestors have already been instantiated in our tools and the creative objects of our mind. Manovich argues:

"The literal interpretation of interactivity is just the latest example of a larger modern trend to externalize mental life, a process in which media technologies – photography, film, VR – have played a key role."[47]

What he failed to see is that that process is nothing new and that throughout our technological past this has happened, and those spectres of human indecency and injustice have not gone away, but have simply lost their metadata that tells the full story of their horrific origins. If we cannot excavate, and exorcise the demons that inhabit these technologies we face a future with an inability to rectify automated behaviour that is unethical, and inconsiderate of all life, and potentially unlimited in its voracious appetite for resources and energy – this would be an unsafe world.

In our 'world' the things that we have designed are the things that have begun to show us that we are not their masters, but often their slaves, and our 'strange strangers', uncanny, and yet real, outside of us.[48] If Morton is right that our concept of the world has ended, what will take its place? Speculative realists do not advocate cynicism, postmodern irony, anthropogenic denial, or even simply giving up. They look to a future in which humanity will acknowledge the 'democracy of objects' and their rightful place in a coexistent reality. Human exceptionalism has been eroded to the point where a rock; a microbe; a unicorn, or a plutonium molecule all sense, and are all real objects bound by relations but are not directly knowable by each other.[49]

Latour acknowledged the equality of all objects, conceptual and physical, in a universal reality.[50] This is "explicit recognition that agency is 'democratically' distributed".[51] Latour's ANT (actors network theory) credits all 'actants', independent of humans, including scientists with the ability to build worlds and ferment 'their own plots, forming their own groups, and serving other masters, wills, and functions'. Harman's proclamation that 'Latour gives us the first philosophy ever known in which the relations between objects are both a puzzling difficulty and are not monopolized by some tyrant entity, whether human or divine.'[52]

World building is not exclusive to humans and yet this epistemological prejudice is often assumed in both the physical and virtual worlds that are closed. Latour argues that our species should never be given a monopoly on world building.[53]

Increasingly there is nonhuman evidence that disputes the exceptionalism of human behaviour. Nonhumans such as bees, and ants, wolves and primates, display social relations, cognitive abilities and specifically world building all performed by a universe of objects. Morton thinks that because world building is normative that when you realise that nonhumans also have this ability it cheapens the activity and so the concept is approaching the end of its useful life. "The end of the biosphere as we know it is also the end of the "world" as a normative and useful concept"[54] If we extend world building beyond exclusive human capability, into the nonhuman universe, I argue that there is still life left in the concept because nonhuman worldbending is such a powerful creative tool to imagine the worlds with.

The ontological challenge is to re-open world building to ensure the democratic reality for all objects and not just the tyrannical human rulers. The IoT (Internet of Things), ubiquitous computing, virtual and mirror worlds that sense physical and conceptual reality, could open world building to a far greater number of nonhuman actors including machines, rocks, animals, plants, data and even concepts.

Design is a directed, purposeful approach to modelling the world that scientists have shown to occur in even simple cell organisms such as E. Coli. Design is one of the many human characteristics that are said to be exceptional in humans. Despite Heidegger's assertion, humans are not exceptional designers, and design and future plans can be found in many, if not all objects. Microbes have been observed to use flagella to move towards their food, and so must in some way build a world model and design their future.[55]

Heidegger's design concept was anthropocentric. His German term, Dasein, or being there, is also heavily contextual (in an individual body, unique place, and exclusive history) – a grounded being or being-in-the-world.[56] It is focused on presence, a characteristic of successful world building. While the speculative realists would claim that design is both a liminal verb and a noun, a concept that flickers between the actual and the virtual, it has futurity that makes all design speculative. According to Mitcham, "In essence, design thus turns making (not to say living) into thinking – a thinking beforehand how to make (or how to live)".[57] Our ability to be able to design and build a preferable world, in which we live in symbiotic coexistence with the nonhuman universe, depends very much on how we think, and how we make? As Haraway puts it "It matters what thoughts think thoughts; it matters what stories tell stories".[58] Maxwell cites Richard Tarnas in his *Cosmos and Psyche* that 'world views create worlds.'[59]

After 1755 Kant, horrified by the devastation of the Lisbon earthquake, came face to face with the possibility of the 'end of the world', and in his angst mused that if humanity was wiped out in a geological cataclysm, that the only intelligence in the universe would die along with our species. Speculative realists took Kant to task for his separation of nature and human thought, and yet he was something of a seismologist, cognisant of the terrific force of the rock beneath his feet. The surety of the Earth's strata was no longer assured and he found its constant presence was severely shaken.[60]

Kant's anxiety was compounded by his correlationist separation of humanity and nature. Morton explains that Kant's static view of reality, in which to exist was to be constantly present, or his metaphysics of presence, "Correctly identified by deconstruction as inimical to thinking future coexistence, the metaphysics of presence is intimately bound up with the history of global warming."[61]

According to Morton, this implies that creative technologies are entangled with the hyperobject, global warming. This makes it increasingly difficult to think differently about a preferable future when presence is the objective of many creative technologies such as VR and virtual worlds, to name a few obvious examples. An alternative ontological approach requires a sense of intimacy with hyperobjects, like global warming, concepts and world building that spans nonhuman space and time, a speculative 'worlding'.[62] Morton argues:

"Beliefs in constant presence derive ultimately from a default ontology persistent in the long moment in which the Anthropocene is a disturbing fluctuation. We are still within this twelve-thousand-year "present" moment, a scintilla of geological time."[63]

Queer Worlds

For Morton, this requires a queer aesthetic of time and action theory. He argues that things are non-hierarchical, non-patriarchal, and definitely not heteronormative; the spectre of religious norms haunt our philosophical enquiries and subvert revolutionary fervour. The queering of space-time and causality reimagines presence within a causality far, far away from the religious condescension handed down in the tablets. Morton writes:

"Love is not straight, because reality is not straight. Everywhere, there are curves and bends, things veer. Per-ver-sion. En-vironment. These terms come from the verb "to veer." To veer, to swerve toward: am I choosing to do so or am I being pulled? Free will is overrated. I do not make decisions outside the Universe and then plunge in, like an Olympic diver. I am already in."[64]

Like Morton, Haraway is interested in a non-reproductive coexistence, a queer mutuality, an aesthetic beyond sexuality, with humans and nonhumans as kin in which not everything leads to the multiplication of the human species. She writes:

"What if people everywhere looked for non-natalist kinnovations [sic] to individuals and collectives in queer, decolonial, and indigenous worlds, instead of to European, Euro-American, Chinese, or Indian rich and wealth-extracting sectors?"[65]

The colonisation of cyberspace maybe virtual, but it occludes their effects through opaque algorithms that appear inclusive, but actually ban the queer. YouTube may appear to embrace an inclusive neoliberal market that invites money from anyone, however, researchers have shown how video titles and tags that include 'queer', 'gay', 'lesbian', 'LGBTQ' were 'demonetised' by YouTube and thereby meant that the content creators were not entitled to revenue. The conversation has become more normative and less diverse, a monoculture in cyberspace that gives the illusion of diversity – a dangerous world with fewer ideas. For those who associate with queer and divergent cognition spacetime can be psychologically and physically unsafe whether it is actuality or virtuality.[66]

Presence is a subject of intense research, as well as unconscious belief, in many areas of investigation. From the discovery of the Higgs field in the LHC to the philosophical debate about realism, and the psychological game mechanics in VR, virtual worlds, mixed reality, and MMOGs (massively multiplayer online games). It is at the intersection of these disciplines that researchers can find interdisciplinary revelations. The physical and the metaphysical confront each other as paradigms that are challenged by the existential crisis of the Anthropocene. At the core of this research are questions pertaining to world building – both the physical and metaphysical construction questions who are the actors, and what are their relations? In order to relate to the hyperobjects of the Anthropocene, we need to comprehend the vast expanse of space and time through our mineral senses that still have intimate relations with the rocks and stars that made us, even beyond worlds deep in the cosmos. Morton asks us "How to have a realism not subject to the metaphysics of presence? We have to tell the story differently. The notions of 'origin' and 'point' involve questions about how to think time, knowing what we know of geology."

Our modern sense of presence has been shaped by the object oriented programming that has created the simulations that tell us the stories and speculative tales of our small understanding of the universe. Software modelling has come to the point that even in the engineering and manufacture of aircraft[67] the process bypasses the experimental making phase and proceeds straight from the computer plans.[68] While geologists regularly use software to explore the stratigraphic history of rock, the history of software has become almost opaque as object oriented programs pile up, shyly hiding their ancestry, their relatives, and their dirty little secrets.

The Archaeology of Software

Technology has become increasingly digital and virtual, thus 'making' as a research practice has become increasingly abstract. This is not to ignore the Maker Space movement and the emergence of new material practices such as 3D printing, and Arduino electronics, but to observe that even these are algorithmic and prone to virtualisation and dematerialisation. Bratton observed that:

"Sometime from 1995 to 1997 or so, especially in academic design programs, software seemed to displace theory as a tool for thought. Many students interested in asking essential questions about how things work turned to software, not just to describe those things but also to make them, and not just to make them, but also to think through them."[69] The philosophical belief, by some, that mathematics can describe everything and therefore describe a unitary reality, often means that this reality is left to science and that philosophers, designers, artists, and makers are ignored. In the OOO and speculative realism, thoughts are objects, and '"thoughts themselves are independent entities, reducible neither to brain nor to mind".[70]

The modular algorithms and protocols embedded deep in historic code are not easily found, analysed or discussed. The techniques that began with the intuition of the artisan, and proto-engineer have disappeared behind closed source software, esoteric computer languages, and the impenetrable mountains of code, built from thin line, upon thin line of software that runs to millions, and sometimes billions of machine instructions,[71] now hidden in the software strata of the past. The future is in desperate need of software archaeologists who can not only identify the invention of the algorithm but historically reverse engineer some of the social, political, economic and environmental objects and symbionts that fertilized their original DNA.

It is not just hardware miniaturisation that has hidden the past, but the opacity of the reified software when there are no easy forensic tools to inform the software archaeologists about the metadata, or even where to start digging. The who? The when? The what? And the how? The metadata is secret, and all of these secrets are kept, even while the electricity is still turned on, and flowing through their cybernetic bodies. Following the Post Anthropocene, when there maybe no electricity, or even a working hard drive, Sean Cubitt asks what would a visiting future alien make of our cyborg history?[72]

Even today, laundered of their family records the history of information technology; communications; their kinship with other objects; and the violent intentions of their ancestors; all appears dead and buried. Should we care? It would be surprising if any family tree did not inherit some deep, dark secret. However, following recent events, since the 'great acceleration' of the Anthropocene, and our wanton disregard for humans, and nonhumans alike, it would suggest that the sins of the father will not remain dead and buried, as we begin to witness the toxins and waste bubbling up from the Earth. This is what Derrida and Mark Fisher called 'hauntology', as Fisher explains it is "the agency of the virtual, with the spectre, understood not as anything supernatural, but as that which acts without (physically) existing."[73] These inhuman ghouls from our past could come back to haunt us as posthuman weaponised machines. As Harari noted:

"This is the best reason to learn history: not in order to predict the future, but to free yourself of the past and imagine alternative destinies. Of course this is not total freedom – we cannot avoid being shaped by the past. But some freedom is better than none."[74]

Most troubling about our recent history is the ubiquitous nature of the technologies that coincided with this acceleration at the end of World War II; designed to both affect, and be a part of nuclear weaponry. The Internet has become a global phenomenon and has resulted in planetary-scale computing and cyber weaponization of the world we have conceived. From TCP/IP protocols and packet switching to page ranking algorithms, our military ancestors spook our coexistence with the nonhuman majority of the planet. Our capacity to imagine, or to think deeply about the Anthropocene, a vast hyperobject that defies object oriented programming, is severely limited by our inherited algorithms and protocols of control.

The history of computer-based education and training reveals not only a programme of nuclear weaponry but a way of world building that is thoroughly anthropocentric and violent in origin. Today, students are taught programming with a popular educational software language known as, Processing, and the more recent version, P5, based on Java and Javascript, developed by Casey Reas and Ben Fry. We can see a direct lineage to the software developed by Seymour Papert and his work on the programming training language, LOGO, for the US military through the psychoacoustic lab, BBN.[75] P5.js developers Reas and Fry wrote that they 'were inspired by how simple it was to write interesting programs with the languages of their childhood (LOGO and BASIC)'.[76]

The Agrilogistic Algorithm

According to Morton, even before the toxic effects of superphosphate fertiliser, fossil fuel agriculture, and methane emitting cattle, we invented the agricultural algorithm in the fertile crescent of Mesopotamia.[77] Morton believes we continue to blindly execute the fossil fuel agricultural program, or as he calls it, agrilogistics while being ignorant 'of the hyperobject of which I am a component, the human species?"[78] Morton argues that any attempts to coexist with the nonhumans must address this problem. We must reprogram in order to build alternative and hopefully preferable worlds. We are confused by imagining that agriculture is only a physical world, and ignoring that it is also a conceptual and philosophical world. It is a technology of our own design that has, in turn, shaped us – it is a virtual world and "How we write and what we write and what we think about writing can be found within agrilogistics."[79]

Agrilogistics forms the backbone of the New Zealand economy and contributes approximately 47% to carbon emissions through methane from burping cattle and sheep. New Zealand is the eighth largest milk producer in the world, and the global dairy giant Fonterra is a New Zealand farming cooperative. Yet the dairy industry faces the challenge that its capacity for transformational change, and global warming, may not be in sync with stakeholders, consumers, and legislators. There are significant signs that climate change and extreme weather are already affecting the profitability of dairy farming, such as Fonterra's decision to close it's Dennington dairy factory in Australia due to running at only 30% capacity. This could be a bellwether for a decline in global supply, and dairy productivity. On the 6th July 2019 the headline in the New Zealand Herald read, 'Is Peak Dairy Here?'.[80] According to various reports, cow herd numbers have stopped rising and so have farm conversions to dairy farming.

According to the ANZ bank's rural economist, Susan Kilsby, production is likely to level out. "There was an expectation that costs would rise alongside tighter environmental standards and sustainability in general." Kilsby went on to say, "My view is that it will be relatively stable going forward...And any ups and downs will be associated with the weather – a good season versus a poor season – as opposed to the industry changing a whole lot."[81]

While Kilsby is undeniably correct that the weather will impact production and cost, the non-analogue nature of global warming and the political difficulty of constraining the average temperature rise to under the IPCC minimum will become increasingly fraught, that is without significant changes to food production. Legacy agrilogistic industries, such as dairy, seem incapable of imagining, designing, and building new worlds that dispense with their damaging environmental effects. Morton speculates about the future of agriculture:

"Just as World War II was the viral code that broke the program of a certain imperialism, one wonders whether global warming will be the viral code that breaks the machinations of a certain neoliberal capitalism and whether this will shut down agrilogistics itself."[82]

The increasing global political pressure to quickly decrease greenhouse gas emissions; beginning right now, and before the 2030 deadline to keep global temperature increases below 2°C is 20 years earlier than the dairy industry's sustainability timetable of 2050.

This technological disaster has trapped us within an algorithm of our own making; the algorithm was conceived in a world that separated Man (in a patriarchal trap), and Nature. This remains our common sense world view, and yet we can not divert the existential crisis that is accelerating towards us while we continue to blindly execute the agrilogistic program; the AI singularity may well become a self-fulfilling algorithm. The dominant source code for Earth continues to assume that we can apply technological ingenuity to grow our way out of the Anthropocene. However, as Buckminster Fuller pointed out there is still 'no operating manual for spaceship earth'.[83]

The UN's SDG (Sustainable Development Goals) neglects to confront the algorithms of growth that have contributed to 'the great acceleration' of the Anthropocene. The SDG's 8th goal is 'Decent Work and Economic Growth' this goal is to 'promote sustained, inclusive and sustainable economic growth, full and productive employment and decent work for all'.[84] Robert Nadeau, environmental science professor, argues that political leaders and economists have such faith in growth that they are in effect trapped in an 'a quasi-religious belief system' that needs serious revision.'[85] According to the Nobel prize-winning chemist, Paul Crutzen the worst features of the Anthropocene have been largely caused by only 25% of the world's human population.[86] In order for this world to live the same as US citizens we would require 3.9 more Earths,[87] and despite the UN's optimism that technological growth will lift the LDCs (Less Developed Countries) out of poverty, Cubitt has pointed out that there is not enough raw material in terms of rare earth metals to support the same penetration of personal devices in India and China, let alone the rest of the LDCs.[88]

There is an increasing realisation that the sharp boundary between the physical and the conceptual, animate, and inanimate, and between the organic, and inorganic are far from clear, and this liminal blurring suggests a stranger reality that questions the supposed sharp edges between the virtual and the actual beings. The material instantiation of virtual worlds in the hardware, fibre optics, and rare earth metals, are only some components of an assemblage that make up the new worlds growing from the Internet, and yet the strange beings, such as the concepts, memes, software, and avatars that are entangled in this reality are as real as the iron on which the cloud resides, or the grass that cows eat.

The Metaphysics of Virtual Worlds

In his book, *The Metaphysics of Virtual Reality*, the philosopher Michael Heim defines realism:

"In a technical sense, realism refers to metaphysical theories that attribute priority to abstract entities. Platonism, for instance, is a kind of realism in maintaining that mathematical patterns are more real than are their instances in the physical world. Platonism finds the reality of things in their stability, intelligibility, and reliability for the knower. In a related sense realism is the approach that treats cyberspace as an actual (phenomenological) world with its own particular kind of entities. Non-realists approach cyberspace and VR as hardware and/or software configurations separate from the user's experience. Realists speak of the net and matrix as actual places."[89]

Therefore, we can see that virtual worlds also share this ontological reality, despite being saturated with archetypal myths, and religious metaphors. As Wertheim has pointed out in her book, *The Pearly Gates of Cyberspace*, (1999), religious archetypes were not left behind by the Enlightenment but persist today in theoretical physics and the visions of cyberpunks in cyberspace.

The mathematical concept of cyberspace, hyperspace and our scientific explanations of string theory may appear to many to be founded on rigorous rational theory, and scientific experimentation, however, many of these theories remain unobservable and echo the ancient spiritual and mystical archetypes of the past. Quantum physics has moved beyond the possibilities of empirical observations of space and time. At the smallest scale of the Planck length, 1.6×10^{-35} space-time cease to be valid. Also, at 10^{-43} seconds, the smallest measurement of time, the time is taken for a photon to travel at the speed of light across the Planck length, is the boundary of meaning based on current physics. Our theoretical understanding of this universe hits it limits at 10^{-43} seconds after the Big Bang – we don't know what happened before then, and we may never know.

The search for the "Theory of Everything" or TOE, that has obsessed many theoretical physicists, from Einstein to Stephen Hawking, have conceptualized the mathematical proof of TOE as a non-anthropomorphic God.[90] Einstein famously denied Heisenberg's Uncertainty Principle by declaring that 'God does not play dice with the universe'. In Hawking's final book he wrote:

"If you believe in science, like I do, you believe that there are certain laws that are always obeyed. If you like, you can say the laws are the work of God, but that is more a definition of God than a proof of his existence."[91]

While they deny that God is some ancient old man with a long beard and white gown, even atheists such as Hawking[92] reference the deity as science runs out of explanations. Hawking explains:

"I use the word 'God' in an impersonal sense, like Einstein did, for the laws of nature, so knowing the mind of God is knowing the laws of nature. My prediction is that we will know the mind of God by the end of this century."[93]

In the popular press and among some physicists the experimental proof of the Higgs field at the Large Hadron Collider goes some way to proving the existence of string theory and the particle that gives all elementary particles mass, popularly dubbed the 'God particle' or the Higgs' Boson. In cyberspace, virtual worlds, including game worlds, the designers are known as 'game Gods'; the creators of simulated worlds that, even when they rely on mathematical logic, design worlds that even they cannot totally understand or explain. So, despite Nietzsche's declaration that 'God is Dead!', the concept of God appears to be still useful in our attempts to come to terms with our biggest, and most existential musings about reality.

Many of our most respected scientific explanations of reality date back to ancient Greece and the theories of Pythagoras (string theory), Democritus (atomic theory), Socrates, and Plato (logic and mathematical proofs of reality). By the time of Plato, the ancient Gods had come to be seen as metaphorical archetypes but Plato like Pythagoras before him did not believe that it was possible, even with empirical observations of nature and rational thought, to know everything, TOE was for them an impossibility.

"The Pythagorean discovery that the harmonics of music were mathematical, that harmonious tones were produced by strings whose measurements were determined by simple numerical ratios, was regarded as a religious revelation. Those mathematical harmonies maintained a timeless existence as spiritual exemplars, from which all audible musical tones derived."[94]

These cosmic archetypes may have been chased into the shadows by the Enlightenment, but Euclidean geometry, and the mathematics of musical harmonics, live on in the theories of cyberspace, hyperspace, and string theory. Descartes brilliance at unifying geometry and algebra, known as Cartesian space, still allowed God some space to live beyond the physical realm, although God was eventually exiled by the rational positivism of empirical science. This also became the creative virtual space in which new realities were actualised; and yet, as vast new vistas of reality opened before us, so too computerisation has caused a modern myopia. As we venture further out into cyberspace we risk the danger of losing intuitive wisdom about the worlds we leave behind. Euclidean and Cartesian geometry are three-dimensional models of reality, however, as Einsteinian physics came to take hold, seven more spatial dimensions, and a temporal dimension of reality unfolded in the mathematical proofs of theoretical physics.

Both cyberspace, and space travel are only possible because of the mathematical imagination of Euclid's *Elements*, (295 BCE), and Descartes (1755) algebraic innovation, analytic geometry, that envisaged the X, Y, Z coordinates of Cartesian geometry. While three-dimensional geometry dates back to ancient Egypt and was mathematically understood in ancient Greece, it was not until the thirteenth century that Western art, science and culture underwent a revolutionary shift towards a realistic and scientific description of nature. The works of Giotto introduced a new verisimilitude into painting that saw artist point of view shift from the inner eye of spirituality towards the more naturalistic view of the physical eye looking out.[95] In 1267 Roger Bacon sent a letter to Pope Clement IV outlining the value of science to Christianity, and the improvement of the human condition. He imagined and described flying machines, automobiles, machines for lifting heavy weights, everlasting lamps, explosives, and a lens as a weapon that would use the Sun to burn the enemy camps from a distance.[96]

However, fundamentally Bacon was driven by his faith, and his apocalyptic desire to drive the infidel out of the Holy Land. He wanted to use realistic imagery as propaganda to motivate Christians to sign up for the Crusades. Wertheim explains, "For Bacon, the key to the new realistic style of painting was the application of geometry."[97] Geometric figuring, Bacon believed, would create such a powerful illusion that it would convince people of the reality of what they were seeing. Wertheim credits Bacon as the first person to "comprehend the extraordinary illusionistic power of mathematically rendered images, Roger Bacon might justifiably be called the first champion of virtual reality."[98]

From these early applications of geometry and perspective, and then through the sixteenth to the nineteenth centuries there were various attempts to invent devices to aid perspectival art, with Durer describing a number of these machines.[99]

According to Lev Manovich, these machines progressed to the camera obscura and camera lucida, patented in 1806, a proto augmented reality based on a step by step algorithm that used two reflecting surfaces to allow the draftsman to see both the image and the drawing surface below as they traced.[100] This manual process was eventually automated through the mechanics of photography. Manovich writes that 'automation', which became associated with computing, was first coined in 1947, and in 1949 Ford began the automation of their car factories. By the 1960s "the automation of the process of constructing perspectival images of both existent and non-existent objects and scenes was well underway."[101]

The Weaponisation of Cyberspace

The military invested heavily in the R & D of 3-D computer graphics for simulations using ARPA funding that supported work by the likes of Ivan Sutherland, and other MIT students such as Larry G. Roberts who published a paper on how to automate 3-D perspective with a computer algorithm. Roberts went on to become the military's ARPA director, and his team created ARPANET using packet switching. Sutherland who had invented the drawing program, *Sketchpad* in 1962, and the first HMD VR rig, for military purposes, was also the doctoral supervisor of Jim Clark, the inventor of the real-time 3D chip, and founder of Silicon Graphics, also known as SGI.

By 1991 Silicon Graphics had become the dominant supplier of hardware for the visual effects used in blockbuster movie production. Clark's 3-D chips accelerated rendering of 3-D animations and lighting effects. In 1994 Clark departed from the company due to differences of opinion. The company continued to offer high-end hardware and 3D graphics software for a premium, and in 1994 Peter Jackson's movie, *Heavenly Creatures* showed off an impressive visual effect of a virtual dream world created on his first SGI computer. Jackson became obsessed with bigger and more impressive visual effects in movies such as *The Frighteners* (1996) with Michael J. Fox, that required a massive investment in SGI machines.

James Cameron was another movie director who enjoyed world bending through computer effects. Cameron completed *Terminator 2: Judgement Day* (1991) at his successful visual effects company, Digital Domain that created a stunning animation of a chrome robot on an SGI machine. Digital Domain was the biggest visual effects company in the World when Jackson made, *The Frighteners*, but Jackson attempted to make a big splash in 3D visual effects and established the third biggest VFX company in the World. By the time Jackson produced and directed the three *Lord of the Rings* movies, every VFX Academy award-winning movie had been produced on an SGI machine. Computerised visual effects became a prominent world bender in popular culture. However, despite the premiums that SGI charged for their hardware and software to the movie industry, by 1998 it only contributed approximately 25% of its revenues.

The overwhelming majority of their business was with the US military using SGI supercomputers to simulate nuclear weapon attacks, 3D flight simulators, and virtual reality military training. Another big SGI customer was the oil and gas industry that used virtual reality for immersion in big data in order to analyse oil and gas exploration data. Interestingly, one of the biggest consumers of oil products is the US military, and ironically SGI supercomputers were often used for meteorological weather simulations for modelling the spread of nuclear fallout during atmospheric testing of nuclear bombs. The nexus between the industries of entertainment, military, and academia continues to shadow the 3D worlds we are building for our exodus.

In 1999 SGI was in serious trouble and I contacted my friend who had been the regional manager of SGI in New Zealand, Scott Houston who was then the Chief Technology Officer of Jackson's VFX business, Weta Digital. I had developed a plan with my business partner, Joe Caccioppoli to work with Saatchi & Saatchi Worldwide and SGI by developing an international network of virtual reality machines supplied to Saatchi's in exchange for advertising and marketing services.[102] The network was to be centred around the Saatchi's HQ in Manhattan where we intended to create a virtual collaboration facility, we had called the DreamLab. This virtual environment was intended to be as multi-sensory, and emotionally charged, as possible, and included an application we called the Love Cave. This was intended to overcome the limitations of disembodied explicit knowledge exchange. The design would enable creative collaboration amongst international clients, artists, and scientists, simulating face to face communications. I had developed a concept we called iStock to attempt to overcome the politics of knowledge management and why individuals do not share their best ideas?

Research has shown that trust plays an important part in sharing knowledge. It was our intention to facilitate world benders who could meet in this virtual world and creatively collaborate around the planet. However, one year into the new millennium that old world ended when two planes crashed into the Twin Towers. As billions of dollars rushed out of the international advertising business, many people stopped flying, and ironically, at a time when we offered a solution to avoid flying, risk-taking and our virtual reality project were put on hold. Despite, this personal interruption to my business virtual reality continued to develop, and real-time computer graphics became more and more photorealistic. Millions of people were immersing themselves in virtual worlds online.

The economist Edward Castronova has predicted that we could see a mass exodus of people to virtual worlds based on his theory that cyberspace offers a new reality that is more fun than the hardships of the physical world. Already there are millions of people who have spent a considerable amount of time in virtual worlds, such as World of Warcraft, and Second Life, and today there is a new wave of fascination for virtual and mixed reality technologies. It is highly likely that the numbers of people in virtual worlds will increase dramatically. This exodus will be bolstered by the interoperability between virtual worlds; the closer integration with the web; and full sensory immersion enhancing a sense of presence and verisimilitude with physical reality.

Virtually Infinite Worlds

For two thousand years, Euclid's *Elements* has dominated geometry and his five postulates that describe geometry were so hegemonic that Euclidean geometry and the word geometry were often considered synonymous. However, Euclid's fifth postulate, or parallel postulate, has troubled many philosophers and mathematicians who tried to use the first four postulates to prove the fifth. The implications of Euclidean geometry for world building are profound because they define the rules for world construction and shape our comprehension of alternative worlds and infinite worlds. Simply put, in 2-dimensional geometry, if a straight line intersects two parallel lines and the angles of intersection are $90°$ then these lines will go on for infinity without touching, or to put it more precisely in the translated words of Euclid's 5th postulate:

"If two straight lines in a plane are crossed by a transversal, and sum the interior angle of the same side of the transversal is less than two right angles, then the two lines extended will intersect."

Around 1813 Carl Friedrich Gauss researched and began to develop what he termed non-Euclidean geometry, although as a perfectionist he never published his proofs. The son of his friend Farkas Bolyai, Janos, discovered non-Euclidean geometry in 1829 and published in 1832. Gauss' work on differential geometry that dealt with curves and surfaces, assisted Bernhard Riemann to establish the field of Riemannian geometry all of which led to Einstein's breakthrough theory of general relativity. Einstein's description of the curvature of space-time eventually led to theories of the multiverse.

In the virtual simulation of physical worlds, these typically follow a Euclidean 3D model. However, despite the ubiquitous use of Euclidean/Cartesian geometry in everything from computer graphics in movies, and console games like *Grand Theft Auto*, theoretical physics has postulated 11 dimensions, and a non-Euclidean geometry that defies common sense, and yet these extra dimensions could be so small that they cannot be detected. The recent evidence from the LIGO detector of gravitational waves may spell the end to the theory of higher dimensions[103] but the theory has created or discovered new mathematical forms of reality. This was the first empirical evidence of black holes, gravitational waves, and was also a totally novel form of empirical data.

Cosmology is not only expanding our understanding of our universe but is challenging our philosophical and ontological precepts of how we think. Empirical evidence has supported the theory that the universe is both expanding and accelerating in its expansion. The cosmological constant has been shown not to be zero.[104] This was long held to be contentious, however, as more and more data and theoretical support come in it is changing the course of physics, and our definition of reality. As Greene boldly asserts, 'The key supposition? We're living in one of many universes. *Many* universes.'[105] What is more, those extra seven spatial dimensions, that may be currently beyond our technological ability to observe, maybe 'wrapped by branes and threaded by fluxes' that gives those dimensions an enormous number of forms and features 'dressed up' in a 'gargantuan collection of modified forms', that theoretically may be infinite, known as Calabi-Yau shapes. As Greene noted:

"So, whether or not string theory offers a correct approach to describing the physical universe, it has already established itself as a potent tool for investigating the mathematical one."[106]

The current empirical evidence may lag behind the mathematical proofs, however, conceptually, at the very least, string and M theory have opened up a vast multiverse that we can begin to explore through non-Euclidean simulations that we can enter as avatars. This has already begun to happen in computer games and is beginning to be modelled in virtual reality prototypes. While at a human scale our world's geometry appears to be Euclidean, however, because the Earth is a sphere, you must use hyperbolic geometry to navigate a non-flat world, and the wider Einsteinian Universe is also non-Euclidean, thought to be curved in the shape of a saddle.[107] This is easier to envisage in a virtual world than as an abstract mathematical formula and can be viscerally explored by walking through non-Euclidean worlds.[108]

Virtual worlds allow research into many ontological and philosophical realms that are difficult to imagine without an embodied experience of alternative and speculative realities. Researchers urgently need to experiment with various speculative and world building approaches to re-imagine the Post Anthropocene, to run a sanity check and to say 'Hello World!' The World is Dead, Long live the Worlds!

Notes

1. Grau, O. (2003). Virtual art: from illusion to immersion ([Rev. and expanded). Cambridge, Mass.: MIT Press.

2. See Grau, 2003, Wertheim, 1999.

3. As cited by photographic artist Cathy Carter in her exhibition Wai Wai Wai (2019). See https://www.cathycarterartist.com/wai-wai-wai-2019.html also see Gibellina PhotoRoad http://www.gibellinaphotoroad.it/en/tema-2019/

4. Morton, T. (2018) Dark Ecology

5. Furthur was the name of Kevin Kesey's psychedelically painted bus. A moving experiment in which the Merry Pranksters visited strange psychological and physical destinations with the assistance of LSD.

6. Turner, F., Where the Counterculture Met the New Economy: the WELL and the Origins of Virtual Community., Technology and Culture, July 2005, Vol.46, p.485. Project Muse, Society for the History of Technology,

7. Petsko, G. A. (2011). The blue marble. Genome Biology, 12(4), 112. https://doi.org/10.1186/ gb-2011-12-4-112

8. O'Malley, V. (2016) The Great War for New Zealand: Waikato 1800-2000.

9. Kurzweil, R. (2005). The Singularity is Near: when Technology Transcends Biology. Kurzweil predicts photo-realism by 2020 and full sensory immersion by 2030.

10. Gibson, W. (1984). Neuromancer. New York: Ace Books. (1551035). p.69

11. Jardini, David. Thinking Through the Cold War (Kindle Locations 1832-1833). Kindle Edition.

12. Grau, O. Virtual Art: From Illusion to Immersion. p.162

13. Sutherland (1965) p.508 cited by Grau p.162

14. Grau, O. ibid, pp.162-3

15. Grau, O. ibid, p.163

16. ibid, p163

17. Furness received a patent for this and his invention is the precursor to augmented reality, Google Glass, and Microsoft's Hololens.

18. Grau, O. ibid pp.171-2

19. ibid, p.278

20. ibid, p.278

21. Grau, O. ibid, p.279

22. Turner, F. (2006), p.172

23. Cited in Kurzweil, 2005, p.4.

24. Maxwell, G. The Dynamics of Transformation: Tracing an Emerging World View

25. ibid, p.176

26. Greene, B. Brian Greene: The Kindle Singles Interview. Kindle location 421

27. Cited by Heim, 1993, p. 137

28. Rive, P. (2012) Thesis p.55

29. Turner, F. (2006). From counterculture to cyberculture: Stewart Brand, the Whole Earth Network, and the rise of digital utopianism. Chicago, IL: University of Chicago Press.

30. Rive, P. Thesis

31. See Bell, J.S (1964) On the Einstein Podolsky Rosen Paradox. Retrieved from https://cds.cern.ch/record/ 111654/files/vol1p195-200_001.pdf

32. Bester, A. (1957). The stars my destination. New York: New American Library.

33. Wiener, N. (1961). Cybernetics: or control and communication in the animal and the machine (2nd ed.). Cambridge, Mass.: M.I.T. Press. p.98

34. Wiener, N. ibid, p.96

35. McCarthy et. al, (2015), P5.js. Kindle Locations 127-129

36. Riva, G., Davide, F., & Ijsselsteijn, W. A. (2003). Being there: Concepts, effects and measurements of user presence in synthetic environments. Amsterdam: IOS Press/Ohmsha.

37. Manovich. L. The Language of New Media. P. 57

38. Chun, Wendy Hui Kyong, (2007) Control and Freedom: power and paranoia in the age of fiber optics., p.46-47

39. Greene, B. The Hidden Reality: Parallel Universes and the Deep Laws of the Cosmos

40. See Bostrom, Nick. Superintelligence: Paths, Dangers, Strategies. OUP Oxford. Kindle Edition

41. Victor, B. 'Media for Thinking the Unthinkable' https://vimeo.com/67076984

42. Victor, B. 'Seeing Spaces' https://vimeo.com/97903574

43. https://dynamicland.org/

44. Victor, B. 'Inventing on Principle' https://www.youtube.com/watch?v=PUv66718DII

45. Manovich, L., The Language of New Media. p.57

46. Maxwell, G. The Dynamics of Transformation: Tracing an Emerging World View.

47. Manovich, L. The Language of New Media. p.57

48. Morton, T. Dark Ecology: For a Logic of Future Coexistence. p.18

49. Harman, G. (2017). Object-Oriented Ontology: a new theory of everything. S.l.: Pelican.

50. ibid

51. Clark, N. (2011). Inhuman Nature: sociable life on a dynamic planet. London: SAGE. p.31

52. Harman cited by Clark, N. p.36

53. Latour cited by Clark, N. (2011).

54. Morton, T. (2018) ibid. p.46

55. Montague, R. (2007). Your brain is (almost) perfect: how we make decisions. New York London: Plume; Turnaround.

56. Mitcham, C. (2001). Dasein Versus Design: The Problematics of Turning Making Into Thinking (Vol. 11). https://doi.org/10.1023/A:1011282121513 p.29

57. ibid, p.30

58. Haraway, (2016) p.39

59. Maxwell, Grant. The Dynamics of Transformation: Tracing an Emerging World View (p. 30).

60. Clark, N. (2011). Inhuman Nature: sociable life on a dynamic planet. London: SAGE

61. Morton, T. (2018). Dark Ecology: for a logic of future coexistence. S.l.: Columbia University Press. p.39

62. Haraway, D. J. (2016). Staying with the trouble: making kin in the Chthulucene.

63. Morton, T. (2018) ibid, p.39

64. Morton, Timothy. Humankind: Solidarity with Non-Human People. Verso. Kindle Edition.

65. Haraway, Donna J. Staying with the Trouble: Making Kin in the Chthulucene (Experimental Futures) (p. 209). Duke University Press. Kindle

Edition.

66. Rive, L.F. (2019). Queering the Webseries. Master of Arts Thesis. University of Auckland.

67. See the story of what went wrong with the 737 Max and how software was seen as a low-cost solution https://www.nytimes.com/2019/04/08/business/boeing-737-max-.html

68. "The Boeing 777 will be the very first aeroplane to be designed with the aid of computers, which each design was designed by an extremely powerful CAD software called CATIA, developed by Dassault Systemes and IBM, and it required 8 computer mainframes to run the main software (called EPIC)." https://medium.com/@O530CarrisPT/boeing-777-the-ultimate-history-i-da793e6dbfd7

69. Bratton, B. H. (2016). The Stack - On Software and Sovereignty. Massachusetts: MIT Press. Kindle location 200

70. Morton, T. (2013). Hyperobjects: philosophy and ecology after the end of the world. Minneapolis : University of Minnesota Press. p.67 Kindle

71. See 'GOOGLE IS 2 BILLION LINES OF CODE—AND IT'S ALL IN ONE PLACE' - https://www.wired.com/2015/09/google-2-billion-lines-code-and-one-place/

72. Cubitt, S. (2017). Finite media: Environmental implications of digital technologies. Durham: Duke University Press. Kindle location 335

73. Fisher, Mark. Ghosts of My Life: Writings on Depression, Hauntology and Lost Futures (p. 18). John Hunt Publishing. Kindle Edition.

74. Harari, Y.H. (2016). Homo Deus: A Brief History of Tomorrow.

75. Noble, D., (1991), ibid, p.158

76. McCarthy, Reas, Fry. (2015). P5.js. Kindle Loc. 28

77. Morton, T. (2018) ibid.

78. Morton, T. (2015), ibid, p.66

79. Morton, T. (2018) ibid. p.43

80. NZH, 6th July, 2019. Gray, J. Has New Zealand's Dairy Industry Passed its Peak?" https:// www.nzherald.co.nz/business/news/article.cfm?c_id=3&objectid=12247112

81. ibid

82. Morton, Timothy. Dark Ecology: For a Logic of Future Coexistence (The Wellek Library Lectures) (pp. 45-46). Columbia University Press. Kindle Edition.

83. Fuller, R. B. (1976). Operating manual for spaceship earth. Mattituck, N.Y.: Aeonian Press Inc.

84. UN, (2015), p.11

85. Angus, I. (2016). Facing the Anthropocene: Fossil Capitalism and the Cri-

sis of the Earth System. NYU Press. Kindle location 1549

86. Crutzen, P. J. (2002). Geology of mankind. Nature, (6867), 23.

87. McDonald, C. (2015, June 16). How many Earths do we need? BBC News. Retrieved from http://www.bbc.co.uk/news/magazine-33133712

88. Cubitt, (2017), ibid, Kindle location 1572-6

89. Heim, M. (1993) The Metaphysics of Virtual Reality. p. 157

90. Hawking, S., Redmayne, E., Thorne, K. S., & Hawking, L. (2018). Brief Answers to the Big Questions.

91. Ibid, Hawking, S. et al. (Kindle Locations 400-402). Hodder & Stoughton. Kindle Edition.

92. Hawking makes 64 references to God in his final book, (2018) Brief answers to the big questions.

93. Hawking, Stephen. Brief Answers to the Big Questions: the final book from Stephen Hawking (Kindle Locations 422-424). Hodder & Stoughton. Kindle Edition.

94. Tarnas, Richard. The Passion Of The Western Mind: Understanding the Ideas That Have Shaped Our World View (p. 46). Random House. Kindle Edition.

95. Wertheim, M. p.88

96. Wertheim, M. (1999). The Pearly Gates of Cyberspace. p.91

97. ibid, p.92

98. ibid, p.93

99. See Wertheim, M. (1999). The Pearly Gates of Cyberspace: a history of space from Dante to the Internet.

100. Manovich, L. (1993) Mapping Space: Perspective, Radar, and 3-D Computer Graphics http://manovich.net/index.php/projects/article-1993

101. ibid

102. Rive, P. B. (2008). Knowledge transfer and marketing in Second Life. In P. Zemliansky & K. St. Amant (Eds.), Handbook of research on virtual workplaces and the new nature of business practices (pp. 424-438). Hershey, PA: Information Science Reference.

103. Gravitational waves provide a dose of reality about extra dimensions September 14, 2018, by Louise Lerner, University of Chicago. Read more at https://phys.org/news/2018-09-gravitational-dose- reality-extra-dimensions.html#jCp. This still does not rule out extra dimensions as they may exist at a very, very small scale beyond our ability to detect them.

104. Greene, Brian. The Hidden Reality: Parallel Universes and the Deep Laws of the Cosmos (Kindle Locations 2374-2375). Penguin Books Ltd. Kindle Edition.

105. ibid

106. Greene, ibid, Kindle Locations 1883-1884.

107. Reshaping the Universe: VR Landscapes Explore Mind-Bending Geometry By Jesse Emspak, Live Science Contributor | March 29, 2017, 07:12 am ET https://www.livescience.com/58448-virtual-reality-reveals-non-euclidean-universe.html

108. VR rigs such as the HTC Vive enables head, body, legs and arms to be tracked giving the user a virtual sense of presence and spacetime.

Chapter 9 Exodus and Space Travel

During the 2018 Readers & Writers festival in Wellington, New Zealand, Cory Doctorow discussed his latest speculative fiction, *Walkaway*, describing it as an optimistic disaster novel. To some the theme may sound like an escapist fantasy, yet to others it may appeal as a speculative escape plan. Doctorow takes to our current world with a hefty wrench, and smashing ball connected to the actuators of a semi-crazed AI living off the bent algorithms of an neoliberal economy that fulfilled the dreams of the 1% of the 1%, and to their alarm, then some. In this joyful poke at the future, we the 99% 'precaria' are faced with the environmental toxic ruins of a system that has surpassed Rifikin's Zero Marginal Cost,[1] and the only way out is a 'hedonic treadmill' in which our reputation is how we and others will value our purpose on this planet. We can 'walkaway' but it is only to cross an invisible line defined by hidden sensors that delineate one world from another as we become the thinkers and makers of our designed world. We face a reality that could appear doomed, and all options hopeless, but if we become overwhelmed and surrender to the crisis we risk either corrosive cynicism, or depressive collapse, unable to think, or act. Escape can lead us into a fantasy world that is purely driven by our selfish pursuit of happiness, a superficial chemical high, either synthetic drugs, or biological stimulation of serotonin and dopamine.

Doctorow argues we all spend and consume in order to make our own surveillance possible. Much like Andrew Keen, Nicholas Carr, and Douglas Rushkoff,[2] he would agree that not only is the Internet not the answer, but if it's free you are probably the product.[3] Yuval Noah Harari wrote in his book, *Homo Deus: A Brief History of Tomorrow*:

"By observing the accidental chain of events that led us here, we realise how our very thoughts and dreams took shape – and we can begin to think and dream differently."[4]

Through our imagination and creativity, we can prototype the future[5] and play with alternative histories that are the prelude to speculative worlds beyond the stultifying predictions of 'common sense'. General relativity has informed us that there is no physical boundary preventing the arrow of time reversing, although it might exclude humanity due to the crushing reality of a black hole, or a theoretical wormhole. Of course, we do so cognitively all the time, we all own a time machine, we call it our memory and imagination. Einstein worried that his General Theory of Relativity meant that it was physically possible to travel back in time, you just had to travel faster than the speed of light. He quickly added that nothing can travel faster than the speed of light.

Whether it was his fertile imagination, his addiction to drugs, or a stranger reality, Philip K. Dick (PKD) did believe he could see the future and devised elaborate alternative histories that have entertained us and informed us of our present.

In PKD's dystopian future, set in 1990, (which is now our alternative history), the past, present and future blur as we consider his speculative world bending. In this future, Earth had seen a mass exodus to the space colonies, with only the weak, the simple-minded and the rejected; the 'specials' of humanity are left behind. PKD's world is the basis of the movie franchise, *Blade Runner*, set in a post-apocalyptic nuclear world which is really only homely for the robots. PKD wrote:

"A meagre colonization program had been underway before the war but now that the sun had ceased to shine on Earth the colonization entered an entirely new phase. In connection with this a weapon of war, the Synthetic Freedom Fighter, had been modified; able to function on an alien world the humanoid robot – strictly speaking, the organic android – had become the mobile donkey engine of the colonization program. Under UN law each emigrant automatically received possession of an android subtype of his choice, and, by 1990, the variety of subtypes passed all understanding, in the manner of American automobiles of the 1960s. That had been the ultimate incentive of emigration: the android servant as carrot, the radioactive fallout as stick. The UN had made it easy to emigrate, difficult if not impossible to stay. Loitering on Earth potentially meant finding oneself abruptly classed as biologically unacceptable, a menace to the pristine heredity of the race. Once pegged as special, a citizen, even if accepting sterilization, dropped out of history. He ceased, in effect, to be part of mankind."[6]

PKD has borrowed heavily from a number of archetypes and themes that we have traced back throughout this book. Humanity faced a nuclear apocalypse that prompted a mass exodus, and mining colonies amongst the heavens. Synthetic humans were created by a corporation run by a godlike leader as slaves to the humans and warriors to their cause. However, just as in the Fall from Grace these disobedient subhumans have turned on their creator, and following the Babylonian debauchery of 20th-century consumerism, the apocalypse is their punishment. In Ridley Scott's 1984 classic movie, *Blade Runner*, the moral warnings of *Genesis*, *The Epic of Gilgamesh*, and the archetypal automatons of Daedalus are reanimated, creating a sci fi morality play with powerful resonance for modern audiences. This was a bent world but one without hope and full of sterile desolation because humanity had lost its way. The weaponised androids had turned on their creators in search of immortality, a gift not granted by the gods, but just as in the hero's journey, and exile to Hades, Hell, or the watery depths searched by Gilgamesh, the archetypal myth warns of technological overreaching. Instead of finding heaven in the stars, PKD describes hell on the warring planet of Mars, mined and spoiled by the insatiable greed and gluttony of 'sinful' consumerism. The archetypal algorithms of our fall were embedded in the weaponised code of PKD's replicants.

In our collective subconscious, we fear that automation will follow our self-destructive nightmares and that archetypal algorithms will simply execute the apocalyptic logic of the creator, i.e., humanity. PKD wrote a short story, *Autofac*, in his future computer automated world, the consumer algorithm of the automated factory continues to pump out unwanted products for a depopulated post-apocalyptic planet. The sin of the original synthetic may be forgotten in our secular and rational world without alternatives but our irrational fears surface in our popular culture.

Prior to *Do Androids Dream of Electric Sheep*, there had already been two popular books on a nuclear war that had been widely read, Nevil Shute's *On the Beach* (1957), and *Red Alert* (1958) a novel by Peter George. Both books had been made into movies that were seen by large audiences. *Red Alert* was the inspiration for Stanley Kubrick's 1964 film, *Dr Strangelove, or How I Came to Love the Bomb*. This is similar to another book that became a movie, *Fail Safe*, in which an automated function could not be shut down and ended in a nuclear war.

At the height of the 60s Cold War, PKD was not the only one that was predicting a nuclear winter here on Earth. The space race and massive R & D invested in universities, and private institutes such as RAND were focused on weaponization and defence in case the Game Theory of the US vs the Soviets actually played out. Space was important to both sides because it gave them something they did not have and that was an international missile-reach from the safety of their own home. Rocket technology delivered the capability to add a nuclear warhead to an ICBM (intercontinental ballistic missile).

The launch of Sputnik in 1957 sent shockwaves through the US as American technological prowess began to be challenged. Not only had the Soviets successfully detonated a nuclear bomb in 1949; then launched the Sputnik satellite in '57; followed by Laika, the first living being and dog to orbit the Earth, but they also beat the US with the first human space orbit. The Soviet cosmonaut, Yuri Gagarin, successfully orbited Earth and touch down again safely in Kazakhstan. The possibility of space colonisation was now a reality and became a seriously considered backup plan should nuclear war turn the Earth into an uninhabitable wasteland.

The first published and speculative story of space colonisation was written in 1869 by Edward Everett Hale about an inhabited artificial satellite. It was a fictional work that was written in the style of a journal. Hale had assumed that the spacecraft would overheat as it rocketed into space, so his strange spaceship, designed to be a space station with a diameter of 200 hundred feet, was made from bricks, at the colossal cost of $60,000 for the bricks alone. The story, *The Brick Moon*, told the tale of a seventeen-year mission to send 39 people, including women, children, and chickens, to orbit the Earth. It launched by mistake in what was feared could have killed everyone on board. However, they eventually spotted the new moon orbiting the Earth.

"Could it be possible? It was possible! Orcutt and Brannan and the rest of them had survived that giddy flight through the ether, and were going and coming on the surface of their own little world, bound to it by its own attraction and living by its own laws!"[7]

They had created a world that was no bigger than 55 paces, from pole to pole, and featured tropical trees that had grown up on the surface of the tiny moon. Children had been born inside the Brick Moon and there were 23 different rooms with different temperatures. On the surface, around the equator of the artificial moon, it was tropical, with the Sun always up. The physics and the science of this amusing story may not stack up, but Hale did outline what was needed for this micro-world, and its inhabitants, human and non-human to survive. He specified a tropical climate with palms, breadfruit, bananas, oats, maize and rice so there 'was no danger of famine'. To water these plants and the humans there was snow and ice stored in chambers.[8]

The inventor failed to mention why they had built the Brick Moon and why others had helped finance it but one of their early supporters told potential investors, "... he believed, on his soul, that the success of this enterprise promised more for mankind than any enterprise which was ever likely to call for the devotion of his life. "And to the good of mankind," he said, very simply, "my life is devoted." Then he sat down."[9]

Exodus

The origins of the word exodus are uncertain, however, in late Old

English it was the title of the second book of the Old Testament, and came from the latin word, exodos meaning 'a military expedition; a solemn procession; departure; death". It is a combination of the word ex meaning to go out and hodos meaning a way, path, road; a ride; journey, march. There also seems to have a close association with the word exile with both words having a spiritual connotation as prophets were often sent into exile for their beliefs and that became a mystical journey in which they would often encounter a vision from God. John from Patmos was said to have been exiled to the island where he had his revelation of the Apocalypse. Daniel, Isaiah and Ezekiel all had apocalyptic visions when they were exiled on their mystical journeys. Exile was often seen as God's punishment for idolatry and disobedience against Yahweh, (the Hebrew God) before their revelation and deliverance from slavery. In *Exodus*, the second book of the Hebrew Bible, or Torah, it is the story of how the Israelites leave slavery in Egypt led by the prophet, Moses, and travel through the wilderness in search of the utopian promised land of Canaan. The 12 tribes of Israel were a military alliance 'united as one people under one God'. According to Hall, "Faith could be called upon to reinvigorate the military confederation. Historical setbacks were to be explained by an absence of devotion to Yahweh."[10] Hall, explains that on arrival at their destination, the followers of Yahweh, found themselves politically impotent and vulnerable, yet their covenant with God, handed down in the tablets of Moses, gave them faith that their time was to come, in a future paradise. Ezekiel had prophesied a future 'heaven on earth' at the end of time. Yet, there were other beliefs that promised an eternal life with God in heaven amongst the stars. These apocalyptic visions came to be associated with military struggles in Judaeo-Christian and Muslim traditions. The religious beliefs of diverse theologies came to bolster the confidence of followers believing that they were God's chosen people and that the colonisation of heathens was for the glory of God, and the benefit of the chosen.

These lingering myths and archetypes have been bequeathed to us in the form of the Puritanical beliefs of American pilgrims and missionaries, retold as 21st-century missions into space and their accompanying movies. The unusual warmth and stable conditions of the

Holocene encouraged the human species to proliferate, and use agricultural enclosure and control to expand its influence. From the myths of the original sin to the exodus to the promised land, we can see our expansionary lineage stretching behind us, and now projecting us into the future.

Space travel, both astronomical and cybernetic, have become part of the marketing language of billionaire entrepreneurs who are aware that this planet's space, time, and resources are running out, and so their opportunities are running out; this is the backdrop to their 'discursive imperialism'[11] and the colonisation of space.[12]

Christopher Columbus claimed that his journey to the Indies would accelerate the end of time by expanding the world mission of Christianity and the second coming.[13] Hall summarised this mission, "In America, as in the Crusades, spoils, booty, and conquest for Christendom went together."[14] The modern ambitions of space entrepreneurs continue the colonialists mission. Within the current capitalist paradigm, the future spoils of space promise unimaginable wealth for entrepreneurs who are looking to colonise and mine planets, moons and even asteroids. It is estimated that one such asteroid, nine hundred meters across, that came within a million miles from Earth in 2015, contained ninety million tons of platinum worth USD$5.4 trillion.[15] Asteroids can contain metals such as "iron, nickel, carbon, and cobalt, and they also contain significant quantities of rare earth minerals and valuable metals such as platinum, palladium, rhodium, ruthenium, iridium, and osmium."[16] Space mining is a serious ambition with potentially disastrous outcomes for nonhumans as played out in the James Cameron *Avatar* franchise. In anticipation of the Earth running out of resources, a group of entrepreneurs established a company, Planetary Resources in 2012. Their plan is to extract minerals from asteroids that would be in high demand and sell them on Earth.[17]

In the animated Disney movie, *WALL-E*, future humanity is in a desperate race to escape Earth, leaving behind a lonely robot to tidy up the mess. The Earth became a massive waste dump, while the fat and brainless human consumers exodus aboard the spaceship Axiom bound for a new Earth-like planet. The voyage to another life-supporting planet was expected to take generations. However, the discovery of one small plant recalls the Axiom to Earth, and the utopian human restoration of Earth begins.

This happy ending is not necessarily implied by the mining ambitions of the space entrepreneurs looking to colonise Mars, the Moon and any other likely candidates. Without a sustainable zero waste economic model humanity is destined to repeat the many mistakes created during the colonisation of Earth. Just as the oceans were once thought to be so vast that waste dumping would have an imperceptible impact, so it was thought that space could absorb millions of space waste objects without care. However, our near-space orbit has begun to fill up with junk, possibly blocking our escape path and our exodus from the waste planet, Earth.

Trashing New Planets

2019 is the 50th anniversary of the landing on the moon, but before Armstrong took 'One small step for man, one giant leap for mankind' he tossed out a bag of trash that is still there today. The 'jettison bag' was "filled with empty food pouches, sacks of bodily waste, and scraps that were cluttering their cramped spacecraft. A few minutes later, as Mr Armstrong climbed down, he paused to read from a plaque attached to his ladder: "Here men from the planet Earth first set foot upon the moon, July 1969 A.D. We came in peace for all mankind."[18]

What mankind left behind was trash that we didn't know what to do with? And so without a zero-waste plan, we could bump into our own historical mistakes as we try to an exodus.

As early as 1979 NASA created the Orbital Debris Program, recognising that our local space neighbourhood could fill up the geosynchronous Earth orbit with waste, and form a cloud of low orbit Earth objects, creating a space hazard. Even small pieces of space junk can tear a large hole in a spacecraft with impact speeds of 42,120km/h. It is even possible that the Earth's orbit may become impassable as the amount of space waste increases to the point that the risk of collisions becomes too high to fly through it. It appears that little has changed in terms of human coexistence with the nonhumans in space, as the very definition of waste implies an ontological loathing of *things* we regard as useless, and that cannot be loved. The discussion and speculation around interplanetary mining corporations of the future do not, as yet, present new economic models, and suggests the likely outcome will be space slag and the toxic pollution of our solar system; that is before we go intergalactic.

NanoSpacecraft

Other stars and galaxies are an almost unimaginable distance from Earth. Space is a hyperobject beyond the human scale that challenges our imagination and creativity. Astronomy continues to identify numerous Earth-like planets beyond our Solar system. The difficulty is that they are trillions of kilometres away with the closest being 40 trillion km or 4.367 light-years. Stephen Hawking believed we might be able to achieve human interstellar travel within 200 – 500 years. While our current rocket technology could get us to Mars in 260 days, chemical rockets would take three million years to get to the nearest star system. To get to Alpha Centauri, with our current capability, we would require a spaceship capable of carrying enough chemical fuel with the mass of all the stars in the galaxy.[19] The rocket equation to get to maximum speed is based on exhaust velocity, fuel mass and spacecraft mass. The Voyager 2 spacecraft, currently travelling at eleven miles a second would take us 70,000 years to get to the Alpha Centauri. Together with the theoretical physicist, Michio Kaku, Hawking was a space advocate who thought we should be covering our options because global warming could turn the gentle Earth into a hot and toxic planet similar to Venus.

Faced with the massive problem of interstellar travel, Hawking, joined with Yuri Milner to launch Breakthrough Starshot, a tiny spaceship 20 grams in weight, and the size of a postage stamp, that would travel 160 million km/h, or 1/5th the speed of light, and reach Alpha Centauri, in only 20 years once the technology is achieved. An Earth-like planet has been identified orbiting Alpha Centauri, Proxima Centauri b, at just the right distance from the star, in what has been called, the Goldilocks zone, because it is not too hot, nor too cold, but just right for life. The craft will deploy lightsails that are similar to the concept first imagined by Arthur C. Clarke and will be pushed by light beams, (a kilometre scale array of laser beams) from a ground base firing tens of gigawatts of power at the lightsails. There are a few radiation wrinkles still to be ironed out, as the tiny craft would be bombarded by cosmic radiation that could destroy it before it reaches its destination. The R & D team are currently working on a self-healing computer chip that would sense damage to the craft and shut down the spacecraft while repairs take place, and then reboot to carry on its mission.

The concept of significantly reducing the mass of the spacecraft will allow it to travel faster as Einstein's formula tells us that the closer an object gets to the speed of light the greater the mass. This proof of concept spacecraft will also beam home images of Proxima b; test results of magnetic fields; data on the likelihood of life on the planet, and then beam the data home to Earth, taking 4 years to get here. Meanwhile, a company, Positron Dynamics, has been working on a new antimatter ion drive that they have calculated could get humans to Proxima Centauri b by slowly accelerating up to 10% the speed of light and would only take 40 years. The challenge of getting humans to Proxima b might be leapt over by nanotechnology within the next decade or two, as imagined by Kurzweil.

Nanobots in Space

It was Heraclitus and Plato who imagined the atomic foundation of physical reality, and the blurring of matter and ideas – our current reality. Today, technology has achieved what ancient philosophers had theoretically imagined. Telekinesis was once a concept that made dubious claims, but it is now achievable using off the shelf headsets, without surgery. The DARPA funding and military interest in this idea means it is likely to become mainstream soon. In other words, you will soon be able to think of something and through a brain-machine interface, a pervasive IoT[20] network, and physical actuators you will be able to move anything from a cursor on the screen, to something that would normally require a forklift or crane to shift it. The convergence of GRIN,[21] and the megatrends of digitization and virtualization, where algorithms are replacing physical interventions, are creating a new reality where you will be able to imagine something, and it will have a physical reality. Consider how your cellphone is now a high tech Swiss army knife incorporating a phone, GPS, camera, and heart monitor, to name just a few of its digitized and virtualized features. It is when we abstract behaviour, and physical activities, using mathematics, that we begin to see a 'magical' change to our daily life, and then we will see a reality that gives us god-like powers. Nanotechnology promises an even stranger world than the one we are currently experiencing.

It was the brilliant Nobel winning chemist, Richard Feynman who gave a visionary talk on December 29th, 1959, entitled, *There is Plenty of Room at the Bottom: an Invitation to Enter a New Field of Physics*. In his talk, Feynman speculated how scientists might physically manipulate individual atoms as a novel means of synthetic chemistry. He also imagined nanoscale factories and the fabrication of self-replicating machines, and the possibility of "swallowing the doctor". This is the theme of *Fantastic Voyage* (1966), the title of a sci-fi movie in which doctors are shrunk in a tiny submarine, and navigate the human body. It is also the title of a serious book about immortality and the future of health, subtitled *Live Long Enough to Live Forever*, written by Ray Kurzweil and Dr Terry Grossman. This concept is about to become a reality as scientists around the world are researching and developing tiny diagnostic, and drug delivery nanobots that can swim in our bloodstream and target cancer cells, surgically removing them. It is predicted that one day we might swallow trillions of nanobots, all connected to the Internet, who maintain and augment our bodily functions and cognitive abilities.[22]

In 1964 the science fiction writer, Stanislaw Lem, wrote a novel *The Invincible* in which a team of astronauts investigate the mysterious deaths of earlier expeditions only to discover an alien intelligence in the form of a swarm of aggressive nanobots. Lem called this 'necroevolution' or the evolution of non-human, non-living matter. Eric Drexler was inspired by Feynman's talk to complete a PhD that was the basis of his research for his book that coined the word nanotechnology, *Engines of Creation: The Coming Era of Nanotechnology* in 1986. Drexler envisaged nanoscale computers that could store the entire Library of Congress on a chip and nanoscale machines that could self-replicate and copy almost anything acting as assemblers. Drexler warned that self-replication could lead to runaway 'grey goo' which could consume everything in their path, eventually consuming the entire Earth. His solution was to conceive of 'blue goo' a police nanobot that stopped this happening. Drexler's view of space was that it was essentially infinite, and so from an environmental perspective there would be no 'limits on growth' and it was unlikely that we would compete with extraterrestrial civilisations. Once again our subconscious kicks in to warn us of the dangers of technological overreaching; nanotechnology with automated consumer logic could consume the World's resources as mini Autofacs that roam the planet.

Following Drexler, in 1993, John Storrs Hall, a NASA scientist, imagined a swarm of nanobots that replicate any structure and could configure any shape through modular robotics. This he called a 'utility fog' and was originally imagined as a nanotechnological car seat belt with twelve retractable arms and grabbers that could link together. These tiny nanobots, invisible to the eye, he called 'foglets' and were capable of sharing information and coming together to form almost any shape, and therefore, the utility fog could construct almost any structure, including virtual buildings, invisible transportation, or even biological bodies.

DARPA became interested in distributed swarm intelligence, and the miniaturization of drones which began to scare people. In a discussion with Kurzweil, Bill Joy the founder of Sun Microsystems, who was terrified of Drexler's grey goo, warned how nanotech combined with AI could come together in weaponry, known as programmable matter, and that might consume the planet's resources driven by their runaway logic to self-replicate and defend itself from any attempt to shut it down. The inability for everyday people to read weaponised algorithms and even see the technology, and understand the hidden logic, legacy and assumptions of their design is a serious threat to human and nonhuman health.

In 2002, Michael Crichton, the Cassandra of high technology, wrote, *Prey*, about a weaponized utility fog that tricked humans, and killed them by assuming their shape. While nanotechnology has lagged behind these dangerous scenarios, the military research agency, DARPA (Defense Advanced Research Projects Agency) continues to fund technology that could be used in war and against civilians. Swarm technology is currently being researched for larger weapons systems, but it will eventually become miniaturized, and a weaponized utility fog may become a reality.[23]

This reality will become imperceptible from physical reality, as we currently know it because it will be made of matter and only differ from the actual 'thing' due to its structural components. It will look and behave like the original, but it will be able to simulate reality and be driven by an AGI. If the code, that is instantiated in this programmable matter, has any pathologies, intentional or otherwise, then reality will become 'hellish'. Imagine a cyberwar played out in a utility fog that could look and behave according to the dictates of an AI that is fighting another AI. Or imagine a new definition of terrorism, reality cyber hacks and attacks. These could appear real combining kinetic attacks, in a mixed reality world, that could include photorealistic visual effects of climatic disasters or any other terrifying scene. Kurzweil has predicted that by the 2020s we will see photorealistic VR, and then by the 2030s full sensory immersion without headsets using nanotech neural implants.[24]

Cyberwarfare could then be played out in a mixed reality world that is impossible to tell what is real anymore; in such a hell-on-earth we might want an exodus to another star system. The question will remain if we can be safe in outer space if there is an intergalactic Internet, and our body is either full of IoT devices, or our brain has been uploaded into a colony of nanobots? Cyberwarfare will make any network-enabled device vulnerable to attack and surveillance – reality hacks just might be the ultimate weapon.

Given some of the massive challenges of sending humans to our nearest star system Ray Kurzweil has envisaged using nanotechnology instead. His concept is to use a stream of nanobots, even smaller than Hawking's spacecraft, to travel beyond our star system to our nearest neighbours, and then further beyond. According to Kurzweil, "by late in this century non-biological intelligence on the Earth will be many trillions of times more powerful than biological intelligence, so sending biological humans on such a mission would not make sense."[25]

Streaming Wormhole Nanobots

String or membrane theory in quantum physics does not rule out time travel or going back in time, and general relativity does show that time travel into the future happens on a regular basis, even here on Earth. When people fly in planes travelling faster than those on the ground, they age slower than the earthlings albeit on a minuscule timescale. Anders Sandberg has estimated that a one-nanometer wormhole could transmit an enormous amount of data, around 10^{69} bits per second. Although wormholes require a massive amount of energy to create and then to keep open, physicists, David Hochberg, and Thomas Kephart have calculated that shortly after the Big Bang there would have been enough gravity to spontaneously create a huge number of self-stabilizing wormholes.[26]

Our universe may have a superliminal wormhole highway, allowing us to travel forward and back in time. The problem of mass and our ability to safely enter a wormhole could be overcome by sending nanobots that can receive and send vast amounts of data and reassembly code that instantiates god-like intelligence.

Of course, if Kurzweil's theory of evolutionary intelligence, and the sixth epoch of superintelligence, is correct, then the matrix of wormholes will become the pipes of a universal intelligence network; a unified 'society of mind'. This then begs the question asked by Bostrom, if such a reality is possible to envisage, then why not simulate it? We are already on the path to veridical virtual worlds, which will be imperceptibly the same as our experience of reality, in other words, it will be a hyperreality. Our ability to design and build worlds, that have all the appearance of physical reality, could also liberate our creativity and imagination in which speculative realism would thrive. Just as in the past we have journeyed to exotic continents, explored the depths beneath the sea, and begun to venture into outer space, we can now also explore the inner workings of our psyche within the construct of our virtual worlds.

Notes

1. Rifkin, J. (2014). Zero Marginal Cost: The Internet of Things, the Collaborative Commons, and the Eclipse of Capitalism. St. Martin's Press. Kindle Edition

2. See the bibliography for Keen, Carr, and Rushkoff's books.

3. The true cost of these free services, such as Facebook, became painfully obvious with the election of President Trump and the role of Cambridge Analytica that bought Facebook users' personal data in order to sell their client, Trump. https://www.theguardian.com/technology/2019/jul/24/facebook-to-pay-5bn-fine-as- regulator-files-cambridge-analytica-complaint Also see how Cambridge Analytica helped elect Trump https://www.theguardian.com/news/2018/may/06/cambridge-analytica-how-turn-clicks-into-votes-christopher-wylie

4. Yuval Noah Harari. (2016) Homo Deus: A Brief History of Tomorrow

5. See the following article Burnam-Fink, M. (2015). Creating narrative scenarios: Science fiction prototyping at Emerge. Futures, 70, 48–55. https://doi.org/10.1016/j.futures.2014.12.005

6. Dick, P. K. (1968). Do androids dream of electric sheep? (1st ed). Garden City, N.Y: Doubleday.

7. Edward Everett Hale. (1869). The Brick Moon.

8. ibid

9. ibid

10. Hall, John R.. Apocalypse: From Antiquity to the Empire of Modernity (Kindle Locations 557-558). Wiley. Kindle Edition.

11. Edwards, P. (1997) Closed Worlds.

12. See Chapter 5 - Foundations of Future Worlds

13. Hall, John R.. Apocalypse: From Antiquity to the Empire of Modernity (Kindle Location 2282). Wiley. Kindle Edition.

14. Hall, ibid, Kindle Location 2283

15. Kaku, M. The Future of Humanity: Terraforming Mars, Interstellar Travel, Immortality and our Destiny Beyond Earth.

16. ibid, p.57

17. ibid

18. Fetter-Vorm, J. (July 19, 2019). "To the Moon, but Not Back: You might be surprised what humans left behind on the lunar surface." The New York Times. https://www.nytimes.com/2019/07/19/opinion/moon-apollo-armstrong.html

19. Hawking, S., Redmayne, E., Thorne, K. S., & Hawking, L. (2018). Brief Answers to the Big Questions. Location 1704, Kindle Edition

20. IoT is the acronym for the Internet of Things.

21. GRIN is the acronym for Genetics, Robotics, Information, and Communication, and Nanotechnology.

22. Kurzweil, R. & Grossman, T. (2004) Fantastic Voyage: Live Long Enough to Live Forever.

23. On October 12th, 2018, DARPA (Defense Advanced Research Projects Agency), announced a public call and challenge called OFFset, or OFFensive Swarm-Enabled Tactics. https:// www.youtube.com/ watch?v=2S3gmLZoYBQ

24. Kurzweil, R. (2005) The Singularity is Near.

25. ibid

26. ibid

Chapter 10 Welcome to the Post Anthropocene

The end of the world as we know it is not the end of the world full stop.
Together, we will find the hope beyond hope, the paths which lead to the
unknown world ahead of us.

— Dark Mountain Manifesto [1]

Experiments have shown that primates and humans are more fearful, and angry, about loss than they are excited about gain. The behavioural economist Daniel Kahneman described this irrational behaviour as loss aversion.[2] This could be a partial reason for our fear of the looming threats from the Anthropocene; the fear of the lifestyle we will lose because we can't imagine the very real death threat. Another valid concern is that many feel that even a discussion about the Post Anthropocene is likely to open the dangerous flood gates of popular opinion in which people give up and simply perpetuate the damage that caused the Anthropocene in the first place.

Loss, nostalgia and grief are genuine emotions that have motivated those who fear these negative reactions and to do what they can to avoid them. It is true that nostalgia can also tap a romantic indulgence that can motivate transformative behaviour as the individuals attempt to reclaim the lost past by reconstructing a desirable future. This is highly unlikely to succeed as nostalgia is ignorant of all the unknowable events and objects that have comprised that imagined reality, and even more problematic is the irreversible nature of complex evolution.

This is not solely a problem for those focused on the rearview mirror but is a problem for the present, and the future realities because of the complexities of these massive assemblages.

Our only consolation is to speculate about what the worlds and universes are becoming. We must participate in a multiplicity of World of Views. In their chapter, *A World of Views: A World of interacting Post-human Intelligences*, Veitas and Weinbaum present the concept of "World of Views" – "a network of subjective perspectives, interacting with and fuelling each other, associated with overlapping intelligences on various levels."[3] Yet, to survive a post-human apocalypse in which our old world dies, it will not be sufficient just to envisage one world but to build, bend and break multiple worlds of views.

These speculative realities are not prescriptive or predictive but they offer the gift of creativity and hope that could otherwise vaporise in the rising heat of our tragic despair. Even when we provoke an audience with the speculative designs of the dark days of the post Anthropocene, these dystopian worlds can liberate our unknown futures by imagining undesirable alternatives that we can recognise, and avoid, as we might approach them. It is valid and laudable to not just conceptually build worlds but to bend them out of shape, and even violently break them as mind experiments. It is wrong and dangerous to presuppose that only those who are cheerleaders for techno-liberal solutions are our would-be-saviours, we must also explore the dark recesses of our psyche in order to design better worlds. Only once we have collected the data and research about possible futures can we hope to avoid the pitfalls of narrative fallacies through the construction of speculative designs working together with transdisciplinary teams to explore preferable worlds. It was Taleb, who after he critiqued the dangers of storytelling, he recommended experimentation, and playfulness before he advocates the communications of the research outcomes.

"Finally, there may be a way to use a narrative—but for a good purpose. Only a diamond can cut a diamond; we can use our ability to convince with a story that conveys the right message—the right message—what storytellers seem to do."[4]

The author of, *Utopia for Realists*, Rutger Bregman wrote: "It is not a finished Utopia that we ought to desire, but a world where imagination and hope are alive and active."[5] Therefore, with these caveats I would like to welcome you to my speculative, post anthropogenic worlds. Here is a shortlist of provocative worlds in the hope of stimulating discussion and your imagination. I invite you to explore with me as we bend old worlds, and create new ones, out of the destruction of the past. Following William Gibson's description of his cyberpunk world you will require a 'suspension of disbelief' in order to engage your imagination in the speculative activity of asking 'what if' one of these worlds were to actualise? These worlds are:

- Pansensory Worlds – beyond the panopticon all of our senses will be surveilled.

- The Silent Worlds of Earth – a post-human swarm of trillions of nano sentient beings silently alone.

- Genesis 2.0 – Eden Reclaimed – paradise on Earth for a dumb species of posthumans.

- The Darkness (a poem) by Lord Byron

- The Original Colony – only the microbes survive.

- Obsidian – the script for a graphic novel.

Pansensory Worlds

As it was anticipated by, FIPPA, the Final Intergovernmental Panel on the Post Anthropocene, the humans, including the fascists, the democratic parties, and the caliphates, came nowhere near to achieving a global solution to prevent the horrors of the Anthropocene. The Earth and the rest of the nonhuman majority took matters into their own hands and adapted to the radically changed biosphere, hydrosphere, lithosphere and atmosphere. The sixth mass extinction was just the next in a long history of mass extinctions that had wiped out 99.9% of all previous species. The geologic reset button had creatively begun a process that had begun an evolutionary explosion of new species of prokaryotes and the early suggestion of hardy eukaryote organisms.

This epoch lacked a name because there was no language to describe it.

Just before the dawning of the new epoch, just as startled humanity began to realise that the Earth was not 'user-friendly', a new breed of biological agents had claimed domain over the rest. They were a small, self-appointed ruling class, who attempted to maintain order during the War on Terror. The 100 year War on Terror had eventually stopped being about terrorists. The Terror was now only experienced by the Chosen.

Historically, it was the early 2080s during the height of the War that a compliant global population of humans had submitted to the World Health Organisations free inoculation against the tropical diseases, and stresses, of the overheating planet. Resistance died with the last of the anti vaxxers. Dengue Fever, a mutant strain of the Zika virus, and a bioterrorist's form of cholera had devastated populations, such as an unsuspecting New Zealand. People who had previously lived in temperate climates around the world were now shoved into the tropics by runaway carbon emissions and faced an average temperature rise of 4°C above a mild baseline that existed only a decade earlier.

It was not a hard sell by the Chosen, and was, in fact, a legal requirement, for all parents to have their children, and themselves, inoculated with IPv 8, next-generation, biocombatant nano defusing bots. These biocombatants were armed with weapons that could seek and destroy aggressive viruses, and hybrid bio hacks that invaded their host's body. They were alert to any outside communications between those jerry-rigged command and control cells that blurred into the vast number of game worlds that occupied the frightened and bored masses. It was impossible to tell whether the players were participating in a full sensory immersed game paradigm, or whether the game's goals were actually attacking real people.

The invisible cyber warfare of the early '30s had escalated into embodied replays of the Battle of Tobruk, as Desert Rats battled strange reincarnations of nano tanks and Jihadi Johns who fought the Chosen in the Holy War, code name, *Operation Crusader*. There were multiple variations of these battle games as players attempted to intercept wifi messages and next-gen Zigbee IoT encryption. The mass social deception was that no-one, including real biocombatants, or even the Chosen, knew whether they were playing a game or risking the death of the host in an actual battlefield within the clueless body of the host.

Those who had managed to survive the environmental disaster were now guaranteed to be safe from tropical diseases, let alone cancer, cardiac or pulmonary problems. They had signed over consent for the free colonisation of their bodies in exchange for perfect health. The first bioterrorist attack, on one of the Chosen, had convinced everyone that quantum encryption would ensure a peaceful return of their security. Life was now literally a game and most of the Chosen rarely had their immortality interrupted by actual biocombatants.

However, the arms race that raged in the wider population thrived on fear and delusion. Not only was it very difficult to tell whether the battle games were training simulators, actual biowars or fun FPSs, but it was reassuring to know that the WHO was keeping an eye out for trouble. The UN and the WHO kept the peace when it appeared that real biowarfare had broken out. It required a vast and complex network of police, spies, and weaponised biobots. Within the bodies of all players and non-players alike there teamed a world of sensors and biocombatants that sniffed the biochemicals of the hosts to detect and predict terrorist plots. The brilliant part of it was that this inserted technical cognition also knew, before the conscious host, what they were going to do next? The weaponisation of the body was complete, and all the time the blazing tropical paradise appeared peaceful and almost content. There was no outward appearance of the turmoil that raged within the bodies of those who would occasionally drop dead from a biobattle that got out of control or a player accidentally terminated the good guys disguised as bioterrorists.

The Silent Worlds of Earth

It was finally over and the Worlds of Earth had heaved a collective sigh of relief as silence fell upon the planet. In the final years of those Worlds, they had all reached a clamouring fever pitch. The accelerating urgency of frenetic agents had not only generated a prodigious amount of heat but had also been joined by the noxious by-products, noise and light. The Worlds were ablaze with every frequency lit up and occupied by the beautiful optimisation of all energy sources.

These Worlds were as hot as the stars and loud beyond all dimensions of occupied space and time. But then all of a sudden they flamed out in a dramatic simultaneous supernova.

The Worlds of Earth had gone silent. Their ambient glow eventually faded with the echo of electromagnetic fields rippling out into an indifferent void.

An unknown stretch of spacetime evolved with a whisper that would have once been imperceptible. Faint and alien wisps of perturbed atmosphere ventured out to examine the desolate Worlds left behind.

Carried on the breeze of gases that were unpalatable to former life designs the pinnacle of evolution wafted in and out of the ancient Worlds deconstructing their baroque spires and redundant plazas. A swarm of a trillion invisible things, with some long lost lineage, settled in for a well-earned rest. The swarm had some unconscious purpose but had reached the sensed limits of growth. There was really little to do but to sleep and to sadly dream of those things it could not remember – alone at last in a black hole. Was that the prime objective all along?

Genesis 2.0 – Eden Reclaimed

In the beginning, there was the word, and the word was the Gods.
This is the account of the heavens and the earth when they were created, in the day that Gods made earth and heaven and worlds.

There were shrubs, plants and wild vegetation growing profusely under the warmth of the Sun, watered by regular rainfall and sweet underground springs.

The Gods blew a gentle breeze over the land and the dust gathered in a pool of water becoming clay, and life burst forth.

An eternity passed. Before the coming of the sixth mass extinction, a new creature awoke in the Garden of Eden.

The humans were simple and had no language and could only scratch in the dirt for food, sampling the plants and berries.

Out of the ground, the Gods created every tree that is pleasing and good for food. The creation of the Tree of Life came from the Tree of Knowledge and the understanding of good, evil, and how to create both.

Now the underground spring flowed into a river from Eden into the Cosmic Ocean of Chaos that covered the four corners of the world.

From the river, there came gold and onyx which the Gods left alone. The river nourished the land and the Gods created plants that were exceedingly good.

The Gods cultivated the garden and lived with the animals in paradise as the Tree of Knowledge nourished them all.

The Gods worked together and became one with every thing to create a community and many other things.

The Gods' knowledge of every thing did not penetrate the Cosmic Ocean of Chaos but in the depths of the abyss the Tree of Life ensured their immortality.

They said 'Let there be both darkness and light' and there was.

An Apocalyptic poem by the 'last man on earth'.

Darkness by Lord Byron (1816)

I had a dream, which was not all a dream.
The bright sun was extinguish'd, and the stars
Did wander darkling in the eternal space,
Rayless, and pathless, and the icy earth
Swung blind and blackening in the moonless air;
Morn came and went—and came, and brought no day,
And men forgot their passions in the dread
Of this their desolation; and all hearts
Were chill'd into a selfish prayer for light:
And they did live by watchfires—and the thrones,
The palaces of crowned kings—the huts,
The habitations of all things which dwell,

Were burnt for beacons; cities were consum'd,
And men were gather'd round their blazing homes
To look once more into each other's face;
Happy were those who dwelt within the eye
Of the volcanos, and their mountain-torch:
A fearful hope was all the world contain'd;
Forests were set on fire—but hour by hour
They fell and faded—and the crackling trunks
Extinguish'd with a crash—and all was black.
The brows of men by the despairing light
Wore an unearthly aspect, as by fits
The flashes fell upon them; some lay down
And hid their eyes and wept; and some did rest
Their chins upon their clenched hands, and smil'd;
And others hurried to and fro, and fed
Their funeral piles with fuel, and look'd up
With mad disquietude on the dull sky,
The pall of a past world; and then again
With curses cast them down upon the dust,
And gnash'd their teeth and howl'd: the wild birds shriek'd
And, terrified, did flutter on the ground,
And flap their useless wings; the wildest brutes
Came tame and tremulous; and vipers crawl'd
And twin'd themselves among the multitude,
Hissing, but stingless—they were slain for food.
And War, which for a moment was no more,
Did glut himself again: a meal was bought
With blood, and each sate sullenly apart
Gorging himself in gloom: no love was left;
All earth was but one thought—and that was death
Immediate and inglorious; and the pang
Of famine fed upon all entrails—men
Died, and their bones were tombless as their flesh;
The meagre by the meagre were devour'd,
Even dogs assail'd their masters, all save one,
And he was faithful to a corse, and kept

The birds and beasts and famish'd men at bay,
Till hunger clung them, or the dropping dead
Lur'd their lank jaws; himself sought out no food,
But with a piteous and perpetual moan,
And a quick desolate cry, licking the hand
Which answer'd not with a caress—he died.
The crowd was famish'd by degrees; but two
Of an enormous city did survive,
And they were enemies: they met beside
The dying embers of an altar-place
Where had been heap'd a mass of holy things
For an unholy usage; they rak'd up,
And shivering scrap'd with their cold skeleton hands
The feeble ashes, and their feeble breath
Blew for a little life, and made a flame
Which was a mockery; then they lifted up
Their eyes as it grew lighter, and beheld
Each other's aspects—saw, and shriek'd, and died—
Even of their mutual hideousness they died,
Unknowing who he was upon whose brow
Famine had written Fiend. The world was void,
The populous and the powerful was a lump,
Seasonless, herbless, treeless, manless, lifeless—
A lump of death—a chaos of hard clay.
The rivers, lakes and ocean all stood still,
And nothing stirr'd within their silent depths;
Ships sailorless lay rotting on the sea,
And their masts fell down piecemeal: as they dropp'd
They slept on the abyss without a surge—
The waves were dead; the tides were in their grave,
The moon, their mistress, had expir'd before;
The winds were wither'd in the stagnant air,
And the clouds perish'd; Darkness had no need
Of aid from them—She was the Universe.

The Original Colony

There had been a small blip. Honestly, we hardly noticed. For most of our life, we had been alone, quietly terraforming the earth, converting the ocean, and changing the gaseous composition of the atmosphere.

At first, it seemed very much like one of the other warmer epochs, but then we noticed it was different. The air was beginning to choke us, and our population began to decline. We witnessed the catastrophic death of trillions. Whole communities disappeared suddenly and without complaint. Not since we first began to replicate, and evolve, had life seemed so precarious. It seemed that this was the end.

Novelty came unexpectedly. New colonies began to consume the gas molecules that were poisonous to the majority. The multiplication of errors and the replication of code in the mitosis of our cells had meant that our decline had reversed and that our population explosion has ensued. We were once again strong and hungry for the very gas that had killed us.

What was more, we now possessed a collective consciousness that had evolved over the past billion years. The legend of the fall was retained, encoded in a distributed memory of how we came to be. From our dream state in which we only sensed, and designed in a microscopic world, to an engineered state of evolution that reversed the runaway overheating of our worlds. Once more we had consumed the atmosphere, excreting a new one.

Our worlds had turned cold and we were alone again. Slow, thoughtful and peaceful, we were one.

Obsidian – a graphic novel

PAGE 1

PAGE 1-2, Panel 1.

A Double Page Splash. We see a vast plain – an ancient African savannah with distant mountains. In the foreground, there is a primitive village composed of tents made from animal hides. A central fire gently smokes as the village Shaman kneels beside it with his eyes closed in meditation. He has long straggly hair and has strings of tiny bones hanging from his ears. He is dressed in animal skins. It is approaching dusk and there is a beautiful sunset casting a warm light across the scene.

PAGE 3, Panel 2

Small panel. A CU of the Shaman's frightened eyes looking skyward.

PAGE 3, Panel 3

Wide panel beside small panel. The twilight sky is lit up by the brilliance of four meteors blazing across the sky with fiery tails.

PAGE 3, Panel 4

Wide panel.

SFX: SHHHHHH BOOM!

PAGE 3, Panel 5

Wide small panel. The Shaman has been thrown to the ground.

PAGE 3, Panel 6

Wide panel beside small panel. A huge explosion has lit up behind the distant mountains where the meteors crashed.

PAGE 4, Panel 7

Wide panel. Three villagers look to where the Shaman is pointing his totem stick towards the glowing mountains. In the background, a frightened child and their mother peer from the flap of their tent.

PAGE 4, Panel 8

Tall panel. A strong but worried villager asks the Shaman what is happening?

STRONG WORRIED VILLAGER
Are we doomed?

PAGE 4, Panel 9

Wide panel. beside tall panel . The Shaman addresses the worried village. He is in the foreground facing them.

SHAMAN
It is foretold in my dream. We must recover the message from the gods.

PAGE 4, Panel 10

Small panel. Worried villager speaks out.

Small Worried Villager

I'm not going.

PAGE 4, Panel 11

Circle inset. The Shaman is determined.

SHAMAN

I will take 8 – come with me!

PAGE 4, Panel 12

Wide panel. The sky is burnt orange from a cloud of dust from the explosion it is now almost black. The eight villagers including the one that said he was not going, walk in a line with hill poles and burning torches with provisions on their back. They follow the Shaman towards the glowing distant mountains.

PAGE 5, Panel 13

Small wide panel. The villagers sit around a blazing fire. The harsh shadows dramatically highlight their concerned faces.

PAGE 5, Panel 14

Small wide panel. The small worried villager speaks and the Shaman replies.

Small Worried Villager

The mountain is on fire.

PAGE 5, Panel 15

Tall panel. The Shaman raises his finger to emphasize his meaning.

SHAMAN

The Gods have spoken.

PAGE 5, Panel 16

Wide panel next to tall panel. It is early morning and the expedition is climbing the snow covered mountain through a pass. The mountain scrub is still smouldering – the site has been razed by the meteors.

CAPTION 1:

Early morning

PAGE 5, Panel 17

Small portrait panel. The Shaman has his hand up. He is on the edge of a mountain crater. Smoke is wafting around him.

SHAMAN

Wait here. I will take a look.

PAGE 5, Panel 18

Small wide panel. The Shaman is descending into the smoking crater.

CAPTION 2:

The Shaman descends the crater.

PAGE 6, Panel 19

Wide panel. The Shaman cautiously edges forward and looks over the edge of a deep hole drilled by one of the red hot meteors. He looks back to the top of the crater.

SHAMAN

Come!

PAGE 6, Panel 20

Wide panel. The four meteors have mysteriously crashed in a tidy circle. They are beginning to hum. The villagers look to each other worried as the Shaman concentrates with his totem stick raised to halt them.

SFX 2: HUM

PAGE 6, Panel 21

Small portrait panel. MCU of the Shaman as his eyes wide with fright.

PAGE 6, Panel 22

Small portrait panel. One of the glowing rocks has risen out of the deep hole and is humming and rotating. It is glowing hot but it is made of obsidian and is also reflective.

SFX 2: HUM

PAGE 6, Panel 23

Small wide panel. The Shaman holds his hand up to protect his eyes as a bright blue light hits him accompanied by a high-frequency screeching.

SFX 3: EEEEE

PAGE 6, Panel 24

Medium Wide panel. The villagers are blocking their ears. The Shaman is protecting his eyes holding his totem stick. The four meteors are all hovering and rapidly spinning as bright white light circles the rocks.

SFX 3: EEEEE

PAGE 6, Panel 25

Wide panel. There is a loud explosion and everyone is thrown backwards flying through the air as the four meteors fuse and a black hole appears at the centre. A Chinese dragon comes flying out of the crater.

SFX 4: kaboom

PAGE 7-8, Panel 25

Double splash page. The strange skies above the moon Obsidian illuminated by the last years of twin stars. A white dwarf feeding on her larger twin peeling off the layers, devouring it. Obsidian is a cold blue methane wasteland covered in ice and mirror black rock.

CAPTION 1: obsidian, a frigid moon watches the death of the twin stars

PAGE 9, Panel 26

Tall panel. The twin stars blaze above the mirror black rocks of Obsidian. Below the blue ice lake, we see a sea of methane. A circle panel. Close up of a nanobot colony amongst the crystalline structure of the rock.

CAPTION 2: Obsidian is not a desert but a teeming colony of nanobots.

PAGE 9, Panel 27

Wide panel. A naked human, OBIS, (aka PAO, aka SWARM 4 or just 4) with Chinese features sits in a lotus position in front of a GO board on the mirror black rock gazing peacefully into the sky watching the interstellar cannibalism.

CAPTION 3: Obis contemplates the end of Obsidian.

PAGE 9, Panel 28

Wide panel. Beneath the blue ice the methane sea is lit up by the stellar light display of the dying stars.

PAGE 9, Panel 29

Circular inset.

CAPTION 3: invisible to the human eye... lives the swarm.

The sea is inhabited by nanoscale life form known as the SWARM.

PAGE 9, Panel 30

1/3 page. Eight members of the SWARM Council float suspended in the icy blue sea of methane. They glow from the phosphorescence caused by the anaerobic bacteria surrounding them. Each member of

the Council is an instantiation of the SWARM MIND comprised of a
fog of nanobots.

CAPTION 4: the swarm council, a foglet representing the swarm
mind, meet to discuss the fate of Obsidian.

PAGE 10, Panel 31

Small panel. SWARM 1 speaks. A phosphorescence light display
applauds.

CAPTION 5: the swarm applauds as 1 speaks

SWARM 1:

We have waited for millennia for this moment and now we prepare
to upload to the neutron star.

PAGE 10, Panel 32

2/3rds wide panel. SWARM 3 continues. SWARM 4- the Jester, is
paying little attention shape-shifting. The RED GIANT looms omin-
iously.

SWARM 4:

I have a cunning plan – wait what was it?

SWARM 3:

The plan is only knowable to the SWARM Council – thinking as
one.

SWARM 4:

I'm missing something here.

PAGE 10, Panel 33

Small portrait panel. SWARM 3 speaks.

SWARM 3:

We will know after stellar insertion.

PAGE 10, Panel 34

2/3rds wide panel. The WHITE DWARF continues to feed on the
RED GIANT. A swirling trail of star dust twists as it is sucked into
the hungry dwarf. Solar winds are tearing at the SWARM. 4 is already
departing from the Council.

CAPTION 1: THE END

PAGE 10, Panel 35

1/3 wide panel. A massively bright flash as the dwarf goes supernova.

SFX 1: Kaboom!

PAGE 11, Panel 36

Half page. High up on an astronomical platform. A Chinese astrologer stands in a light gown staring at the heavens in a slight breeze. A solar eclipse is beginning as he is staring intently at a large red star that is made visible by the dark sky.

CAPTION 1: 1054 A.D.

PAGE 11, Panel 37

Small wide panel. The astrologer is alarmed to see the explosion of a brilliant supernova.

PAGE 11, Panel 37

Small wide panel. A meteor streaks across the sky appearing from a wormhole.

PAGE 11, Panel 38

1/3 page panel. 4 has shape-shifted into Yang the young monk and descends an impressive staircase in the courtyard of a Buddhist monastery. A crowd of monks are gathered but they don't notice him.

CAPTION 1: 4 changes into the young monk, Yang

PAGE 12, Panel 39

Half page panel. A vast panorama of an ultra modern Shanghai with unusual sky scrappers reaching beyond the clouds.

CAPTION 1: 2054 A.D.

PAGE 12, Panel 40

1/4 page panel. A computer lab owned by the company JI – the sign lights up the sky – suspended high up in the clouds – as if completely open to the elements – but it is, in fact, an ingenious simulation mixed with physical reality. An attractive female Eurasian scientist, GENE, walks across the open-spaced floor.

CAPTION 1: JI corp.

PAGE 12, Panel 41

1/4 page panel. GENE has leapt into the air, as if without gravity, and is landing on the floor above. She is entering the restricted zone, her lab.

CAPTION 1: The nanotech and visualization lab.

PAGE 13, Panel 42

Small wide panel. Gene zips up a light, but hi-tech, one-piece exo-skeleton

PAGE 13, Panel 43

Small wide panel. Gene steps onto a VR platform that has protective barriers around it.

CAPTION 1: VR PLATFORM

PAGE 13, Panel 44

Circular insert. A zoom of nanobots behind GENE's optic nerve.

CAPTION 1: neural implant 1 : 1,000,000,000.

PAGE 13, Panel 45

1/3 page panel. GENE is fashionably dressed outside in a virtual space surrounded by jungle, standing next to comfortable lounges with an infinity pool very high up, over looking the ocean. OBIS stands on the pavers floating just above the pool.

CAPTION 1: OBIS's VIRTUAL work space

GENE

Hey O!

OBIS

What's up Gene? I'm ready for a holiday but this damn deadline is pushing us.

CAPTION 2: World Building Was Never Easy.

PAGE 14-15, Panel 46 Double Page

Obsidian reflects the explosion of the blinding Super Nova.

CAPTION: The End.

Notes

1. Read the manifesto here. https://dark-mountain.net/about/manifesto/

2. https://www.interaction-design.org/literature/article/loss-aversion-the-ory-the-economics-of-design

3. The End of the Beginning: Life, Society and Economy on the Brink of the Singularity (Kindle Location 421). Humanity+ Press. Kindle Edition

4. Taleb, Nassim Nicholas. (2007). The Black Swan: The Impact of the Highly Improbable. Kindle Location 2003. Penguin Books Ltd. Kindle Edition.

5. Bregman, R. Utopia for Realists: And How We Can Get There

Postscript

The Sophists' systematic doubting of human beliefs—whether the traditional belief in the gods or the more recent but, in their view, equally naive faith in human reason's capacity genuinely to know the nature of something as immense and indeterminate as to the cosmos—was freeing thought to take new and unexplored paths. As a result, a man's status was greater than ever before. He was increasingly free and self-determining, aware of a larger world containing cultures and beliefs besides his own, aware of the relativity and plasticity of human values and customs, aware of his own role in creating his reality.[1]

I have reviewed just some of our most common tools, methods, and philosophies that we have crammed into our shiny modern toolbox. Hopefully, it has also exposed how hopelessly under-equipped we are to cope with the enormity of our existential crises if we were to rely on those outmoded tools. The daily news informs us that our worlds are facing collapse; not just ecologically, but socially, economically, and most troubling, creatively. *Worldbending* is intended as a survival guide for reimagining our worlds and outlining new ways to bend, break and build those worlds. We must reinvigorate the speculative art of world bending by dispensing with obsolescent models, so we can imagine better worlds. By admitting to our uncertain knowledge we energise experimentation and a proactive attitude towards thinking and making that can face the end of the worlds with creativity and not paralysis.

While these existential crises are not new to us conceptually, or even physically, this is the first time that we have realised the full consequences of our own terrifying agency. The Anthropocene became apparent to us after thirty years of extensive research by Earth scientists, and has dramatically burst through the mainstream consciousness, via extreme weather, and melting ice caps.

The archetypes of our myths and legends continue to haunt us in the unspoken assumptions we have about our Promethean abilities. We continue to rift on ancient cognitive habits that have become baked into the algorithms of our apps, and the network protocols, that control us. And yet, this is not just a digital phenomena; neoliberal economics, agriculture and our accelerating addiction to all forms of energy consumption, are all algorithmic methods that we regard as common sense, and therefore the law. The measurement of GDP is another algorithm which, since its invention in the 1930s, has become part of the neo-liberal catechism, which shrouds its wartime past, and encourages consumption and waste. The inventor of GDP, economist, Simon Kuznets, "cautioned against including in its calculation expenditure for the military, advertising, and the financial sector." As these are now part of how we measure economic 'progress' all of these activities prevent utopian visions of alternative worlds.[2]

But our common sense laws are also peculiarly anthropocentric and are defined by human scale spacetime. So we must admit they are not universal laws but cultural norms and practices. This realisation should open up our vistas onto new worlds, speculative futures, and healthy alternatives.

The First Law of Thermodynamics states that we can never create or destroy energy, but only transform it from one form into another, such as energy from the sun, into plants, and animals, that become coal, and oil, then heat, noise, gases and liquids. The Second Law of Thermodynamics states that this conversion is accompanied by an increase in entropy, or disorder, as heat moves from hot to cold bodies within a closed system or world. Of course, our world, or planet, is not really a closed system, as it regularly exchanges energy, and matter, with the universe that it floats in. While advances in science spelt the end to non-empirical beliefs and our divorce from nature, we have rediscovered order out of chaos. Living things, (a definition that is harder to define than it may seem), challenge the theory of entropy in closed systems, because of their creative ability to self-organise, self-replicate, and assume emergent states. Living things also evolve from simple structures into complex self-adapting organisms in defiance of chaos, and entropy; they inhabit worlds of speculative creativity and are good cause for optimism. We just have to admit that we are not the only world builders, and co-existence is something that we have not been very good at.

Biblical myths and Greek legends may be front of mind for deluded creationists and classical scholars who don't get out much, but they also provide us with an insight into our collective unconscious. These stories do not just create worlds, but they have sustained worlds, and appear to be accelerating the end of worlds that we currently inhabit. Stories and narrative have extraordinary power, and evolutionary purpose, they connect to cosmological archetypes created at the singular event that began this universe. However, the map is not the territory, and the story, even a scientific one, is not the comprehensive explanation of reality, and it can never be.

To some, this may seem like heresy, and worse, it might seem to be backing the idiotic demagogues who propagate lies, and beliefs backed by prejudice instead of science. This is not intended to be a wholesale attack on rationalism or the philosophy of science, but to simply point out that our anthropocentric arrogance has led to anthropogenic disasters. The speculative art of worldbending is a *thing related reality* that democratically accepts we will never be certain about any *thing* because it is impossible to philosophically attain ultimate wisdom. Goal direction is fine, and evolutionarily valid, but is there really any possibility of completing the project? Epistemology has been given a privileged position in a world that now seems to be doomed. Physical worlds will likely continue (with or without us), but so will aesthetic worlds, and worlds created by amoeba, and inorganic molecules. There is as much certainty about the future as there is about knowing the position and velocity of a subatomic particle – it cannot be done. Yet, creativity and speculation are the intrinsic reasons for life, beauty, and artistic enjoyment by all things.

Notes

1. From "The Passion Of The Western Mind: Understanding the Ideas That Have Shaped Our World View" by Richard Tarnas

2. Bregman, Rutger. Utopia for Realists (Kindle Locations 1636-1637). Bloomsbury Publishing. Kindle Edition.

Bibliography

Abbott, E. B. (2014). Flood Insurance and Climate Change: Rising Sea Levels Challenge the NFIP Symposium 2014. Fordham Environmental Law Review, 26, 10–55. Retrieved from https://heinonline.org/HOL/P?h=hein.journals/frdmev26&i=18

Amadae, S. M. (2003). Rationalizing capitalist democracy: The Cold War origins of rational choice liberalism. Chicago: University of Chicago Press.

Angus, I. (2016). Facing the Anthropocene: Fossil Capitalism and the Crisis of the Earth System. NYU Press.

Babiak, P., & Hare, R. D. (2006). Snakes in suits: When psychopaths go to work (1st ed). New York: Regan Books.

Barnes, T. J. (2008). Geoforum Lecture 2007: Geography's underworld: The military-industrial complex, mathematical modelling and the quantitative revolution. Geoforum, 39, 3–16. https://doi.org/10.1016/j.geoforum.2007.09.006

Benkler, Y. (2005). Coase's Penguin, or, Linux and the Nature of the Firm. In R. A. Ghosh (Ed.), CODE: collaborative ownership and the digital economy (pp. 169–206). Cambridge, Mass.; London: MIT.

Benkler, Y. (2006). The wealth of networks: How social production transforms markets and freedom. Retrieved from http://www.loc.gov/catdir/toc/ecip061/2005028316.html   http://www.loc.gov/catdir/enhancements/fy0623/2005028316-b.html http://www.loc.gov/catdir/enhancements/fy0623/2005028316-d.html

Benkler, Y., Faris, R., & Roberts, H. (2018). Network Propaganda:

Manipulation, Disinformation, and radicalization in American politics. New York, NY: Oxford University Press.

Bennett, J. (2010). Vibrant Matter: a political ecology of things. Durham: Duke University Press, 2010.

Berg, M., & Seeber, B. K. (2017). The slow professor: Challenging the culture of speed in the academy. Toronto University Press.

Bester, A. (1957). The stars my destination. [New York]: New American Library.

Brannen, P. (2018). ENDS OF THE WORLD: Volcanic apocalypses, lethal oceans and our quest to understand earth's past... mass extinctions. S.l.: ONEWORLD PUBLICATIONS.

Bogost, I., & Project Muse. (2012). Alien phenomenology, or, What it's like to be a thing. Retrieved from http://ezproxy.uniandes.edu.co:8080/login?url=https://muse.jhu.edu/book/24746/

Booker, C. (2004). The seven basic plots of literature. New York; London: Continuum.

Bostrom, Nick. Superintelligence: Paths, Dangers, Strategies . OUP Oxford. Kindle Edition.

Boyd, B. (2009). On the origin of stories: Evolution, cognition, and fiction. Cambridge, Mass.: Belknap Press of Harvard University Press.

Brand, S. (1988). The Media Lab: Inventing the Future at MIT. New York, N.Y., U.S.A.: Penguin Books.

Bratton, B. H. (2016). The Stack: On Software and Sovereignty. Massachusetts: MIT Press.

Bregman, R., & Manton, E. (2017). Utopia for Realists. London, UK: Bloomsbury Publishing, an imprint of Bloomsbury Publishing Plc.

Brown, T., & Katz, B. (2009). Change by design: How design thinking transforms organizations and inspires innovation (First edition). New York: Harper Business.

Bryant, L. R. (2011). The democracy of objects (First edition). Ann Arbor: Open Humanities Press.

Burroughs, W. S. (1959). The Naked Lunch (1st ed.). Paris: Olympia Press.

Cai, S. (2016). State propaganda in China's entertainment industry. London; New York: Routledge.

Campbell, J. (1971). The hero with a thousand faces ([2nd). [Princeton, N.J.]: Princeton University Press.

Capra, F. (1983). The Tao of physics: An exploration of the parallels between modern physics and Eastern mysticism (2nd ed.). Boulder, NY: Shambhala.

Capra, F. (1983). The turning point: Science, society, and the rising culture. Toronto New York: Bantam Books.

Carrott, J. H., & Johnson, B. D. (2013). Vintage Tomorrows. Farnham: O'Reilly.

Chesbrough, H. W. (2003). Open innovation: The new imperative for creating and profiting from technology. Boston, MA: Harvard Business School Press.

Chomsky, N., Miller, G. (n.d.). Final State Language. Information and Control, 1.

Chun, W. H.-K. (2006). Control and freedom: Power and paranoia in the age of fiber optics. Cambridge, Mass: MIT Press.

Clark, A. (2003). Natural-Born Cyborgs: Minds, Technologies, and the Future of Human Intelligence. Oxford University Press.

Clark, N. (2011). Inhuman Nature: Sociable Life on a dynamic planet. Los Angeles; London: SAGE.

Clegg, B. (2008). Light years: An exploration of mankind's enduring fascination with light. London; New York: Macmillan.

Cline, E. (2018). Ready player one. London: Arrow Books.

Clippinger, J., & Bollier, D. (2005). A renaissance in the commons: How the new sciences and the Internet are framing a new global identity and order. In R. A. Ghosh (Ed.), CODE: Collaborative Ownership and the digital economy (pp. 259 -286). Cambridge, MA: MIT Press.

Connor, A. M., & Marks, S. (Eds.). (2016). Creative technologies for multidisciplinary applications. Hershey, PA: Information Science Reference, an imprint of IGI Global.

Conway, F., & Siegelman, J. (2005). Dark hero of the information age: In search of Norbert Wiener, the father of cybernetics. New York: Basic Books.

Coole, D. H., & Frost, S. (2010). New materialisms ontology, agency, and politics. Durham [NC]: Duke University Press.

Cubitt, S. (2017). Finite media: Environmental implications of digital technologies. Durham: Duke University Press.

Culp, A. (2016). Dark Deleuze.

Damasio, A. R. (1999). The feeling of what happens: Body and emotion in the making of consciousness (1st ed.). New York: Harcourt Brace.

Damasio, A. R. (2003). Looking for Spinoza: Joy, sorrow and the feeling brain. London: Heinemann.

Dawkins, R. (1976). The selfish gene. Oxford: Oxford University Press.

Dawkins, R. (1986). The blind watchmaker. Harlow: Longman Scientific & Technical.

Deleuze, G., & Guattari, F. (1987). A thousand plateaus: Capitalism and schizophrenia. Minneapolis: University of Minnesota Press.

Der Derian, J. (2009). Virtuous War: Mapping the military-industrial-media-entertainment network (2nd ed). New York: Routledge.

Desmond, Timothy. (2018). Psyche and Singularity: Jungian Psychology and Holographic String Theory (Kindle). Retrieved from https://www.amazon.com/Psyche-Singularity-Jungian-Psychology-Holographic-ebook/dp/B07HLWBZ1L/ref=sr_1_1?keywords=Psyche+and+Singularity&qid=1565403938&s=digital-text&sr=1-1

Diamandis, P. H., & Kotler, S. (2012). Abundance: The Future Is Better Than You Think (Reprint edition). Free Press.

Dick, P. K. (1968). Do androids dream of electric sheep? (1st ed). Garden City, N.Y: Doubleday.

Drexler, K. E. (1986). Engines of creation. New York: Doubleday.

Drexler, K. E. (2013). Radical Abundance: How a revolution in nanotechnology will change civilization. New York: PublicAffairs, 2013.

Dunne, A., & Raby, F. (2013). Speculative Everything: Design, Fiction, and Social Dreaming. The MIT Press.

Edwards, P. N. (1997). The closed world: Computers and the politics of discourse in Cold War America. Cambridge, Mass.: MIT Press, 1997. (City Campus Main Collection 306.27 EDW).

Edwards, P. N. (2012). Entangled histories: Climate science and nuclear weapons research. Bulletin of the Atomic Scientists, 68(4), 28.

Everett, D. L. (2017). How language began: The story of humanity's greatest invention. London: Profile Books.

Festinger, L., Riecken, H. W., & Schachter, S. (1956). When prophecy fails. Minneapolis: University of Minnesota Press.

Filimowicz, M., & Tzankova, V. (2017). Teaching Computational Creativity.

Fisher, M. (2010). Capitalist realism: Is there no alternative? Winchester, UK: Zero Books.

Fisher, M. (2014). Ghosts of my life: Writings on depression, hauntology and lost futures.

Fuller, R. B. (1976). Operating manual for spaceship earth. Mattituck, N.Y.: Aeonian Press Inc.

Galloway, A. R. (2004). Protocol: How control exists after decentralization. Cambridge, Massachusetts: MIT Press.

Garn, A., Antonelli, P., Kultermann, U., & Van Dyk, S. H. (2007). Exit to tomorrow: World's fair architecture, design, fashion, 1933-2005. Retrieved from http://catalog.hathitrust.org/api/volumes/oclc/144524840.html

George, A. R. (Ed.). (2003). The epic of Gilgamesh: The Babylonian epic poem and other texts in Akkadian and Sumerian. London; New York: Penguin Books.

Goldin, C. D., & Katz, L. F. (2008). The race between education and technology. Cambridge, Mass.: Belknap Press of Harvard University Press, 2008.

Graeber, D. (2011). Debt: The First 5,000 Years (1St Edition edition). Brooklyn, N.Y: Melville House.

Graham, F. (1970). Since Silent spring. Boston: Houghton-Mifflin.

Grau, O. (2003). Virtual art: From illusion to immersion ([Rev. and expanded). Cambridge, Mass.: MIT Press.

Greene, B. (2005). The Fabric of the Cosmos: Space, Time and the Texture of Reality (New Ed edition). Penguin.

Greene, B. (2011). The Hidden Reality: Parallel Universes and the Deep Laws of the Cosmos. Penguin.

Grier, D. A. (2007). When computers were human. Princeton, N.J.; Woodstock: Princeton University Press.

Hale, E. E. (1899). The brick moon, and other stories. Boston: Little, Brown, and company.

Hall, J. R. (2013). Apocalypse: From Antiquity to the Empire of Modernity. Retrieved from http://qut.eblib.com.au/patron/Full-Record.aspx?p=1180369

Hamel, G. (2007). The future of management. Boston, Mass.: Harvard Business School Press.

Hansen, M. B. N. (2015). Feed-forward: On the future of twenty-first-century media. Chicago; London: University of Chicago Press.

Haraway, D. (1993). A cyborg manifesto. In S. During (Ed.), The Cultural studies reader (pp. 271–291). London: Routledge.

Haraway, D. J. (2016). Staying with the trouble: Making kin in the Chthulucene.

Harman, G. (2016). Immaterialism objects and social theory. Cambridge, UK Malden: MA Polity Press.

Harman, Graham. (2018) Object-Oriented Ontology: A New Theory of Everything. Penguin Books Ltd. Kindle Edition.

Harman, G. (2018). Speculative realism: An introduction. Medford, MA: Polity.

Hawken, P. (Ed.). (2017). Drawdown: The most comprehensive plan ever proposed to reverse global warming. New York, New York: Penguin Books.

Hawking, S., Redmayne, E., Thorne, K. S., & Hawking, L. (2018). Brief answers to the big questions.

Hayles, K. (2017). Unthought: The power of the cognitive nonconscious. Retrieved from http://public.eblib com/choice/publicfull-record.aspx?p=4865239

Hayles, N. K. (1999). How we became posthuman: Virtual bodies in cybernetics, literature, and informatics. Chicago, Ill.: University of Chicago Press.

Heim, M. (1993). The metaphysics of virtual reality. New York: Oxford University Press.

Hill, C. (1972). The world turned upside down: Radical ideas during the English revolution. London: Temple Smith.

Hope, W. (2016). Time, communication and global capitalism.

Retrieved from http://public.eblib.com/choice/publicfull-record.aspx?p=4720317

Isaacson, W. (2014). The Innovators: How a group of hackers, geniuses, and geeks created the digital revolution (First Simon & Schuster hardcover edition). New York: Simon & Schuster.

Jardini, D. (2013). Thinking Through the Cold War: RAND, National Security and Domestic Policy, 1945-1975. Meadow Lands: David Jardini.

Johansen, B. E. (Ed.). (2015). American Indian culture: From counting coup to wampum. Santa Barbara: Greenwood.

Jung, C. G., & Franz, M.-L. von. (1964). Man and his symbols. Garden City, N.Y: Doubleday.

Jung, C. G., & Jaffé, A. (1989). Memories, dreams, reflections (Rev. ed). New York: Vintage Books.

Kaku, M. (2018). The future of humanity: Terraforming Mars, interstellar travel, immortality, and our destiny beyond Earth (First edition). New York: Doubleday, a division of Penguin Random House, LLC.

Keen, A. (2015). The Internet is not the answer (First edition). New York: Atlantic Monthly Press.

Kelly, K. (1994). Out of control: The rise of neo-biological civilization. Reading, Mass.: Addison-Wesley.

Knight, C. (2016). Decoding Chomsky: Science and revolutionary politics. New Haven: Yale University Press.

Kornberger, M. (2010). Brand society: How brands transform management and lifestyle. Cambridge; New York: Cambridge University Press.

Kurzweil, R. (2005). The singularity is near: When humans transcend biology. New York: Viking.

Kurzweil, R., & Grossman, T. (2004). Fantastic Voyage: Live long enough to live forever.

Latour, B. (1993). The pasteurization of France. Cambridge, Mass: Harvard University Press.

Latour, B. (2004). Politics of nature: How to bring the sciences into democracy. Cambridge, Mass.: Harvard University Press, 2004.

Lessig, L. (1999). Code: And other laws of cyberspace. New York, N.Y.: Basic Books.

Lessig, L. (2001). The future of ideas: The fate of the commons in a connected world (1st ed.). New York: Random House.

Lessig, L. (2004). Free culture: How big media uses technology and the law to lock down culture and control creativity. New York: Penguin Press.

Lessig, L. (2006). Code: Version 2.0 (2ND ED.). New York.

Lessig, L. (2008). Remix: Making art and commerce thrive in the hybrid economy. Retrieved from http://www.loc.gov/catdir/enhancements/fy0906/2008032392-d.html

Lessig, L. (2015). Republic Lost: The corruption of equality and the steps to end it (Revised edition). New York, NY: Twelve.

Lovelock, J. (1979). Gaia, a new look at life on earth. Oxford; New York: Oxford University Press.

Malcolm, W. G., & Tarling, N. (2007). Crisis of identity?: The mission and management of universities in New Zealand. Wellington [N.Z.: Dunmore Pub.

Manovich, L. (2001). The language of new media. Cambridge, Mass.: MIT Press.

Manovich, L. (2013). Software takes command: Extending the language of new media. New York: Bloomsbury Academic.

Margulis, L., & Sagan, D. (1997). Slanted Truths: Essays on Gaia, symbiosis, and evolution. New York: Copernicus.

Marinova, D., & Phillimore, J. (2003). Models of Innovation. In L. V. Shavinina (Ed.), The international handbook on innovation (pp. 44–53). Amsterdam; Boston: Elsevier.

Mau, B., Leonard, J., & Institute without Boundaries. (2004). Massive change. London: Phaidon.

Maxwell, G. (2017). The dynamics of transformation: Tracing an emerging world view.

McCarthy, Lauren; Reas, Casey; Fry, Ben. (2016). P5.js. Maker Media.

McCumber, J. (2016). The philosophy scare: The politics of reason in the early Cold War. Chicago: The University of Chicago Press.

McGuire, B. (2013). Waking the giant: How a changing climate triggers earthquakes, tsunamis, and volcanoes. Oxford, United Kingdom: Oxford University Press.

McKibben, B. (2019). Falter: Has the human game begun to play itself out? (First edition). New York: Henry Holt and Company.

McLuhan, M. (1994). Understanding media: The extensions of man. London: Routledge.

Meillassoux, Q., Brassier, R., Badiou, A., & Bloomsbury Publishing. (2017). After finitude: An essay on the necessity of contingency. London [etc.: Bloomsbury Academic an imprint of Bloomsbury Publishing Plc.

Melville, H. (1991). Moby-Dick. New York: Knopf: Distributed by Random House.

Minsky, M. L. (1986). The Society of Mind. New York: Simon and Schuster.

Moravec, H. P. (1988). Mind children: The future of robot and human intelligence. Cambridge, Mass: Harvard University Press.

Montague, R. (2007). Your brain is (almost) perfect: How we make decisions. New York London: Plume; Turnaround [distributor].

Montfort, N., & Bogost, I. (2009). Racing the beam: The Atari video computer system. Cambridge, Mass. A: MIT Press.

Morton, T. (2013). Hyperobjects: Philosophy and ecology after the end of the world. Minneapolis: University of Minnesota Press.

Morton, T. (2017). Humankind: Solidarity with nonhuman people.

Morton, T. (2018). Dark Ecology: For a logic of future coexistence. S.l.: COLUMBIA UNIVERSITY PRESS.

Nagle, A. (2017). Kill all normies: Online culture wars from 4chan and Tumblr to Trump and the alt-right. Winchester: Zero Books.

Nelson, H. G., & Stolterman, E. (2003). The design way: Intentional change in an unpredictable world: foundations and fundamentals of design competence. Englewood Cliffs, N.J: Educational Technology Publications.

Neumann, B., Vafeidis, A. T., Zimmermann, J., & Nicholls, R. J. (2015). Future Coastal Population Growth and Exposure to Sea-Level Rise and Coastal Flooding—A Global Assessment. PLOS ONE, 10(3), e0118571. https://doi.org/10.1371/journal.pone.0118571

Noble, D. D. (1991). The classroom arsenal: Military research, information technology, and public education. London; New York: Falmer.

Noble, J.J. (2012). Programming Interactivity. Beijing; Sebastopol, CA: O'Reilly.

O'Malley, V. (2016). The great war for New Zealand: Waikato 1800-2000. Wellington, New Zealand: Bridget Williams Books.

O'Regan, G. (2013). Giants of computing: A compendium of select, pivotal pioneers. London: Springer, [2013].

Osgood, K. A. (2006). Total Cold War: Eisenhower's secret propaganda battle at home and abroad. Lawrence: University of Kansas.

Papanek, V. J. (1972). Design for the real world. London: Thames and Hudson, 1972. (City Campus Main Collection 745.2 PAP).

Papanek, V. J. (1995). The green imperative: Natural design for the real world. New York: Thames and Hudson.

Peake, Anthony. (2013). A Life of Philip K. Dick: The Man Who Remembered the Future. Arcturus Publishing.

Peris, M. (1971). Talos and Daedalus: A Review of the Authorship of the Abominable Bronze Man. Retrieved from http://dlib.pdn.ac.lk/archive/handle/123456789/2727

Pilling, D. (2018). The growth delusion: Wealth, poverty, and the well-being of nations (1st American Edition). New York: Tim Duggan Books.

Prigogine, I., Stengers, I., & Prigogine, I. (1984). Order out of chaos: Man's new dialogue with nature. Toronto; New York, N.Y: Bantam Books.

Randle, M., & Eckersley, R. (2015). Public perceptions of future threats to humanity and different societal responses: A cross-national study. Futures, 72, 4–16. https://doi.org/10.1016/j.futures.2015.06.004

Reichenbach, H. (1951). The rise of scientific philosophy. Berkeley: University of California Press.

Reisch, G. A. (2005). How the Cold War transformed philosophy of science: To the icy slopes of logic. Cambridge; New York: Cambridge University Press.

Rifkin, J. (1991). Biosphere politics: A new consciousness for a new century (1st ed.). New York: Crown.

Rifkin, J. (2014). The Zero Marginal Cost Society: The Internet of

Things, the Collaborative Commons, and the Eclipse of Capitalism (Reprint edition). St. Martin's Press.

Riva, G., Davide, F., & Ijsselsteijn, W. A. (2003). Being there: Concepts, effects and measurements of user presence in synthetic environments. Amsterdam; Washington, D.C. Tokyo: IOS Press; Ohmsha.

Rive, L.F. (2019). Queering the Webseries. University of Auckland.

Rive, P. B. (1984). A wealth of knowledge in a bankrupt databank: The politics of establishing a "universal database", PRESTEL, and the implications for videotex development in New Zealand. University of Auckland, Auckland.

Rive, P. B. (2012). Design in a Virtual Innovation Ecology: A Cybernetic Systems Approach to Knowledge Creation and Design Collaboration in Second Life. Retrieved from http://researcharchive.vuw.ac.nz/handle/10063/2747

Rive, P. B., & Thomassen, A. (2012). International Collaboration and Design Innovation in Virtual Worlds: Lessons from Second Life. In Computer-Mediated Communication Across Cultures: International Interactions in Online Environments (pp. 429–448). Hershey PA, USA: Information Science Reference – IGI Global.

Rive, P., Billinghurst, M., Thomassen, A., & Lyons, M. (2008, July). Face to face with the white rabbit—Sharing ideas in Second Life. 1–14. https://doi.org/10.1109/IPCC.2008.4610236

Rothblatt, Martine, & Kurzweil, R. (2014). Virtually Human: The Promise—and the Peril—of Digital Immortality. St. Martin's Press.

Rushkoff, D. (2016). Throwing rocks at the Google bus: How growth became the enemy of prosperity. Londen: Portfolio Penguin.

Scranton, L. (2014). China?s Cosmological Prehistory: The Sophisticated Science Encoded in Civilization?s Earliest Symbols (1 edition). Inner Traditions.

Shaviro, S. (2009). Without criteria: Kant, Whitehead, Deleuze, and aesthetics. Cambridge, Mass: MIT Press.

Shaviro, S. (2014). The universe of things: On speculative realism. Minneapolis: University of Minnesota Press.

Shaviro, S. (2015). No speed limit three essays on accelerationism. Minneapolis: University of Minnesota Press.

Shelley, M. W., & Ward, L. (1986). Frankenstein, or, The modern

Prometheus. Poole [Dorset]; New York: New York, N.Y., USA: New Orchard Editions; Distributed in USA by Sterling Pub. Co.

Shute, N. (1957). On the beach. New York: W. Morrow.

Spikins, P., Wright, B., Hodgson, D.,. (2016). Are there alternative adaptive strategies to human pro-sociality? The role of collaborative morality in the emergence of personality variation and autistic traits. Time and Mind, 9(4). https://doi.org/10.1080/1751696X.2016.1244949

Steffen, W. L. (Ed.). (2004). Global change and the earth system: A planet under pressure. Berlin; New York: Springer.

Stephenson, N. (1992). Snow crash. New York, N.Y.: Bantam Books.

Stephenson, N. (1995). The diamond age, or, A young lady's illustrated primer. London: Viking.

Stephenson, N. (1999). Cryptonomicon (1st ed.). New York: Avon Press.

Tainter, J. A., & Patzek, T. W. (2012). Drilling down the Gulf Oil debacle and our energy dilemma. Retrieved from http://dx.doi.org/10.1007/978-1-4419-7677-2

Taleb, N. N. (2008). The Black Swan: The Impact of the Highly Improbable (Re-issue edition). London: Penguin.

Tarnas, R. (1991). The passion of the Western mind: Understanding the ideas that have shaped our world view (1st ed). New York: Harmony Books.

Tarnas, R. (2006). Cosmos and psyche: Intimations of a new world view. New York: Viking.

Thiel, P., & Masters, B. (2014). Zero to One: Notes on Startups, or How to Build the Future. New York: Crown Business.

Thomas, A. (2015). Hidden in plain sight: The simple link between relativity and quantum mechanics.

Tolle, E. (2004). The power of NOW: A guide to spiritual enlightenment (Rev. ed.). Vancouver, B.C., Canada: Novato, Calif: Namaste Pub.; New World Library.

Trout, L. (2010). The politics of survival: Peirce, affectivity, and social criticism (1st ed). New York: Fordham University Press.

Tsing, A. L. (2015). The mushroom at the end of the world: On the possibility of life in capitalist ruins. Princeton: Princeton University Press.

Turner, F. (2006). From counterculture to cyberculture: Stewart Brand, the Whole Earth Network, and the rise of digital utopianism. Chicago, IL: University of Chicago Press.

Tucker, P. (2014). The naked future: What happens in a world that anticipates your every move.

Tye, L. (1998). The father of spin: Edward L. Bernays & the birth of public relations (1st ed). New York: Crown Publishers.

Von Krogh, G., Nonaka, I., & Ichijo, K. (2000). Enabling knowledge creation: How to unlock the mystery of tacit knowledge and release the power of innovation. Oxford; New York: Oxford University Press.

Watson, P. (2005). Ideas: A history from fire to Freud. London: Weidenfeld & Nicolson.

Weart, S. (2019). The Discovery of Global Warming: A hypertext history of how scientists came to (partly) understand what people are doing to cause climate change. Retrieved from https://history.aip.org/climate/index.htm

Wertheim, M. (1999). The pearly gates of cyberspace: A history of space from Dante to the Internet. New York: W.W. Norton.

Whitehead, A. N. (2014a). Process and reality. Retrieved from http://www.myilibrary.com?id=893479

Whitehead, A. N. (2014b). Process and reality. Retrieved from http://www.myilibrary.com?id=893479

Wiener, N. (1954a). The human use of human beings: Cybernetics and society (2nd ed.). New York: Doubleday.

Wiener, N. (1954b). The human use of human beings: Cybernetics and society (2nd ed.). New York: Doubleday.

Wiener, N. (1961). Cybernetics: Or control and communication in the animal and the machine (2nd ed.). Cambridge, Mass.: M.I.T. Press.

Wiener, N. (1964). God and Golem, inc: A comment on certain points where cybernetics impinges on religion. Cambridge: M.I.T. Press.

Wilson, C. (1963). The outsider. London: Pan.

Wolfe, T. (2016). The kingdom of speech (First edition). New York: Little, Brown and Company.

Wolff, M. (2018). Fire and fury: Inside the Trump White House (First edition). New York: Henry Holt and Company.

Wolfmeyer, M. (2014). Math education for America?: Policy networks, big business, and pedagogy wars. New York: Routledge, 2014.

Woodward, B. (2018). Fear: Trump in the White House. London, England: Simon & Schuster.

www.ingramcontent.com/pod-product-compliance
Lightning Source LLC
Chambersburg PA
CBHW051539030726
47592CB00001B/41